Occasional Views, Volume 2

Other Books by the Author

Occasional Views, Volume 2

"The Gamble"

and Other Essays

Samuel R. Delany

WESLEYAN UNIVERSITY PRESS
Middletown, Connecticut

Wesleyan University Press
Middletown CT 06459
www.wesleyan.edu/wespress
© 2021 Samuel R. Delany
All rights reserved

Manufactured in the United States of America
Typeset in Monotype Baskerville, Mona Lisa Recut,
and Futura Now by Nord Compo

For acknowledgments of previously published essays, see page 357

Library of Congress Cataloging-in-Publication Data
Identifiers: 2021003527 | ISBN 9780819579775 (cloth) | ISBN 9780819579782
    (trade paperback) | ISBN 9780819579799 (ebook)
Subjects: LCGFT: Essays.
LC record available at https://lccn.loc.gov/2021003527
LC ebook record available at https://lccn.loc.gov/2021003528

5 4 3 2 1

For
Luise White
Jane Gallop
Teresa de Lauretis

Contents

Illustrations for chapter 24 follow page 326

Occasional Views,
Volume 2

Quest Diagnostics

QUEST DIAGNOSTICS INCORPORATED

REPORTED: 06/01/2004   11:30

PATIENT INFORMATION
DELANY, SAMUEL R

DOB: 04/01/1942 Age: 62
GENDER: M

REPORT STATUS **Final**

ORDERING PHYSICIAN

Test Name	In Range	Out of Range	Reference Range	Lab
URINALYSIS W/ALBUMIN (Continued)				
URINALYSIS, COMPLETE (Continued)				
WBC	None		<or=5 cells/hpf	
BACTERIA	None		None Seen /hpf	
RBC	None		<or=3 cells/hpf	
MICROALBUMIN, URINE				TBR
CREATININE, RANDOM URINE	1227		mg/L	
MICROALBUMIN, URINE	7		0 - 30 mg/g Creat.	
CHLAMYDIA/GC DNA, PCR				TBR
C.TRACHOMATIS DNA, PCR			Negative	
			No acceptable specimen was received	
N.GONORRHOEAE DNA, PCR			Negative	
			No acceptable specimen was received	
HIV-1 AB W/CONFIRM., NY				TBR
HIV-1 AB, EIA		Nonreactive,	Nonreactive	

No HIV-1 antibodies detected.
A nonreactive test result does not exclude the possibility
of HIV-1 infection, since seroconversion is variable.
If clinically indicated, repeat testing of a new sample(s) in
three months is suggested.

Government regulations require the assurance of patient
confidentiality. New York State Public Health Law,
including Article 27F, details for providers their
responsibility and authority regarding partner/contact
notification.

HEMOGLOBIN A1C		7.1 H	Percent	TBR
			Reference Range: Non Diabetics < 6.0%	
STREPTOCOCCUS, GRP A CULT				TBR
STREPTOCOCCUS, GRP A CULT		Final		
STREPTOCOCCUS, GRP A CULT				
			No group A streptococci isolated	

Performing Laboratory Information:

TBR Quest Diagnostics One Malcolm Avenue Teterboro NJ 07608 Laboratory Director: William E. Tarr, M.D.

DELANY, SAMUEL R - 43821044

Page 2 - End of Report

Report from a test for HIV, other STDs, and strep throat: June 1, 2004. See note 2, following this essay.

1

The Gamble

1.

What is the nature of the gamble?

Twenty-five years ago I would have answered that question fairly simply: "I'm gambling on science." Today, that's a lot more difficult to say. Is science what scientists say? Is science what doctors say? Is science what the people who write forms (for insurance companies, for patients, for doctors, for "the public") say, in order to qualify what they say to go along with the reigning wisdom?

2.

Today, when you get an HIV test, and the test comes back negative, the form from the Diagnostic Center that runs the test says:

"HIV—1 AB W/CONFIRM., NY
"HIV—I AB, E/A nonreactive, no reactive
"No HIV-1 antibodies detected.

"A non-reactive test result does not exclude the possibility of HIV-1 infection, since seroconversion is variable. If clinically indicated, repeat testing of a new sample(s) in three months is suggested."

In short, the test would seem to prove nothing. It only defers the knowledge of infection by three months, or, indeed, to whenever the next test is administered.

Neither the indication "HIV–" nor the words "HIV negative" occur anywhere on the test results. The term is, indeed, a fiction—a reassuring term of distinction that has been more or less demanded by patients, and that, indeed, doctors have largely accepted—to counter the equally fictitious narrative of the testee who, once he or she is tested, is, by the very force of the act, pulled into a population to which health itself is totally and forever denied but rather deferred, test after test after test, until, presumably, death.

I think this is a perfectly reasonable reading of the text on the paper one receives, of some of the rhetoric that moves around it. The test itself and its results I have no problem accepting as science. The question is: To what extent is the rhetoric around it science?

3.

I got my first HIV test in June of 1988, when I was forty-six years old, six years after I'd first heard of AIDS. It was at the end of a three-year period during which I was certain that I had AIDS. But the results were negative. As well, after the lesions that had appeared on my lower legs in April of 1985, there had been no other symptoms—and the first time I went to a doctor since I'd been convinced I'd been infected, he diagnosed the lesions as a "psoriasis-like" condition (and not the Kaposi's lesions that, for three years, I'd assumed they were), which have since been much improved with a cortisone cream.

For the next seven years I got tested twice a year. Again, in all cases, by the conventions of that reigning fiction, I was "HIV–." Since 1988 I have been tested once a year. In all cases I have been "HIV–." I am now sixty-two years old. My most recent test results were returned on June 1, 2004.

4.

Here is a statement lifted from a conversation recorded in my journal with a twenty-nine-year-old Pennsylvania AIDS educator from late in 2003: "I assume there must be about ten million cases of AIDS minimum, in the United States alone—maybe one out of ten has been detected. The tests are inconclusive— they say so right on the paper they send back to you. I figure that, whatever the official figures says, you can assume there's a case of AIDS somewhere in the country, for every test that's been given"—though I note with three afternoons of research online, I have not been able to come up with the number of

ELISA tests performed since they were made available in 1984. The Centers for Disease Control and Prevention (CDC), whose most recent figures date from December, 2002, says that in the United States there were 880,575 tests—that is to say, slightly under a million.

Is there anything "scientific" in what this young man says?

Talking to another young man, in April of 2004, also an AIDS educator, I recorded the following in my journal: "I've been instructed by my supervisor to tell my clients that one out of five people in New York City has syphilis."

Is there anything scientific in either of these claims?

In a recent issue of a *New Yorker*-sized glossy magazine for women, a health column bylined by a "Dr. Beth" refers to the "virus that causes syphilis." Since most (responsible, reputable) medical texts tell us that syphilis is caused by a spirochete (*Treponema pallidum*), is this in any way scientific?

Is there anything scientific about: Acupuncture?

Chinese herbal medicine? Reiki? (A mode of "energy healing" in which the practitioner moves his or her hands over the patient's body, gathering or moving around the "energy," "concentrating" the "good" energy and "discarding the "bad"—usually without touching the patient.)

Not to mention astrology, tarot cards, and "certified" TV psychics.

The husband of a good friend practices a number of these. "And enough of it works," she says, "so that I have no difficulty believing he's providing a useful and needed service. Besides, he's an extremely responsible man, too. If he thinks for a moment there's a medical problem involved that falls outside his purview, he's very quick to tell you to see a Western doctor." Nevertheless, this same woman was horrified when her best friend of many years in the Midwest was diagnosed with breast cancer and insisted on spending a year in "alternative" medical treatment. "I really had to ask myself how much Tom—yes, and I—had contributed to that. Indeed, it was only when her third herbalist, after three weeks of treatment, announced that the cancer was not responding and demanded she see a Western doctor, that she finally consented. A double mastectomy and a long session of chemotherapy later, the woman is still alive.[1] "But," said my friend, "you just don't know."

And where is the science in all of this?

When "Western doctors" regularly suggest that patients try alternative methods, either because they suspect that the patients want to, or that it won't hurt, what has happened to the "scientific"? When I was discussing this with a friend, he said: "Well, some of it seems to make people feel better. What do you want? An article in *Scientific American*?"

To which my personal answer is: You're damned right I do—and that's only after half a dozen other refereed articles in notable, respected medical journals have appeared.

5.

I am gambling on the high probability that AIDS is not spread orally, i.e., by mouth-to-penis contact or by penis-to-mouth contact, with or without the passage or ingesting of pre-cum or cum: I am gambling on the fact (a word I use rarely) that studies I have read in reputable scientific venues that strike me as responsibly operationalized show no evidence that the virus can be passed through oral sex (mouth-to-penis; penis-to-mouth) between human males.

What do I mean by responsibly operationalized? First and foremost, that no hearsay is accepted as evidence within the study proper.

Consider the following logic: If what we are trying to determine is transmission routes for HIV (which behaviors will pass the virus on and which will not), then the one thing we cannot under any circumstance accept as evidence is asking someone who has been diagnosed as HIV-positive what sexual behavior transmitted the virus to him or her. The reason we can't accept such statements as evidence is because to accept them assumes that the answer to our question is known, rather than unknown.

It has nothing to do with whether the informant is right or wrong, mistaken or accurate, honest or lying. Rather, it introduces material that throws off the statistical balance of the portrait of behaviors.

A study that seeks to give an accurate statistical picture of which behaviors lead to seroconversion and which do not, has to start with a sampling of people all of whom test negative. Then, these people must be regularly asked about (and the answers tabulated in writing) the specific sexual acts each indulges in, over a period of time—three months, six months, a year. Finally, they must all be tested for seroconversion *again*, and the behaviors must be tabulated against the seroconversions and lack of seroconversions.

To my knowledge this sort of study—I call it a monitored study, which is to say, it accepts only monitored evidence and excludes hearsay—has only been done three times in the United States. The results of the first and largest of these studies was published as far back as 1987. Though the study was done in America, its results appeared in the British medical journal *The Lancet* for Saturday, February 14: "Risk factors for seroconversion to human immunodeficiency virus among male homosexuals," by Kingsley, Kaslo, Rinaldo *et alia*, which I republished as an "Appendix" to my novel *The Mad Man* (Kasak Books, 1995). It involved 2,508 gay men, all of whom were sero-negative at the start of the study. At the end of six months, there had been ninety-eight seroconversions among them.

Briefly, ninety-five of the men who seroconverted had indulged in receptive anal intercourse at least once. For the three others there is a chance of "misclassification," i.e., they either did engage in receptive anal sex or were misreported. (Something about the study itself makes this a reasonable suggestion: the men's reports were incomplete or the questions were poorly administered—easy enough to occur in two-and-a-half-thousand cases.) Five seroconverts, indeed, had engaged in receptive anal intercourse only once during the six months of the study. As well, another population of 147 men in the study only engaged in receptive oral sex, none of whom seroconverted. The study concluded that "Receptive anal intercourse was the only sexual practice shown to be independently associated with an increased risk of seroconversion to HIV in this study . . ." and "The absence of detectable risk for seroconversion due to receptive oral-genital intercourse is striking."

Since the Kingsley, Kaslo, Rinaldo study there have been two other such studies—one published in *JAMA* (*Journal of the American Medical Association*) in 1990. The test sample was a thousand male homosexuals from San Francisco. The third test became available online in 2000, with several hundred participants. The statistical portrait of transmission routes is the same for all three studies. No anomalies are reported between them, though the monitoring processes were notably different. In the *JAMA* study, the participants were monitored only at the beginning and the end of the study, but not throughout the entire period.

6.

Why is basing one's behavior (i.e., indulging in no unprotected anal intercourse with men whose HIV status is not known, but freely indulging in unprotected oral sex) on such studies still very much a gamble—so great a gamble that one could not reasonably suggest that anyone else take the same one?

First, three studies are simply not enough to change a high probability into anything like a scientific certainty. But no more studies have been done. (No studies at all have been done with heterosexual women, so that there is no statistical evidence at all available that AIDS can be transmitted to women though vaginal sex—though there are barns full of hearsay.) Regularly, people send me "studies" in which the statistics wildly contravene those of these reports: this one with six hundred participants, seven of whom "developed AIDS from oral sex" (and the tester has no doubt about their "honesty"), or a friend of a friend (name unknown) who "certainly got it orally." In all cases, however, it is fairly clear that these are hearsay, at least in the manner described above. Someone, however honest, is making a judgment—either the tester or the participant— from statements gathered about infection *after* seroconversion.

Two points: seven out of six hundred (more than one percent) contravenes the statistic of the monitored studies that have been done so wildly that any statistician would have to raise an eyebrow. Second, in none of the cases that have been shown to me does the set up of the "test" seem even vaguely aware that hearsay *must* be operationally weeded out of the "evidence" if the study is to be meaningful.

7.

Let me state it right out: There is another aspect of the "gamble" that is equally problematic to discuss—indeed, it is *why* I want operationalized information based on refereed articles in respected medical journals. A gamble suggests that, for whatever set of reasons, you make your choice, you stake your claim, and you stick to it. You don't change in the middle.

Unfortunately, however, life does not work that way.

But because it doesn't, that is precisely *why* I want the information that I base the explanations of what goes on in my life to be rigorously operationalized. All information that falls outside such rigorously operationalized standards, we call hearsay.

I accept hearsay evidence into my life and base some of my behavior on it all the time. When I decide whether to go to see a movie or not, the evidence that goes into my decision is ninety percent hearsay. I am also blatantly aware that from fifty to ninety-five percent of that hearsay evidence is likely to be not the estimation of friends who have actually seen the picture and returned with a considered judgment, but comes rather from the movie marketers themselves, who have spent hundreds of thousands of dollars on newspaper advertisements, posters, and TV commercials to make the film's presence known and to make it seem of interest at whatever level they can. That is to say, not only is it hearsay, it is blatantly biased hearsay, with a hugely commercial motive that completely swamps any concept of truth or accuracy.

If the problem of biased hearsay were just a matter of movies, then life would be a wonderful thing. But in a consumer society, biased hearsay controls pretty much the entire field of evidence I have to make my decisions on for pretty much any commodity I purchase or expose myself to; it *is* the field of the arts, popular to high-brow. It *is* the field of all household utilities, foods, and daily comforts. It is entirely the field of politics.

What happens to medical knowledge in such a society? What happens when there is a disease, such at AIDS, which can be contracted in the pursuit of public pleasure and is still incurable, if not quite as irrevocably fatal as it was a decade ago?

8.

Highly operationalized evidence is what allows planes to fly, antibiotics to kill bacteria, car engines to turn over, mills to grind (exceedingly small or otherwise), TVs to work, cloth to be woven, lights to come on when we flip the switch, cellphones and computers to function, food to come out of cans unspoiled—and books to be readable, on all levels. (I know of no one in the book business, writing, publishing, printing, who is not aware of the falling off of the professional competency in proofreading over the last twenty-five years—which is purely a lowering of operationalized standards.) One might even say that a web of operationalized evidence nets the society we live in within a grid of expectations that even the most skeptical philosopher might call "truth" (or something close to it); we trust it practically from the moment we first glance at a clock in the morning, before rising from bed, and throughout the day, along with whatever work is done, whatever play is indulged in.

Sometimes this grid fails. Perhaps it is simply a phenomenon of the contemporary world: But whenever we believe we have fallen out of the grid, hearsay inflates at a rate that to call exponential is the most inadequate of metaphors.

9.

The last time, during "public sex," when someone whom I'd never seen or met before put his cock up my ass and came, was during the spring of 1981. It was in a place called Fantasy Land, on the corner of Eighth Avenue and Forty-Seventh Street, in the same building as a pornographic movie theater, then called the Hollywood. From the street, you entered a minuscule lobby where the freight elevator for the building opened up. You rode up to the fourth floor and got off in a room that was a small gay bookstore, which also sold male videos and sex toys. For the $3 admission, you went through a door into a loft space that had been decorated to look like Central Park's "Rambles" at night: park benches, park lights, plastic bushes, and usually half a dozen guys wandering around who had come there a few minutes before—though people rarely *did* anything, at least when I was there.

Off to one side, around a corner and on a raised platform, stood a wall of padlocked gym lockers, a wrack of weights, and a bench press—presumably this was for those who fantasized sex in a high school or college locker room. I don't believe I ever saw anyone even hanging out in this area.

To the back was a stairwell leading down into another loft area on the floor below, this one was fairly roomy. The walls were black. A jukebox stood to one side, near a couple of pinball machines (not plugged in). Padded with industrial carpeting, a number of waist-high shelves were fixed to two of the walls—with ladders up to a second tier, as though they were bunk beds. At one side was a glass-fronted concession counter, which was completely empty. My sense is that this was an area the owners had not yet completed—perhaps it was to be a "gay bar" or a "theater lobby." Because you could sit or even stretch out on the shelves around the wall, it's the only place I ever had actual sex, or saw people having actual sex in the dozen-odd times I visited.

In November 1981, I was a stocky thirty-nine-year-old—with glasses.

One Thursday afternoon at about four-thirty, when I had dropped in for the afternoon, a fairly ordinary-looking Hispanic fellow, in a tweed cap and tan slacks, half a dozen years my junior, came onto me very heavily—and, soon, had my jeans down about my ankles and, as we stretched out on one of the shelves, grunting and thrusting, shot his load up my ass. As I recall, he was not particularly friendly. I think, once he was finished, he smiled and asked if I was all right. But by the time I had my pants up, he was gone. I recall thinking, as I sat on the rug-covered ledge, "I could have done without that."

Generally, I tend to get off on what gets my partner off. By and large, however, getting fucked is not my particular thing. During a sex life in which I was easily averaging between a dozen and three dozen encounters of one sort or another a week, I was probably indulging in insertive anal sex perhaps ten times a year, and receptive anal sex perhaps twice a year. The overwhelming number of my encounters—and the ones I enjoyed the most—were oral, with receptive to active three to one.

Perhaps four months later, I heard my first mention of the "gay cancer," Kaposi's sarcoma, which had begun appearing, only in the last few months, with unprecedented frequency among gay men.

10.

Sometime in 1983, after I had heard half a dozen mentions of it on various news reports, I asked a doctor about AIDS. He was a young man in his early thirties, who had recently finished his residency and was working in a clinic that specialized in cancer research. "Kaposi's sarcoma?" I asked him. "What is it? They keep referring to lesions, but where do they show up?"

"I think it's some kind of skin cancer," he said. "This stuff they're talking about is supposed to be transmitted sexually: I would imagine the lesions show up around the genitals."

Is there anything scientific in the young doctor's statement?

11.

Kaposi's sarcoma is a cancer of the mesodermic capillary linings. Often about the size of mussel or clam shells, its irregular purple lesions show up on the skin, anywhere on the body, arms, face or torso, though most often they appear on the lower legs.

Three or four years after I spoke to my young doctor, the above would be a "scientific fact" most urban gay men would "know."

12.

Chip, how many unprotected oral receptive encounters have you had since 1982?

I can't be sure, but I would say a conservative estimate is that between 1982 and '88, when I started at the University of Massachusetts, I was having between three and five hundred encounters a year. Between 1988 and 2000, the number probably went down to about a 175 a year: Heavy cruising was limited to the summers. Since I've been teaching in Philadelphia, thanks to venues such as the Sansom Theater and the Forum, it's probably gone back up to at least 250 a year. Roughly that makes somewhere between 5,800 and 7,000.

While my HIV test is not, certainly everything else I have said above must be considered hearsay: I could be crazy. I could be mistaken. (Few of these encounters—or what I did during them—I wrote down.) I could be making it all up—from either the best, or from the worst intentions.

For what it's worth, however, mistaken or not, I perceive what I say as "the truth."

13.

In the warm late afternoon of May 8, 2004, in Philadelphia, I wandered down Twelfth Street's red brick sidewalk to the corner of Pine Street, by the occasional boxed glass windows slanting out from the cellars of the old houses, under the trees, to Giovanni's Room, the gay bookstore on the corner, where, later that evening, I was scheduled to read from my autobiography *The Motion of Light in Water* (Ultramarine, 1988), which in 2004 had just been returned to print by the University of Minnesota Press. I had told a number of my students at Temple University that the reading was at seven o'clock. Dutifully, they'd promised to come. A month before, my doctor had changed my hypertension medication—putting me back on an ACE-inhibitor, Lisinopril; and, as when I had taken Vasotec, a few years before, I had developed a slight but persistent cough: 5 percent of people who take it do. It seemed to be my pattern. Most of the time it was okay, but two or three times a day it produced a two- or three-minute coughing fit: not what you wanted to happen in the midst of a reading. When, at about five-thirty, I stepped up into the bookstore, I told the clerk I'd just wanted to stop by to tell them that everything was on track.

But, even as I was talking with the clerk, with her blonde-tipped hair and nose ring, I noticed the flyer lying on the counter that announced my reading said 6:30 p.m.

Yes, the reading was not at seven but a half an hour earlier. That's what had gone out on all the announcements to the various local papers.

"Oh, dear," I said. "I'm glad I stopped by, then."

I figured I had time to go home—I lived a block-and-a-half away—grab a quick shower and change my clothes. While I wondered how many of my students would come in half-an-hour late, that's what I did. At six-thirty, in the circle of folding chairs set around the gray rug in the upstairs space, among the wall bookshelves, only five people had turned out to hear me. One was a young sociologist from Temple, John, who had come with a friend, and one, Jeff, was a thirty-one-year-old English graduate student friend. The other two were a young, pleasant-faced couple, male and female.

With my audience of four (plus the owner and a book clerk), the reading took about forty minutes. *No one* came in at seven. A fairly lively discussion bloomed afterwards, however, which ran on another forty minutes among the half-dozen of us there. When it was done, the sociologist, John, and his friend and Jeff cornered me and suggested that we go off to get some dinner at a bar/restaurant called Fergie's a few blocks north, just up from Walnut on Sansom Street.

As we were walking up the tree-lined sidewalk, the leaves silent in summer under the darkening sky, John introduced me to his friend, a little blond bull of a weightlifter, probably in his middle thirties. He wore an orange T-shirt and marine fatigue pants. His head was shaved and he had a boyishly friendly face. "This is B.J. He's a prostitute and porn star. I had him in to talk to my class last week . . ." And little B.J. gave me a warm handshake in a large meaty hand.

Our graduate student, Jeff (straight and currently having some problems with his live-in girlfriend, which is why she hadn't come), looked quite as surprised as I felt—though I did a better job of not showing it. (Only two weeks before at the CUNY Graduate Center up in New York someone else had been introduced to me more or less the same way.) The conversation with B.J. that evening was memorable: B.J. was HIV positive—and had been so for the last ten years, he was quick to tell us. He is certain he picked up the virus through oral sex: "Oh, yeah. Lots of people say you can't get it orally. But, believe me, I'm walking proof that you can."

In what is certainly more than a hundred conversations over the last twenty years with people who were HIV positive, while I have talked with numerous people who were fairly sure you could get the virus orally, B.J. is the first person I personally have spoken with who claimed to have gotten it that way.

The conversation went on through dinner—not an argument, by any means. I am, after all, gambling. (I picked at B.J.'s and John's long, limp French fries, darker than McDonald's. B.J. and Jeff each took a polite handful of my stained-gold popcorn shrimp.) I could always be wrong. I did a lot of questioning and a lot of listening.

Elbows on the dark wood table under the shadows from his pumped-up forearms, B.J. was very knowledgeable about the biochemistry of the human immunodeficiency virus—though he knew about none of the three transmission route tests and was surprised to find out what they actually said. He was surprised that I knew a fair amount about the biochemistry too: which protein receptors the virus affixes to on the cell membrane, which proteins it has to push aside in order to do it.

Most of that information I first learned when my daughter, who is now thirty, was in the ninth grade and doing a school report on the organic chemistry of HIV; much of it came from a very thorough *Scientific American* article that we had read and reread.

I'd typed up her report for her. But just because that information is seventeen years old does not mean it's out of date, any more than is Kingley, Kaslo, Rinaldo *et al.*

As a gay porn star and prostitute—and probably because, frankly, he's gorgeous—B.J. has had a *great* deal more sex than I have, by a large factor. And it's been a lot wilder. The number of encounters I've had in the last ten years you could—for B.J.—easily multiply by three, five, seven . . . We found this out quickly, at dinner. Much of his professional work was before he seroconverted, back at age twenty-three though he has given up on neither profession. He is rigorous about performing with condoms. He, too, calls himself an AIDS educator (as well as a sex worker), and says that he is deeply concerned with getting information out to people.

When Jeff and I finally walked John and B.J. back to John's ground-floor flat, and we had left them at John's apartment, with its piles of books around the walls, I said to Jeff: "Oh, you know—I just thought what I really should have asked B.J. Was he ever in an orgy or orgy-like situation, around the time or in the months before he seroconverted, either on a job or during a film shoot, where someone who had taken a load of cum in his mouth might have licked out his asshole within five, ten, or fifteen minutes. I think *that* would have to count for getting the virus anally—though he might have been unaware of it, or not even noted it—because no one stuck a dick up his ass. Of course that's something that, if it happened to him, he might not even have remembered it. But I *still* think, from the kinds of things he was talking about in his general sex life, there's a greater statistical chance that he picked up the virus that way than that he got it through sucking. The problem is, straight people—who, alas, are the ones doing most of the research—don't think of questions like that."

Under darkened trees, Jeff said: "Jesus Christ, Chip—I have never heard people talk about sex the way you guys were talking about it!" He had been silent all through the heated and vigorous dinner conversation about numbers, positions, encounters, when and where . . . "I mean, never—in my life. Over a hundred partners a year . . . I didn't even know there was sex like that. I mean, people actually doing it. My God—And you say you're on the *low* end of gay activity, because you're getting old . . . !"

I wasn't even sure he'd heard my question.

14.

A few days later, I left Philadelphia specifically to go up and visit an old fuck buddy of twenty years standing in upstate New York. He met me in his truck at the train station, and we went to get a motel room. For the past two years (and past two years alone), we have been having unprotected anal sex. Why? Because he really likes it. Somewhat to my surprise, I found I really like it too—though, since 1981, he's the only one I've ever done it with. He has showed me his HIV test: It reads the same as mine, and he too gets tested every year. He swears up and down that he has not been fucked since he was twenty. For half a dozen character-related reasons, I believe him. Now in his mid-forties, he's pretty set in his sexual ways—though what he does, he does spectacularly well. He's a working-class white guy, Catholic, with a thing for older black men. A hot and heavy six-week affair back when he was twenty-eight and I was forty-five now simmers along at a couple of phone calls a month and two or three meetings a year—often less. He still lives in a trailer park with his parents and a shifting population of cats, nieces, and nephews of several shades and ethnicities. (His older sister had/has the same predilection for non-Caucasians as he does; and grandma loves them all—and has raised most of them.) Those two or three times a year I have sex with him, it's wild and wonderful and a great change from my main squeeze of fourteen years. And sometimes you really just have to trust people, especially if they are old friends—and this is someone who is an older friend than even my steady life companion, with whom sex is regular, always oral, and, because it's what both of us really like a lot as day-to-day fare, is always reassuring and emotionally fulfilling.

In terms of the gamble, however, one could easily say the unprotected anal sex that has crept into my last year-and-a-half visits with my fuck buddy is insane—or that it introduces an insane factor. I will be the first to admit it. But there it is. Factor it in.

15.

A day after leaving upstate New York, back in Philadelphia I dropped in at the Sansom Street movie theater, where I sucked off three guys. One came in my mouth. Two didn't.

16.

Over the next week I developed a major sore throat. This, I thought, has got to be strep. And when, on my way to my office at school, I mentioned that I had a bad sore throat to another one of my graduate students, he told me: "I had strep throat just about a week ago. It's going around—half a dozen of my students have had it."

The fact that it was apparently a factor in recent school life greatly relieved me. Schools and work are places where things like that spread like prairie fires. Still, it was not till the last couple of days of the month when I finally visited my doctor's office back in New York with no encounters at all between then and now: just as responsible as you'd expect a sixty-two-year-old professor to be. Not that I was always thus. (By now, even swallowing olive oil felt like sandpaper over my lower throat and larynx.) Yes, my throat was very red, my Indian Family Practitioner told me, as she sat back after peering in with her conical light.

"What about oral gonorrhea?" I said. (While, between the age of nineteen and twenty-six, I had twelve cases of gonorrhea, since 1968 I've had no STDs that I know of, save three or four cases of a specific urethritis, though I have been tested for syphilis and gonorrhea dozens of times. But you have to be certain.) "It's not thrush or anything like that, is it?" I asked. Like lesions on the lower legs, oral thrush is often an indicator of AIDS.

"No," she told me. "It's certainly not thrush. That you can check visually. It could be Chlamydia, though. We usually test for both gonorrhea and Chlamydia at the same time."

That afternoon, of course, the doctor's office was out of gonorrhea testing swabs, though they had the Chlamydia ones. So, at a white-topped testing desk by the stand-up scale, besides walls of files with colored tabs, another nurse—this one male, solid, handsome, and dead black—thrust a couple of long wooden white-tipped swabs into my throat, one for Chlamydia and one for strep—and I got another HIV test.

"Look," the Practitioner told me, returning, "I'm going to proscribe you an antibiotic that, if it's either of those, will clear it up: Zithromax and Cipro. Take them both at once; and if that's what you've got, you'll be over it in a day or so."

And so, that evening, at Albert's Pharmacy on Eighty-Sixth Street, across from the sprawling new CVS that is pushing Mr. Pommerantz, in his tiny business, toward retirement (his bald head visible just over the top of the boxes piled high on his second counter, in front of which Jennie, his brassy, big-hearted Hispanic assistant, has been helping him run the place for thirty years now), beside the glassed-in shelves of vitamins and holistic medicines and copper bracelets and strap-on magnets (which, he says, all but the vitamins, are embarrassing junk, but which he must sell because people ask for them), I picked up the big red pill and the big white one, and downed them on the way home.

A few days later, the test was back.

It was negative for strep throat.

It was negative for Chlamydia.

No sample had been submitted for gonorrhea.

It was negative for HIV antibodies.

In forty-eight hours the sore throat was gone—or at least it had retreated back to the faint cough that is the standard side effect of some people—like me—to ACE inhibitors.

17.

I hope you can see why I consider my sexual life a gamble. I hope you can see why I would not even begin to think of suggesting that anyone else gamble in the same way. Until many more tests are done—including especially a rigorously monitored test that starts out with only HIV-negative men who engage only in *oral* sex—the results are simply not conclusive.

I enjoy a certain kind of pleasure. I gamble on getting it.

So far, over six or seven thousand receptive condomless oral encounters since c. 1982, I've been lucky. No AIDS. No Chlamydia. And *possibly* one case of oral gonorrhea (the only time the doctor's office was out of swabs), though I note that in the two weeks I had the sore throat, neither a genital discharge nor urethral soreness developed—which is simply not characteristic of gonorrhea, whether initially contracted orally or genitally. (Usually, such symptoms develop within three or four days.) Thus, there's a high possibility it was some other bacterial infection that happened to respond to the Cipro and/or Zithromax—though what it was for sure, we will never know.

One thing that is part of what I am gambling on, however, is the scientific evidence that exists: and, yes, I am ignoring all hearsay, including accounts such as B.J.'s. I do not think he is dishonest. I believe, rather, that when people think that you can get AIDS orally, a certain number will also believe that

that's how they got it. It doesn't make it any less a gamble—and possibly makes it more so.

In the past, often science has been like that.

—August 2004
New York

NOTES

1. Several years later this woman indeed died of breast cancer.

2. Facing the first page of this essay is an illustration—yes, a photocopy of a medical form—that illustrated the article as initially published in both Spanish and English in the journal *Corpus* (Institute for Gay Men's Health, 2005), edited by Robert F. Reid-Pharr, who is now at Harvard University. On the form itself, there are three redacted lines and one redacted name, that of the doctor who had authorized my HIV test to see if I had AIDS.

Eventually I delivered the essay as a lecture for Gay Pride Day at Dartmouth College, where only one person got up and left, in what I assumed was discomfort over, or disagreement with, what I had been saying. Because her feelings/thoughts were expressed as a protest rather than a comment, it is hard to know for sure.

What I want to talk about here are the redactions. When I handed in the article, they were not blocked out. When it was published I was surprised by them. Eventually I believe I discussed the matter on the phone—though I cannot remember with whom, only that it was not with editor Reid-Pharr—and this is my memory of what I learned.

The name of the doctor, Dr. Steven Tamarin, had been blocked out because they could not get in touch with him to clear if it was all right for them to print the document with his name visible. I told whoever it was that the reason they couldn't was that he had been dead for a number of years. (Indeed, he had died of a heart attack less than two hours after I had spoken to him on the phone, one Thanksgiving eve, but that's another story . . .) So there was no chance of his objecting.

The other redacted lines were other diseases he was having me tested for—chlamydia was one; I don't recall what the other was. Did I have any symptoms, or did Dr. T. think I might? No. But he did know the kind of life I was living, so he thought: Let's be on the safe side. And the tests had come out negative. (For what it's worth, I've been tested for chlamydia as many times as I've been tested for AIDS, since, after a six-year period of being sure I had it, I bit the bullet, as it were, and started regular testing in June 1988. I never had chlamydia at all.)

So why were they redacted?

Because the editors thought it might be distracting from the point of the article, which was about HIV tests . . .

And this is my point: Here is a medical form that shows nothing but the truth. But a lot of it was suppressed. And it is in the suppression of truth where misinformation—often dangerous misinformation—blooms.

Misinformation flowers where truth is suppressed—what people really wrote, really said, what they really did—whether it is harmless or helpful.

2

A Note on John Ashbery

One begins by looking for the properly nuanced encomium, "the finest . . . ," "the most significant . . . ," only to remember that, in his own
rhetoric, the poet (born in 1927) vigorously eschews a certain non-ironic
nineteenth-century transcendentalizing—not of the sublime, but verbal
laziness and cliché dishonesties about the sublime—which, hindsight tells
us, once we pass World War II, is after all pretty useless. The demise of
such rhetoric—if not the demise of the discourse that went with it—cleared
space for everything from the Beat Generation to Black Mountain and the
various West-Coast renaissances, Berkeley and San Francisco, as well as the
New York School, at whose center Ashbery initially seemed located, to the
anti-essentialist critical waves, structuralism and poststructuralism, and the
general Heideggerean fall-out.

An attempt to repoeticize the modern world, a few folk have called it,
early and late; but as the mid-century catastrophes revealed more and more
clearly what barbarism lay buried so shallowly in that "heroic" rhetoric,
American poetry made another of its periodic retreats to the "language
really used by men."

Ashbery, Koch, O'Hara, and Schuyler name some East Coast peaks of the
process in alphabetical order.

In the 1960s I kept occasional company with young poets and writers excited
by the experimental playfulness of *The Tennis Court Oath* (1962). In my novel *The
Mad Man*, I tried to give a brief portrait (page 257 in the Voyant edition) of
that excitement when an older poet, Almira Adler, recollects Timothy Hasler's
enthusiasm over Ashbery's second generally available book. (The relatively
limited Tibor de Nagy edition of *Turandot and Other Poems* I don't count—and

usually, on his book pages, neither does Ashbery, though the poet Alfred Corn included its publication among the most important avant-garde events in the twentieth century.)

Myself, I have no particular care, or more than the most provisional interest, in whether Ashbery wrote the eponymous poem for *The Tennis Court Oath* during or after a reading of Carlyle's three-page account—pages 170 to 172 in the current Oxford paperback of *The French Revolution*—of that meeting, in a light drizzle, on Old Versaille's Rue St. Francois, on June 20, 1789, where six hundred raised their right hands with President Bailly. Still, they are two fascinating texts to read against one another: Carlyle's urges us to foreground those elements that turn Ashbery's into a rich meditation on the thoughts and general subjectivity surrounding the making of any commitment, the swearing of any oath, whether of fidelity to a lover or of engagement to a political constitution. After its 1962 publication by Wesleyan University Press, and even more so after its second printing in 1967, many young writers took it as a call to arms for precisely the experimentation of the sort that had been foregrounded throughout Ashbery's first broadly disseminated anthologistic home, his ten-odd pages in Donald Allen's *New American Poetry, 1945–1960* (Grove Press, 1960).

In 1969, a random rereading of "The Instruction Manual" from *Some Trees* (1956) and "These Lacustrine Cities" from *Rivers and Mountains* (1966) would catapult me into an entire reconception of a novel that swallowed five years of my life (*Dhalgren*, 1975). And Paul Carroll's interview with Ashbery about the poem "Leaving the Atocha Station" would hone the edge of an aesthetic that had been ceded me in grosser form by dancers James Waring and Douglas Dunn, by way of an 8:45 a.m. encounter with dancer Freddy Herko at the bottom of the steps at the Second Avenue subway station on Houston Street: Revision is always an option, but what's most necessary is that you *do* it—if only so you'll have something to revise. At least, that's how I heard it back then.

Here's an early poem from Ashbery's book *The Double Dream of Spring* (1966): "Parergon" (page 55), which does engagingly many of things that the young Ashbery did so well. From Derrida's discussion of it in *Truth in Painting*, you'll recall that a "parergon" (literally, something that accompanies the work) is a frame, but a frame with an ambiguous status. We never know, just from the word, whether the parergon is a frame like the frame of a painting, surrounding the work and separating it off from the rest of the world, or whether it is a frame in the sense of the frame of a house, which pervades the work, supporting it from within (like canvas stretchers) and allowing it to stand coherent and manifested before the world.

In Ashbery's "Parergon," two relatively calm and quietly descriptive verse paragraphs would appear to frame a quoted passage, "the few words one knows."

We are happy in our way of life.
It doesn't make much sense to others. We sit about,
Read, and are restless. Occasionally it becomes time
To lower the dark shade over it all.
Our entity pivots on a self-induced trance
Like sleep. Noiseless our living stops
And one strays as in a dream
Into those respectable purlieus where life is motionless and alive
To utter the few words one knows:

"O woebegone people! Why so much crying,
Such desolation in the streets?
Is it the present of flesh, that each of you
At your jagged casement window should handle,
Nervous unto thirst and ultimate death?
Meanwhile the true way is sleeping;
Your lawful acts drink an unhealthy repose
From the upturned lip of this vessel, secretly,
But it is always time for a change.
That certain sins of omission go unpunished
Does not weaken your position
But this underbrush in which you are secure
Is its doing. Farewell then,
Until, under a better sky
We may meet expended, for just doing it
Is only an excuse. We need the tether
Of entering each other's lives, eyes wide apart, crying."

As one who moves forward from a dream
The stranger left that house on hastening feet
Leaving behind the woman with the face shaped like an arrowhead,
And all who gazed upon him wondered at
The strange activity around him.
How fast the faces kindled as he passed!
It was a marvel that no one spoke
To stem the river of his passing
Now grown to flood proportions, as on the sunlit mall
Or in the enclosure of some court
He took his pleasure, savage
And mild with the contemplating.
Yet each knew he saw only aspects,
That the continuity was fierce beyond all dream of enduring,

And turned his head away, and so
The lesson eddied far into the night:
Joyful its beams, and in the blackness blacker still,
Though undying joyousness, caught in that trap.

In this dreamlike progression of phrases, with the logic of association (i.e., grammar, rather than referential argument) in control, what frames what? And in which manner? The return of words like "dream" and "crying" at the ends of their respective lines, the oppositions "life" and "death" or "mild" and "savage" suggest some sort of conceptual frame. The attempts to grasp one and watch it slip away while another comes to the fore is one of the poem's principal pleasures.

In 1972, in my tenth-floor room at the Albert Hotel, on the rather ratty orange spread the hotel provided for the double bed, in the midst of a ten-month residency, I took out all five of the generally available Ashbery volumes then published and reread them, end to end. Then I reread them again, but got sidetracked comparing the order of the telutons in Ashbery's slender *canzone* in monometers, dimeters, and trimeters with those in Auden's pentameter "Canzone."

The order was identical.

The single time I met the poet was at an April 1976 party Judith Johnson Sherwin gave, to celebrate Marilyn Hacker's National Book Award for Poetry for *Presentation Piece*. (Like Ashbery's *Somes Trees*, Margaret Walker's *For My People*, James Agee's *Permit Me Voyage*, and George Starbuck's *Bone Thoughts*, Sherwin's *Uranium Poems* had been a Yale Younger Poets selection, some years before.) I was particularly tickled to overhear Marilyn saying to Ashbery, "I noticed that the order of repetition in the end-words of your 'Canzone' in *Some Trees* is the same as Auden's. I hadn't realized, when I first read them, that there were a number of canzone forms."

At which then silver-haired Ashbery chuckled: "Well," he said, "where do you think I got mine?"

Ashbery has produced some of the most incredibly and unassumingly serviceable prose for writing about poets and poetry in particular and art in general of any critic writing in the United States. As a critic, he has a healthy respect for biography and—I would even say—gossip. (Though, as the co-author with James Schuyler of the charming bit of joyousness *A Nest of Ninnies* [1969], how could he not?) Without ever abusing it, he employs a fine understanding of the way life really *can* make poets and their work more interesting. Whether he is writing about Raymond Roussel (the gay experimentalist with his bosom female companion), Henry Darger (with his cartoon little girls with penises, his physical isolation, and his obsessive, many-thousand-page fantasy novel), Laura Riding (with her spine-shattering leap from the window), David Schubert (with his schizophrenia and tubercular death at thirty-three), or Joan Murray (with her own isolation and early death), in Ashbery's essays they live by means of the ways he embeds them in the fictions arising from such clear accounts of, and intelligent quotations from, their work—even as he offers us Schubert's own warning: "I hate to feel that a poetry is so inextricably tied up with the tragedy of the poet that it cannot lead its own life." In a critical clime still far more under the sway of the anti-biographical prejudices of the New Critics than many of us are aware of and most of us will admit, Ashbery has that sane and wholly measured love of gossip without which—come on—literary studies could not endure.

Ashbery is a contemporary poet whose work is fun, thought provoking, and again and again exciting, as well as beautiful, in ways that—again and again—trouble any easy reading of poetry, as they trouble those contemporary poetry readers who let ourselves slip into any such easy reading. He is a writer I have always been glad was here.

—*September 7, 2004*
New York and
Philadelphia

3

Samuel R. Delany, by K. Leslie Steiner

"K. Leslie Steiner" is Samuel R. Delany's critical alter-ego, invented in London in 1973 for an essay called "The Scorpion Garden Revisited," a discussion of my novel *Hogg*. As explained in my preface to the essay collection *The Straits of Messina* (1989), the writings of K. Leslie Steiner are an answer to the question "Wouldn't it be nice to have someone say all the fine and brilliant things about my work I so desperately would like to hear . . . ?"

After a difficult thirty-six-hour labor, on April 1, 1942, at seven o'clock in the morning, Samuel Ray Delany, Jr., was born at Harlem Hospital on Lenox Avenue and 138th Street, in New York City's black ghetto. Because he was cyanotic, there was some suspicion he might be brain damaged.

The youngest of four daughters, Delany's mother, Margaret Carey Boyd Delany (June 16, 1916–March 2, 1995), was a short, level-headed, intelligent woman—exactly five feet tall—who'd met her husband while she worked for the Works Projects Administration (WPA). For a while, after her marriage to Samuel Delany, Sr., Margaret worked as a stenotypist. At her husband's urging, she got her own license as a funeral director, though she never practiced.

Samuel R. Delany, Sr. (May 6, 1906–October 1, 1960), was the youngest of ten children in a family of black educators and professionals involved with the black Episcopal College, St. Augustine's, in Raleigh, North Carolina. In 1923, at age seventeen, Samuel Ray Delany had followed his older brothers and sisters to New York. After a first marriage at nineteen to a young woman named Mary, of which his family generally disapproved, followed by a brief stint owning a haberdashery on 138th Street with a St. Augustine graduate, William K. Bell, he became a successful Harlem undertaker, initially in partnership with an older black man, a Mr. Levy. Delany bought out Levy in 1938, the year of his second marriage to Margaret, but kept the name of the funeral establishment, Levy & Delany's, which he moved to 2250 Seventh Avenue, between 132nd and 133rd Streets, across the avenue and one block up from the old Lafayette Theater (a supermarket by the time of Samuel Junior's childhood; later it would become a church). Often Delany Senior said he owed Levy a great debt: "He showed me almost every way possible *not* to run a successful funeral business!" In a November 1978 talk Delany Junior delivered at the Studio Museum of Harlem ("The Necessity of Tomorrows"), he said:

> I wonder, with my father dead twenty years now, if the two of them found any irony in the suggestion of the Jew and the Irishman running what, by the middle of the 1940s, was considered a rather swell Harlem funeral establishment. At any rate, the irony was misleading. Both were black men. Both owed their ethnic patronymics to the whites who had owned their grandparents, their great-grandparents.

The name Levy & Delany appears in stories by Langston Hughes and other black writers chronicling Harlem in the 1940s and '50s. Managed by his nephew and several younger business acquaintances, the business persisted—under that name—for more than twenty years beyond Delany Senior's death at age fifty-four from lung cancer. A tall, slender, handsome man, the senior Samuel was even-tempered in his work but often angry and anxious with his family. He was talented in both art and music and taught his son to play the violin.

Delany Senior's own father—young Delany's grandfather, Henry Beard Delany—had been born in slavery in Georgia in 1857 and was seven in 1865 at the time of emancipation. (The middle name, Ray, which Delany Junior and Senior shared, came from an older brother of Henry Beard's.) Henry Beard's memory of the great event was of running excitedly around the house of his Scottish masters, wearing a small apron, which, untied, flapped around him. Along with the other slaves, he shouted, "I'm free! I'm free!" but, inside, he was unsure what "free" meant. Against the law, little Henry Beard had already been taught to read and write by his owners. (Often he would say, "Once emancipation came, we were so busy trying to survive, there would have been no time for me to learn.") By his death, in 1928, he had become Vice Principal of St. Augustine's (today we would say Vice Chancellor), and white and black ministers together had elected him the first black suffrage bishop of the Archdiocese of North and South Carolina. Both W. E. B. Du Bois and Booker T. Washington were his friends and oft-times visitors to the college. Activist and entertainers Paul Robeson and Cab Calloway, Nobel Prize winner Ralph Bunche, Secretary of Housing and Urban Development Robert Weaver, and singer Marian Anderson were all friends of his children. Delany Senior's mother, Nan Logan, had been a teacher and eventually Dean of Women at St.

Augustine's, as well as the mother of Henry Beard's ten children, of whom, as we have already said, Delany Senior was the youngest.

Margaret's father, Samuel Hugo Boyd, had been Chief Red Cap at Grand Central Terminal during the twenties and thirties. (Delany Senior had spent some time working as a red cap at Grand Central Terminal, where Samuel Hugo, deciding that he was a reliable young man, had brought him home to meet his family.) Traveling about the country in his teens, Samuel Hugo had run an elevator for a while in the Callahan Building in Dayton, Ohio, at the same time as black poet and novelist Paul Laurence Dunbar.

Born in the 1870s, Samuel Hugo was, of course, too young to have any memories of slavery. Frequently he told this story about his slave-born father, however, to his children and grand children. The June-day emancipation was a hot one in Virginia. As a boy Samuel Hugo's father was sitting in a hogshead beside a road with another, older slave for the shade, when a white officer on horseback rode past, reigned up, and called down, "You're free, old man! You're free!" The elderly black man leaned forward and declared, "Oh, thank you, sir! Thank you, sir!" The intensity with which the old man expressed it was the first indication Samuel Hugo's to-be-father had of the significance of the coming transformation for his people. Among the adult Samuel Hugo's closest friends was Matthew Henson, the black explorer and writer who had accompanied Admiral Peary to the North Pole and who had reached the pole a day before Peary.

Margaret Delany's mother, Sara Fitzgerald, had followed her own mother, Ophelia Fitzgerald, a fancy pastry cook from Petersberg, Virginia, to New York City by boat, to work as a maid in 1898, when she turned eighteen. (Sara's father, Archie Fitzgerald, Jr., a laborer, had died of a stroke, working in the fields in the hot sun, when she was a child.) Sara Ophelia and Samuel Hugo Boyd had been childhood sweethearts in Petersburg. Soon Sara was living in the first house in Harlem open to blacks working for the Germans in the neighborhood—a rooming house on 132nd Street between Seventh and Lenox, owned by a white woman married to a black man, literally around the corner from where her youngest daughter's family would live, forty years later. (This is not to be confused with the apartment house on 133rd between Fifth and Lenox whose white landlords, two years later in 1904, evacuated all the white tenants and moved in single black male laborers, which started protests and even riots in the neighborhood. Some people tried to fence the house in. Often this is cited—incorrectly—as the first house where blacks lived in Harlem.) Samuel Hugo came to New York in 1902. He and Sara were married in 1904. All four Boyd daughters (one died in infancy) were born at home, on Morris Avenue in the Bronx. Born in 1880, Sara Ophelia Fitzgerald Boyd had her own tales of slavery times, from her mother Ophelia Fitzgerald. (Sara Boyd and Samuel Hugo lived for long periods with all three of her daughters. After her husband's Christmas Eve death from stomach cancer in 1950, Sara Boyd eventually lived with Delany's mother, Margaret, till her own death at a 102 in 1982.) The eight-year-old Ophelia had had a cruel master who often punished her unfairly. Once, when her master was ill in bed and a guest had stopped by to see him, he ordered the little girl to bring the guest a glass of water, but, because she was angry with him, just outside the door, she stopped and spit in the glass, then came in and handed it to the visitor. After the visitor left, the master called the little girl to him. "I saw what you did," he said. "I want you to know, as soon as I get up out this bed, you will get another whipping!" Well, Sara would comment, with a twinkle that mimed the way her mother had told the tale to her, she just made sure he never got up!

The implication (though neither Sara nor, apparently, her mother had ever confirmed it) was that the little girl had proceeded to poison her white master to escape the coming flogging—for, indeed, coupled with his own illness, the man had died.

"Did she really *kill* him . . . ?" Sara's half-dozen grandchildren would demand, as indeed Ophelia's own children had probably demanded in their own childhood.

"A little girl kill a grown man? Oh, I really couldn't say. I just don't know!" But when, a month or a year later, they would ask her to retell the tale, Sara Boyd would tell it with the same wicked twinkle. In later years, young Samuel often thought it a particularly interesting story from a woman who would go on to be a much sought-after cook of wedding cakes, fancy pies, charlotte russes, cookies, éclairs, and fine pastries, especially by white clients, both in the South and in the century's early years in New York City. Another story, this one of his maternal great-grandfather, an ex-slave with brick red hair and freckles, who went without shoes all year long, told how Archie, Sara's grandfather, had sat on his porch with his bare feet on the railing and a loaded shotgun across his lap, arguing off half a dozen white men, who'd stormed into his yard "looking for a nigger to lynch," while little Sara and her sister Martha crouched inside the country shack, peeking out under the blue speckled curtain, through the window. But, along with another family lynching story from his father's family that he made use of in both his fiction (*Atlantis: Model 1924*) and his nonfiction ("The Semiology of Silence"), these were among the tales that came to Samuel Junior as part of his black heritage.

A bright and outgoing child, young Samuel grew up in the two floors over his father's Harlem funeral parlor on Seventh Avenue between 132nd Street and 133rd. When Samuel was four, his mother enrolled him in the Vassar Summer Institute for Gifted Children, at Vassar College, in Poughkeepsie, New York. Mother, son, and infant daughter Sara stayed for the six-week summer session,[1] not far from Hopewell Junction, where Samuel Senior had built a modest summer home (four rooms, an attic, and an unfinished cellar), and where each Labor Day, from several years before he was born until Samuel Junior was sixteen, the family held an annual barbeque. An eighty-pound pig was roasted on an outdoor grill throughout the night. The next day upwards of a hundred family and friends would gather to drink and eat barbeque, along with tubs of coleslaw, boiled corn, potato salad, and endless homemade pies, to tell stories and generally enjoy themselves.

When young Samuel was about ten and his younger sister Peggy eight, Margaret went to work as a New York City Public Library clerk. Before the Schomberg Collection of Negro Literature received its own building on 135th Street, Margaret Delany was the senior clerk in charge of the Collection and also of the library's Russian Collection, in their joint home on the second floor of the Countee Cullen branch library on East 125th Street. Later she worked in the Film Department of the newly opened Donnell Branch on Fifty-Third Street, across from the Museum of Modern Art and, in the years just before her retirement, at the St. Agnes branch on Amsterdam Avenue, across the street from where her son now had his own apartment.

The number of Samuels in the family may have encouraged Samuel Junior to change his name. Until he was ten, his aunts, uncles, and cousins usually called him Little Sam or even Sambo, to distinguish him from his father, Samuel, and his maternal grandfather, Samuel Hugo. In the summer of 1952, in the first year at his second summer camp, Camp Woodland, Delany gave himself the nickname Chip, which stuck for the rest of his life.

With his sister, Delany attended largely white, private schools (Horace Mann Lincoln, The Dalton School) and went to Sunday school and Sunday services at the black Episcopalian Church, St. Philips, in whose basement, where now he went Wednesday nights and Saturday mornings to choir rehearsal (for a season he was an altar boy), the Broadway cast of Gertrude Stein's *Four Saints in Three Acts* had rehearsed with choreographer Frederick Ashton and director John Houseman over the winter of 1933–34.

(Henry Beard died in 1929, a baker's dozen years before Samuel Junior was born.)

Early interests in both science and the arts led Samuel to the Bronx High School of Science, in 1956, where almost immediately he began to write seriously and to make friends with others with similar interests.

Delany spent his adolescence writing novels, composing music; and when, in 1954, his family moved from over the funeral parlor on Seventh Avenue to Morningside Gardens, at the west edge of Harlem just above Columbia University, he even choreographed several dances that were presented at the General Grant Community Center. There, when he was seventeen, he taught remedial reading to an after-school class of Puerto Rican young men—the more remarkable, since he suffered from severe dyslexia, a condition not acknowledged at the time but which had already caused his frustrated parents to retain half a dozen special tutors and even psychotherapists to deal with the discrepancy between his obvious verbal ability and his appalling spelling and writing. Like many bright dyslexics before and since (the condition has plagued a number of writers, including Gustave Flaubert, William Butler Yeats, and Virginia Woolf), Delany was slowly developing strategies to get around it, most of which were, as they had been with these other writers, a matter of endless revisions, endless rewriting.

Shortly after his father's death in 1960, the eighteen-year-old Delany dropped out of his first year of City College and, at nineteen, married a talented eighteen-year-old poet, Marilyn Hacker, who had also gone to the Bronx High School of Science and then, as a fifteen-year-old early admissions student, had gone on to New York University, which she finished in three years. At their apartment on East 6th Street in the newly named East Village, Delany wrote his first science fiction novel, *The Jewels of Aptor*—completed when he was nineteen. Working as an editorial assistant at Ace Books, Hacker first brought the manuscript to the editor-in-chief's attention, saying she had found it in the slush pile. In December 1962, when he was twenty, Ace published it. Over the next six years eight more Delany science fiction novels appeared, including a trilogy of novels, today known by their collective title, *The Fall of the Towers* (1963, '64, '65). The trilogy was followed by *The Ballad of Beta-2* (1965), *Babel-17* (1966), *Empire Star* (1966), *The Einstein Intersection* (1967), and the highly acclaimed *Nova* (1968), two of which—*Babel-17* and *The Einstein Intersection*—won Nebula Awards from the Science Fiction Writers of America as best SF novels of their respective years.

The period was not placid, however. In winter of 1963, after a breakdown brought on largely by overwork, Delany spent three weeks in Mt. Sinai mental hospital. The winter following his release, Delany and Hacker entered a three-way relationship with a young man a year their senior from Lakeland, Florida (Bobby Folsom was twenty-four). When, at the advent of Folsom's wife, Darlene Folsom (twenty-eight), the menage broke up, Delany and Folsom took off together to work on shrimp boats in Aransas Pass, Texas, on the Texas Gulf, just south of Corpus Christie. After the briefest attempt by the three to get back together in New York, Folsom returned to Florida (and a twenty-year jail term), and Delany and Hacker separated. Hacker chronicles all this in her sequence of poems, "The Navigators," included in her first collection, the National Book Award–winning *Presentation Piece*. The sequence takes its title from the "triple" relationships described among the spaceship navigators in Delany's sixth novel *Babel-17*. The affair's tale takes up the last third of Delany's Hugo Award-winning autobiography *The Motion of Light in Water* (1988).

October 18, 1965, on an Icelandic Airlines flight Delany flew to Europe for six months with a friend, Ron Helstrom, whom he had met during the summer when he'd worked as a header and cook on shrimp boats on the Gulf Coast. *Empire Star* had been written in New York City over eleven days that August to finance the trip.

After visiting Luxemburg for a week and Paris and Venice for two weeks each, Delany, Helstrom, and a third friend, Bill Baluziac, whom they'd met on the plane over, spent most of the next four months in Greece, first in the Cyclades, then on the mainland, while Delany worked on his novel *The Einstein Intersection* (1967: then called *A Fabulous, Formless Darkness*). By way of Munich, London (where he met fellow SF novelist John Brunner and the writer/editor Michael Moorcock), Reims, and Luxembourg, Delany arrived back in New York on April 15, 1966.

Hacker and Delany separated and rejoined several more times over the next eight years. Delany was gay—he had been aware of his sexual preferences since age ten—and while this was not a central node of tension between Delany and his wife, certainly it contributed to what tensions there were. During this time, Hacker pursued several relationships, most importantly with a young half–Native American poet named Link (Thomas Luther Cupp, 1947–1973). Link had been an adolescent protégé of the San Francisco poet Jack Spicer and, when he and Hacker began their friendship, was the twenty-one-year-old lover of twenty-eight-year-old poet and critic Hunce Voelcker. For a while Hacker and Link lived together in San Francisco, on Perine Place. Soon Link began a relationship with a young man from Georgia half a dozen years his senior, George Ponder, and Hacker moved into a flat two houses away at 1067 Natoma Street, upstairs from a middle-aged black woman named Helen, who actively practiced witchcraft.

After becoming a major member of the gay theater collective, The Cockettes, that bloomed in the late 1960s and early '70s under the creative genius of Hibiscus (aka George Harris), Link died of cholera and malnutrition during an extended trip to Cambodia in 1974. (Link and Hacker wrote the vast majority of the lyrics to one of The Cockettes' most ambitious shows, *Pearls Over Shanghai*, with which the group opened their New York tour, though the collective nature of the enterprise meant they were uncredited.) Hacker's other major relationship during this time was with an older Englishman, the "D. G. B." of a number of her poems from those years, who first visited San Francisco in 1971 and whom Hacker followed to London at the end of the year.

Shortly after Delany returned from his Greek stay, by way of London and a while hitchhiking through northern France to reach the airport at Luxembourg, he was living with a young baritone, Ron Bowman, at 33 St. Mark's Place in New York. On March 11th of 1967, Delany's 1966 novel *Babel-17* won him his first Nebula Award from the Science Fiction Writers of America as best SF novel of its year.

He was two weeks away from his twenty-fifth birthday.

Over the 1966–67 Christmas/New Year's season, for three weeks Delany returned to London, to see Moorcock, Brunner, Judith Merrill, and meet Thomas M. Disch, J. G. Ballard, Brian Aldiss, John Sladek, and Pamela Zoline. Back in New York Delany finished writing his ninth novel, *Nova*. By June, Bowman broke up the St. Mark's Place apartment. During another brief stab at getting back together with Hacker, Delany turned his first published short SF work, the novella *The Star Pit*, into a two-hour radio drama for Baird Searles's Mind's Eye Theater, on WBAI-FM, directed by Daniel Landau, in which Delany played the main character. With special effects by a young musician, Susan Schweers, the radio drama premiered during the Thanksgiving week of 1967, just after Delany himself had joined a commune, centered around a rock group he'd been working with, The Heavenly Breakfast, composed of Steve Wiseman, Schweers, Bert Lee (later of the Central Park Sheiks), and Delany himself. By now Hacker had gone to San Francisco to rejoin Link.

The Star-Pit was broadcast annually for more than ten years over WBAI-FM in New York City, and even today, on Jim Freund's *Hour of the Wolf*, gets broken out every few years as an exemplar of ambitious radio drama.[2]

A dozen years later, the notebooks from this period yielded Delany his third nonfiction book, *Heavenly Breakfast: An Essay on the Winter of Love*, which—especially since its 1997 republication by Bamberger Books—has become a popular teaching text in universities around the country, for classes dealing with the '60s and alternative life styles.

Just after the Heavenly Breakfast disbanded, *Nova* appeared in the spring of 1968. Longtime SF critic Algis J. Budrys wrote in a *Galaxy* review:

> Samuel Delany, right now, as of this book, *Nova*, not as of some future book or some accumulated body of work, is the best science fiction writer in the world, at a time when competition for that status is intense.

The book had been completed in the two months after Delany turned twenty-five. He was now twenty-six, though many people, including Budrys, were under the impression he was several years older. Delany won two more Nebula Awards for short fiction. "Aye, and Gomorrah . . ." (1967) won the award in 1968 for best SF short story, the same year as *The Einstein Intersection* won for best novel. Two years later, "Time Considered as a Helix of Semi-Precious Stones" (1968) won Delany his fourth Nebula while he was living in San Francisco, again with Hacker. By then the story had also won a Hugo Award. Both were included in Delany's first short-story collection, *Driftglass* (1969).

The end of 1968 and the beginning of 1969 saw Delany's first two experiments in pornography. Written shortly before he took off from New

York to San Francisco, the first was a novel called *Equinox*, completed in
September '68 but not published until 1973 (under the title *The Tides of Lust*,
by Lancer Books). A night-long critical session over the manuscript with
Michael Perkins convinced Delany that a great deal more, however, might be
done with the genre than he'd tried so far. Delany delivered his talk "About
5,750 Words" at that year's Christmas meeting in New York of the Modern
Language Association and, on New Years' Eve, flew to San Francisco to
rejoin Marilyn.[3] His major project, at that time, was his novel *Dhalgren*, but,
after stalling on the first chapter in the West Coast city, Delany directed a
production of Jean Genet's *Les Bonnes*, in French, with William Alvin Moore[4]
as Claire, Gerald Fabian as Solange, and Marilyn Hacker as Madame. The
production played for three weekends in a theater space Delany and Hacker
set up in their front hall (with Link running lights): *Le Théatre du sorbet*. On
opening night, after the show the cast and crew, along with house-mate Paul
Caruso, served the audience lemon sherbet and coffee. Besides directing,
Delany designed and executed the unit set: the elaborate chairs, tables, fireplace, windows, a vanity, and wall sconces for Madame's boudoir were elab-
orately drawn with thick black marker on large fragments of white paper,
which were stapled to the working chairs and tables the actors used, or were
hung on the dark gray walls. That audience included many poets and artists
then working in the city—among them Robert Duncan, Paul Mariah, Bill
Anderson, Knute Stiles, Ebbe Borregaard, Jack Thibeaux, Joanne Kyger,
George Stanley, Lewis Ellingham, John Ryan, Deneen Peckinpah (novelist
niece of the film director Samuel Peckinpah, whose first novel Delany was
instrumental in getting published), Richard Brautigan, Nemi Frost, and
James Alexander—with Gerald Fabian faithfully fulfilling Genet's exhorta-
tion that in every performance the set be covered with colorful bouquets of
real flowers, supplied to Fabian from the weekly discards of a florist friend
across the river in Berkeley. Relieved by cascades of yellow, blue, white, and
purple flowers—as well as a pair of startling red rubber gloves—the stark
black and white sets and costumes were highly effective. After three weeks,
the production moved to a church basement theater, where it ran on weekends for another three months. Finally, it was recorded and broadcast (still
in French) over KPFA-FM, in Berkeley. Another theatrical project from the
same period was a ten-minute super-eight-millimeter film, *Tiresias*, in both
color and black and white, which Delany wrote and directed with Robert
Mooney filming (the single copy has since been lost). Again it starred Hacker,
Moore, Fabian, and Mooney's then-lover Peter Rooney.

Dhalgren was still undergoing a great deal of conceptual reorganization at
this time; so, from March through the end of June, with many of Perkins's
comments in mind, Delany wrote out in longhand a draft of a pornographic
novel, *Hogg*, filling most of four notebooks and part of a fifth, before plunging

into the reconceived *Dhalgren* that summer. Despite the subscription date at its end, *Hogg*'s first draft was finished perhaps days before the June 27 Stonewall riots in New York.

In an interview article by Anthony Miller in the *Los Angeles Times*, Delany has described *Hogg*: "It's the last pre-Stonewall gay novel written in America . . . It's very much a book that comes out of the anger of a gay man who wants to tear the whole thing down. Once Stonewall comes, once there was a concerted gay-liberation movement and there was a way for these disruptive energies to channel in more constructive ways, I don't think I could have thought *Hogg* at all."

The book was rewritten several times over the next few years, though it was not changed substantially in terms of plot. It was only published twenty years later, however, in 1995, by Fiction Collective-Two's Black Ice Books.

In the last years of the 1960s and throughout the '70s, Delany wrote and published a series of critical essays on science fiction, which turned on the idea of science fiction not as a particular kind of text, but rather as a discourse—in his words, "a way of reading, a way of making certain texts make sense." At the same time, his critique was deeply grounded in the material reality of the genre: printing practices in pulp magazines, editorial conventions and history, biographical occurrences in the lives of writers, editors, and the particularly committed readers who put on SF conventions and published SF fanzines since the thirties. On the strength of these early essays, Delany and Hacker were invited by Paperback Library to put together a journal on the model of the highly successful *New American Review*, then out from Signet Books. Between 1970 and '71, four issues of *Quark* appeared, before the publisher Hy Steerman withdrew his support. On his return to New York, Delany wrote two issues of *Wonder Woman* comics for DC Comics, the second of which was the first of a six-issue story arc. Changes in administrative policy made Delany lose interest in the project, when DC scuttled the rest of the story arc.

Delany essays from the period that received particular attention included "About 5,750 Words" (1968), *The American Shore* (1975)—a book-length essay on a single SF short story ("Angouleme," by Thomas M. Disch), a study which to many SF scholars seemed a paragon of involuted theoretical tortuosity, but still stands in the landscape of SF criticism today, a daunting crag to be sidestepped by some or to be scaled by others—as well as an examination of Ursula K. Le Guin's seventh novel, "To Read *The Dispossessed*" (1976), its title a play on Louis Althusser's book-length essay, "*Lire* Le Capital."

In 1972, during a year living at the Hotel Albert back in New York's Greenwich Village, Delany made another film, *The Orchid*. Produced by Barbara Wise, in sixteen millimeter, it was thirty-five minutes long, in sound and color. Again with Gerald Fabian in the lead role, Delany shot the film over twelve days in February, with a cast of approximately fifteen. The production employed the Wises' then seventeen-year-old son, David Wise, as cameraman. Already a talented film-maker, David's work had been shown at the Museum of Modern Art. Delany edited *The Orchid* in his room on the tenth floor of the Hotel Albert. It was finished that summer, with an original score by John Herbert MacDowell. Premiered at the World Science Fiction Convention in Chicago that September (Delany himself was not present), it caused a riot. Outraged fans tried to shout the film off and even pulled down the screen.

On Christmas Eve, at Marilyn's entreaty, Delany flew to London, again to get back together with his wife, who by then was running a successful rare-book business with her partner John Sims in the King's Road Market in London's Chelsea. In April of that year, at an SF convention in Bristol, their daughter was conceived. In London Delany rewrote *Dhalgren* one more time and, at Hacker's insightful urging, added the last chapter, "The Anathēmata." Delany also wrote (or better, constructed from his journals) his thirty-thousand-word essay "Shadows," published in two issues of the journal *Foundation*. As well, he rewrote *Hogg*. In the ten months before and just after the birth of their daughter Iva Alyxander Hacker-Delany at Queen Charlotte's Maternity Hospital in Hammersmith, he also wrote *Trouble on Triton*.

Shortly after this time, Delany took an active part in the *Women in Science Fiction Symposium* (published 1975), organized by Jeff Smith, with Joanna Russ, Louise White, Kate Wilhelm, Suzy McKee Charnas, Ursula K. Le Guin, Chelsea Quinn Yarbro, Vonda McIntyre, James Tiptree Jr. (Alice Sheldon), Virginia Kidd, and others.

Almost a year after Iva's birth, just before Christmas of 1974, Delany, Hacker, and Iva returned together to the States. In September, as a result of an exchange of letters, critic Leslie Fiedler had invited Delany to take a position as visiting Butler Chair Professor at SUNY Buffalo for the following term. Late that December, Iva, Delany and Hacker saw the first printed volumes of *Dhalgren* in a Kennedy Airport book rack, even before they arrived in customs, and as they came out, they saw, slouched back wide-kneed on a chair in one of the waiting areas, a U.S. sailor in uncharacteristic winter whites, reading a copy.

That Christmas they stayed with Delany's mother. In January, Delany went on to SUNY Buffalo. Hacker returned to London with their infant daughter. Four months later in April of that year, Hacker's first volume of poems from Viking Press, *Presentation Piece* (1975), won the National Book Award for Poetry. She returned to New York to accept the prize at the award ceremony at Lincoln Center and, sending Iva with Delany up to Buffalo, began a reading tour—which included an evening's reading and reception Delany arranged at Buffalo. Then, with Iva, once more Hacker returned to London.

Delany was now thirty-two and a father. His eight-hundred-seventy-nine-page science fiction novel *Dhalgren*, from Bantam Books, had been the product of five years' work. The novel deals with the disaffected young, black and white, and the tensions between them, unto interracial rape—yet always with an uncharacteristic take. Its hero is an amnesiac half-breed Native American, who hitchhikes to the burned-out city of Bellona, where talent, celebrity, and even the performance of laudable and praiseworthy acts others might call heroic turn out to be largely a matter of chance, mistake, or social misapprehension. These socially created images—illusions, really—are wholly apart from, and sometimes in direct opposition to, the will of the characters. Easily the most controversial SF novel of its decade, *Dhalgren* portrays graphically—and sympathetically—both homosexual and heterosexual behavior. Rather than spaceships and interstellar travel, many of its images come from the burned-out inner city of the sort Delany's old neighborhood Harlem had become, back in New York, and which now blighted block after block of most major American cities.

As one reads over the negative reviews today, it's clear the most angering aspect of the novel was that it presented a view of the world counter to the heroic individualism at the center of so much science fiction adventure. But both inside and outside the science fiction world, there were many positive reactions: "I have just read the very best ever to come out of the science fiction field," Theodore Sturgeon began his March 1975 review of *Dhalgren* in *Galaxy*.

Over the next dozen years *Dhalgren* sold more than a million copies, netted the writer a good-sized mailbag of enthusiastic fan letters, was turned into a rock opera by a young Los Angeles composer, Quentin Llorentes; and, in *The Libertarian Review*, critic Jeff Riggenbach wrote in 1981:

> A nearly 900-page tour de force of a novel, *Dhalgren* still seems to me, after five years and two thorough readings of its extensive text, to stake a better claim than anything else published in this country in the last quarter century (excepting only Gass's *Omensetter's Luck* and Nabokov's *Pale Fire*) to a permanent place as one of the enduring monuments of our national literature.

Delany's next novel *Trouble on Triton* (1976: originally published as *Triton*) tells the story of a man in the twenty-second century, born on Mars and living on Neptune's larger moon, who decides midway through the book to deal with his numerous personality problems by becoming a woman. Many consider the book to synthesize Delany's concerns in *Dhalgren* with the color and adventure of his early science fiction. *Triton* has been repeatedly discussed in contemporary considerations both of utopian and gender questions and was eventually reprinted by Wesleyan University Press with an introduction by Kathy Acker.

Trouble on Triton led directly to Delany's next major enterprise, a series of eleven tales—including short stories, several novellas, and a near-four-hundred-page novel—which together fill four volumes. The series is called *Return to*

Nevèrÿon. Set in the distant past, rather than the future, the stories are leisurely, developed with care, and written in a style combining precise analysis with colorful description. They tend to turn on intriguing paradoxes: What if a man who has committed himself to ending slavery in a primitive culture is sexually excited by the accoutrements of slavery—whips, chains, and iron slave collars? What are the parallels—and differences—between a fatal, sexually transmitted disease that comes to a primitive city at history's dawn and the spread of AIDS in New York City over 1983 and the first months of 1984? This last, *The Tale of Plagues and Carnivals* (1984), was the first novel about AIDS from a major publisher in the United States.

Among science fiction readers, *Return to Nevèrÿon* (which consists of *Tales of Nevèrÿon* [1978: five stories]; *Neveryóna, or: The Tale of Signs and Cities* [1982: novel]; *Flight from Nevèrÿon* [1985: two stories and a short novel]; and *Return to Nevèrÿon* [first published as *The Bridge of Lost Desire* (1987): two novellas and a reprise of the opening story)]), was as controversial as *Dhalgren*, if not more so. In the midst of the series, even though the mass-market paperback sale for each of the separate volumes was in the two- and three-hundred-thousand range—quite respectable for a mass-market book—for a couple of years Delany was effectively blacklisted by the then-largest American bookstore chain, Dalton Books, along with Barbara Hambly and Tanith Lee, two other fantasy writers whose works dealt, as did Delany's, with gay material. When Dalton Books explained that they would no longer be stocking any Delany, Delany's publisher Bantam Book declined even to read the manuscript of the fourth and final volume in the series, *Return to Nevèrÿon*. When the book was eventually published in hardcover by Arbor House in 1987, the editor, Delany's long-time friend David Hartwell, changed the title to *The Bridge of Lost Desire* as a marketing strategy to dissociate it, in the minds of bookstore stock buyers, from the contaminated series, even though, by now, as a result of letters and articles in a number of gay newspapers, the ban on Delany (and Hambly and Lee) had been lifted when Dalton Books was sold to Barnes & Noble. Indeed, one way to look at the growing conservatism throughout publishing in particular and the book business in general during those years was simply as a response to the collapsing and merging of U.S. publishing itself. By the end of 1987, pretty much all of Delany's fiction—as had most fiction by what the industry then called "mid-list" writers (i.e., writers like Delany with high critical reputations and substantial and faithful audiences in the hundreds of thousands, whose books still failed to break into the two-million-plus sales of the bona fide paperback "Bestseller")—had been dropped from the catalogues of publisher after publisher.

Delany's essays on SF continued to appear through the 1970s and '80s, however. Some scholars found them richly suggestive, others intricately frustrating. After his term as visiting Butler Chair Professor at Buffalo in 1975, Delany spent

a few months again living at the Hotel Albert in Greenwich Village, then moved
into a fifth-floor Upper West Side apartment, where, with a term out here or
a term out there as a guest university teacher, he lives to this day. Though they
had officially separated in 1975, Delany and Hacker only divorced in 1980.
In 1977, on a July 14 of torrential rains in New York City, Delany met Frank
Romeo at the Variety Photoplays Theater. Soon the two men were living together. During his eight years with Romeo (a singer [part of a trio, The Trout,
with Cassandra Morgan, and his brother Tony Romeo] and director of two
short films in the 1980s, *Bye Bye Love*, and *The Aunts*, which Delany produced,
scripted, and edited) there were two more multi-week trips to Europe, one by
air to Paris and another by boat to Antwerp. The first year they visited Rome
and made a return-trip to Greece. The second, they revisited Rome and took a
train trip to Romeo's family village in the Abruzzi mountains, Calomel. In 1981
the two men took another train tour, this time of the United States, through
Meridian, Mississippi, to New Orleans, with a detour by car among the can-
yons and national parks of the Southwest (the Grand Canyon, Arches National
Park, Zion National Park, Bryce Canyon, Canyon Land), Death Valley, and a
few of the surrounding ghost-towns, then by train again to Los Angeles, San
Francisco,[5] Vancouver, Chicago, and Montreal. On the train with Frank, com-
ing down from Canada, Delany completed the handwritten draft of *Neveryóna*.
That journey would also mark the landscapes of Rhyanon and Velm in *Stars in
My Pocket Likes Grains of Sand* (1984).

During these years, Delany held several visiting academic positions:

For two weeks in November 1972, he was a visiting writer at Wesleyan
University's Center for the Humanities.

For spring of 1975, as mentioned, he was visiting Butler Chair Professor at
SUNY Buffalo.

(In 1976 Delany began a project with artist Howard Chaykin that, two years
later, in 1978, would be published as the 106-page graphic novel, *Empire*.)

For a term in 1977 he was a Senior Fellow at the Center for Twentieth
Century Studies at the University of Wisconsin.

For two weeks in 1978 he was Writer in Residence at SUNY Albany.

In 1984 Delany published *Stars in My Pocket Like Grains of Sand*, set many
years in the future amidst an interstellar society of some six thousand worlds,
in which all intelligent living beings are known as women and womankind—
much the way humanity was once known as man and mankind. But even the
meanings of "she" and "he" are completely other in these far-future days. The
story details the love between two men, one, Marq Dyeth, an ultra-sophisticated
and well-traveled "industrial diplomat," and the other, Rat Korga, the most
ordinary of uneducated workers, who happens to be the lone survivor of a
world which has destroyed itself through a violent political process called "cultural fugue." Even before the book was published, Delany's publisher wanted

a sequel to the novel. Not very enthusiastically, Delany agreed to do a second volume to complete the story of Marq and Rat. Though he planned it out and even began writing it, and here and there (in *Reflex Magazine* and the *Review of Contemporary Fiction*) sections of the sequel have appeared, the book was never finished. In January 1985, the eight-year live-in relationship with Frank came to an end. A few months later Delany was honored with the Pilgrim Award from the Science Fiction Research Association of America, for excellence in SF scholarship. His essays continued to appear in *Science Fiction Studies* and, even more frequently, in the *New York Review of Science Fiction*.

In 1987, for the fall term Delany was a Senior Fellow at Cornell's Society for the Humanities and roomed on the Cornell campus in Telluride House. While there, he was interviewed by then-undergraduate Kenneth R. James. A second, written interview with James would appear in *Silent Interviews* (1994). In December 1987, while still at Cornell, Delany was invited to join the faculty of the University of Massachusetts as a (full) Professor of Comparative Literature, where he began teaching in September of 1988. Earlier that year, Delany's autobiography *The Motion of Light in Water: Sex and Science Fiction Writing, 1957–1965*, came out. In 1989, when he had been at the University of Massachusetts for a year, the World Science Fiction Convention in Boston voted the book a Hugo Award for best nonfiction title of its year. On the strength of this book, his last ten years of science fiction, and his Nevèrÿon tales, in 1989 the *Lambda Book Report* included Delany among its "Fifty Men and Women Who Have Done Most to Change Our Attitudes Toward Gayness in the Last Hundred Years." The same year he won a life-time achievement award from the Dark Room, Harvard University's black students collective.

For three weeks in 1993 he was a visiting Senior Fellow at the University of Michigan's Humanities Center; in the same year he was a visiting professor at the University of Kansas, at Lawrence, where he spent an afternoon and evening with William Burroughs.

For two weeks in September 1995, he was Distinguished Writer-in-Residence at the University of Idaho in Moscow, Idaho. In the same term he was Cole Visiting Honors Professor at the Honors College of Michigan State University at East Lansing, Michigan. In November of that term, for two weeks, he was a Senior Fellow at the Atlantic Center for the Arts at Daytona Beach, Florida.

In 1997, in New York, Delany was honored with the Kessler Award from the Center for Lesbian and Gay Studies (CLAGS), and delivered that year's prestigious annual Kessler Lecture, ". . . Three, Two, One, Contact: Times Square Red." Four months later, "Times Square Red" was delivered as a Chancellor's Distinguished Faculty Lecture at the University of Massachusetts, on his receipt of the University Chancellor's Distinguished Faculty Medal.

During his second year at the University of Massachusetts, Delany published an article, "Twilight in the Rue Morgue" (*Transition* 54), examining the work of historian of science and culture critic Donna Haraway; another, "Street Talk / Straight Talk" (*Differences. A Special Issue on Queer Theory*), was sharply critical of AIDS research and the dissemination of medical information.

In October of 1991, after he delivered his keynote lecture, "Aversion/ Perversion/Diversion," at the Fifth Annual Lesbian and Gay Studies Conference at Rutgers University, from the thousand attendees squeezed into the auditorium that evening Delany received a boisterous standing ovation. Almost equally successful was his presentation of "The Rhetoric of Sex / The Discourse of Desire" as a two-hour long evening lecture at the Massachusetts Institute of Technology.

In 1990, during the first of two terms he spent as Head of the Comparative Literature Department, while he commuted back and forth between Amherst, Massachusetts, and his New York City apartment, Delany met and befriended a thirty-six-year-old homeless man, Dennis Rickett, who sold books from a blanket on Seventy-Second Street. In February of 1991, Dennis and Delany began to live together.

Though Delany's fiction was by now all but unavailable in the United States, Grafton Books in England was keeping the four volumes of *Return to Nevèrÿon* in print, as well as *Dhalgren* and some of his other works. Delany's collected short fiction, *Driftglass/Starshards*, appeared from Grafton in 1993. And at Wesleyan University Press, editorial director Terry Cochran spearheaded a major move to bring Delany's fiction back into print in this country, starting with *Tales of Nevèrÿon* in 1992. Meanwhile, a new novel (expanded from an old story), *They Fly at Çiron* (1993), was published in an elegant limited edition and a trade edition by Ron Drummond's Incunabula Press in Seattle. Wesleyan followed the Nevèrÿon books with a collection of Delany's written interviews, *Silent Interviews: On Language, Race, Sex, Science Fiction, and Some Comics*, which appeared in summer 1994, and, two years later, *Longer Views: Extended Essays* (1996) appeared with an introduction by Kenneth R. James.

The years in Massachusetts saw still two more trips to Europe. In 1992 Delany was a guest at a Science Fiction convention in Oslo, Norway, with Angela Carter, Brian Stapleford, and Brian Aldiss. The following year he spent two weeks at Berlin's Akademie der Künste, giving a seminar on science fiction to a group of young visual artists, mostly involved with film, which he co-taught with his one-time Clarion student William Gibson.

Besides *They Fly at Çiron*, Delany completed two other notable pieces of fiction during his eleven years at the University of Massachusetts. The three stories in *Atlantis: Three Tales*, appeared in a limited edition from Incunabula Press in 1995, and shortly afterward in a trade edition from Wesleyan. The first and longest story, "Atlantis: Model 1924," is a meticulously researched historical novella about a black adolescent, based closely on Delany's father, who moves to New York from North Carolina in November 1923 to stay with his older brothers and sisters, in the course of which he meets the poet Hart

Crane in an early May walk across the Brooklyn Bridge, where he also observes a possible drowning in the East River below. (To write the story, Delany read the weather reports for every day covered by his tale; as well, he researched the moon's phases for those nights.) The text uses a number of experimental techniques to present the story. A section was excerpted in *The Norton Anthology of African-American Literature* (1997). In honor of the publication of that prestigious anthology, along with Ntozake Shange, David Bradley, Jamaica Kincaid, and Rita Dove, Delany read at the 92nd Street YM/YWHA in New York in November 1998.

Delany began work on "Atlantis: Model 1924" in spring of 1992. In October of that year, independently and unknown to Delany until several weeks after it was published, a young newspaper reporter, Amy Hill Hearth, wrote an article for the *New York Times* "Metro Section," about Delany's aunts, Sadie and Bessie Delany (his late father's eldest sisters), both now over a hundred. The article elicited an extraordinary amount of mail. It was decided to turn the tapes that Hearth had recorded into a book. The following year, 1993, Kodansha International published *Having Our Say: The Delany Sisters' First Hundred Years*, by Sarah and A. Elizabeth Delany with Amy Hill Hearth, with considerable publicity.

The book became a bestseller and stayed at the top of the nonfiction best-seller list for almost two years. For the remainder of their lives—and three more books—Bessie and Sadie became national celebrities. The book was made into a Broadway play and finally a TV mini-series.

Delany's novella was completed in 1993. In it, Bessie and Sadie appear as "Corey" and "Elsie," along with younger versions of a number of Delany's other paternal aunts and uncles. Though it was published in the midst of the excitement over *Having Our Say*, Delany refused to let any publicity suggest a relation between the two books. This may, indeed, have slowed the growth of appreciation for Delany's novella. There are a number of places where the books touch on the same or similar family stories.

While teaching at the University of Massachusetts, and working largely over a summer that Rickett and Delany spent in Canaan, New York, as guests of their friends Leonard Gibbs and Sam DeBennedetto, Delany wrote much of the first draft of his novel *The Mad Man*.[6] It appeared in hardcover in 1995, to be revised twice, first for the paperback edition of 1996 and even more extensively for the Voyant Edition trade paperback of 2002.

In 1998, Delany left the University of Massachusetts for a professorship in the English Department of SUNY Buffalo's Poetics Program, the same university he'd taught at on his return from England to this country in 1975. In 1999 his UMass Distinguished Faculty Lecture, ". . . Three, Two, One, Contact: Times Square Red," prefaced by a new "ethnographic" memoir of his experiences in the Times Square theaters of New York City, appeared as *Times Square Red,*

Times Square Blue from New York University Press, and immediately broke into the bottom of the *Village Voice* bestseller list. Only a few months later, a graphic novel, with a script by Delany and drawn by artist Mia Wolff, *Bread & Wine*, appeared from Juno Books. It tells much of the story of Dennis and Delany's first meeting, during the time of Dennis's homelessness, and how the two men began to live with one another. At the end of the same year, Wesleyan released *Shorter Views*, another hefty collection of Delany's essays, lectures, and interviews. That same year, after educator Jill Lauren had published an account of Delany's (and his daughter Iva's) dyslexia in her book *Succeeding with LD* (1997), Delany was honored by the Mary McDowell Learning Center in Brooklyn, a school for dyslexic children, where Delany came and spoke informally about his battle with the learning disability.

Between Christmas and New Year's Eve, 1999, Delany gave an evening-long reading at the Judson Poets' Theater at the historic Judson Church on Washington Square South, during which he read to a highly enthusiastic audience from a number of his works, including his autobiography *The Motion of Light in Water*, *Bread & Wine*, *Times Square Red*, *Times Square Blue*, "Atlantis: Model 1924," and *The Mad Man*. It was filmed by a twin-camera crew, led by filmmaker Eric Solstein. An extremely effective videotape of the reading, *Atlantis and Other New York Tales*, is available through Voyant Publishing. In 2000, *1984: Selected Letters* also appeared from Voyant, a selection of letters Delany wrote in the year Orwell made famous, with another highly useful introduction by Kenneth R. James. Writing about it in the *Harvard Gay and Lesbian Review*, Michael Bronski said that the collection "reads like an eighteenth-century epistolary novel." In January of the same year, after only a year and a half, Delany left suny Buffalo to begin teaching at Temple University in Philadelphia, where he'd been invited to be professor of English and Creative Writing.

In 2001, in cooperation with Wesleyan University Press, Vintage Books released a new trade paperback edition of *Dhalgren*, which soon went into four printings. (The third printing and those following have many minor corrections, making this the most accurate edition to date.) One of Delany's responses to 9/11, his story "Echoes," appeared in *110 Stories: New York Writes after September 11th* (New York University Press, 2002), edited by Ulrich Baer.[7] This was followed the next year with the Vintage Books editions of *Babel-17* and *Empire Star* (in one volume), and *Nova*. In April of 2002 he was briefly in France for the Utopiales Festival in Nantes. In July of the same year, while Delany himself was at a family reunion in Los Angeles, during a banquet in Lawrence, Kansas, he was inducted into the Science Fiction Hall of Fame. In April 2003 Vintage Books published a complete collection of all Delany's significant science fiction and fantasy stories (omitting only those in *Return to Nevèrÿon*) under the title *Aye, and Gomorrah, and Other Stories*. Between the summers of 2001 and 2005, he taught at the Jack Kerouac School of Disembodied Poetics at Naropa in

Boulder, Colorado, and also—2003—at the Clarion SF Writers' Workshop in Seattle, where he had taught many times before. Several other articles and interviews, including a detailed textual exegesis of the second chapter of the Book of Genesis ("Eden, Eden, Eden," in *Chain #11: Public Forms*, edited by Jena Osman and Juliana Spahr, Philadelphia, 2004)[8] and a comparison of possible sources for elements in the work of Joanna Russ in the films of D. W. Griffith ("Joanna Russ and D. W. Griffith," in *PMLA*, Summer 2004), as well as lengthy interviews in Lou Anders' *Argosy*, Lisa Moore's *Lambda Book Report*, and the first issue of Steve Erickson's *Black Clock*.

Delany's most recent fiction is a short historical novel, *Phallos*, which details the life, loves, and adventures of a young gay man, Neoptolomus, from the island of Syracuse, during the reign of the Roman emperor Hadrian in the second century AD. Recently released from the army and on a commercial mission sponsored by a wealthy Roman patron to the Nile-side city of Hermopolis in Egypt, inadvertently Neoptolomus becomes involved in the assassination of the emperor's young lover, Antinous, as well as the theft of a jewel-encrusted phallus from an idol representing a nameless god in a temple on the city's outskirts. An exciting chase follows to regain the purloined object, with, as well, the goals of life, love, material wealth, and secret wisdom, which takes our hero from Rome to Athens to Byzantium, and back to the Pillars of Hercules. The tale is both a self-contained adventure, and a historical coda for Delany's "prehistoric" *Return to Nevèrÿon* series.

Also in 2004, Wesleyan University Press brought out a new edition of *Stars in My Pocket Like Grains of Sand*, and in December 2005 they issued a new Delany collection, *About Writing*.

Delany's work has been the subject of a number of books: Douglas Barbour's *Worlds Out of Words: The Science Fiction Novels of Samuel R. Delany* (Brans Head Books, 1979), Michael W. Peplow and Robert S. Bravard's *Samuel R. Delany: A Primary and Secondary Bibliography, 1962–1979* (Twayne, 1980), Jane Weedman's *Delany: A Starmont Guide* (Starmont House, 1982), George E. Slusser's *The Delany Intersection* (The Borgo Press, 1983), Seth McEvoy's *Samuel R. Delany* (Unger, 1984), and Damien Broderick's *Reading By Starlight* (Routledge, 1995). Although not packaged as a single-author study, the first half of Broderick's book is an overview of "modern science fiction" largely contoured by Delany's theories and demonstrating their influence; the second half concentrates on Delany's fiction directly). 1984 also saw a special "Science Fiction Issue" of *The Black American Literature Forum* (edited by Joe Weixlmann), with critical and bibliographical articles on Delany by Sandra Y. Govan ("The Insistent Presence of Black Folk in the Novels of Samuel R. Delany"), Robert Eliot Fox, and an astute overview of *Dhalgren* by Mary Kay Bray, "Double Consciousness in Delany's *Dhalgren*." (The issue contains as well articles on Octavia E. Butler and Stephen Barnes.) *Ash of Stars: On the Writing of Samuel R. Delany* (University

Press of Mississippi, 1996), edited by James Sallis, contains informative essays by Mary Kay Bray, Ray Davis, Marc Gawron, Kenneth James, and Kathleen Spencer, among others. Sallis also edited a section of the Fall 1996 edition of *The Review of Contemporary Fiction* (Vol. 16, no. 3) devoted to Delany's work. (The other half of the issue focuses on Edmund White.) The late Mary Kay Bray's essay, "To See What Condition Our Condition Is In," on *Stars in My Pocket Like Grains of Sand*, and David Samuelson's attempt to survey Delany's critical ideas, "Necessary Constraints: Delany on Science Fiction," appear in both the journal and the Sallis *Ash of Stars* collection. The other contributions are different. May, 2004, saw a single-author study of Delany's work from Wesleyan University Press, by Jeffrey Tucker of the University of Rochester, *A Sense of Wonder: Samuel R. Delany, Race, Identity, and Difference.*

Books containing substantial chapters on Delany's work include Thomas M. Moylan's *Demand the Impossible: Science Fiction and the Utopian Imagination* (Peter Lang, 1986), Robert E. Fox's *The Conscientious Sorcerers: The Post-Modern Fiction of LeRoi Jones / Amiri Baraka, Ishmael Reed, and Samuel R. Delany* (Greenwood Press, 1987), Earl Jackson, Jr.'s *Strategies of Deviance* (Indiana University Press, 1995), and Carl Freedman's *Critical Theory and Science Fiction* (Wesleyan, 2000). As well, Ross Posnock's *Color and Culture: Black Writers and the Making of the Modern Intellectual* (Harvard University Press, 1998) closes with a chapter-long reading of "Atlantis: Model 1924." Other books that discuss Delany's work at some length include Hazel Carby's *Race Men* (1999: Harvard University Press, Cambridge); Paul Robinson's *Gay Lives: Homosexual Autobiography from John Addington Symonds to Paul Monette* (University of Chicago Press, 1999); and Reed Woodhouse's *Unlimited Embrace: A Canon of Gay Fiction, 1945–1995* (University of Massachusetts Press, 1998) contains a lucid discussion of *The Mad Man*. Walter Benn Michaels's *The Shape of the Signifier* (Princeton University Press, 2004) contains an interesting discussion of Delany's Nevèrÿon tale "The Game of Time and Pain." Madhu Dubey's *Signs and Cities* (University of Chicago Press, 2004) not only takes its title from Delany's *Neveryona, or: The Tale of Signs and Cities,* but contains some highly interesting remarks about a number of his works, most extensively—as does Steven Shaviro's *Connected* (University of Minnesota Press, 2003)—the book *Stars in My Pockets Like Grains of Sand.*

NOTES

1. Delany's sister's given name is Sara. Since birth, she has gone by the nickname Peggy, which is the nickname for Margaret, the name of their mother, who always wanted to be called Peggy but never was, so this became the nickname of her daughter, who still uses both Peggy and Sara.

2. The radio play *The Star-Pit* can be heard online at: www.pseudopodium.org /repress/TheStarPit/index.html

3. At the flat she and Paul Caruso had been ceded by longtime San Francisco artist Nemi Frost.

4. At the time, he was still known as Bill Brodecky, aka William A. Brodecky.

5. Where, at 1067 Natoma Street, they met with Joel Coen (of the Coen Brothers), who said he'd look at Frank's films, but Frank was unable to follow through, and Delany was feeling less and less like running interference for him. So they went on with their trip, and because Frank never mentioned it again, Delany did not push him to move on it. If he had, this would have produced a major argument.

6. Other parts were written at the summer home of Barbara Wise in Wellfleet, Massachusetts, and still others were written in New York City.

7. The story "911: Echoes" is also included in Delany, *Occasional Views*, Volume 1 (Wesleyan University Press, 2021), 367–68.

8. The essay "Eden, Eden, Eden" is also included in Delany, *Occasional Views*, Volume 1, 68–83.

4

More and Less Than Human

While it *was* the decade in which segregation in the nations' schools was finally declared unconstitutional by the United States Supreme Court, the 1950s do not have a particularly good reputation either for women's rights or for disability rights. Indeed, they seem to be oddly linked, when we consider the highly popular *New Yorker* short story by Elizabeth Spencer, "The Light in the Piazza" (1958),[1] mounted as a musical a few years ago at Lincoln Center in New York. It tells the tale of an American mother, Margaret Johnson, in Florence, with her twenty-six-year-old daughter, Clara, who, due to an accident some years before, has a mental age of ten. Clara catches the eye of a twenty-three-year-old Italian, Fabrizio Narcarelli. The story's burning question—whose positive outcome clearly the writer expects us to hope for—is whether the engagement will be irreparably contracted before the young man and/or his family notices that his fiancée is not just feminine and child-like, but mentally challenged. At what is supposed to be the comic high point of the tale, Fabrizio's father is far more upset about discovering the age difference (mistakenly he thinks his twenty-three-year-old son is twenty; and is cupidinously interested in the $15,000 legacy Clara's mother has promised, if he will allow the wedding to go forward) than Clara's mental condition—which has slipped by him as much as it has by his smitten son. The point of the story would seem to be something close to a serious posing of the question (to use the language of the decade in which the story was written): Is mental retardation an adequate metaphor for femininity? Or, indeed, can femininity be adequately represented by mental retardation? Or, as someone three nights ago at dinner challenged my interpretation: Isn't it just wonderful that Italians are so patriarchal there's no meaningful difference between the two states, femininity and mental retardation, to *them*—in any case, by today's standards, it's a pretty appalling message.

Clara is, indeed, the only mentally retarded person in Spencer's tale—in which most of our sympathy is clearly supposed to go to her somewhat self-deluded mother (who, yes, learns that being self-deluded finally doesn't matter very much, when, [a] you're a woman and, [b] you're dealing with Italians). Most ideological critics, among whom I would count myself, have learned that, among narrative symptomatologies, the fictive trope of the single black, the single lesbian or gay man, the isolated woman, the single Jew or single disabled person against a field of the "unmarked," is usually a narrative strategy for repressing the representation of group oppression that, in most cases, can only be fought collectively.

Mental retardation, in its several forms, among disabilities is one that is most anxiety producing among the "temporarily abled" population, possibly because it seems today the least redressable by protheses. Many even might claim that it goes to the heart of what it is to be human. Shortly we will look at how and why—and also look at a novel that comes to what, I hope, for many, will suggest some surprising (or at least unexpected) conclusions about just such questions.

Five years before Spencer's highly popular and rather appalling story—besides being a musical, it was also a popular, if inane, film—Theodore Sturgeon wrote a science fiction novel that, among other things, deals with *several* mentally challenged characters, who relate to one another, and also to a range of "normal" characters, and whose relationships suggest a very different world view from Spencer's.

More Than Human began as a long story, published in 1952 in *Galaxy Magazine*, called "Baby is Three." The "baby" of the title is a Down syndrome child, born to an aging farm woman and her husband, Mr. and Mrs. Prodd. He will never mature beyond the age of three. And, in terms of the plot, he is certainly the most important character in the book.

The novel, which appeared a year later, was extended both forward and backward from the original story, with a prologue almost as long, "The Fabulous Idiot," which tells the story of *another* mentally challenged young man who lives a feral existence in the woods, and after a brutally traumatic run-in with a literally sadistic father and his socially isolated sixteen-year-old daughter, which results in the daughter's death at her father's hands and the young man's brutal beating, until in retaliation he kills the father, and is then himself rescued from the edge of death by the kindly farm couple and is slowly, over several years, taught minimal socialization.[2]

Eventually, the young man, Lone, goes off in the woods where he collects four more children, including the Down syndrome baby, whom he raises and protects until he is accidentally killed by a tree falling on him in the forest. Besides this sixty-page prologue, Sturgeon also added a concluding sixty-nine-page novella, "Morality"—in which the images of the disabled that were so strong in the book's first two-thirds take a back seat; and, in the eyes of most critics since, the whole novel becomes much less interesting.

More Than Human is not an unknown novel: for close to fifty years after it was written, it was considered by many as the greatest—or among the greatest—science fiction novels ever written. But although the novel has sustained a fair amount of attention, especially in the first thirty years of its history, I have never seen it discussed from the point of few of the disabilities of at least four of its seven central and five supporting characters. Indeed, all the disabilities entailed *are* forms of retardation.

Besides Baby, of the three little girls, Bonnie and Beanie, and Janie, Janie would appear a particularly smart and mature child of eight, when Lone, remembering how Mrs. Prodd first offered him food, finally consents to feed the starving girl and her two charges, Bonnie and Beanie, black twins, several years younger—neither of whom, in the novel, ever learns to talk.

Indeed, the ability to speak and communicate is, for many, the sine qua non of humanity.

One of the reasons—it would be disingenuous not to state it—that *More Than Human* is rarely or never discussed as a novel about disability is that the central characters all have extraordinary compensating powers: a kind of projective telepathy for Lone, an idiot savant brain for Baby, like a "faultless computer" or an "adding machine," telekinesis for Janie, and teleportation for Bonnie and Beanie. These move the story over into fantasy. But, if the fantasy is bracketed, which, for much of the novel it is fairly easy to do, such an interpretive violence yields some interesting points.

After Lone's death, when Lone's children, two of whom are apparently normal, and one of whom is the Down syndrome child, or "mongoloid idiot," and two of whom are the twins who cannot speak, are living with Miss Kew (the other highly neurotic daughter of the murderous father), the two central incidents which the children perceive as problems are, first, with the twin girls: because they are black, Bonnie and Beanie are not allowed to eat with the other children. "They're like our sisters," Gerry and Janie tell their guardian. Miss Kew informs them: "We don't have little colored girls as sisters," to which they return the pragmatic answer:

"*We* do!"

The next problem is when "Baby" is taken off to live in a home.

Before his death, Lone has given his wards two instructions. First, they must always stay together. Second, unless it contradicts the first instruction, they must do everything their new guardian, Miss Kew, tells them to—and, by extension, everything her black housekeeper Miriam tells them. But in both these cases, the first instruction is violated.

The children mount a terrorizing campaign against their benefactor. In both cases, they are quickly successful—and Gerry notes that their triumph in the case of the black twins promotes a marked change, for the better, in the attitude of Miriam, the otherwise loyal black maid, toward them.

But even if the children's means are in the realm of the paranormal, we have to admit that there is something out of the ordinary about a novel that portrays five children, two presumably "normal" and three of whom are mentally challenged, who fight—and fight successfully—to get the Down syndrome child returned from an institution, after he has been taken away from them. Indeed, in the midst of the fight, their current guardian, Miss Kew, yells at them: "Stop it! Stop it! Stop talking about that mongolian idiot! It's no good to anyone, not even itself. How could I ever make believe it's mine!" (96).

That is the point at which the remaining children infest the house she lives in with rats.

For those familiar with the book, I believe, by the way, this is the key to the solution of the incredibly complex psychoanalytic puzzle Sturgeon presents us in Part II of his story—and (looking ahead for a moment) with which I shall end this paper.

Eventually one of the children kills the woman who expresses these sad, but certainly easy to imagine, comments and gets away with it—indeed, well *after* the baby is returned.

Sturgeon's justification for all this is simply that intelligence per se is *not* the sine qua non of humanity; but what is wanted, rather, is the ability to provide some aspect of care—specifically food and warmth—and a sense of community and belonging against which even speech itself is secondary, if the communication of feelings can be achieved by other means.

Needless to say, this is a very different view from Spencer's, in which socially impoverished templates of "normality" are held up in the hopes that they can be counterfeited by the mentally challenged so that no one really has to know or be more than minimally inconvenienced.

*   *   *

Sturgeon is known as a stylist and as a particularly "poetic" writer. Yet, as is often the case with successful "poetry" in fiction, much of that effect comes from particularly careful observation, rendered economically, rather than complex rhetoric. For example, here is a passage often sighted as a description of a sixteen-year-old girl's perception of the coming of spring. Evelyn, you'll remember, is an innocent who has been raised in isolation in the woods by her father and sister. Here she is, shortly before she meets and falls hopelessly in love with hard, flat, blank-faced Lone—and is murdered in a rage by her angry father, Mr. Kew, for the offence,

> It was spring, the part of spring where the bursting is done, the held in pressure of desiccated sap-veins and gum-sealed buds are gone, and all the world's in a rush

to be beautiful. The air was heavy and sweet; it lay upon the lips until they parted, pressed them until they smiled, entered bodily to beat in the throat like a second heart. It was air with a puzzle to it, for it was still and full of the colors of dreams, all motionless; yet it had a hurry to it. The stillness and the hurry were alive and laced together and how could that be? That was the puzzle.

Save that "second heart," there's not a metaphor there. Indeed, half of its effect is that we keep expecting phrases to be metaphorical—"the colors of dreams"—only to realize they're perfectly referential. If you do look over the list of metaphors I have provided below, however, you will see that Lone's inner core is compared to a peach pit and an egg yoke. I believe that this relates, if only subliminally, to the "second heart" that Spring infuses into Evelyn's throat. The conduction between is what brings them together. But this starts us looking through the web of comparisons that, again and again, Sturgeon presents us with—all of which are quite as exactly observed as his non-metaphorical writing. Very few are cliché or on the point of death: At one point, Lone "sweeps his gaze" across the Prodds' farm, but that is about as close to stock language as Sturgeon lets himself come.

An idea controls many of the metaphors in my list: an intellectual discursive structure that the story dramatizes from end to end. That idea is: We have to learn how to care for other people in a human community, and learning *how* to care for people who, themselves, have rarely or ever been cared for takes *time* and *patience*. Not everyone can do it—and not everyone can do it every time.

The first teachers of this complex lesson in the book are the farming couple, the Prodds. They lavish their care on wounded, feral Lone. Paradoxically, a good deal of what allows them to give this sort of care and education is their own desire for a beautiful and perfect child—"Jack," the fantasized son whom they have imagined and prepared for throughout the years of their marriage, even as they grew old and remained childless. The care they give to Lone, the patience they show, the years it takes them to teach him to speak the few words he finally masters, or even to foster in him enough concentration to pick up a ball of red yarn and simply look at it—Mrs. Prodd recognizes this as a "miracle," when he does it—is all in excess of their own fantasies about caring for their nonexistent son. But when their own child is finally born, the Down syndrome baby, there *is* no more excess. It has all run out. There is hardly enough initial humanity left to raise the infant. Mrs. Prodd dies, presumably of grief, and Prodd himself loses his grip on reality; and while he manages to feed his son through the weeks before Lone takes him from the farm, we know—and Lone knows—that Prodd himself will not survive much longer. For all the kindness and care the farmer has been able to show to Lone over eight years, the loss of his wife and—more—the loss of his fantasy-perfect son have been too much.

In the metaphorical system Sturgeon uses for his characters, we find animal images and architectural images and tool images for the human; we find one part of a human being compared to another part—as though the world will always slip outside of the rigors of non-metaphorical observation. Though not many, we even see those metaphors that today's specialist in disability studies can find so troubling, metaphors lifted thoughtlessly from the disabled—blind, deaf-mute, brainless—used to describe actions of the abled and the disabled that go awry for their various reasons. (This was, after all, the 1950s.) But there are also synesthetic metaphors: "a dazzle of birdnotes," as well as oxymoronic ones: "the spring air" is "a soundless shout." Yet, things must be passed on—must be learned and must be taught. And those necessary things, which form community, are often in excess of any specific plan or intention of any specific character. It is that particular excess to human intention that *forms* their humanity.

In Sturgeon, the metaphors are precisely what is in *excess* of the precise—i.e., they carry the larger cares and worries, anxieties and whimsies, of what is human.

Sturgeon was highly aware of this. The giving and the sharing of food—especially to the hungry, to the starving, to the emotionally starved and impoverished—is a constant throughout Sturgeon's work. His earlier novel *The Dreaming Jewels* (1950), about a carnival full of "freaks" who must work together to defeat the carnival owner, who also happens to be a not-very-typical "mad scientist," organizes much of its most effective plot and action within the same discourse of community and caring. The differently abled and the temporarily abled must all care for each other. They must entertain each other. And they must exchange things that we would call art across gender lines, age differences, and ability boundaries.

More Than Human is, however, the more complex of the two books—and that is because it is not only about the warmth and wonder of community. It is also about the dangers and stifling conformity inherent in community: If the first part and much of the second is about the "good" community, the great question of a significant part of the second part of the novel—which we have not yet touched on, but which I hope you will all take a look at, if you haven't read it already—is why, when all the children have gotten what they want—when they are, indeed, together, and are, by their own standards, happy—why must Gerry, the newest of the children, kill their guardian Mrs. Kew and bring this seeming goodness to an end? In just what way are they opposites and how do they lace together? For Sturgeon goes to great lengths to point out that the "good" community and the "bad" community can be extraordinarily alike in their emotional coloring. But like the opposites that enlace to form the spring air, "That is the puzzle."

—*December 27, 2006*
New York

LIST OF METAPHORS (AND SIMILES)
ASSOCIATED WITH THE CHARACTERS
IN THE FIRST SECTION ("THE FABULOUS IDIOT")
OF THEODORE STURGEON'S
MORE THAN HUMAN (1953)

LONE, JANIE, BONNIE & BEENIE, PRODDS, BABY, ALICIA KEW, EVELYN KEW

Hunger = lightning

Fear = flicker

Shin = cold chisel

Ribs = fist

Lone = animal

Human center = peach stone, egg yolk

Perception of babies = his own language (Lone is mute)

Body movement = wallowing

Effort = blindly, Insistently

Call = Carrier & signal

Connection between inner and outer self = conduction

Spring air within her = a second heart

Evelyn hears = a dazzle of bird notes

She sees the woods = misted with wonder

Her hair = Iron order

Her hands scamper

Spring air = a soundless shout

Excitement = she bites into it

LOAN, JANIE, BONNIE & BEENIE, PRODDS, BABY, ALICIA KEW, EVELYN KEW

Her attack on her father = a bullock with tiger claws

Fear = fog, clammy and blinding, with a thirsty edge, hard and purposeful

Lone's body soaking up nourishment = a cactus absorbing water

Lone's first weeping = shrill & tortured

Stance = jackbooted

"Decent as a deacon"

Play = squeak, claw

Glances = deliciously frightened (appear so to Janie)

their rompers = little flat crabs

Lungs = a toy steam engine

Divesting = shucking

Rompers = a steep climb (aeronautical image)

Communication = twitter

Her place in the park = sanctuary

Communication = squeaks, whimpers

Janie's containment = a round toothpick

Lone = a halfwit (as others see him while he is with the Prodds)

Sound of Lone sharpening his scythe = (slow) water boiling, (fast) a shrew dying

Lone's gaze = sweeps the farm

Lone sees farm = water held in a basin

Wrongness = squirrel with feathers, wolf with wooden teeth

Janie freezing to death = a top slowing down

LOAN, JANIE, BONNIE & BEENIE, PRODDS, BABY, ALICIA KEW, EVELYN KEW

Bonnie & Beanie saving Janie = little animals moving over her face

Useless action = trying to piece together broken china

Lone's world when the children call him = dreamlike, enchantment, somnambulant, kindle, inferno of conflicts, walks blindly, receive cruel blow over eye, hunger

Lone's pique at children = edged and spicy mixture of anger and amusement

Lone's relief on meeting them = great surge, "setting down a 40-pound pack after 40 years"

Lone's speech = harsh and ill-toned, like that of a deaf-mute"

Beenie, with her mouth opened = potbellied stove with the door opened

Lone eating in forest = "licks his fingers by way of desert"

Janie walking toward stewpot = "With the exact air of a lady crossing a drawing room toward the bonbons"

The desire to feed the children = "an emotion . . . reached up from his solar plexus and tugged at this throat"

Retuning self-awareness = Like coffee soaking upward through a lump of sugar

The effectiveness of Prodd's tone of voice = his broken hay rake

Eyes = upholstery tacks

Tongue-tied

Skin = the color of mustard

Hair = horse-hair

Baby = adding machine

Prodd = prancing around the farm

Lone & All the Children = occupants of a slag-heap of brainless but faultless
computer at the edge of mankind; monstrous; different; mountain pinnacle/
mountain foot

NOTES

1. Elizabeth Spencer, *The Light in the Piazza and Other Italian Tales* (University of Mississippi Press, 1996).

2. Theodore Sturgeon, *More Than Human* (Ballantine, 1953).

5

Acceptance Speech at Temple University

Delivered on April 20, 2008, at Mitten Hall in Philadelphia upon receipt of Temple University's Faculty Award for Research and Creative Achievement, presented for *Dark Reflections*.

The conflicts between university teaching and creativity are worthy of a scholarly sub-discipline. Somewhere Goethe writes, "Once a man does something truly admirable, the entire universe conspires to see that he never does it again." Well, there are moments when those of us who make poems, stories, paintings, and music, and—at the same time—teach, must feel we are Goethe's defining exemplum. But that is also a reason that an award such as this is so warming, and even significant.

I'd like to thank my life-partner of nineteen years, Dennis Rickett, who could not be here today, but is waiting for me to phone and tell him how it all went.

And I'd like to thank all the writers—of fiction and nonfiction: the poets, the composers, and the actors, the dancers, the artists in whatever medium—at Temple University. You, of course, are the reason this award exists. A particular winner in a particular year is only a tiny thing in that.

I would like to thank as well my chair Shannon Miller and my colleague Joan Mellen, both of whom wrote so eloquently on my behalf; and the awards committee for its generous choice; and the entire Temple faculty, English and otherwise, and all our students, graduate and undergraduate; and the staff of Temple; I want to thank President Ann Weaver Hart, whom I have not met until today, and Dean Teresa Soufas, who has been so supportive of the graduate and undergraduate creative writing program here, and security guard Dawn Brook, who steps out of her guard booth to smile at me in the morning as I arrive at Anderson Hall, and the Ritchie Jamalli's, senior and junior, from whom I get my daily coffee and my Diet Peach Snapple. Anthony Trollope once wrote that the man who provided his coffee in the morning could arguably be considered indispensable to, if not co-author of, all Trollope's books. Sometimes, leaving Ritchie's in a cold drizzle, with a warm paper bag in my hands, I feel much the same about my work of the last nine years since coming to Temple. I want to thank Bob Graves, and everyone else on the maintenance staff, who help dispose of the cascade of scrap paper that tumbles from my office each week, and Linda Tran who, at the Thai/Vietnam Kitchen in the Anderson Food Court, sells me my aromatic pho Thai, which makes my office smell richly and wondrously of basil for two hours in the afternoon; in short, I want to thank all the individuals—again, faculty, students, and staff, Sharon Logan especially, Belinda Wilson Hagans, Rose Wint, Mary McCoy, Kim Jackson, and Gloria Basmagian (of whom we are all thinking), the people who keep *my* world from falling to pieces, and the undergraduate student workers, among them Kristan Ott—all the individuals who constitute our Temple community, a community whose complex inter-relations, direct and indirect, comprise the multiple and material discourses that *are* Temple, discourses that finally and formally inform this award with its meaning.

Good thoughts to you all, for all good things.

Thank you—.

—2008
Philadelphia

NOTE

Dark Reflections also received a 2008 Stonewall Book Award and was chosen for *Best African-American Fiction 2009*, edited by Gerald Early and E. Lynn Harris (Bantam Dell, 2009).

6

Fiction's Present: A Brief Note

> The question of the present inflection of fiction is Janus-faced,
> looking aside to the novel's radically changed political, economic,
> technological circumstances and back to its history of achievement
> and problems.
>
> —from the *SYMPLOKĒ* call for papers for "Fiction's Present."[1]

The "call for papers" begins with an interesting comment. For me, it brings to
mind that when Bakhtin noted that, by the beginning of the twentieth century,
all artistic genres had been novelized, he was at the beginning of a process that
allows us to say today that, by the twenty-*first* century, all artistic genres have
been "film-ized." That process takes us through more than half a century of
novelized films that finally did as much as any social phenomenon to remove
the novel proper from a certain preeminence in the job of social representation. One remembers the scene in Tim Robbins's historical film *Cradle Will Rock*
(2000), in which, after New York art students riot over the destruction of Diego
Rivera's overtly left-leaning Rockefeller Center mural, Nelson Rockefeller and
William Randolph Hearst, who up until now have supported this representa-
tional, highly social art, do a coldhearted about-face and decide from now on
to support only abstract art with no overt social messages, to avoid this kind
of disruptive political response.[2] The ironic point is not whether any such con-
spiratorial conversation ever actually took place at such a financial pinnacle,
but rather the scene's revelation of a social truth—a moment in what Fredric
Jameson might call the "political unconscious"—that explains why, indeed,
in an art field supported by those with more money rather than those with

less, natural selection is finally going to favor the abstract. It happens for the same reason that, if epic singers are going to be supported by ninth-century BCE kings and princes, you're going to end up with the *Iliad* and the *Odyssey* rather than *Germinal* and *Giants in the Earth*. The same turning away from the larger social portraiture of the interrelations of the classes is evident in Julie Taymor's totally gorgeous film, from two years later, that focuses on Rivera's wife, painter Frida Kahlo (*Frida*, 2002).[3] Today, of course, a critical discourse is in place that rushes to read the two films as pejorative mutual critiques. In the light of Taymor's film, Robbins's looks like an emotionally button-pushing, finally rather preachy socialist tract. In the light of Robbins's film, Taymor's reduces to a kind of tragic-glamorous fairy tale presented as objective reality, but that rigorously cuts out the larger social context making the other film signify: different buttons pushed.

But, one wonders, why can't the two films be read as supporting one another—expanding on one another, enriching one another? Finally, what would prevent a new, hypertextualized novel, say, from embracing both approaches? But it would require a creative discourse that paid much more attention to rhetorical texture than the novel usually does, in either case, to plot—and in which rhetorical texture would be seen as a site for the generation of meaning in itself rather than as merely a supplementary intensifier.

Novels that aspire to broad-scale social representation are rarer and rarer—even as commercial fiction relies more and more heavily on plot, and even as it trains its readers to ignore style.

From *Père Goriot* to *Invisible Man*, from Dickens to Flaubert, one thing the novel has done is explain—dramatically—how areas of society interact and affect each other, in terms of what this interaction inflicts on individuals and their strivings and desires within their own social spheres, or as they move from sphere to sphere. Paradoxically, both Marx and Freud, who start out by enriching the range of explanations of how our strivings and desires function, both in the family and the state, may have finally managed to swamp the novel, because we now know that what explains these things is, finally, too complicated to "dramatize" in other than a truly simplistic fashion.

Finally, the novel (with the short story leading the way) becomes a kind of extended "haiku" run to seed, where from time to time the artist asserts, yes, there is an explanation somewhere behind it all, but it is much too complex and, finally, boring to go into at any length while presenting the glimmer and flicker of the here and now, the shadows of memory and association in the forever lost.

Over eighty-two years, *Ulysses*'s shift from eccentric experiment to the central text of the contemporary novelistic tradition indexes the rise of the novel as extended haiku, or in the case of *Ulysses* itself, eighteen extended haiku, each presented with some interesting technical filigree to keep one involved in an implied but never-stated exploration—behind the fabulous verbal surface—of what Gertrude Stein several times called "the daily island life."

The opening decades of the twentieth century are marked by a kind of forking into two rivers: Stein starts us off along one, which leads up through Perec and a lot of today's playful writers, and Joyce leads the other, which carries us, frankly, to I'm-not-sure-what. It is a river that, by today, includes lots of ambitious, unreadable novels that really do try to explain things, as Joyce's work itself, once past *Dubliners* and *Portrait*, locates itself in the "unreadable" precincts first mapped out by Walter Pater's *Marius the Epicurean: His Sensations and Ideas*, which also ceded Virginia Woolf the vacant lot on which to erect *The Waves* and the novels that followed.

> Can the novel establish itself in the present of global capitalism without abandoning its formal distinctiveness?[4]

Bakhtin's point is that the novel is already established. As a discourse, it is quite firmly in place, which is why we go on writing them. But we may need to trace out other subcurrents through its history in order to reawaken our formal interests.

Such a subcurrent that presently fascinates me is the one that takes in Baron Corvo's *Hadrian the VII* (1905), G. K. Chesterton's *The Man Who Was Thursday* (1908), Richard Hughes's *A High Wind in Jamaica* (1929), Djuna Barnes's *Nightwood* (1936), Malcolm Lowry's *Under the Volcano* (1947), Vladimir Nabokov's *Pale Fire* (1960), and Joanna Russ's *We, Who Are About to . . .* (1978), as well as other novels in which great effort has gone into making the prose crystalline, vivid, and readable (without stylistic pandering), in order to allow a more or less lucid narrative structure to speak of things that most fiction, whether innovative or not, usually leaves unsaid.

The novel's existence as a discourse (like the poem's) is the existence of a discourse that allows its texts to make sense (i.e., fundamentally it is a critical discourse). But when, indeed, we compare the critical discourse of fiction to the critical discourse of the poem, the discourse of the poem right now seems willing to welcome within its discursive boundaries a lot more material that does not "make sense"—with the result that, by and large, right now the poem seems more vigorous, healthier than the novel, at least to me.

> Unreadable novels can revitalize the style of the novel. But readable novels are what revitalize its structure.[5]

Perhaps in this statement, both "readable" and "unreadable" need to be in scare quotes. Certainly, they are wildly inexact terms for what I mean—since most novels that are written to be readable, I cannot read, while a few "unreadable" novels for me make the most interesting reading.

> Does fiction continuing the tradition of modernist innovation have any reality for emergent political groups and cultures?[6]

The place where poetry trips up is in trying to prove that, yes, all of that "experimentation" is politically significant, if not actively subversive.

I think, for both the novel and the poem, the answer to the question above should be a blunt "no." We will get farther if we accept that "no" than if we try, however subtly, however dogmatically, to convince more and more people that it does.

There is an expanded version of that "no," of course. It is this: The relatively small group of people that can, when it wants to, trace out the subversive allegories in all that stylistic difference just is not large enough or, frankly, powerful enough to make a difference, because it is dealing with a critical construct rather than the reading experience of (most of) the texts with which it deals. Indeed, this is precisely the point where the apolitical aspect of art, which critics from de Man to Bloom are always stressing, comes home, and should be welcomed.

I think of myself as the model consumer—if not an ideal one for innovative art. I am a self-styled marxist, which is relevant only in that I think I am moderately politically sensitive. I like innovative fiction and poetry as genres. I buy them in bookstores. I enjoy sitting back and reading them.

I still enjoy the narrative. I enjoy the ways that the rhetoric constitutes and disrupts that narrative. And when the rhetoric enhances the narrative, the insights, the intellectual content, and the structural richness of that narrative, as it does in the fiction of Guy Davenport, William Gass, Robert Glück, Charlotte Bacon, or R. M. Berry, as a reader I am at my happiest. At that point, frankly, I stop perceiving the fiction as traditional or innovative and simply think of it as very good writing.

But unless I enter into a particular type of dialogue with the textual rhetoric *per se*—a dialogue that something in the text has invited me to enter—as a rule I do not usually read the rhetoric itself as political. I read it as some sort of formal constitutive/commentary on or of the narrative, i.e., primarily as aesthetic.

I do think new art teaches us to read new discourses—and a changing society is always presenting new discourses to its citizens in order to help them negotiate the world. But I firmly believe that that is a task art only accomplishes at the level of groups of artworks. One work by itself never relates to politics in that way.

—*c. 2003*
New York

NOTES

1. Quotation from the *SYMPLOKĒ* call for papers on "Fiction's Present."

2. *The Cradle Will Rock*, directed by Tim Robbins (1999; Burbank, CA: Touchstone Home Video, 2000), DVD.

3. *Frida*, directed by Julie Taymor (2002; Burbank, CA: Miramax Home Entertainment, 2011), DVD.

4. From the *SYMPLOKĒ* call for papers.

5. From *SYMPLOKĒ*.

6. From *SYMPLOKĒ*.

7

Two Introductions for Junot Díaz

I

Read at the Lannan Foundation, Santa Fe, New Mexico, on Wednesday evening, January 21, 2009.

I'd like to thank Christie Masura Davis and the Lannan Foundation for inviting me here to Santa Fé this evening to introduce Junot Díaz.

But, first, let's look at his language:

It leaps, it lolls about, it lingers on the street, it lunges into the precincts of paraliterature, plundering comics and science fiction and fantasy for its kerygma and mythological comparisons, its superlative metaphors and exemplaries, the way Cyril Connolly's "Mandarin" writers mine Shakespeare, mythology, and the Bible for their hypograms and paralogisms. It plunges through an already existing Spanglish and a more traditional Spanish, so that—especially when we get to the novel of Oscar's brief and wondrous life—if we are not a native Spanish reader, as I am not, then each must compile her or his own paradigm of personal wonderings, to put up against Burgess's clockwork glossary or Heinlein's harsh mistress's Russian roister:

Colmado—(*bodega* to us long-time New Yorkers) that little corner store, but idiosyncratically often part of the house itself.

Carajo—the hell with it, when, for whatever reasons, you can't find what you want at *el colmado.*

Chancletas—the cheap flip-flops you wear when you can't afford Tevas, that you hit the kids with, if you have to.

Verguenza—something you haven't a speck of: shame.

Galletazo—as in *Dale un galletazo*, give her a smack; or, as a recent online *cabrón* translated it, "a bitch-slap," or, in the Harlem dialect I was brought up with, "up side yo' head"; or, more neutrally, "an open-handed slap," what you might use *"una delas chancletas"* for.

Of course, it's the neutrality of language Diaz wants to get away from. His is weighted, loaded, not to slow it, but to fuel it with a rollercoaster's energy, to send it careening around the hidden formalities and symmetries of his topic.

The beginning and ending of Oscar's saga mirror one another: The younger Oscar is to Ana Obregón as an older Oscar is to Ybón Pimental. Where Manny, the Gulf War returnee, stands in the way of the adolescent consummation, the Captain is the adult adulterator of Ybón and Oscar's love.

Between them are strung the stories of an island—or half an island, the Dominican Republic side of Hispañola. Most memorably that's the stories of its women: La Inca, Oscar's grandmother, his sister Lola, and his mother, Hypatia Balicia Cabral. For Oscar and, in her way, Lola, relive his mother's early life as a victim of the Trujillo dictatorship, in a diabolical intergenerational repetition compulsion, where we can only watch its events interweave with an unsettling psychological succinctness, in which every effort of the former to protect the latter from these lethal horrors ("beaten, set on fire, left for dead"), once endured and barely survived, ensure that the children cannot escape the same fate—the *fukú*, the fatalism that fuels the fall of *all* the West's tragedies.

For a while, though, let's put *Wao* away and look at something that, at first, might seem smaller. Let's give a nod to "Nagocios," business, negotiations— that Díaz mini-epic that sits, like Joyce's "The Dead," a daedal text that twines together the intricacies of *Dubliners*, to climax the deftly inter-crafted dramas of *Drown*.

What emerges from what's submerged in this whirlpool of a story?

A twenty-four-year-old father, Ramón, leaves his family—his wife and three children—in the Dominican Republic, to come to America. The defection is ambiguously positioned: yes, he happens to be having an affair about which his wife is deeply unhappy. But the whole business—the negotiations with his father-in-law for money to finance the trip—are absorbed into the general Dominican diaspora.

The stories in *Drown* have learned their necessary lessons of stylistic econ-omy and reticence from Raymond Carver without which working-class fiction could simply not be taken seriously in the decade of their writing. But, even besides the shift of their scrupulous virtuosity over onto the observed reality of Dominican life in New York, Miami, the Island, or northern New Jersey, some-thing else was going on that made these tales—and this tale in particular—very much its own.

The repeating form of fatalism we have mentioned in *Oscar Wao* is here in embryo. In his years in the States, Ramón begins a second family, even while, now and again, he retains his allegiances to his first. But in the end, to reunite with the former, he must abandon the latter. And from this double rupture, the adult son of the first concludes the tale with a visit to his father's abandoned second wife.

I found this story devastatingly effective—and deeply moving. There is nothing in it that is not prepared for dramatically. In this novella, the way Ramón is trapped into all his flights is worthy of any of the great nineteenth-century social novelists. Social habituations stymie his efforts in a way that, at least once, even he can recognize as a racism he cannot challenge. It's played out in such a low-key and muted manner that it slides from under the name to join the inevitable, the unconquerable, which the determination to endure alone can conquer.

The third child in a family of five, Junot Díaz was born in Santa Domingo in December, 1968. He came to this country in 1974. He attended Kean College in Union, New Jersey, then Rutgers University, and received his MFA from Cornell University, in 1995. His stories have appeared in *The Paris Review, Best American Short Stories* of 1996, '97, '99, and 2000, *African Voices*, and *The New Yorker*. Among many honors he has received a John Simon Guggenheim Fellowship, a Lila Acheson Wallace *Reader's Digest* Award, the 2002 PEN/Malamud Award, and the Rome Prize from the American Academy of Arts and Letters. In 2007 his novel *The Brief, Wondrous Life of Oscar Wao* won the National Book Critics Circle Award for best novel of that year and, in April 2008, the Pulitzer Prize for Fiction. Please, join me this evening in welcoming Junot Díaz.

—*January 2009*
New York,
Philadelphia,
Santa Fe

2

Read at the presentation to Junot Díaz of the Norman Mailer Distinguished Writing Prize at the Norman Mailer Gala, held at the Central Branch of the New York Public Library on Thursday evening, October 17, 2013.

Years ago, Susan Sontag wrote that a writer who is loved is in an unstable position historically. When we fall out of love with an Edgar Allan Poe, a Charles Bukowski, or an Algernon Charles Swinburne, often we feel we have betrayed ourselves by loving them in the first place. Their excesses, their sentimentalities, their narrownesses are now all we see. One of the two American writers we are honoring tonight—indeed it might be said of both—is becoming a loved writer; and the one whose award I have been asked to present tonight is a writer for whom, since the appearance of his Pulitzer Prize–winning novel *The Brief, Wondrous Life of Oscar Wao*, that process has moved quickly and accelerated astonishingly, not only for his novel, but for his two extraordinary books of short stories—*Drown* and *This is the Way You Lose Her*. Possibly in response to this, a very few of my graduate students have taken to saying, dismissively, oh, Díaz's writing is just more slice of life about the poor and the underprivileged—that's not really art. To this I want to pose the defense Baudelaire marshaled against similar attacks focused on Flaubert's *Madame Bovary*, in a set of articles the poet wrote in 1857 defending the novel many wanted to dismiss as mere "realism," a cluster of descriptive details with no other interest than that they were, indeed, there:

> Realism—a repulsive insult flung in the face of any analytic writer, a vague and formless word which for the ordinary man signifies not a new means of creation, but a minute description of trivial details.

In exactly the way Baudelaire's comment suggests for Flaubert, Díaz is a writer of astonishing analytical power, whose command of observed life yields him a dramatic medium at once scintillating and coruscating: for it is only when observation and a reason to observe work together that we can be truly shaken by their aesthetic reinforcement. (Flaubert himself wrote in a letter to George Sand that, while he had sympathy for no one, he hoped to have compassion for all.) Tonight, I am pleased, honored, and humbled to present Junot Díaz with the Norman Mailer Distinguished Writing Prize—and whose writing, for its inventiveness, its liveliness, its observational accuracy and the force and compassion of its analysis of our lives, I love, today, unreservedly and unapologetically, no matter the reactionary glibness of a few of my more sophomoric graduates.

—*October 2013*
New York

8

A Lost Lady and Modernism: Willa Cather

I don't know the source of this insight, but I first heard it at Cornell University during a conference on modern opera in 1986 or thereabouts. Someone giving a paper on Claude Debussy's *Pelléas et Mélisande* (1901) made the point that many works of modernism retell one of two tales, the story of Oedipus or the story of Parsifal—and sometimes both. In this young music scholar's characterization, Oedipus ("the lamed man") is the smart bastard who, when he meets the riddling sphinx, seems to know all the answers. Parsifal ("the pure fool") is the dumb bastard (in the sense of unable to speak), who, when he first observes the ceremony of the Grail, doesn't know the questions to ask; he must go away, learn what they are, then return to try again. (I wish I remembered the man's name so I could credit him for the observation.)

It's fairly easy to map Willa Cather's *A Lost Lady* (1923) onto the Parsifal story—or, to make it even easier, onto the fragmented version of it in T. S. Eliot's *The Waste Land* (1922).[1] Eliot's poem had been published and become an instant literary cause célèbre a year before Cather's elegant and resonant novella—or long short story—appeared in its own volume from Alfred A. Knopf, Inc. It can bear either genre mark as easily as novel.

I'm comfortable using Wagner's version, however. An opera lover, Cather knew her Wagner, as in those days most intellectuals did. In the very long note below, the basic point is that the Parsifal story most people knew then and know today doesn't come from medieval times. It's Wagner's own construct. While loosely based on a set of late medieval poems—by Chretien de Troyes, Wolfram von Eschenbach, and even Thomas Malory's prose *Le Morte d'Arthur*—it follows none slavishly. And none of the sources mirror any other with exactitude. Whether Cather had the story in mind when she wrote her own can only be a speculation that possibly helps a reader organize the incidents and the other fictive material.

Instead of starting her story with a young man's inadvertent bow-and-arrow killing of a swan in the sacred woods of the Grail Castle, Cather begins, after a brief historical prelude, with the sadistic torture and destruction of a woodpecker. Later, a series of untutored young men who rotate through the "Parsifal position" in her tale poach wild ducks, with tacit permission, from Captain Forrester's beautiful and uncultivated marshlands.

Like Kundry and Isolde at the beginning of their respective music dramas, Marian Forrester is early on associated with healing when she takes Niel Herbert, Judge Pomeroy's nephew—our point-of-view character for much of the tale's remainder—into her home with his broken arm (a result of the deplorable woodpecker incident) and later when she cares for her dying husband.

The major notion both works share—Eliot's and Cather's—is that the current world is a moral waste, an ethical ruin, a world where, as Cather writes on her opening page, things are "so much greyer to-day than they were."[2] The backstory of Cather's short novel occurs during the explosion of railway activity that would lead up to and follow the 1869 establishment of the first cross-country railroad.

But to say only this much is to miss the distinction of so many novels postdating the political/industrial ferment between 1830 and 1855 in Europe and after the Civil War in the United States, up to the 1950s or even the 1960s—the period we call modernism.

That earliest of psychological novels, *La Princesse de Clèves* (1678), or, at the picaresque extreme, *Don Quixote* (1605, 1615)—inarguably premodernist—both begin with praise for a time fifty-odd years before the writer's present, when true glory and authentic nobility were common in their respective lands—Madame de Lafayette to set it out as an example for her readers and to help explain her heroine's final high-minded climactic choice and Cervantes to mock gently its deleterious influence on the weaker minds of his own day. If modernism manifested itself only in the high value set on the past, then the entire novel genre must be called modernist!

Among elements that seem particularly modernist in so many novelists from Gustave Flaubert on, however, is the writer's decision not to use this temporal discrepancy simply as a framing device to highlight the tale's significance but rather, after (arbitrarily) the revolution of 1848, to pull that discrepancy between past and present under the narrative spotlight in order to give a dramatic analysis of *how* the novel's world got from one condition to the other. Flaubert's famous 1864 epistolary statement of purpose about the book he was to publish five years later, *L'Éducation sentimentale* (1869), is the benchmark: "I want to write the moral history of the men of my generation—or, more accurately, the history of their *feelings*. It's a book about love, about passion; but passion such as can exist nowadays—that is to say, inactive."[3] Certainly something close to this could be said of George Meredith's *The Ordeal of Richard Feverel* (1859) and *The Egoist* (1879), as it could be of Samuel Butler's *Ernest Pontifex: The Way of All Flesh* (1904) or even Somerset Maugham's (appallingly sexist!) *Of Human Bondage* (1915). This concern with both moral history and inactive passion is what urges us to characterize Cather's work as modernist—especially in her later work, where Flaubert's influence,[4] not only stylistically but thematically, is strongest.

Even more than its rhetorical flourishes, Leopold Bloom's inactive passion for Gertie McDowell, the Night Town whores, and Molly is one of the themes (as unpopular as thematics are in our current critical landscape—I won't say Waste Land for several reasons, primary among them that I don't believe it is; in the same way one is never outside metaphysics, however, one is never outside thematics) that tethers *Ulysses* to the modernist project, as does Jay Gatsby's inactive passion for Daisy Buchanan (*The Great Gatsby*, 1925), and Jake Barnes's for Brett Ashley in *The Sun Also Rises* (1926), three and four years after Cather and Joyce.[5] What stalls the consummation of desire in so many modernist works (as much in "The Dead" [1914] as in *Ulysses* [1922]) is the modern condition itself, with its expanded options, personal and social, for both men and women, its demand for artistic honesty in conflict with propriety, its new possibilities for articulation and the concomitant responsibility to listen—and the past's failure to provision the characters for the change. This passive passion—or, more accurately, this passion forced by both circumstances *and* psychology to hold off awhile and remain incomplete—marks many of these works, among them Cather's, in similar ways—so that dawn or death must come before that passion can be fulfilled.

Cather's own answer to the question, what exactly happened to bring this change in the world about? is almost always one form or another of the observation: The money went elsewhere. But the details of its going, its going's effect on people and their values, or the kinds of people the going of money allows to rise to the top of the social mix (and the kinds it lets sink to the bottom) are the material of her dramas. Cather is not such a reductionist as to believe that money, or the movement of money, *makes* certain behaviors occur. She understands that different people will always behave in different ways. But she is harshly aware that it creates the conditions of possibility and of the considerable pressure such conditions can exert, especially on women.

In *A Lost Lady*, Ivy Peters is a heartless youngster a decade before a changing economy moves the remaining citizens of Sweet Water to judge his brand of cutthroat lawyering necessary, efficient, and popular. This heartlessness is what Peters's blinding of the bird is there to dramatize—as well as to anticipate his own eventually destructive effect on our older Kundry, Marian Forrester. Marian enjoys the good life quite as much while her husband is alive and wealthy as she yearns for it once he is dead and she is financially reduced. All three men we see her join herself to, starting with her husband, the Captain, have a roughness and a brutality about them that, apparently, she finds attractive in a way—surely sexual—that, equally clearly, she does *not* find in the point-of-view character's (Niel's) sensitivity and good looks, however much she likes him and his company from boyhood on—a liking inextricably mixed with his blind willingness to submit to her social manipulations on one occasion after another, because he finds her so fascinating, both when she is a rich woman and later when she is a relatively poor one. But all these men have clear relationships to money. Changes in economic conditions are what allow certain people, who, given their personal values, are prone to one sort of behavior or another, to do well or to do poorly by means of them or—in the case of her husband, Captain Forrester, then Frank Ellinger, and even, we will later learn, her long-dead one-time fiancé, Ned Montgomery, and finally Ivy Peters himself—to come together with Marian.

The first uncomprehending observation Niel/Parsifal has of the ceremony of the Grail knights is on the evening he is first invited to a formal dinner by Marian Forrester, when the Captain is still alive and the railroad society is still aswirl about them. His second chance to observe it comes years later at the dinner party Marian gives long after the Captain is dead and Marian's own fortunes have been much reduced, during which she tries to pass on some of her social knowledge and cultural style to the young legal Turks of Sweet Water.

Throughout the novel, however (with Cather, one almost wants to write "of course"), Cather's central concern is Kundry/Marian, the half-cursed, half-blessed protectress of the Grail, who—in Wagner—serves the Grail knights and, with her relation to the dying Grail king, Amfortas, and the evil magician, Klingsor, in the second act, is the most problematic character, both in terms of performance and interpretation, as much sorceress and seductress as she is Magdalene and martyr.

Much of the life in Cather's fiction comes from the writer's love of her central women. She loves to observe them; she loves to describe them; she loves to watch them move socially; she loves to see the people they gather around themselves and loves to overhear their conversations—and she loves to analyze what motivates them as well as their failings and missteps in a society that often puts them in impossible positions. Their generosity of spirit and character again and again draws her to them—whether the innocent Czech immigrant Ántonia Shimerdas on the Nebraska prairie (*My Ántonia*, 1918) or Myra Henshaw (née Driscoll) during her socially rich life in New York in the artistic community around Madison Square or her later penury with her devoted husband in a San Francisco residence hotel (*My Mortal Enemy*, 1926), or Thea Kronborg, the committed artist of *Song of the Lark* (1915).[6] At the same time, Cather is aware that much of what is most attractive about these women is their response to circumstances, so that those circumstances constitute both their glory and their tragedy.

These women are a series of warm, knowledgeable, and exciting—and finally fascinating—Kundrys for a succession of innocent young Parsifals, who
appreciate them from a position of passive passion. (Both in her great novella
My Mortal Enemy and in her short story "The Joy of Nelly Dean," the part is
taken by young women instead of a young man—teacher or newspaper reporter, both; starting in her teens, Cather was a reporter for much of her young
womanhood.)

A Lost Lady is strewn with conservative tropes, and Cather has the good conservative's awareness of the importance of money (or, as a marxist might put
it, of the economic register) and its relationship to happiness and the good life
for pretty much everyone, up and down the social ladder. As Marian Forrester
herself puts it, "Money is a very important thing. Realize that in the beginning;
face it, and don't be ridiculous in the end, like so many of us" (*Lost Lady*, 114).
Cather's world is not the sociologist's three-tiered pyramid of upper, middle,
and working class. Rather it is "two distinct social strata . . . : the homesteaders
and hand-workers who were there to make a living, and the bankers and gentlemen ranchers who came from the Atlantic seaboard to invest money and to
'develop our Great West,' as they used to tell us" (*Lost Lady*, 9–10). Movement
between the two levels is possible, but difficult; and it is always accomplished
with some awkwardness.

Good manners are primarily a convenient method for hierarchizing people's behavior—but at different times they hierarchize it in different ways.

Twenty-five years his wife's senior, Captain Daniel Forrester, Marian's husband, is a self-made man. He has acquired his money in railroading, and years
ago he returned to Sweet Water with his new, second wife, the socially sophisticated and charming Marian, whose life he saved and who married him, one
first suspects, out of gratitude. They are without children—and whether the
marriage even has a sexual side or not is left (conservatively) out of the picture.
But he enjoys his wife, her elegance, her good-natured charm, her command of
culture and manners, and he supports it with his rougher version of the same.
He is a self-confident man whose "repose was like that of a mountain. When
he laid his fleshy, thick-fingered hand on a frantic horse, a hysterical woman, an
Irish workman out for blood, he brought them peace; something they could not
resist" (*Lost Lady*, 49). This three-way conjunction—beast, woman, workman
(presumably to most fiction-reading Americans of the time, because he is Irish,
drunken)—needs only the addition of "child in a tantrum" to complete its survey
of the subaltern individuals who both throw into relief and recognize Forrester's
personal superiority—the position Niel is just leaving at the story's start.

Yet for all Forrester's noblesse, we must remember: Captain Daniel Forrester
rides through Sweet Water in a carriage called a "democrat." When our point-
of-view character, Niel, and the black servant the Forresters sometimes borrow
from Judge Pomeroy, Black Tom, take over Captain Forrester's care in his last

days, and the two men lift him into his bed, the Captain thanks them with, "Thank you, Niel, thank you, Tom" (*Lost Lady*, 141). Other than the hierarchy of thanking the white man first, the response would seem to be—and is intended to be—democratically equal.

At a telling climax in the novel's part 1, among the catastrophes that bedevil the end of the nineteenth century, a savings bank fails in Denver. One of the bank's biggest investors, Captain Forrester impoverishes himself so that the "Poles and Swedes and Mexicans" (*Lost Lady*, 91) who have invested their life savings—at the time Mexicans were considered by many white Americans not human—won't be defrauded of their money. Other failing banks are regularly paying fifty cents or less on the dollar to their clients, but Forrester makes sure that the clients of his bank—even the Mexicans—get back every penny, though to do so he personally must end up a relative pauper.

Besides simply refusing to pay out from their own moneys, other bankers are saving their own necks by transfering much of their own holdings into their wives' names. Captain Forrester refuses this tactic. One result is the great respect he receives from his wealthy friends and even his own lawyer, Niel's uncle, Judge Pomeroy. For a few years after Forrester's death, Judge Pomeroy charges Marian Forrester nothing for looking after her interests, out of respect for her husband's generous gesture to the American people. But while this saves her some money, it doesn't provide an income. Only investments can do that—or a good second marriage. Eventually, under the influence of the story's putative villain, ("Poison") Ivy Peters, the young, hard-hearted and scheming lawyer in the town of Sweet Water, Marian wounds Judge Pomeroy deeply by taking her business away from him and abruptly transferring it to the unprincipled and frankly vicious Peters, who has promised to invest what funds she has so as to give her at least a minimal income. Apparently, Peters makes good his promise, though he does so without any of the scruples Pomeroy or Forrester himself would have maintained in selecting what to invest in.

We have mentioned the book's introductory allegorical incident. We rehearse it here: While playing in the Forrester marsh with some other boys, before age and social conventions have separated out the poorer from the better off, sensitive young Niel watches eighteen-year-old Ivy Peters blind a live woodpecker by slitting open its eyeballs in order to impress Niel and the other boys with him, including the working-class German twins, ten-year-old Rhein and Adolph Blum—who in a decade will be twenty-year-old poachers when Ivy Peters is a twenty-eight-year-old lawyer. Trying to find her nest, the sightless bird injures herself greatly and, presumably, dies off stage. In an attempt to put the woodpecker out of her misery, Niel tries to climb the tree where she hides, but he falls and breaks his arm.

Niel is taken into the Forresters' great house, where Marian cares for him until the doctor arrives. The twins and Peters are not invited in and must wait outside because they are not of Niel's social class. This begins Niel's life-long infatuation with Marian Forrester—a kind of low-key and particularly American replay of Frédéric Moreau's intoxication with Madame Arnoux in Flaubert's *L'Éducation sentimentale* (1869), a book, as we know from her essays in *Not Under Forty*, Cather respected greatly.

By the novel's end, however, the adult Peters would seem to have "blinded" Marian Forrester as well to the old-fashioned values of human fairness that her late husband and Niel's own uncle, Judge Pomeroy, represented. Peters has done this in the course of becoming Marian's lover, as once before, during the last years of her marriage, Frank Ellinger had become her paramour, even while Captain Forrester was still alive—much to Niel's disgust in both instances.

Though Niel comes to suspect more and more that these moves were made with the ailing Captain Forrester's knowledge, if not approval, for Niel this represents not the sophisticated adjustment of the upper class to practical matters of human appetite but a further moral failure in which it is hard not to suspect, as well, personal currents of jealousy and self-hatred that Niel might feel toward his own passivity and inability to take advantage of Marian's clear and repeatedly hinted-at feelings for him, despite all the manipulations that lie, just as clearly, beneath her actions; the passivity of Niel's own passion may be read, at least in the aesthetic structure of the novel, as a version of the Captain's own condition. Certainly, the strokes Captain Forrester suffers, coupled with the fact that he is already twenty-five years older than his wife, may have left him infertile, a condition that possibly plagued him—or her—even earlier.

In chapter 5 of part 1, some years after the incident with the injured bird, we learn directly of Marian's first infidelity to her husband. The revelation occurs in a strange and even haunting scene. Formally, the placement of the scene feels slightly awkward, yet that awkwardness contributes to both its verisimilitude and its strangeness: Marian has invited Niel to dinner the night before to entertain young Constance Ogden, a homely girl about his own age (like Anton Chekhov, Cather is a careful describer of faces), who clearly has her eye set on the dashing and romantic—and also rather brutal—Frank Ellinger. Niel is invited back the next day to keep Constance company, while Frank and Marian leave the disgruntled girl at the house with Niel while the Captain is asleep upstairs.

Marian and Frank take the sleigh off to cut cedar boughs to decorate Marian's house for Christmas; they take the small sleigh, with the excuse that the pole is broken on the larger one that would have accommodated all four of them.

We might expect the well-made tale that the novella seems to have started out as to continue with Niel's point of view or possibly to switch to Peters's—a young man who, that first night, was not invited to dinner. Instead, however, we switch to the point of view of young Dolph Blum (one of the German twins), who is now nineteen or twenty and who, with his gun, is hunting on the Captain's land. He comes upon the empty sled. Suspecting something interesting might be going on, he hides and sees Frank embrace Marian:

When the blue shadows of approaching dusk were beginning to fall over the snow, one of the Blum boys, slipping quietly along through the timber in search of *rabbits*, came upon the empty cutter [sleigh] standing in the brush, and near it the two ponies, stamping impatiently where they were tied. Adolph slid back into the thicket and lay down behind a fallen log to see what would happen. Not much ever happened to him but weather.

Presently he heard slow voices, coming nearer from the ravine. The big stranger who was visiting the Forresters' emerged, carrying the buffalo robes on one arm; Mrs. Forrester herself was clinging to the other. They walked slowly, wholly absorbed by what they were saying to each other. When they came up to the sleigh, the man spread the robes on the seat and put his hands under Mrs. Forrester arms to lift her in. But he did not lift her; he stood for a long while, holding her crushed up against his breast, her face hidden in his black overcoat.

"What about those damned cedar boughs?" he asked, after he had put her in and covered her up. "Shall I go back and cut some?"

"It doesn't matter," she murmured.

He reached under the seat for a hatchet and went back to the ravine. Mrs. Forrester sat with her eyes closed, her cheek pillowed on her muff, a faint, soft smile on her lips. The air was still and blue; the Blum boy could almost hear her breath. When the strokes of the hatchet rang out from the ravine, he could see her eyes flutter . . . soft shivers went through her body.

The man came back and threw the evergreens into the sleigh. When he got in beside her, she slipped her hand through his arm and settled softly against him. "Drive slowly," she murmured, as if she were talking in her sleep. "It doesn't matter if we are late for dinner. Nothing matters." The ponies trotted off.

The pale Blum boy rose from behind the log and followed the tracks up the ravine. When the orange moon rose over the bluffs, he was still sitting under the cedars, his gun on his knee. While Mrs. Forrester had been waiting there in the sleigh, with her eyes closed, feeling so safe, he could almost have touched her with his hand. If it had been Thad Grimes who lay behind that log, now, or Ivy Peters? (*Lost Lady*, 66–68)

The scene—and the chapter—concludes with a paragraph of backstory:

But with Adolph Blum, her secrets were safe. His mind was feudal; the rich and fortunate were also the privileged. These warm-blooded, quick-breathing people took chances,—followed impulses only dimly understandable to a boy who was

wet and weather-chapped all the year; who waded in the mud fishing for *cat* [cat-
fish], or lay in the marsh waiting for *wild duck*. Mrs. Forrester had never been too
haughty to smile at him when he came to the back door with his *fish*. She never
haggled about the price. She treated him like a human being. His little chats with
her, her nod and smile when she passed him on the street, were among the pleas-
antest things he had to remember. She bought *game* of him in the closed season,
and didn't give him away. (*Lost Lady*, 64 –65; all emphases added)

Because she does not give away the secret of his poaching, the assumption is
that, quid pro quo, Dolph Blum will not give away Mrs. Forrester's love affair
with Frank. And we do not see Dolph again in the novel until he comes—at
the back door—to pay his respects when Captain Forrester dies, with a gift
of game for the house. But even more is going on in this scene, at least for
the careful reader. Correspondences are established here, however, between
the Forresters and the Blums that are crucial for understanding Sweet Water's
social coherence.

To begin, let's look only at food.

Even more so than Black Tom (who after all probably lives and eats in the
house of the Judge), the Blum family is certainly the poorest that we know of
among Cather's portraits of Sweet Water residents. What do *they* eat? From
the above passage, we can surmise: rabbit, catfish, wild duck, and other game.

And what do the Forresters eat? We have already seen, in the dinner party
that this scene follows (and will see again, when a poorer Marian prepares yet
another dinner), that they eat a "fancy" duck meal. The first one is prepared
presumably by Mary the Bohemian cook; the second, Marian—now unable to
afford kitchen help—takes great pains to prepare herself. And we know that,
over the years, the Blum boys have sold her and her cook their fish and game
at the Forrester's back door.

Following the French model, pork, fish, duck, goose, turkey, rabbit, and
game in general, along with lamb, mutton, and organ meats (liver, hearts,
sweetbreads, and brains) are the food of *both* the American aristocracy *and* the
American peasant class—with, indeed, the latter providing most of it to the
great houses—where "Mary, her Bohemian cook" (that is, a Czech immigrant,
as in Cather's lyric novel of impoverished immigrant life on the prairie, *My
Ántonia*) is a talented member of that peasant class itself.

Beef and chicken are, as Cather will wryly explain through Niel in a scene to
come, the meats of the middle classes and the petite bourgeoisie—who, except
in certain locales, tend to distrust fish, game, and organ meats, both for practical reasons of storage and for the social discomfort their lack of familiarity and
complex tastes suggest.

Besides the content, however, when the whole is lifted out of context in the
way we have, a formal aspect to this scene ceases to be so apparent, though it

is implied in the rhetorical question Cather ends with: "If it had been Thad Grimes who lay behind that log, now, or Ivy Peters?" The Blums are the part of the working class that knows its place (on Cather's social scale), and the German rural poor are presumably as content with it as the rich are, not to mention the "Poles and Swedes and Mexicans"—at least the ones fortunate enough to be banking at Captain Forrester's Denver bank during the crash. Thad Grimes and the other Sweet Water boys are members of social classes who are suffering social changes because they are not economically tethered in that same way to the nation's fluctuating wealth. Thus, they are more likely to fall victim to the gossip-drenched pettiness of small-town *schadenfreude* and *ressentiment*. This is also, of course, one of the things that turns the larger social equation into more than a bit of a fairytale—which is what happens when the most economically powerful characters' behavior in a narrative becomes too idiosyncratic. (That is what gives us tragedy.) But Cather is aware of this, which is how she makes her story into a socially relevant fairytale. We must at least consider the values, even if we don't buy the notion of their being common enough in certain social strata to make a difference, since that is after all, exactly what she herself says is the case. Because they weren't common enough, presumably the vanishing of these values has brought the world to its "so much greyer" present. Without laying the blame directly at the feet of capital itself, this is about the best one can do—and nothing in her argument contravenes the potential argument that capital is the force that has demolished such values. Cather has simply chosen to cut the world up, in her fiction, in a way that doesn't foreground capital's role in it directly. To do that dramatically, she would have needed characters who worked in Forrester's bank and in other banks, as well as dramatic portraits of characters who banked at both and been interested in showing the comparative effects and interrelations of those effects on each and over time. That was simply not her fictive focus—though it's not something she denies. On the contrary, what she has to say about them—the result of those forces—is largely true. Her social message seems to be a conservative one: treat all classes fairly in economic terms, and the cultural distinctions that arise will be purely to maintain social order. Karl Marx's warning—that under capitalism economic fairness is unsustainable as long as greed, blindness, and unregulated profit (surplus value) are possible or commonplace—persists even while Marx's predicted effects have already intruded and fueled the story's progress; Cather is not interested in bringing these effects in their specific workings to the forefront of her tale. But they are there in the background. Nor does she misrepresent them. One can enjoy Cather today in the same way Marx himself enjoyed Honoré de Balzac; or, indeed, Walter Benjamin could enjoy Flaubert.

To reiterate: *A Lost Lady* appears to start off as a kind of well-made novella with a plot very similar to any number of French farces. But the scene quoted is where it shifts from that model and where Cather signals she is after something different from what might reasonably be expected: that, indeed, we *should* have expected Ivy Peters to have stumbled upon Marian's infidelity. Full of *schadenfreude*, in a well-made tale, Peters would have told Niel, who at first would not have believed him. The hostilities between the two boys, already in place, would deepen. Later, in a scene that the novel actually presents, when Niel does catch Marian with Frank (on one of his winter visits to the Forrester house), he realizes that there is a possibility for him to become Marian's lover. The story's resolution would have been the working out of whom—Niel or Ivy—would consummate his relationship with Marian.

But this is not the story Cather wants to tell.[7]

Niel's passion is fundamentally the inactive passion of modernism (and he wants Marian's passion to be inactive as well, which is why he cuts the wires when she starts to rage at Frank on the phone and feels that, by doing so, he has saved her); that is, the impediment to passion's consummation that stands in the fiction as a symptom or symbol of the change that has occurred in the world between generations, at least from the point of view of the younger.

Concomitantly, as with Captain Forrester and Frank Ellinger, Ivy Peters's brutality and values, which, in the changing world of the story, are more and more the ones that make for success, are also, apparently, the stuff of his sexual attractiveness and thus seal his relation with Marian, the same way that Niel's outmoded values, with misunderstandings and understandings intricately interwoven from his historical naiveté about the genealogy of those values, possibly set him outside Marian's sexual interests.

Held up against the *Parsifal* story, Captain Forrester is Cather's Fisher King, whose health is somehow intimately connected with the health of the land. Each time a major failure of values (that is, financial) occurs in the country, Forrester suffers another stroke and becomes sicker and sicker—until he dies. At that point, the land is literally lost. Peters takes over the beautiful and romantic marsh, where the Captain and Marian once loved to wander and the Blums went poaching in return for fish and game.

Peters drains it and turns it into a productive wheat field.

The irony of the novel, of which Cather seems aware, is that the hierarchy good manners impose basically eases the social machine along and allows it to function smoothly: who can come into the great house, who cannot, who can dine there, who would feel deeply out of place in such a social gathering—all this presumably having nothing to do with the worth or lack of worth of a man or woman, for example the German twins, who, as they get older, retain "poach rights" on Forrester's land because they don't take too much and know they must not set foot in the door, though they regularly bring Marion some of the game and fish for the privilege, sometime for money, sometimes as gifts. She is fond of them as she is fond of Niel and possibly of Ivy, too—though Niel's social connections with his uncle the Judge allow him to come through the front door, while Ivy's, the twin's, and Thad Grime's do not—at least in the book's part 1. That would seem the job of Marian, as Captain Forrester's wife, gently and kindly to keep everyone "in his proper place" (*Lost Lady*, 153) and, moreover, to make sure each is comfortable in that place. As in the case of the failed savings bank, we have seen, at least ideally, this hierarchy is presented as benign when it comes to dealings before the law or with economics, given the constraints of the capitalism they all live under.

Unfortunately, the thing that produces the outsized nostalgia that infects the younger generation, whether represented by Niel *or* by Peters, is the way those young men have misjudged that benign quality. Because they have not learned it or even re-created it, as Captain Forrester did, through a life that took him from young army officer (one doubts he was ever a private) to railroad baron, both of them believe that those who are accorded first place *by* the hierarchy of manners—because they are richer or better born, or even better educated—really *are* better persons than those who labor and toil with their hands and do not have other cultural advantages. For this generation, the hierarchical pattern is not just for social convenience and preservation of comfort. To them, it bespeaks a spiritual ontology. Defrauding Poles, Swedes, and Mexicans is acceptable because they *are* only Poles, Swedes, and Mexicans. (Cather waited until her last novel, *Sapphira and the Slave Girl* [1940], to attempt to treat the black/white version of this situation.) But we can see where her personal allegiances lie, even when she writes (sympathetically) about people such as the Captain and Marian Forrester, who would never dream of receiving a black man, such as Black Tom, socially—though neither would they ever think of defrauding him in a bank on whose board of trustees the Captain was a powerful member, because Black Tom has a place in the greater social matrix that supports their lives. Patronizing as it is, at least this view acknowledges these people exist and have some rights. It even goes so far as to make clear that if Captain Forrester is a man with such a vision of the country, he may well be a minority of (or close to) one, so that, as American as his attitude might be, only a relatively small group of people could benefit.

This is why politically such structures have to change.

The paradox of the situation, which—at least in the world of the novel—possibly only Marian herself appreciates (and which Niel, the point-of-view character, is too naïve to see) is that once Forrester is dead and she is no longer Captain Daniel Forrester's wife but his widow, Marian's job is no longer to stabilize things through her elegance, charm, and knowledge of what is *comme il faut*. The values her husband once represented have died with him.

Years after the Captain's death, the financially much-reduced Marian prepares a roast duck supper for eight, which she cooks herself as part of a strategy to civilize some of the coarser young folk of Sweet Water, including Ivy Peters and his sister, Annie.[8] The young men who are most of her dinner guests even though they all have professions now, are precisely the ones who would not have been allowed in her house as children—and their silence and awkwardness at the meal is the proof of how out of place they would have been if, by accident, they had been invited in. One of her motives for inviting Niel is that she feels he will be a good influence on them, showing them how to make dinner table conversation, how to divide his attention equally among all the guests, an art whose finer points Niel has already mastered during earlier visits with his uncle to the Forresters'. At first Niel thinks the project is both silly and doomed. (These young people are the people who, in the words of W. H. Auden's "Caliban to the Audience," "eat blancmange and have never said anything witty.")[9] That proper social dinner table behavior is learned—or can be learned by such young men who are now practically adults—is not part of Niel's experience. Because he learned it as a child, he assumes it is something normalized in an individual by birth—either you have it or you don't. Also, Niel does not realize that the roughness and sexual energy that Captain Forrester possessed came from the fact that he had *acquired* such knowledge, rather than been born to it. (One can assume Frank Ellinger's own rougher origins somehow account for his own animal energy and probably comes by the route of experience rather than birth.) While he is still contemptuous of the young men around him, Niel regains some sympathy for Marian as he watches her strive to bring off the supper ("He sighed as he thought how much work it meant to cook a dinner like this for eight people—and a beefsteak with potatoes would have pleased them better! They didn't really like this kind of food at all. Why did she do it?" [*Lost Lady*, 161]). One can only wonder, if—for all the elegance of the china, silver, glassware, and the general presentation—at least one reason they might not like it is that it is too close to dinner at the Blums', which is perhaps something they do know about from their own middle-class pasts.

As the meal draws on, however, Marian wins all of their sympathies with her tale of how Captain Forrester saved her life before they were married. Cather prefaces her internal tale, however, with a paragraph of Niel's memory of his uncle's account of the scandal that preceded it:

> When Marian Ormsby was nineteen, she was engaged to Ned Montgomery, a gaudy young millionaire of the Gold Coast. A few weeks before the date set for their marriage, Montgomery was shot and killed in the lobby of a San Francisco hotel by the husband of another woman. The subsequent trial involved a great deal of publicity, and Marian was hurried away from curious eyes and sent up into the mountains until the affair should blow over. (*Lost Lady*, 164)

Marian follows this with her own story of how, on a mountain-climbing adventure with another young man, Fred Harney, whom she had persuaded to take her down the face of Eagle Cliff. Their rope breaks. In the fall, Fred is killed. Both Marian's legs are broken and, among the rescue parties, Captain Forrester's reaches her first. The trail is too dangerous and narrow for a litter. The men take turns carrying her. With her broken legs, "she suffered terribly—fainted again and again" (*Lost Lady*, 165). Through the pain, however, she still notices that Captain Forrester is the most sure-footed, that he takes the most dangerous parts of the trail, and that she suffers least when she is over his shoulder as he carries her back to safety. After further details, when she is healing, he asks her to marry him; and, of course, she says yes.

After her story, Niel thinks: "She had, after all, not changed so much since then. Niel felt tonight that the right man could save her, even now" (*Lost Lady*, 166). With this expansion of what we know about the relationship between Marian and the late Captain, and its prologue about Ned Montgomery, the reader has another layer of evidence that Marian is attracted to men who act before they think and whose strengths lie in their oneness with the physical, rather than the intellectual, world, whether their actions are for good—like the Captain's—or for ill—like every other man we see her actually involve herself with. The right man is presumably one who, like the Captain, has the social values Niel himself is nostalgic for. The tragedy was that age eventually rendered a man who habitually acted well without thinking into a man who could no longer act at all—with the result that nothing was left. Thus Marian's straying had begun; and at this point Niel knows its entire history, except its last leg in Sweet Water and its final, post–Sweet Water resolution.

Still, neither Niel nor the reader realizes how far the parallels between the two dinners extend. During the first dinner, Marian had invited Niel to entertain the homely Constance so that Marian could have the dashing Frank Ellinger to herself though Constance had been already smitten with him.

Eventually, Constance *would* marry Ellinger—and their marriage comes along to shatter Marian's affair with Frank, which would serve as part of the unhappy "second-act" education that Niel gets between his two significant visits to the Grail castle.

Despite Marian's efforts and great pain, which Niel alone sees when, back in the storm, Marian comes to his office to use the long-distance phone line to tell Frank her feelings, Niel saves her from herself—at least he thinks he does—by cutting the wire just as she begins to raise her voice to Ellinger and tell him that she never wants to see him again. But this time, at the second dinner, Niel will learn that Marian has invited him in the same way that she had invited him to the first, this time to occupy Ivy Peters's sister, Annie, so that Marian can have time alone with Annie's brother, who has, as had Ellinger in years past, now become Marian's lover. Again and again, young Parsifal does not realize how he is being manipulated by Captain Forrester (in his double role as both Klingsor and the Fisher King) or by Marian/Kundry.

Though it is only the most ghostly suggestion in the text, probably this is the time to mention that, despite his love for Marian, the all but asexual Niel may, indeed, be gay—which possibly explains why he never thinks of making the relation sexual the way first Ellinger and then Peters (who, after all, is only two years Niel's senior) have no problem with. If Niel (or, indeed, Marian and Niel) are aware of such sexual preferences and those preferences are left out of the narrative foreground (as Cather tended to do, say, in her most widely known short story, "Paul's Case"), it might mean that some of his hostility towards her comes from the fact that he realizes she is using his platonic affection for her own highly nonplatonic ends.

Perhaps this hostility blinds Niel to the fact that the two generations, his own and the Captain's, are much more alike than he realizes—and that, indeed, all social behavior is learned and thus can be used properly or improperly. The only thing you can use it to judge people with is not how valuable a person is, but rather how well or badly they have learned it. To follow this rigorously, though, we would have to take those homoerotic suggestions and use them to queer Cather's text and show up Niel's perception of the fallen present as illusory or, at least, simply the triumph of people justifying to themselves the taking of a path of least resistance rather than one that leads to the greatest good for the greatest number, in which Niel is finally as much involved as is Peters.

Soon after the second dinner, Niel catches a glimpse of Ivy Peters through the Forresters' kitchen window, embracing Marian while she is rolling out bread on the breadboard (that is, at a task her Bohemian cook would have undertaken in the days when Marian could afford to hire one). That is the moment when Niel and the reader realize this is a replay of the situation with Frank Ellinger. Niel is disgusted. He throws the roses he was bringing for Marian into the mud, leaves, and never sees her again. This replay with Peters has a similar outcome to that of her affair with Frank Ellinger—with Marian abandoned a few years later by the callous young Peters, who (as Frank Ellinger did with Constance) goes off to marry a younger woman. Finally, in the novel's closing pages, news comes back that, off in Brazil, Marian has at last found some happiness with a rather grumpy English husband, who apparently needed her social graces and who could provide her the kind of life she had craved all through her marriage to Captain Forrester and after his death.

Marian Forrester is a woman who "preferred life on any terms" (*Lost Lady*, 169). The problem of life in Sweet Water for someone with Mrs. Forrester's breeding and vitality is a problem Chekhov cites in story after story. As Marian herself tells Niel on the stormy night, minutes before her long-distance breakup with Frank Ellinger in Niel's office, after she reads in the Denver paper of Frank's marriage to Constance: "'Nothing will happen over there. Nothing ever *does* happen'" (*Lost Lady*, 131–32). The Grail castle, the site into which stasis and castration constantly retreat, always masquerading as the seat of power, is the center of the Waste Land.

Usually when we speak of modernism, we focus on the development of fictive strategies in the presentation of the subject. The later modernists—the high modernists, as they are called—such as Proust, with his cascades of subjective analysis, and Joyce, with his stream of consciousness and his rhetorical innovations in *Ulysses* and *Finnegans Wake*, all go directly back to the pillars so frequently cited as the supports of modernism: Charles Baudelaire (the sensual ugliness of the modern world, poetically often indistinguishable from its beauty), Wagner (the mythic-historic complexity underlying the modern world and the psychological complexity it takes to negotiate it), and Flaubert (the sensory potential and the structural richness and ironic juxtapositions narrative art can summon in presenting all of these).

Baudelaire initiated an artistic tradition that went on to celebrate, whether in poetry, painting, narrative, or even music (Maurice Ravel's *La Valse*, for example) the horrors of the present day, wherever we locate them. (Baudelaire was a champion of both Wagner and Flaubert.) Wagner gives us the first grand model *for* the subject, that Sigmund Freud and Friedrich Nietzsche will basically adjust, refine, and even add to—but will not fundamentally change in its overall form—through a theoretical elaboration of how the subject is to be presented in his music dramas; the words represent what the character is saying or thinking consciously, the melody represents the character's thoughts and feelings about what he is saying, while the orchestra gives the range of his feelings about what is going on, both conscious and unconscious, historical and associational. Famously and directly, this will lead, though the intermediary of Paul Desjardin's *Les Lauriers sont coupés*, to Joyce's *Ulysses*. (For a reminder, Desjardin was the secretary of the *Review Wagnerian*, in Paris, and his project was to write a novel of bourgeois life that did in language what Wagner had done in music. On reading Desjardin's elegant little novel, Joyce—already deeply influenced by Wagner—consciously and carefully took the Wagnerian psychological project several steps further (in a direction that, in her diaries, Virginia Woolf recognized was one that had been laid out by Walter Pater— the Pater of "A Child in the House" and *Marius the Epicurean, His Sensations and Ideas* [1885]).

But this is not the modernist current—the rhetorical attack on the presentation of the subject—in which we locate Cather's work.

Academic criticism tends to fixate on this stream, as it circles around the Wagner/Joyce axis. But, by the same light, it tends to find materialist explanations ("the money has gone elsewhere") vulgar, though they are no less an overriding current of modernism for that. In both Cather and Flaubert it is the respect for things, natural or man made—and the physical beauty that can inhere in them—that governs both the style and the narrative structure of their fiction. In both authors, the stories always imply, if not state, how those objects mesh together to becomes the socioeconomic world and how they reach, retain or slip from their positions, as well as the values they can remind the people around them of, because of the positions they once had or still have. Their dependency on the world of objects might be called materialist, rather than "realist": aesthetic materialist for the style and that familiar old notion, historical materialist, for the complex and ironic narrative structure, all governed by an increasingly paratactic reticence. Though neither Cather nor Flaubert were marxists, their lives overlapped with the same world he'd lived in. Thus they saw much of what he saw. Such marxist explanations—I am by no means the first to state—decenter "man" as the controlling agent of his own fate quite as much as Copernicus (or, later, Freud). Modernist criticism tries to look at the Flaubertian current and its problematization of the relation between aesthetics and realism (the first -ism by which Flaubert was dismissed by his contemporaries), as if it were only the origins of Théophile Gautier's and, later, Oscar Wilde's *l'art pour l'art*. Still, there is a huge social side to both Wilde and Flaubert that much present-day criticism tends to elide. (See *all* of Wilde's nonfiction and many of Flaubert's letters to his *maître* George Sand.)

Flaubert said there were *two* imperative sides to literary talent. One was the ability to write cleanly and carefully at the level of the sentence—the popular part of Flaubert in today's schema because it is presumably somewhat more or less teachable. I don't know whether it is, if only because of its intricate relation to the other side: That is the ability of the artist to chose *what* was important at a given moment to write about. Without either one, Flaubert felt, the writer might as well pack it in and give up.

That was as clear as he was willing to articulate his project which, on the pages he left us, seems so quietly revolutionary when we read them closely.

However unpopular—or at least ignored—the second idea is, today, the root of the notion that the great writer, whether Vladimir Nabokov or Leo Tolstoy, William Gass or Wyndham Lewis—or Willa Cather—*does* have something of significance to say, which is, in itself, an inescapable tenet of modernism. But if it is to be said, especially in the novel, it cannot be said in synopsis. It must be dramatized. And that is what Cather does and what seals her into the modernist pantheon amidst all her other modernist concerns and influences.

At one point we might assume that Cather was thinking of having Marian eventually succumb to tuberculosis; or at least that she wanted the reader to consider it as a possibility. Toward the beginning of the story, when young Niel is thinking about Mrs. Forrester, he recalls "some legend about a weak chest and occasional terrifying hemorrhages. But that seemed doubtful, as one looked at her—fragile, indeed, but with such light, effervescing vitality" (*Lost Lady*, 39). Above and beyond the tell-tale hemorrhages, the feverish "vitality" of the tubercular is a standard literary trope for the disease itself. Presumably we are to guess, from this, that such a demise will be Marian's eventual fate. But this is not what the novel recounts. (If she has TB, certainly in the 1860s or 1870s she will expire within a few years. But she doesn't.) It seems to be there so that anyone too appalled with what the novel actually says has something to satisfy them if they need it. Marian is a "lost lady" in at least three fundamental senses. She is—first—a lady who loses her reputation as the good and wonderful woman who, as she loses her husband, loses "her faculty of discrimination; her power of easily and graciously keeping everyone in his proper place" (*Lost Lady*, 152), at least in Niel's judgment. But that loss has been brought about by socioeconomic change, and—second—she is also the lady whom Niel himself has lost; clearly she was taken with him. The present-day reader has to wonder why, if he is as smitten with her as he seems, Niel himself makes no attempt to realize an affair with her. But, by her own choice, Marian has given up any responsibilities she might have once felt for most of the values that Niel, his uncle Judge Promeroy, and her husband held dear—and, very possibly, Niel himself misunderstands, to the extent he assumes with Ivy Peters that good manners hierarchize not just convenient behavior but the actual worth of human beings. (Despite Peters, she does not "like" defrauding Native Americans—which, by implication, Peters has been doing.) The Captain, Cather makes clear, knew about his wife's infidelities and apparently lived comfortably with them. That is how he fulfils the castrated Klingsohr position as well as that of the castrated Fisher King. Potentially, Niel might have assumed that position—that of the "castrated" Fisher King, who presides over the health of the land. Because of his misunderstanding, however, gay or straight, he cannot ask of Marian (as presumably Captain Forrester once could, if not Ellinger and Peters), "Can you love me?" By the end, nevertheless, in the tale's very last pages, Marian is— the third meaning of the title—lost to the entire slut-shaming, bourgeois machinery that constructs such unfair and cruel judgments on women in the first place—and we, if not Niel, are left to read it as a triumph or, at the very least, a positive, deserved fate. That ability to break out of the prison of custom and propriety might well have been all the violence he needed to become attractive to Marian—to pose the question that, in his own terms, might have saved his lost lady. Although he is too much the prisoner of propriety and ignorance to voice it, almost all readers today can intuit that—though it would likely have been as unusual a relationship as that of Marian and Captain Forester's—her answer would almost certainly have been, like Molly's, at the heralding of dawn in *Ulysses*, "Yes."[10]

—*2014*
Philadelphia and
New York

NOTES

1. Jessie Laidlay Weston's *From Ritual to Romance* (1920), which, T. S. Eliot tells us, gave him "not only the title, but the plan and a good deal of the incidental symbolism of the poem" (T. S. Eliot, "Notes on 'The Waste Land,'" in *Collected Poems 1909–1962* [New York, 1963], 70), is a fascinating scholarly hodgepodge that swoops through everything from a survey of various versions of medieval Grail stories and related Arthurian legends on through tarot cards and Morris dances. Many of her arguments basically take the form "while there is no evidence of a connection, nevertheless . . ." and off we go again. Like so many others at the time, including Eliot, she was very taken with the work of James Frazier in his multivolume *The Golden Bough*. Weston explains in her introduction that her book grew out of an earlier project, *Legends of the Wagner Dramas* (from 1896, two years before G. B. Shaw's *The Perfect Wagnerite*), which had already inspired her to several volumes on various knights and two volumes on *The Legend of Sir Percival*, before she returned, in *From Ritual to Romance*, to wrap things up. The last book she published during her lifetime, *From Ritual to Romance* won Weston the Crawshay Prize. I doubt, however, if very many people would have retained much interest in Weston's work more than a decade beyond its publication if Eliot hadn't given it such priority among his *Waste Land* notes.

If one turns to Weston's index entries on the Waste Land, the Fisher King, Adonis, Attis, and Osiris (the names Eliot cites in his famous—or infamous—end notes), we have a meditation on a composite version of the story about which Weston initially writes, "a prototype, containing the main features of the Grail story—the Waste Land, the Fisher King, the Hidden Castle with its solemn Feast, the mysterious Feeding Vessel, the Bleeding Lance and Cup—does not, as far as we know, exist" (Jessie L. Weston, *From Ritual to Romance* [Doubleday, 1957], 3). In short, the modern "version" with all these elements is what the writer of the graphic novel *From Hell* (1999), Alan Moore, calls a "super-position," or a modernist construct if you prefer (Alan Moore, "Appendix II," in *From Hell* [Top Shelf Productions, 2006], 16).

Even if there is a Wagnerian Parsifal tale lurking in *The Waste Land*, it seems pretty much restricted to the second-act confusion-cum-education of the poem's main speaker, an education that falls between Parsifal's first and second encounter with the Grail knights. Recall, Parsifal had both male and female aspects that, at one point, Wagner thought to exploit by having a woman take over the part once Parsifal—"the pure man" or "the pitied fool," false etymologies both, as even Wikipedia assures us today: throughout his career Wagner was particularly fond of them—becomes enlightened by compassion. Thus the sexual duality of Tiresias—"a mere spectator and not indeed a 'character,' . . . yet the most important personage in the poem, uniting all the rest" (Eliot, "Notes on 'The Waste Land,'" 53)—can, in the poem, still be mapped onto Parsifal as well. In the same way it can also stand as a characterization of the point-of-view figure or even the narrator of a number of Cather's novels, even as it supports Eliot's later admission that the notes were intended to be ironic—if not parodic—bogus scholarship (Eliot's, not Weston's), as well as the sneaking suspicion that, given enough paired aspects and events, Parsifal's nonexistent prototype will resonate with almost anything, including Oedipus (via the blind hermaphroditic seer), and vice versa. That's what is so interesting about such constructs, even if they are not complete in any single folk version and really came into existence largely as a result of Wagner's tinkering; at least this one did.

Part of Wagner's project in *Parsifal* was to dramatize that all religions were fundamentally one—and thus all cultures were fundamentally related. This was one reason Wagner was so eager to have the Jewish conductor Hermann Levi premiere his opera at the *Festspielhaus* theater that King Ludwig had built for the composer at Bayreuth—as a dramatic gesture to the cultural unity he saw as undergirding all men. (The idea may have been among Frazier's inspirations.) After much soul searching and several serious conversations together, for Wagner's anti-Semitism was already well known, Levi finally let Wagner win him over. He conducted the opera. For the rest of his life Levi was a Wagner defender and supporter. He was one of Wagner's pallbearers after the composer's death.

Though he dominates the second act of Wagner's final music drama, the evil magician Klingsor does not even get an index entry in Weston's book. In Wolfram Von Eschenbach's *Parzival*, Klingsor is an auxiliary character, a duke who castrates himself in order to become one of the Grail knights but who is rejected nevertheless; see Wolfram Von Eschenbach, *Parzival*, trans. and ed. A. T. Hatto (Penguin, 1980). (Presumably he goes off and sulks.) Thus, he functions as a sort of double of the wounded Grail king, Amfortas, who is already a figure of castration. This doubling is a familiar feature of stories gathered from folklore, all the way back to the *Iliad*. To most readers of that exemplary military epic, today the exploits of the warrior Diomedes read much like doublings of the exploits of Achilles, often incident for incident, sentence for sentence, which, here and there, suddenly display some notable differences. The most parsimonious explanation we can assume is that Diomedes and Achilles began as versions of the same story, probably even about the same person, but over time various tellers began to incorporate various differences, as tends to happen with stories about folk figures. When these stories were collected, editors, after deciding which were primary and which secondary, included both versions so as not to waste either, and the protagonists were given different names. A version of this process may explain the various enhancements/ displacements of the Klingsor stories. In his novel *Heinrich Von Ofterdingen* (1802), Novalis makes Klingsor a worldly poet (in this case, a double of the poet himself) who engages the naive young poet, Henry, in provocative dialogues and tells him suggestive fables for much of the novel's second half, which may have prompted Wagner to continue with the idea of making his Klingsor the steward of Parsifal's erotic education. (See Novalis, *Henry von Ofterdingen*, trans. Palmer Hilty [Waveland Press, 1990]). Currently Klingsor Syndrome is the psychiatric name for the desire for or act of self-castration. And in the most recent production of Wagner's *Parsifal* at the Metropolitan Opera that I saw, back in April of 2013, the director mounted the opera's second act to great effect by having it take place in a stage-wide pool of blood, in the center of which stood Klingsor's throne, while the flower maidens danced and sang around him, their virginal white draperies more and more stained with red throughout the act as the costumes became dyed with Klingsor's presumably endlessly flowing symbolic bodily fluid—an even more extreme doubling of the wounded Amfortas of act 1 and act 3. The Wagner/Novalis correspondences have often been noted. It was a truism of late nineteenth-century music criticism that the astonishing extended *nachtmusik* of *Tristan und Isolde*'s act 2 was essentially Novalis (specifically his *Hymns to the Night*) set to music.

2. Willa Cather, *A Lost Lady* (Grosset & Dunlap, 1923; Vintage, 1972), 1; hereafter abbreviated *LL*.

3. Gustave Flaubert letter to Mademoiselle Leroyer de Chantepie, October 6, 1864, in *The Letters of Gustave Flaubert, 1857–1880*, trans. Francis Steegmuller (Harvard University Press, 1982), 80.

4. See Cather's delightful and informative essays in Willa Cather, *Not Under Forty: Studies of Literary Personalities and Certain Aspects of Literature* (Alfred A. Knopf, 1936), which—today—I'd recommend to any aspiring writer over fifteen!

5. Don't discount publishing restrictions, either. Stories of *active* passion in those years were generally frowned on and—as well—were illegal to print and distribute in the U.S. That only loosened up in the (pre–Hays Code for films) 1930s. Though published in 1922 and read by intellectuals with a Paris pipeline, in this country *Ulysses* was a banned book, after all, for slightly more than a decade after it had appeared in France—until December 6, 1932—and was first available in the country in an American edition only the following year.

6. Read *The Song of the Lark* (1915)! Read it! Re-read it! It dramatizes so much about the historical structure of art—especially opera—in America!

7. E. K. Brown and Leon Edel, *Willa Cather: A Critical Biography* (Alfred A. Knopf, 1953), 228–29.

8. According to *Mrs. Beaton's Book of Household Management*, the nineteenth-century Bible of good manners, any evening meal between "the number of the graces [three] and the number of the muses [nine]" was an "intimate supper." (If guests were entailed, a table of two was not allowed.) More than nine was "a formal dinner party." And don't you forget it.

9. W. H. Auden, "The Sea and the Mirror: A Commentary on Shakespeare's *The Tempest*," in *Collected Poems*, ed. Edward Mendelson (Random House, 1976), 328.

10. James Joyce, *Ulysses* (Alfred A. Knopf, 1992), 783.

9

Interview with Matthew Cheney

Matthew Cheney: What led you to want to write nonfiction about science fiction?

Samuel R. Delany: As a child I was an omnivorous reader. I read *War and Peace* when I was thirteen and *Ulysses* when I was seventeen. Between them I devoured Faulkner and Proust. It's not bragging, nor would I recommend it to any bright kid. Vast amounts of everything I tried to take in went wildly over my head. Still, for most of the book Tolstoy's heroine, Natasha, is between thirteen and sixteen—so easily you could read its hundreds and hundreds of pages as if it were a young adult novel gone to seed. And that's what I did. (By the novel's end, after seven more or less off-stage years of marriage with Pierre, she's a fat, sluggish, older woman of twenty-three, who's lost all her charm and vivacity!) *Not* the way to read *War and Peace*, let me tell you!

Nevertheless, I had some astonishing experiences, and I quickly learned that reading fiction produced in me two highly distinct pleasures. One was the pleasure of story. But far more intense was an extremely vivid, all-but-transcendentally intense experience from some of the words themselves. One I still recall—yes, from the opening pages of *Ulysses*—was Joyce's description of Buck Mulligan's hair like pale, grained oak . . . and suddenly Mulligan, fleshy, jovial, course, and blond, was momentarily in my third-floor bedroom with me in Harlem on Seventh Avenue just up from 132 Street.

It was amazing!

Another came from the science fiction writer Theodore Sturgeon, in his story "Granny Won't Knit," I believe, where a young boy experiences a moment of sadness, and Sturgeon wrote something like, "A hand rose up inside his head and scratched down the inside of his face, making his eyes water," and my own face got chills as my own eyes teared.

I found language doing this in Lawrence Durrell's *Justine* and the other three novels of *The Alexandria Quartet*. I found it doing this in James Agee's *A Death in the Family* and in science fiction writer Alfred Bester's *The Stars My Destination*. I found it in Virginia Woolf's *Mrs. Dalloway* and *To the Lighthouse* and *The Waves*, and Djuna Barnes's *Nightwood* and *Spillway* stories, and Richard Hughes's *A High Wind in Jamaica* and *In Hazard*, and Nabokov's *Lolita*.

I noticed, too, that I found almost none of this in novels translated from other languages, even when the introductions suggested that, in the original, this is precisely what made the books great. Now why was that . . . ?

I also noticed that, in a writer like Ray Bradbury (and many others, inside and outside science fiction, with the reputation for writing "poetically"), sentence after sentence came close to doing this, but somehow it was as if the writer blinked at just the wrong moment or let his attention wander, so that some slight verbal awkwardness slipped in and the effect didn't quite came off with the intensity it had with these other writers, writers who went on to include William Gass and Guy Davenport, Thomas Brown and Thomas de Quincey, Shakespeare, Shakespeare, Shakespeare (yes, say it once more), Shakespeare, Joanna Russ, Baron Corvo, Mark Twain, Willa Cather, Herman Melville, and Stephen Crane . . .

By now you'll have noticed how many of them—Sturgeon, Russ, Bester—*are* science fiction writers.

Basically, I wanted to produce such effects. Then, I wanted to write about *how* language produced them. Really, that's what's behind an essay like "About 5,750 Words." The ideas about "levels of subjunctivity" are there only to justify the initial analysis of how and when, in the phrase that the first half of the piece analyses, that wonderful spark—for some readers—leaps the gap and manages to illuminate another world.

Cheney: Of your essays, "About 5,750 Words" is probably the one I've seen most frequently cited by SF fans and critics, particularly its ideas of "levels of subjunctivity" within written texts. This essay, though, dates from very early in your career, and I imagine you would not want a reader to stop there among your critical writings. How do you feel about that essay now? What should a reader who found "About 5,750 Words" insightful continue on to read?

Delany: Recommending your own work is always a dicey game. That is to say, once I'd written a handful of science fiction novels, by the late '60s I was noticing things that made the language of the SF story unique. So, in a series of essays over the next decade—"Science Fiction and Literature," "*Dichtung und* Science Fiction" (essays you'll find in next year's rerelease of *Starboard Wine*)—I began to write about these differences. Certainly the one where I pulled out most of the stops, as it were, was the first one, "To Read *The Dispossessed*," in *The Jewel-Hinged Jaw*. (The title is a phrase I took from Thomas Disch's wonderful SF novel *Camp Concentration*. Disch and Zelazny are two other writers that should be on that list.) Yes, I had begun to realize that there was a tenuous connection between the way language was used in the tales that did this and that odd story pleasure—but a connection subtle enough to fill volumes. I also noted how many of the ones who did this in things written after 1870 seemed to revere Gustave Flaubert, in French, as if he'd taught them something important. And I had begun to note how they worked to keep their language as clean as possible so that nothing got in the way of these effects when they came about—as though, yes, the verbal context around them was everything . . . or close to it.

Cheney: In that central essay currently in *The Jewel-Hinged Jaw*, "To Read *The Dispossessed*," you offer some strong criticisms of Le Guin's novel—a novel that won major awards and is often cited as a classic of science fiction. Are such accolades misplaced, do you think?

Delany: Not at all. Le Guin's novel is wonderfully ambitious, and, as I write towards the end of that essay, what Le Guin's novel tries and fails to accomplish, very little American fiction even makes a stab at. I say: Read it. Revel in it. Learn from it.

Cheney: What is the origin of the last essay in the book before the appendices, "A Fictional Architecture That Only Manages with Great Difficulty Not Once to Mention Harlan Ellison"? Was Harlan Ellison annoyed that you went to such effort not once to mention him?

Delany: Harlan has never expressed any annoyance about that essay at all. I would be very surprised if he did. His name in the title is a mark of what an extraordinary presence he was in the field when I wrote the piece. That was the time he was putting together and publishing his genre-changing anthology *Dangerous Visions*.

I think it would be rather difficult for someone—someone a part of the SF community of writers, readers, and fans—who didn't live through that period, from 1965 through '71, to have a sense of how ubiquitous Ellison's name—and the energy associated with it—was.

The essay is basically an experiment in autobiographical impressionism. That's all. It functions as a contextual sketch of what the life I was living at the time felt like, especially those first trips to Europe—for all the people who had awarded the Nebula to *The Einstein Intersection* and enjoyed the journal entries scattered through it.

Cheney: The new edition of *The Jewel-Hinged Jaw* includes two appendices, one an open letter to Leslie Fiedler that was originally part of the main text of the book, and the other a piece called "Midcentury: An Essay in Contextualization." What led you to create the appendices in the new edition? What does "Midcentury" contextualize?

Delany: In the first edition, the letter—not *exactly* an open letter to Fiedler—was the book's introduction, under the title "Letter to a Critic." It was full of specifics about publishing at the time with names and figures. Today the companies themselves no longer exist. The numbers are entirely other. So it's now been relegated to a historical appendix.

"Midcentury" is a back-look at the 1950s—originally written for the volume I helped (ever so slightly!) Josh Lukin edit, *Fifties Fictions*—out of which the ferment of the 1960s blossomed. Perhaps more important, it's an attempt to talk about how whole sets of ideas move into—and out of—a culture, so that for a while certain things are much easier to understand—and certain others become much harder. In what's getting close to seventy years, I've seen this happen three or four times. The current retreat from science in this country—I've already seen several books on the topic—that the "information explosion" is prompting, coupled with the overload of the usual "epistemological filters" (my own term), is one of the most important and potentially damaging. It manifests itself in everything from denials of global warming and its effects, denials of evolution, the—by the same process—denials of the Holocaust, and the rise of fundamentalisms—as well as the superceding of science fiction by fantasy fiction. I believe all are facets of a single trend, in which increased population and the failure of social benefits to keep up with them on several levels are the greatest drivers.

Cheney: The last sentence of the very first paragraph of text in *Jewel-Hinged Jaw* is "This book is not an introduction to its subject." Aside from having a general interest in science fiction, what does a reader need to appreciate these essays? (My mother wanted to get a better grasp of it all, so I pointed her toward Jonathan Culler's *Literary Theory: A Very Short Introduction*. She said it helped.)

Delany: One of the things that hamstrung early SF criticism is that *every* book was a general reader introduction. (These are both Blish and Knight, despite their brilliance and originality.) Well, I wasn't a fourteen-year-old newcomer getting ready to read my third SF novel, looking for a definition I could give to some high school teacher who'd challenged me for wasting my time. When I was into my twenties and had been a publishing writer for half a dozen years, that's not whom I saw roaming the halls of convention hotels by the hundreds. We knew its history. We'd read hundreds upon hundreds of examples. We'd published—and read—thousands and thousands of pages of fanzine articles and reviews, and—as a group—had read them since the 1930s, the '20s. I wanted a book *I*—that is to say, we—could read and enjoy. So I wrote it.

I hope the book, especially in this edition, is self-contained. That's one of the reasons for not including the mega-essay "Shadows." (Thirty thousand words; "Midcentury" replaces it as an appendix.) As you say in your own introduction, "Shadows" is available as an appendix to my Wesleyan collection *Longer Views*, where interested readers can find it. Also, "Shadows" is a kind of show-offy piece that requires you to have at least some familiarity with much of the burgeoning intellectual work of the 1960s and early '70s—or at least to recognize names that were "hot" back then—from intellectual pop figures like Korzybski, to Ryle, Charbonier, and Edmund Leach, but who are no longer particularly current; or current in the same way. Moving it to another book also removes the greatest barrier to general understanding in the collection.

Cheney: Finally, the question all good book bloggers are required to ask: Read any good books lately?

Delany: My last ten months have been taken up entirely with my current novel, *Through the Valley of the Nest of Spiders*. I haven't had time to read my name on the mailbox as I come into my apartment house!

During that time I taught some interesting classes, however, and for them I had to read and reread some intriguing works—some of which I've mentioned. Longus's *Daphnis and Chloë* was one. Madame de La Fayette's *La Princesse de Clèves* was another. We read Cyril Connolly's stunningly fine *Enemies of Promise*—a book all writers need to read—and Melville's "Bartleby the Scrivener" and "Benito Cereno"; Joanna Russ's novella "Souls"; Joseph Conrad's *Heart of Darkness*, a short novel that can't be read too frequently; Willa Cather's *My Mortal Enemy*, ditto; Djuna Barnes's *Nightwood*, double ditto (I've been through it more than thirty-five times at this point, and it metamorphoses completely for me each time I do); James Joyce's "The Dead"; and, yes, Richard Hughes's *A High Wind in Jamaica*.

Then there's the novel I send everyone to read who asks me such a question: Gustave Flaubert's *Sentimental Education*.

As either reading or rereading, with time to think about them, that should keep anyone busy for a few months.

—August 12, 2009
New York

10

On Three Novels

Great House, So Much for That, and
Parrot and Olivier in America

Great House, by Nicole Krauss

I'm glad Sabina got her notes on *Great House* in before I got mine into a form I felt I could send you. I like to see such discussions start with the positive.

I think all she points to is there.

Also, I think her analysis is incomplete, and the things she omits are so overwhelming as to make these virtues seem very small by comparison.

* * *

I have strong feelings about *Great House*. I dislike it intensely. My objections are formal. Perhaps I am articulating in detail what Andre means when he says that it is a book of death that begins in literature and stays there.

For me *Great House* fails in two major ways. I start with the writing, which I find artificial, inflated, and largely colorless for great stretches. Here is a passage from page 37, picked at random, when, in the first movement, "All Rise" (I), Nadia writes about her husband "S," during a period when her own writing is going badly:

> . . . I went on as before, only not as before, because now I felt a creeping shame and disgust with myself. In the presence of others—especially S, to whom I was of course closest—the feeling was most acute, while alone I could forget it a little bit, or perhaps ignore it. In bed at night I recoiled to the furthest edge, and sometimes

when S and I passed in the hall I couldn't bring myself to meet his eyes, and when he called my name from another room I had to exert a certain force, a strong pressure, to goad myself to answer. When he confronted me I shrugged and told him it was my work, and when he did not press me on the subject, laying off as he always did, as I had taught him to do, giving me a wider and wider birth, I secretly grew angry at him, frustrated that he did not notice how dire the circumstances were, angry at him, and perhaps even disgusted.

Oscar Wilde noted with such "characterization," the effect is not to individualize your character. Rather, said Wilde, the more of such characterization you write, the more your character comes to sound like everybody else. This is why you must be so sparing, so selective in its use when you write fiction today. The contradictions within such a cascade of observations are not particularly incisive, and when they go on in this mode for page-long and two-page-long paragraphs (she went on as before, but not as before . . . she was disgusted . . . perhaps she was *even* disgusted; these rhetorical gaffs and cascades of received language—"bring myself to meet his eye," "pressed me on the subject," "I had to goad myself," "a wider and wider birth"—virtually constitute the book's prose), it becomes mere noise and blurs all specificity. Krauss is neither Proustian nor Jamesian in her insights. In this book, at least, she is bland and verbose. Add to this her affectation of not using separate paragraphs for dialogue, and running all conversations together in these same undifferentiated paragraphs, and the result is 289 painful pages that are all sound but have neither grace nor precision.

The second way the book fails is its major structure. A couple of years ago, Krauss published a very good book—*The History of Love*. But this new one has all the marks of a despairing writer, wondering what she should do now, and who finally settles on cobbling together a handful of short stories, some of them decent but some not very good stories at that, writing some extensions, backwards and forwards, in the hope that this will form a book. Here and there, some of the rewriting gives a semblance of a shared theme—in this case, a desk, which she makes a symbol of the reconstitution of Jewish culture in Israel after the country's 1948 declaration after the Israeli–Arab War. But it is painfully apparent that this book was constructed (I can't even say written) under the commercial rubric that novels sell and short stories don't. Attempting to bow to it, writers take a bunch of stories and do as much rewriting (or better, over-writing) as they can to convince readers that it's really a novel.

It's not.

And it won't be, without a *lot* more work! It's apparent to any reader with the least ability to analyze what they are reading *that* it's not. In a much differently constructed novel, some of this writing would have been interesting in exactly the ways Sabina notes. But that is purposefully to ignore well over half the pages of the book and the narrative context they set up and what that context does to the range of affects that is our reading of *Great House*. Giving such a performance a prize will do the book, ourselves, and literature no service at all. Because the writer knuckled under to mammon in a move that obliterates most of what aesthetic integrity the individual pieces once had is not a reason for a prize, though I am sure lots of publishers would be delighted if we did give it one—not just Krauss's—and would go around congratulating each other for years. ("We told ya' that was the way to do it. Looka these sales figures . . . !")

I have all the sympathy in the world for the writer who gets him- or herself into this evil trap, which all but precludes the writer writing anything first rate or even worth reading. But we cannot give a prize like the National Book Award out of sympathy.

The book's innumerable subsequent problems grow out of this initial decision and the inadequate attempts to write connecting material that would make it seem as if it were a single work. But the basic construction shows through again and again, and when the cracks *have* been successfully covered over, things grow even more murky. To read its clumsinesses and narrative absurdities and awkwardnesses as ambition is risible. Joanna has said that images echo through the book—and they do. But this is because Krauss could not develop those images; she could only repeat them, tale to tale.

Great House is not a novel. It is not a good collection of stories. It is not a collection of good stories—thanks to the rewriting and the often inappropriate (and wildly inept) material now interlarded throughout. In synopsis, almost any idea can be made to sound rich and fecund, but it is the execution that finally determines its worth. And the execution here would be sub-publishable if the writer didn't already have a track record.

With much cobbling together and new material added to suggest the repeated theme of a desk with nineteen compartments in its back, it's eight short and long stories. They take place in New York City, London, Israel . . . More accurately, *Great House* is three pairs of short stories, all in the first person—a deadly choice given her form—and a stand-alone ("Lies Told by Children"), with a coda composed of fifteen more first-person fragments assembled from the book's narrators. Each pair has a different cast of characters, a different location, and a different central problem. One or two of them may even have been written *for* the "novel." But finally, they do not make the rest cohere.

The first tale, "All Rise, I" is narrated, as we have said (as is "All Rise, II"), by Nadia, and *to* a Judge, who may (or may not), indeed, be Judge Dov, the son of Aaron, whom we meet later in the "True Kindness" duo of tales, and who, after a devastating incident in the Israeli army, when, as a young soldier, Dov violates a fundamental army principle by leaving a wounded comrade to die in the desert. Finally Dov leaves Israel itself, after receiving a vituperative letter from the father of his comrade, blaming Dov for the death of his son, and goes to England to study law, where he becomes—indeed—a successful Judge. He only returns on the death of his mother to stay with his father, whom he has never gotten along with, but with whom he wants to spend time and, possibly, make some sort of amends. Krauss divided this tale in two (as she does the others), with the first part giving Dov's eccentric childhood and painting the terrible relationship he has with bullying Aaron.

The concept of "true kindness" is an interesting one. Krauss locates it with the Israeli Red Cross (I think!). It's the kindness that you offer to the dying, without strings—the kindness which you know can never be repaid. This is, presumably, what Dov has returned to Israel to offer his aged father. It is the most interesting idea I took from the novel. But it is given in a page—and the long dramatization that precedes it does not make it particularly stronger.

The problem with this story—or pair of stories—is that it has nothing to do with the great desk that, thanks to the rewriting, is the symbolic center of the entire book. Yes, that desk comes to reverberate interestingly and becomes the center of a feeling of resonant mystery. My objection is not that it (or Krauss) fails to provide any answers. Rather, finally it organizes no particularly interesting questions.

In the first story, Nadia receives the desk from a young Chilean poet, Daniel Varsky. They have an affair. Daniel leaves, to write her a series of postcards. The desk stays with her. She marries "S," becomes a successful writer. Then the postcards stop—and there is a great deal about Pinochet and disappearings in Chile. But nothing is resolved.

The book is rife with meaningless loose ends. I mention only one: Nadia divorces "S" and eventually she finds a book of her husband's, a collection of stories signed to him by another author, Lotte Berg, who will—two stories on—become the subject of another story ("Swimming Holes," I), this one set in London; Berg is *another* Jewish woman novelist, this one living on London's Hampstead Heath; the book identifies Nadia's husband as a young man who, in that later tale, long before marrying Nadia, sought out Berg because he admired her work and eventually became a figure of whom Berg's husband became obsessively jealous, a jealousy that fuels the penultimate story in the book, "Swimming Holes, II." The identification of this young man as "S" (definitely a second-reading detail—it would be almost impossible to catch it on a first) tells us nothing meaningful about either story, unless it was just that "S" had a thing for women novelists—which is about par for Krauss's sense of psychological complexity.

Eventually a young woman who claims to be Varsky's daughter comes for the desk, takes it way, and vanishes. Later in the second installment ("All Rise, II"), someone comes looking for the desk, and Nadia, now fifty or so, takes a trip to Jerusalem, in hopes of finding it again.

If one has never read another one of such things, I can see how the collection might seem briefly interesting. But I cannot imagine that we haven't all read dozens of these semi-commercial hodgepodges, the more pathetic (e.g., Michael Cunningham's *Specimen Days*) when they are produced by writers who *have* written good work, such as Krauss (or, indeed, Cunningham).

As well, all eight sections/stories are in the first person. While two are supposed to feature a successful woman fiction writer—"All Rise, I," and "All Rise, II"—there is little interest or sustained individuality to the presumably separate voices. Indeed, out of the eight, only two sections come close to escaping this: "Lies Told by Children"—the last story in part I—and "True Kindness"—the opening story in part II.

The second story in part II, "All Rise" is somewhat better—or at least easier to follow—than the others, but the plot is so cliché that all we can finally do, with this version set in Israel, is nod and turn-away, embarrassed: an older woman (of fifty!), Nadia throws herself at a handsome young criminal of twenty or twenty-one in Jerusalem, who she thinks is trying to seduce her, only to find that the idea of sex with her physically repels him and he was only trying to get her to buy a replacement desk for one she has given away in the past. The text brings little to the basic situation, however, that has been a topic of classic—and simply better—tellings of the same basic tale so many times before: *The Roman Spring of Mrs. Stone*, *The Lonely Passion of Judith Hern*, *A Streetcar Named Desire*, *Good Morning Midnight* . . .

This one isn't vaguely in their league.

In the book's first tale ("All Rise, I"), Nadia, then a young poet destined to be the successful author of seven-plus novels, tells of her life over twenty-seven years on New York's Upper West Side, the same neighborhood in which, incidentally, I live today and in which I am writing these notes. It's a wonderfully colorful place. Thirty-six years ago, when I first got here (a couple of years prior to Nadia), it was even more so, with an extraordinarily diverse population, black, Latino, Asian, and the remnants of a politically radical set of Jewish thinkers and writers. When I came, Isaac Bashevis Singer had not yet won the Nobel Prize for literature and regularly I would see him browsing in the local bookstores, which extended down below Columbia University at 116th Street. Singer lived here until his death in July of 1991, and was a most distinguished neighbor. While writing this, I had to break for a trip to the bank on Broadway. When I returned, I listed the most interesting things and people I had seen in that few minutes—the marathon runners in their black and green spandex and their mylar cloaks given out by the city (it was Marathon Sunday), who filled the street along with their friends and admirers, clutching the red, green, and silver plastic around their necks and holding their water bottles; the elderly ladies in their hats, with their walkers, their long coats against the November chill, sitting on the island in the middle of Broadway with their black and

Latino paid companions; the booksellers lined up at their tables along the edge of Broadway in front of Zabar's, young mothers angling to get their strollers into the entrances of, here, McDonalds, or there, the new vegan "Peace Foods" restaurant, with a green framed window and spider plants draped behind the glass—six months ago it had replaced the pizza parlor on the corner of Eighty-Second for practically fifteen years—kids with their skateboards were coming from the park, a bevy of high school students were texting their friends vigorously as they strode in a phalanx down the street, at the end of the block the seventy-year old Asian maintenance man (Sam—his name is the same as mine) was finishing up his duties with the garbage cans of the doctors' building with its curved iron stairway, painted ivory, up to the second floor, just across the street from the bronze doors of Holy Trinity.

These are all from one ten-minute trip—and they don't even mention the street fairs set up on Amsterdam and Broadway, five and six times a summer, for the last twenty years.

Save two obligatory mentions of a babkhah from Zabar's, you will find neither these nor anything like them or any part of them anywhere in the first forty-five pages of *Great House*, which presumably picture Nadia's life in these same streets over some twenty-seven years! Their omission makes the area seem like a grim north English industrial neighborhood.

But such omissions go along with the flat, flat writing.

Maybe you bought it.

I couldn't.

(Again and again, page after page, I found it impossible to tell any southern Mediterranean home in Israel from the kitchen of some north Jersey suburb. In a good two thirds of the book there is no specific world present—other than in London, and then only barely.)

For me the entire novel momentarily rose to a new level of interest when, at the beginning, Daniel tells Nadia that the desk he gives her had briefly been used by the poet Federico García Lorca—and I anticipated that the tale would take us into the coils of the Spanish Civil War, and the 1936 firing squad and the gay poet, dead at thirty-eight, in his unmarked grave. But a few pages on in the story, someone on the phone tells Nadia that her desk was not used by Lorca after all, and with that authoritative fact, the story lost most of its interest for me.

As E. M. Forster notes in his 1927 study *Aspects of the Novel*, plot per se can have only one virtue: to make the reader want to know what happens next. Similarly, it can only have one failing: It does *not* make the reader want to know what happens next. It can accomplish this pricking of readerly curiosity elegantly and intricately as in a Jane Austen novel—by setting up a clean and clear narrative rhythm that allows readers to predict enough of what's coming next to make them hungry to learn how it's going be carried out. Or it can accomplish it energetically, if clumsily, as does Emily Brontë's *Wuthering Heights*—by presenting a cascade of emotions and incidents, but with each new scene written strongly enough to cast clear illumination on all that has gone before, making the reader yearn for this progression of illumination through the chaos. *Great House* would appear to take the Emily Brontë method, but without ever providing more than the weakest illumination. Rather, things become so entangled that are themselves so far apart, they finally seem to have no bearing on one another, so that vast parts of the construction have nothing to do with what it's actually about, and even intelligent and sensitive readers become indifferent to the performance.

It's boring—which is fiction's cardinal sin.

Sabina's statement that the book is not about "a desk, or about a piano, or about incidental furniture" or even a mystery, is right—exactly so; and part of what is wrong with the book is that it *is* that desk and the narrative around it that holds many of its pages to "the Jewish experience." So many pages *are* about the desk and so much of the book's energy is spent in suggesting mysteries that Krauss, here, displays neither the novelistic skill nor interest to solve, soon many readers cease to care.

I was one of them.

I was bored. I persevered through it—twice.

I don't think it was worth it, and it was less so the second time around than the first. Most of the things Sabina mentioned, I *did* get on first reading. (A small few of her points struck me as over-readings, but I'll wrack those up to her individualistic critical approach.) When a book gets better on the second reading, it's the sign it's a good one; when a book gets worse, it's the sign it's a bad one—and the second time through I saw all the creaking machinery, the forced parallels, with every possible correspondence shoehorned into some metaphor or other, and the correspondingly flat, flat characters, iced over with that dreadfully vapid prose, many of the characters millimeters off from ethnic clichés, with none of the richness of lived life to bring them alive, the endless oedipal tensions, the interminable loose ends, which, because I *had* read the book before, I knew now would go nowhere and meant nothing. To me, they seemed, by and large, less rather than more significant on the second time through.

In "Swimming Holes, II," after her death, Lotte Berg's husband, Arthur (Mr. Bender), searches futilely for the fate of a child his wife put up for adoption before he met her. In the end, when he is given a paper with a possible name, he tears it up and decides not to look further—a gesture which will be mirrored at the very end of the book when Krauss at last draws the curtain just before Leah opens the final cabinet on the desk with the mysteriously returned key—which is about the same level of anti-climactic gush as the 101-year-old heroine of the film *Titanic*, throwing her diamond necklace back into the sea at the end.

I've already told how Nadia, in an earlier tale, narrated how she sees the handsome young lay-about, with black hair and a motorcycle, whom she is smitten with—the spitting image of Varsky, in fact. Though everyone tells her he is a thief and has a young girlfriend, he—Adam—seems to like her, and, after a failed visit to an elderly man whom I assume is a narrator of one of the other stories, Aaron (father of our Judge, remember), to learn some information, he offers to help her get a replacement for the desk she is looking for.

Though, by shooting down the Lorca connection, Krauss shot down my major interest in her tale, I still was curious about the connection between Varsky and the desk. But when, as I read on over the next two stories, I learned that (1) Krauss did not know the answer to that one, and (2) she did not seem at all interested in putting out the inventive energy to find out, as (3), the next two tales had taken me as far as page 198 without any progress in the major questions at all. This is when I decided that the book—at least as a novel—was incompetent.

G. E. Lessing in the eighteenth century said that genius was the ability to put all one's talent into the service of a single idea—and it is the scattered feel, the failure to summon the sense of singularity (which for all its clumsinesses of another kind, is a singularity I *do* find—or find, for me, much more strongly—in Karen Tai Yamashita's *I-Hotel*) that makes me feel that Krauss's book is, to put it gently, *not* a work of genius.

Nor have I, with a second reading, changed my mind.

That said, stories four (the last in part I) and five (the first in part II) would have been decent tales by themselves had they not been presented sunk in the rest of the nonsense, which just makes them difficult to read, because by that time we are looking for them to answer questions posed by earlier material—questions that Krauss herself was probably completely uninterested in when she wrote them. It is the second reading that allows you to appreciate them for the potentially good stories they might have been without all the baggage trying to fake a novel.

Story four, "Lies Told by Children," was, for me, the strongest tale in the book. In London, not far from the Freud Museum, the adult son and daughter of an Israeli antique collector and seller, George Weizs, lives in an old Victorian house crammed with their father's acquisitions, while he is away buying and selling his stock. The daughter, Leah, is an aspiring pianist. The son, Yoav, is at Oxford, where he meets the narrator, a young American woman also studying at the English university. The story is basically the tale of Yoav and the narrator's affair and how the absent father dominates his children.

In general, in this story the writing is clearer than in the first four stories, which, by comparison, seem largely like attempts to fill up paper. Even so, there is no real climax or resolution, save that the father makes an unexpected return and the narrator, uncomfortable with the whole arrangement, leaves.

Weizs is the character closest to the symbolic center of the novel (if we acquiesce to Krauss and read it as such). He has taken on the job of reconstructing, in present-day Israel, rooms from various Jewish homes in Europe from before the war. He has promised to get the desk for Aaron—or someone. (It's not clear.) But his obsession with this task has basically destroyed the possibility of any normalcy in his children's lives.

It's a good idea—even a good idea for a novel. It doesn't work in this one, however, because we never see him actually do it for any length of time. He is just not on stage enough. The book is about everything else under the sun—as I say, it's a collection of disparate stories that Krauss has tried to write into a coherence that they don't possess. She would have had to write a long, long section in which we saw George working to fulfill his task, which was paired with the intense desire of some one to have such a reconstruction carried out, in which that desire was made emotionally and novelistically palpable. But—like the answer to Arthur's search and the secret of the desk's last cabinet—it's not there.

One can interpret such absences forever.

But we can't award them prizes, unless they show far more signs of having been positioned with conscientious novelistic skill, rather than by happenstance.

A prelude at the tale's beginning—which feels much more like the bleary writing in the rest of the book—has already made clear that, years later, Leah—Yoav's sister—phones the narrator in America and asks her to return to her brother, who is losing it. The bulk of the story is a flashback. I confess, I am unclear whether she does or does not return. But the fact is, it's another element that makes no difference one way or the other to anything that happens later.

The first story of part II, "True Kindness," is the military tale that follows the back story of the conflict between Dov and his bullying father, Aaron, that is given us in the first "True Kindness" tale in part I. The second "True Kindness" tale is set in the Arab-Israeli conflicts of the late 1960s. The basic story tells how Dov, in the army, abandons a fellow comrade in the desert, thus contravening a primary principle of the Israeli army: never abandon a fellow who is still alive. But Dov was in a position where, if he had carried his friend, or if they had both stayed where they were, both would have died. This way, at least one of them lives.

When he returns, to his home in Jerusalem, Dov is deeply depressed by the incident. (From the former story, we know there is a fundamentally strained and basic temperamental difference between father and son.) From a bomb that goes off in the street, killing and wounding many, we learn the meaning behind the term "true kindness." True kindness is the kindness offered to the dying, where there is no chance of their paying back the good deed. This is the kindness that Dov has returned to offer his own father, in his own twilight years.

Indeed, it is an important and interesting concept—for me the most interesting in the book.

The problem is that, for all its importance as a human theme, it seems to have nothing to do with the novel up until now *because* it has nothing to do with the much discussed and mobile desk. Unfortunately, these are the connections that the rest of book sets up, clearly and incontrovertibly. Despite all the plotlets that Krauss has written to bind them together, none of the stories feels as if it was integrated with any of the others. Unless this is supposed to be some sort of anti-novel (in which case, I shall admit, I completely misread the book), I find it impossible to read the feelings of dissociation between the sections as other than an almost endless succession of glaring narrative flaws. And the inserted connecting material makes it impossible not to want to bring them together.

Even in what I felt were the narratively strongest parts of the book, such as the two tales I have just discussed, moments of dissociation crop up within them as well:

Yoav and the narrator are making love on the living room rug in the old London house:

> My shoes came loose, and the pants slipped free. Then he took off the rest of his own clothes. At last we were naked. But instead of continuing in the vein we'd been going in, Yoav switched course and started to roll. An actual somersault with me attached. Once we'd gone around 360 degrees, he started to roll again . . . We were like two people practicing for the circus. You're hurting my neck, I whispered. (134)

This is ludicrous as well as anatomically impossible. A page later, Yoav is recording in writing every little move and gesture the narrator makes. Another of these moments—this one in "Swimming Holes, I"—is Lotte's daily dawn swims all year long in one of the lakes on Hampstead Heath—even if it is frozen over in winter and the ice has to be broken away. Back in 1966 and '67, when I had friends in Hampstead with whom I stayed when I was in London, I heard about such Polar Bear Club carryings on. I always assumed this was some sort of London urban legend. But whether real or fanciful, in Krauss's book there's no mention of bathing suits, towels, changing cabins, hot showers afterward, anything else to give a sense of veracity to these daily ice dips. These moments of anatomical absurdity or psychological unlikelihood are possibly to be read as "postmodern irony" or even moments of "magic realism." If they are intended as comedy, however, to me they fall flat. But it's far more likely that the writer's narrative invention simply hit a snag at such points and produced a moment of idiocy. The fact is, they are silly, narratively indigestible, and throw one out of the tale.

All Sabina describes is basically there, I feel. But I also can say confidently that Sabina is describing the Emperor's very skimpy underwear as he huddles in the wind—a few bits of interesting underpinning for the structure. In this case, however, *Great House* has no walls—and the Emperor has no clothes.

—*November 12, 2010*
New York

So Much for That, by Lionel Shriver

So Much for That is a postmodern (but pre-Obamacare) dark fairy tale about the debacle of American health insurance.

A not very productive yet serious maker of silver and metal jewelry, flatware, tongues, and the like, Glynis Knacker has been diagnosed with mesothelioma—which interrupts her husband's long contemplated trip to an island ninety miles from Zanzibar, called Pemba, to live out the rest of his life in an African beach town.

Shepherd Armstrong Knacker's family and friends are dubious about this move. Shep has amassed a portfolio of about $771K from his handyman business in Westchester, which, a few years back, he sold for an even million. Shep had stepped down as boss and owner to the position of "just another worker" in the company. The new boss is a narrow-minded tyrant and former employee, and Shep has decided to drop all—home, friends, and family—and leave it behind. His wife and two late adolescent children can come along or move in with relatives. He has already brought the plane tickets—when Glynnis drops her medical bombshell.

Fundamentally, Shep is a good guy. As well, he loves his feisty wife. His own family and in-laws depend on him for endless loans, and he's the guy who always picks up the tab when out at dinner with friends. The guys at work really depend on him, especially his long-time best friend, Jackson Burdina—Burdina is a Basque name which means "steel"; but many of the names in this book (Shepherd, Armstrong . . . not to mention a handyman and a jeweler named Mr. and Mrs. *Knacker*) have ironic or allegorical overtones.

With his wife Carol, Burdina lives down the Westchester road from Shep and Glynis. They have two daughters. The elder, Flicka (yes, named after the children's horse book), has an ultimately fatal disability, FD (sometimes called Riley-Day syndrome, also known as familial dysautonomia), a genetic anomaly that effects only perhaps three hundred people in the world. It sounds like a real nightmare, combining the worst of cystic fibrosis with the neurological degeneration of multiple sclerosis. Among her other infirmities, Flicka can't cry. Their second daughter, Heather, is an understandably neurotic younger sister, who is fat, attention starved, and not very bright. Both are a trial for their parents, especially their mother, Carol.

Bills and—by extension—health insurance have already been a great problem for the Burdinas, and will be a factor in what will become a fatally crippling complex that includes a gambling problem (which we hear about but never really see) and an inability to manage credit cards.

Health insurance will become an all-but-fatal problem for Shep, over the year of his wife's treatment.

As the book makes clear with cruel irony, Shep's assets are whittled down from $771K to under $4K, by which point he has been fired from his job and lost his insurance coverage to boot. We learn his dwindling bank balance at the head of various chapters, along with the date, as the book—from December 2004 through February 2006—progresses.

And what have Shep and Glynis gotten for their expenditures?

Besides a grueling year of bills, sleeplessness, and the job of being his own accountant as well as the twenty-four-hours-a-day caregiver for his wife, on top of insensitive family members and deranged friends and Shep finally getting fired for taking too much time off to take care of his wife—without treatment at all, Glynis might have been expected to survive a single year.

With regular poisonings from chemo that render her practically a zombie, she is able to survive a year and three months.

"Well, at least," says her physician Dr. Goldman (another allegorical name), during one of the book's more satisfying confrontations at the end, "we gave her three good months." Altogether those three "good" months have cost over two million dollars and left Shep broke.

"No," answers Shep, who has been cleaning up Glynis's vomit and stained bedding, carrying her into and out of the toilet, wiping her privates when she is finished using the facilities, and watching her crawl pathetically up the steps, "they weren't good."

Now we come to the major question: What kind of *novel* is this?

The first thing I have to say is that *So Much for That* has as close to a happy ending as such a book *could* have. Thanks to a lawsuit Glynis insisted on bringing against the company, Forge Craft, who possibly exposed her to asbestos, back when she was an art student, when all seems lost Shep and Glynis receive an $800K settlement—slightly more than Shep began with, a year and three months ago.

Shep picks up his wife, his children, abducts his octogenarian father from the nursing home he is been confined to, and—with the Burdinas—decamps for Africa after all.

On the other side of a grueling thirty-six-hour flight, Glynis gets a week or so of glorious weather with her husband, before she dies in his arms, with the help of the same morphine (provided by Dr. Goldman in that final confrontation) she would have had in the hospital. In Africa, Flicka gets an undisclosed number of years of air conditioning—as well as good weather—before, one morning, she simply does not wake up. Octogenarian gramps rallies to where he can take three-mile walks on the beach—and dies falling from a tree branch, reaching after a mango. Finally, at the end of a suitable number of years, Carol gets Shep's "really, really big dick," which is apparently what she has demurely wanted all along.

The book's final seventy-six pages (from page 357 to page 433 [the end]), their flight to Africa and their times in tropical Pemba, are actually quite fun— if you don't look too closely at what's gotten them there. The filmic models for Shriver's tale are the old 1940s Jimmy Stewart standbys, *Mr. Deeds Goes to Town* and *Mr. Smith Goes to Washington.* Indeed, had Shriver stayed more faithful to such models, it would have been more fun and probably more intellectually satisfying. Characters move about practically as in a Jane Austen novel, to have their chance at encountering each other—Flicka with Shep, Flicka with Jackson, Flicka with Glynis; Shep with Flicka, Shep with Carol, Shep with Jackson . . .

The motto under which such works operate is the motto from the Jewish Midrash, "*emet yeshalom yasood ha'ollam*": *Peace and truth are the foundation of the world.*

Well, "truth" specifically is what does not triumph in this tale. When the legal deposition falls due, which Glynis has been trying to put off, Shep tells his wife— who is exhausted and weakened from chemotherapy—that if she wants to save him and her family, she must lie.

And she does, brilliantly and magnificently. But as Shriver writes, and as Glynis and Shep now both know, the company which they bilk (Shriver's word) out of $800K had never done his wife "a speck of harm." Forge Craft, who made the asbestos-utilizing tools in the 1950s and '60s that quite possibly caused Glynis's cancer, are not the real villains, as both Shep and Shriver point out.

Which brings us to the next flaw in the book. If the problem the novel had presented to us was simply that of one unbelievably successful working-class family head in Mt. Kisko, smitten like Job by God, what Glynis's lies reduce to a purely personal solution might have been acceptable. But the book has spent pages and pages and *pages*, especially in the first half, explaining that this is not an individual problem. It is systematic and socially endemic.

The book's own treatment of it has made us aesthetically hungry for, at least, a gesture toward a social—rather than a personal—solution.

It would have required some far cleverer plotting, however, than the flimsy, largely off-stage *deus ex machina* lawsuit that the book provides to turn things against some actual upper echelon insurance CEO and allowed us to watch him get his comeuppance as well as give Shep back his money. (The job Shep did gratis for the CEO's Latina cleaning woman—herself with an infirm mother—which prompts her to steal for Shep the papers proving the insurance company lied when they turned down his appeal for the medication two months before Glynis's condition developed past the point where . . . etc., etc.) But as portrayed, I simply didn't believe that, on top of all his other time-consuming responsibilities with the insurance billing, Shep could have negotiated the paperwork for a lawsuit, no matter how good a lawyer Rick Mystic—the last of our allegorically named characters—happened to be. After all, the putative villains of the piece, at least some of those CEOs, probably live only a handful of miles in the other direction down that Westchester road from Jackson and Carol Burdina. In a book like this, leaving the actual villains entirely offstage—even as you resolve things for what's held up, with lyrical descriptions of beaches and helpful natives and soft breezes, as "The Good" (or the "*peace*" part of "*peace and truth*" in your search for the foundation of the world)—is just cheating (as much so as side-stepping "the truth").

So Much for That is what was once called an "encyclopedic novel"—*Moby-Dick* on whaling, *Twenty Thousand Leagues Under the Seas* on oceanography, *The Hunchback of Notre Dame* on twelfth-century gothic architecture—a genre in which pages and pages of nonfiction are summarily dropped into the book, bringing the story to a dead standstill. Traditionally it was a genre much loved by the nineteenth-century bourgeoisie—because they could believe they were learning something useful when they read it and not just wasting their time reading . . . well, fairy tales.

Basically, it didn't survive the Flaubertian revolution that occurred when Gustave wrote his own encyclopedic novel on the revolution of 1848, *Sentimental Education*, with maximum hypotaxis and minimum editorializing—that is, *everything* was dramatized: in many chapters, three or more things (elements from three or more story lines) were dramatized at once. Nothing was allowed to creep into paratactic sermons, whether delivered by characters or the author.

In what the English translator of the Penguin edition, Robert Baldick, has rightly called the most influential European novel of the nineteenth century, and which takes you inside the palace, while the peasants are throwing the throne out the window into the courtyard, even as it gives the smell of their B.O., you won't get as close-up a view of the goings on in a revolution as you do in Flaubert, even in a firsthand account like Marx's *Eighteenth Brumaire of Louis Bonaparte*.

In the past fifty years, indeed, the encyclopedic novel has weathered far more cynical clutches at bestsellerdom than *So Much for That* (see *Airport, Hotel, High-Rise* . . . and other pale recalls of the encyclopedics).

I wonder if that hasn't contributed to some of the high hopes people might have entertained for Shriver.

Finally, however, more Flaubert and less raw data would have been really helpful here: at one point, while walking in the park with Shep, Shep's buddy Jackson (who is Shriver's major mouthpiece) improvises for us an entire *chapter* of a nonfiction book (he invents new titles regularly, and we hear them all) he is planning to write on the economics of insurance companies or some such. My first reader's response was, "All right. Let's see what you can do."

But a page into it, I was rolling my eyes heavenward, impressed only with Shriver's Ayn-Rand-like *hutzpah*. The fact is, even when the reader agrees with the position expressed in these nonfiction screeds, which, yes, can sometimes be redeemed with wit (or *especially* when the readers agrees, which by and large I do), since Flaubert this stuff has no place in the novel.

And the writer's quipping in the text itself (which a couple of times Shriver tries) how boring all this must be doesn't help.

If such outpourings have any use as characterization, a couple of lines to suggest their verbal and emotional texture, followed by an ellipsis and a mention of how long they droned on, is quite sufficient—another technique invented by Flaubert.

This brings me to the next problem: As I read along through the first two hundred pages, gulping down monologues and essayistic chunks and impassioned expositions (even Shep's new boss, the thuggish Randy Pogatchnik—"at one time an employee so lazy and sloppy that they'd been on the verge of firing the guy before . . . a callow, loudmouth, ignorant twit" [10]—gets to give a three-quarter-page monologue, neither ignorant nor callow, detailing how Shep's growing medical expenses are driving up his *own* health insurance premiums for his other workers, just before firing the man for taking one too many personal days to get his wife to some debilitating chemo appointment), I kept being reminded of an Alan Bennett play. Long passages of the book are actually written with some art, although the writing is not consistently high. (A week before, I had read Bennett's delightful *The Habit of Art*, about a fictive encounter between oft-times collaborators Benjamin Britten and W. H. Auden, in which everyone debates wittily and movingly the meaning of opera.) From time to time, especially when bolstered by intelligent dialogue, such badinage can be redeemed by cleverness. Shriver strains my sense of the basic intelligence of the characters, however, especially of Jackson and Shep; and only slightly less of Glynis and Flicka.

But this is not a seventy- or eighty-page play script, which can be performed over a two- or three-hour evening. It's a four hundred-fifty-page novel. As is often the problem with idea-driven narratives—and as sometimes happens even with a master such as Shaw—the main characters, Shep, Glynis, Jackson, Carol, and Flicka, are as deep as thimbles. The secondary characters, Glynis and Shep's children, Zachary and Amelia, Shep's sister Beryl and their father

Gabriel, are wholly flat. Each has a single personality trait, well drawn, but without complexity.

Within such limitations, there's little or no psychological veracity.

Shep, whom we are told (and shown) is constitutionally incapable of getting angry at anyone, nevertheless manages to read Dr. Goldman the riot act in a final confrontation scene and argue a prescription out of him for a controlled substance (morphine!) *after* his wife is no longer covered—yeah, *sure* he does—through sheer aggression.

And Jackson, after a botched surgical penis-enlargement(!), which results in his wife *and* the first prostitute he hires online both rejecting him sexually because it looks so awful (coupled with a lot of debts and the aforementioned offstage gambling problem), castrates himself with a meat cleaver on a kitchen cutting board, then puts a gun in his mouth and blows out his brains. Whether the writer is male or female, this is an adolescent anxiety fantasy hiding behind John Irving–style smuttiness—nobody, of course, considers cunnilingus, though satisfying his wife *seems* to be what Burdina is so hung up about. It totally over-balances the book and is finally just unbelievably and ineffectually over the top.

After her and her daughter's gruesome discovery of Jackson's suicide, Carol tells Flicka: "Perhaps he wanted to die before you did, and couldn't face being in the world without you." Nice try. But we never see Jackson go through any such thought processes in the pages we spend with the brooding man, even when he's thinking about his daughter, whom, we are repeatedly told, he loves. Yes, his death brings most (though not all) of the book's preachiness to an end; but it's too little too late.

This brings me to my final catalogue of problems that sink this novel for me as a contender for Best of the Year. Again and again Shriver writes her way up to one or another scene that a reader might expect to be emotionally weighty, at which point she elides the scene itself and takes the story up after the scene is done with, as if to say, "All such encounters are alike and without individualizing complexity"—a risky statement for any novelist either to make or to imply—"and thus I need not bother with it." Perhaps Shriver feels that is a way to avoid sentimentality. But I think it is more likely that she was simply afraid to confront the material.

At any rate, Shriver does this on page 22: i.e., she skips the scene in which Glynis actually confronts Shep with her mesothelioma diagnosis. It's just not there. (By extension, she also omits Shep's actually first changing of his mind about Africa.)

In the same way, on page 91, Shriver omits Shep's incredibly self-centered sister Beryl's reaction to learning of Glynis's cancer. Again, we go right up to it—and leapfrog over it. We must make due with bitter Glynis telling Shep how much she enjoyed telling her—though what she actually said or what Beryl said back, we never hear.

On page 101 we get three distanced sentences, from Shep, indeterminately after the fact, covering Zach's and Amelia's response—their children's—to the news from their mother ("Amelia cried. Zach didn't. I think he took it harder") but we don't see the scene itself, where or when it occurred, or what anyone actually looked like or, of course, felt.

On page 117, we have the briefest of indirect accounts of Amelia's not showing up for her mother's operation; but we get none of Glynis's direct feelings at the time. (In keeping with the tropes of the encyclopedic novel, as soon as she emerges from her post-operative morphine haze, atheist Glynis is immediately embroiled in a religious debate with her born-again mother who wants her to accept Jesus and acknowledge the necessity for prayer, which goes on for a few pages, with no mention of Glynis's absent daughter.) And on page 426 all Shep's—or anyone else's—response to Glynis's actual death, not to mention any account of the funeral or her burial—are omitted.

If three—or even one—of these scenes had been fully presented, the withholding of the others might have come off as an interesting aesthetic reticence. But we never learn to trust Shriver in such situations. (Burdina's self-castration and suicide come off like tasteless slapstick. No writerly trust is engendered there.)

As it is, these omissions—because so frequent—finally register as a writerly tic. If you can convince yourself they're art, fine. I thought they were novelistic laziness, however, or, worse, novelistic affectation.

Indeed, only once in the book did I experience a moment of emotional identification: long-suffering Shep has been waiting on Glynis's every whim, no matter how unreasonable. Once she notices, she starts making her requests more and more difficult to fulfill. He makes one kind of rice for dinner. She wants another. He goes out, gets it, prepares it, and she takes one bite—and pushes it way. Finally, a bitter Glynis berates him with her disgust at all he's done for her, his endless compliance with her unreasonableness, in an attempt to make him angry. Instead, she can only make him cry—but at least Glynis can turn around and comfort him when he does, so that finally she can feel capable of doing *something* positive (pages 303 and 304). Yes, it's effective. But that's not a lot for four-hundred-fifty pages.

Other problems with the book? Given all the research clearly done to bolster this portrait of the American insurance nightmare, which so many Americans must go through, Shriver gets a couple of legal points wrong when she extends her argument to nursing care: If you are, indeed, paying for your own nursing care, as Shep must do with his aging father in the New Hampshire home, Twilight Glens, and you run out of money, as Shep is terrified will happen, the government is required to go on supporting you at the same level. It can't force you to put your relative into a cheaper place. Indeed, that's one of the few humane aspects of our welfare system. If it could—or if it could appropriate your money when your elderly relative, him- or herself, can no longer pay, my mother's final eight years in a fairly comfortable nursing home, at six thousand five hundred a month, would have rendered me and my sister penniless. What happened, however, as per the law, is that once my mother's own savings were eaten up (after three and a half years) and my mother was officially penniless, the state took over the bills for the remainder of her life.

It meant only that my sister and I received no monetary inheritance from her, on her actual death in October 1995, though she had started with a fairly healthy $300k in the bank, which, if she *could* have spent it as a healthy woman, would have given her a pleasant life, with some left over.

So Much for That is 356 pages of alternating suffering and preaching, relieved by bits of domestic comedy, followed by a 75-page feel-good resolution.

(I literally do not know how Shriver wanted me to experience Burdina's suicidal subplot. To me, it felt silly, out of character, and unbelievable. There *are* suicidal personalities—probably we've all known several. [I've had them as both roommates and friends.] But plucky garrulous Burdina doesn't have such a personality. They've been brilliantly dealt with in contemporary works, like Marsha Norman's *'night, Mother*, Michael Cunningham's *The Hours* and its post-Edwardian model, Virginia Woolf's *Mrs. Dalloway*—not to mention Charles Dickens's Ralph Nickleby and Victor Hugo's Inspector Javert. But if hardship alone could drive you to off yourself—even sexual hardship—then Glynis and Shep would have probably done themselves in by the sixth or seventh month of their ordeal. Burdina's auto-castration and self-slaughter are novelistic bathos that left me with no real emotional response and simply threw me out of the tale.)

Read *So Much for That*. Probably you'll enjoy it—I did, especially the conclusion.

Because of the character flatness throughout the novel, however, and the emotional holes Shriver felt obliged to scatter through the telling, in her pursuit of irony or of something else I just didn't understand, I have to judge *So Much for That* finally as an entertainment, a somewhat crippled fairy tale that suffers from being at once both preachy and without meaningful moral weight.

In short, for all its concern with a crushingly real problem, it's no more serious—or skillfully constructed as a presentation, much less any hint of a solution—than the last explosion-filled adventure that boomed across the big screen, where, despite the damage and mayhem they have wrecked around themselves, the heroes manage to get away with it in the end.

—*November 6, 2010*
New York

Parrot and Olivier in America, by Peter Carey

And here is a still further clarified version of my take on *Parrot and Olivier.* I do think, inadvertently, we picked three poor books among our five finalists, finally because—probably—we were rushed, and we were all trusting each other. This is too bad, but it happens. I can live with either *I-Hotel* or *Lord of Misrule.* I think Jaimy Gordon's is much the better novel, but if we feel social ambition is a necessary element for the kind of seriousness we are looking for, I can live with Tei Yamashita. (I think both are good books of their kind.) But I'd really like to see us do the right thing and choose not the "most interesting" despite overwhelming flaws, but the best. And the best to you all—Till our truffleless lunch at Bouley. —Chip

* * *

I confess I start with a disadvantage. The historical novel is rarely one I turn to for enjoyment—unless it takes on a specific historical problem and promises an interesting take on it.

Thus, I am not Carey's ideal reader.

I did not enjoy this book. Its back-and-forth-in-time plotting seemed unnecessarily baroque and not to any effect. The revelation of what I can only call Parrot's alternate childhood as a girl in Australia was interesting, but—since we'd already spent so much time in what was supposed to be his childhood in England (and told in the first person at that)—finally it wasn't very credible. Since Parrot was not writing for a specific audience (the way Olivier was writing largely for his mother), his withholding of the Australian information for the first two-hundred-twenty-five odd pages seemed more gratuitous than not. We get a sequence where Parrot has his mad-cap adventures as a twelve-year-old boy in England in which a one-armed M. Tilbot is a passing character. Then Olivier observes Parrot in France and he is now in Tilbot's employ as an engraver and spy. Similarly, the revelation of the hate Parrot bears for Tilbot, which only occurs past page 200, seemed gratuitous, since Tilbot repeatedly saves the boy's life and neither beats him nor is harsh with him. If there is supposed to be a non-articulated sexual side to their relationship, which occasions the hostility, I didn't get it, since Parrot is so forthcoming with specific descriptions of his own heterosexual carryings-on. If that's the explanation, the book is coy to the point of idiocy. Tilbot tells Parrot he wants him to go to America to keep an eye on the young nobleman, Olivier—the two eponymous title characters have been narrating alternating chapters. "Why don't you take your painter girlfriend and her mother?" suggests Tilbot. Following this, we get a scene in which Parrot's painter girlfriend throws him out of her artist's garret in Paris, when he tells her his patron, Tilbot, wants him to go to America and he suggests she accompany him. Then we go back in time and find out how, exactly, Parrot met Tilbot, when they were both fleeing across the wilds of Dartmoor. Next, we're on a boat to America, and—from the text of a letter by Olivier to his mama—we learn, in passing, that Parrot, also on the boat, *has* taken his girlfriend and her mother on the ship to America anyway—but what, then, was the point of the scene that so definitely put an end to the idea, unless it's supposed to be a funny reversal of fate? In the same way we went back and filled in the material missing from Parrot's young life, now we fill in the missing time from Parrot's ejection from Mathilde's garret and his finding a room in a poor quarter of Paris and the boat trip where we learn Mathilde has changed her mind. This is unnecessarily baroque story-telling. Either one likes it for itself or one doesn't. I didn't.

Because both POV characters write in the first person, the story lacks a sense of grounding and the emotions all seem overblown, in an attempt to be historical or interesting. And without some still point in these endlessly turning occurrences (this is another book that never suggests a coherent world for me, for all the colorful descriptions), they became tiring. Young Olivier is a fairly sympathetic character. He doesn't know any better and has had so little life experience we can excuse his noble arrogance, and enjoy a certain charm, energy, and curiosity which make him of interest. Adult Olivier, however, is just a reactionary prig, who, while believable, is a bore. The adult Parrot is interesting: He is an experienced fellow who has had a rough-and-tumble life—and his artistic talent gives him something of a center, though I wish it had been made more of and not presented as a flat given, the skill of a mimic but no art. (This is one reason the Philadelphia revelations about Parrot's time as an engraver in Australia fall so flat.) Terrified of everything, young Parrot is all but intolerable, however, and not terribly sympathetic. He is too frightened of *everything* to be interesting. And he comes back again and again and again. . . . Still, I never got a sense of what turned one—the boy—into the other—the man. Even the wife and child in Australia (in the last hundred pages—a little late, don't you think?) didn't do it for me.

For the first third of the novel Parrot is either (as an adult) blind with jealousy or (as a child) practically paralyzed with terror, while Olivier is just disdainful of everyone and everything. None of the three emotions is a particularly interesting lens through which to observe the world—especially when written in the first person. That Carey comes off as well as he does is a credit to his skill; but novelistically, it's a poor choice and doesn't make for interesting reading.

I don't want to give the impression that I think novels have to follow rules. They don't. But there are certain storytelling choices that present certain problems which the writer must acknowledge and think of writerly ways to overcome. When the writer does this, you have a wonderful book. *Parrot and Olivier* runs into problem after problem, however, and pretty well founders under them. The only one it makes a stab at wrestling with in some sort of interesting way is the drawn out, mosaic presentation of the Robert-Louis-Stevenson-*Kidnapped*-style survival on the moor, a là David Balfour and Alan Breck Stewart, in the persons of Parrot and Tilbot. In fact, it holds up pretty well to its model, though it lacks Stevenson's precision and emotional clarity. And there are no Catrionas or Barbara Grants in the book, alas.

The women characters we do have are totally wasted. Neither Parrot nor Olivier ever talks to any of them—save words of consolation or love; or outrage. But the women are never given a chance to talk *about* anything. One is aware that Carey is aware he is portraying a highly sexist era, but again and again, after he has done so, he relaxes into it just a little too comfortably, and the women vanish from the stage for thirty or fifty pages. Olivier's mother is probably the strongest, as presented, in her very few pages on stage. And though Mathilde is a painter in the age of Élisabeth Vigée Le Brun (and Rosa "The Horse Fair" Bonheur), and apparently a rather sharp businesswoman, Parrot never addresses a word to her about either art or life. After the hugger-mugger on the docks, where she is presented as a neurotic twit, Parrot carries her off to the New World the way a woman might pack a vibrator in her rucksack to take on a vacation—then goes ballistic any time others pick it up, when she's left it lying around, to use for themselves. But neither Christine, nor—in the last hundred pages—Amelia Godefroy ever *do* anything that affects anything in the novel, except be sexually fascinating or available (or unavailable). Her teaching enterprises are interesting, but, like Mathilde's painting, finally they *do* nothing in the tale. Olivier goes through endless conniptions to get Amelia a copy of Molière (he wants *Tartuffe* but ends up with the *Versailles impromptu*, which, disappointingly, is a pantomime without words), which she doesn't particularly want. Probably Amelia is her most articulate when she's off-stage playing the cello.

Carey's writing is lively and colorful and often fun to read for itself. But by the same token, equally often it doesn't cleave to the topic or character. There are sentences that are lovely. But there are others that would curl George (*The History of English Prose Rhythms*) Saintsbury's toes. And there are a fair number whose doggedly repetitious beats would makes at least Saintsbury say they weren't prose at all. But then, Saintsbury was eccentric about such things.

Finally, the whole book is too recomplicated and—strangely—claustrophobic (the boats, the prisons, even the Philadelphia library [my favorite scene] and the Connecticut mansion [my least favorite]) and emotionally ungiving to hold my interest.

Unless I'm getting some major psychological insight I haven't gotten before, I can give your ordinary, heteronormatively jealous male (or female) about a page-and-a-half—then I close the book; especially when the character is blathering on about him or herself. (This is the stuff of low farce, not high comedy. To work, it's got to be a lot cleverer than Carey makes it. Otherwise, it's just—that nasty word—sexist button pushing.)

This ain't Proust.
It ain't Stendhal.
It ain't Collette.
It ain't Wilde.
It ain't DaPonte,
It ain't Chaucer.
Again, I wanted a world, and I didn't get one.

Despite the regular alternation of narrators between John Larrit, aka Parrot and Olivier de Gramont, the story feels as if it was put together by the seat of Carey's pants. It's not well constructed. There's a lot of narrative awkwardness, and several parts are unclear. At page 200 of his 380-page book, we are still getting multiple-page-long stretches of back story that all should have fallen into the first fifty or sixty pages. It's not clever. It's just slipshod, and serves to dilute any emotional identification or sense of narrative speed. Over these same pages, the only strong emotions Parrot regularly experiences are rabid jealousy or terror, as—in his passages—Olivier's basic humor is aristocratic disdain: none of the three is the best fictive lens through which to observe the world, so that that both characters tend to grow dull. (Historically the novel works at its best when the world is seen through the glass of desire.) This is not the sort of novel you should have to read twice—and you do.

This is not a complete consideration of the novel, by any means. But finally, it is just too dense and *too* multilayered to be of interest—at least to his reader. ("Multi-layering" is a strategy to give the world of the book resonance and a sense of volume—but if there is no world, it doesn't accomplish anything.) By the end—hell, by page fifty—it had grown truly tedious.

The point of the book is that Parrot and Olivier become friends, but nothing actually done by either really has an effect on the other. Rather they just change with time and exposure, which makes the novel itself largely irrelevant. It's a very dull book.

As I said, these are only some of my thoughts.

—*November 17, 2010*
New York

11

The Paris Review Interview
by Rachel Kaadzi Ghansah (Uncut)

The first time I interview Samuel Delany, we meet in a diner near his apartment on New York's Upper West Side. It is a classic greasy spoon that serves strong coffee and breakfast all day. We sit near the window, and Delany, who is a serious morning person, presides over the city as it wakes. Dressed in what is often his uniform—black jeans and a black button-down shirt, ear pierced with multiple rings—he looks imperial. His beard, dramatically long and starkly white, is his most distinctive feature. "You are famous, I can just tell, I know you from somewhere," a stranger tells him in the 2007 documentary *Polymath, or the Life and Opinions of Samuel R. Delany, Gentleman.* Such intrusions are common, because Delany, whose work has been described as limitless, has lived a life that flouts the conventional. He is a gay man who was married to a woman for twelve years; he is a black man who, because of his light complexion, is regularly asked to identify his ethnicity. Yet he seems hardly bothered by such attempts to figure him out. Instead, he laughs, and more often than not it is a quiet chuckle expressed mostly in his eyes.

Delany was born on April 1, 1942, in Harlem, by then the cultural epicenter of black America. His father, who had come to New York from Raleigh, North Carolina, ran Levy & Delany, a funeral home to which Langston Hughes refers in his stories about the neighborhood. Delany grew up above his father's business. During the day he attended Dalton, an elite and primarily white prep school on the Upper East Side; at home, his mother, a senior clerk at the

New York Public Library's Countee Cullen branch, on 125th Street, nurtured his exceptional intelligence and kaleidoscopic interests. He sang in the choir at St. Philip's, Harlem's black Episcopalian church, composed atonal music, played multiple instruments, and choreographed dances at the General Grant Community Center. In 1956, he earned a spot at the Bronx High School of Science, where he would meet his future wife, the poet Marilyn Hacker, on his very first day.

In the early 1960s, the newly married couple settled in the East Village. There, Delany wrote his first novel, *The Jewels of Aptor*. He was nineteen. Over the next six years, he published eight more science fiction novels, among them the Nebula Award winners *Babel-17* (1966) and *The Einstein Intersection* (1967). Even then, his exploration of issues of sexuality, ethnicity, and gender—like the polyamorous love between three spacecraft navigators in *Babel-17*, or alien colonization and the relationship between the marginalized and history in *The Einstein Intersection*—distinguished him from other authors working in the genre. Even when set in fantastic worlds, like the Star-Pit, a city that squats at the galaxy's edge, or Nevèrÿon, an ancient, dragon-filled land whose inhabitants are just learning to write, Delany's work mirrors the generational shifts and concerns of his times.

In 1971, he completed a draft of a book he had been reworking for years. *Dhalgren*, his story of the Kid, a schizoid, amnesiac wanderer, takes place in Bellona, a shell of a city in the American Midwest isolated from the rest of the world and populated by warring gangs and holographic beasts. When Delany, Hacker, and their one-year-old daughter flew back to the States just before Christmas Eve in 1974, they saw copies of *Dhalgren* filling book racks at Kennedy Airport even before they reached customs. Over the next decade, the novel sold more than a million copies and was called a masterpiece by some critics. William Gibson famously described it as "a riddle that was never meant to be solved."

When we talk, Delany still seems humbled by that novel's success, yet he mentions more than once that it did not change his life in any real way: he still struggled to publish his more controversial works. One of these was "The Tale of Plagues and Carnivals," from the *Return to Nevèrÿon* series, four volumes comprising eleven interlocking stories and novels. Written in 1984, it was the first work of fiction about AIDS published by a major publisher, Bantam. During the mid-1980s, Dalton Books, then the largest bookseller in America, refused to stock his books or those of other science fiction and fantasy authors who dealt with gay content, since novels in those genres are often read by high-school students. As a result, Bantam backed out of publishing the fourth book in the series, and much of his older work wasn't reprinted. Delany, however, turned to small presses and academic publishers, and to date he has nearly forty books in print.

Over the course of almost a year, I met with Delany eight times. We never returned to the diner; as we finished that first interview, the waitress told us they would be closing forever that afternoon. One of our longest interviews was in a café-bar in Philadelphia called Woody's, whose walls were bordello red. Young men milled about in leather vests, and someone kindly picked up our bill. I had been reading Octavia E. Butler's essay "Positive Obsession," in which she mentions that when she started out as a writer of science fiction, Samuel Delany was the only black author known to be writing in the genre. "What good is science fiction to black people?" Butler asks. "What good is its tendency to warn or to consider alternative ways of thinking and doing?"

I pose these questions to Delany, and he responds excitedly: "Science fiction isn't just thinking about the world out there. It's also thinking about how that world might be—a particularly important exercise for those who are oppressed, because if they're going to change the world we live in, they—and all of us— have to be able to think about a world that works differently."

—Rachel Kaadzi Ghansah
(Additional questions by Jenny Davidson)

*   *   *

Samuel Delany requests that this interview be dedicated to Joanna Russ (1937–2011).

Paris Review: Between the time you were nineteen and your twenty-second birthday, you wrote and sold five novels, and another four by the time you were twenty-six, plus a volume of short stories. Fifty years later, considerably more than half that work is still in print. Was being a prodigy important to you?

Samuel R. Delany: As a child I'd run into Wilde's witticism "The only true talent is precociousness." I took my writing seriously, and it seemed to pay off. And I discovered Rimbaud. The notion of somebody just a year or two older than I was, who wrote poetry people were reading a hundred, a hundred fifty years later and who had written the greatest poem in the French language, or at least the most famous one, "*Le Bateau Ivre*," when he was only sixteen—that was enough to set my imagination soaring. At eighteen I translated it.

In the same years, I found the Signet paperback of Radiguet's *Devil in the Flesh* and, a few months after that, the much superior *Le Bal du Comte d'Orgel*, translated as *Count d'Orgel* in the first trade paperback from Grove Press, with

Cocteau's deliciously suggestive "introduction" about its tragic young author, salted with such dicta as "Which family doesn't have its own child prodigy? They have invented the word. Of course, child prodigies exist, just as there are extraordinary men. But they are rarely the same. Age means nothing. What astounds me is Rimbaud's work, not the age at which he wrote it. All great poets have written by seventeen. The greatest are the ones who manage to make us forget it."

Now that was something to think about—and clearly it had been said about someone who had not expected to die at twenty of typhoid from eating bad oysters.

Paris Review: What was your daily routine like in those days?

Delany: At six-thirty or seven I'd get up, scramble Marilyn some eggs—she was eighteen, I was nineteen; we'd been married that August—make toast and coffee. She'd go out to work, and I'd start writing. I'd work all day, with a couple of breaks for extracurricular sex in the local men's rooms and a stop at the supermarket for dinner makings. Right before five, I'd start cooking again. In general, I believe I work a lot harder today than I did then. Today I'm a five-o'clock-in-the-morning riser. Although I do stare at the wall a lot.

Paris Review: Stare at the wall?

Delany: I think of myself as a very lazy writer, though other people see it differently. My daughter, who recently graduated from medical school, once told me, "Dad, I've never known anyone who works as hard as you. You're up at four, five o'clock in the morning, you work all day, then you collapse. At nine o'clock, you're in bed; then you're up the next morning at four to start all over again."

Gide says somewhere that art and crime both require leisure time to flourish. I spend a lot of time thinking, if not daydreaming. People think of me as a genre writer, and a genre writer is supposed to be prolific. Since that's how people perceive me, they have to say I'm prolific. But I don't find that either complimentary or accurate.

Paris Review: Do you think of yourself as a genre writer?

Delany: I think of myself as someone who thinks largely through writing. Thus I write more than most people, and I write in many different forms. I think of myself as the kind of person who writes, rather than as one kind of writer or another. That's about the closest I come to categorizing myself as one or another kind of artist.

Paris Review: When did you decide that sex was important to your work?

Delany: For my work? Hell, for my life! Although I didn't start taking advantage of the public sex available to gay men till I was eighteen, with a moderately successful trip to the New Amsterdam movie palace on Forty-Second Street. No lightning flashed. No bells clanged. But it was useful to learn that it was available and could make me feel better about small stretches of my life.

Not a full decade on, when I was twenty-seven, Stonewall happened. Many of the political conclusions that became generalized with Stonewall—such as coming out of the closet to end the nightmare of gay blackmail—I'd arrived at in theory at eighteen or nineteen. But I didn't start acting on them seriously until I moved to San Francisco on New Year's Eve 1968. The existence of a public movement can change the way you arrange the details of your private life—one of the effects of discourse.

Paris Review: You describe learning, as a young teenager, that a sexual fantasy you hadn't yet written down could be eked out for a number of days or even weeks, whereas putting it on the page—using what you call "the whole narrative excess we think of as realism"—would make it briefly far more exciting, but then leach it of all subsequent erotic charge. Do you still feel that tug between the urge to put something into language and the urge to fend off writing?

Delany: I still feel that style is important for reading pleasure, and sex is important for pleasure in life. Each appeases a different type of desire. And while I find nothing shameful in taking direct erotic pleasure from reading or writing, I don't think they entail a necessary relation. The processes you have me describing are contingent psychological processes. Neither marks one end nor the other of any necessary or even philosophical relationship. Do I still feel the tug between the urge to put something into writing and the urge to fend it off? Less so as I get older. I shall always be able to come up with new fantasies. As long as there are people walking around in the street, as long as I have books to read and windows to look out of, I'm not going to use them up. I assume the universe will go on providing me with many more. The man I've lived quite happily with for twenty-two years provides me with much of my sexual satisfaction, physical and psychological. But, no, not all—thank *Deus sive Natura*, to borrow a phrase from Spinoza. Nor do I provide all his. What an unachievable responsibility!

For both heterosexuals and homosexuals, monogamous fidelity is either a romantic fantasy or a penance you agree to subject yourself to as compensation for having been allowed to have any sex at all. It's just not very realistic. Some people can do it, the way some people can give up meat—or, indeed, become celibate. But there's nothing either natural or healthy about it for primates, men or women. And to think there is, rather than to put real thought and work into how to negotiate multiple partners intelligently, with as much honesty and sensitivity to other people's feeling as possible, is naïve.

Paris Review: In your writing, you seem fascinated with cities and the contact they provide. Where does that come from?

Delany: Doubtless from living in them. I was born in Manhattan. I grew up in Harlem, a block away from what was then the most crowded block in New York City, according to the 1950 census. Something like ten thousand people lived in one city block. Probably that means it was more crowded than Calcutta or Singapore or Yangon—places we think of as inhumanly crowded today. The city gets you used to crowds, used to people relating to one another in a certain way, like strong and weak interactions between elementary particles. The strong interactions only come into play when the particles are extremely close, less than the distance of a single atomic nucleus. Those are the interactions readers want to see in novels. At the same time, paradoxically, cities can be dreadfully isolating places. The Italian poet Leopardi wrote in a letter to his sister, Paulina, about Rome, that its immense public spaces didn't contain people; they fell between people and kept them apart.

Paris Review: When you write about Harlem, you give it the allure and glamour of the Jazz Age but also describe how rarefied and suffocating its bourgeoisie could be.

Delany: Wonderful as it could be, that world was proscribed in some very strict ways. I was a kid who liked art and theater and dance and music, but if you lived in Harlem, high culture was somewhere else, and it wasn't black. When I was a child, the Metropolitan Opera had no black singers. I was twelve, when, at the start of 1955, Marian Anderson first sang the part of the sorceress Ulrica in Verdi's *Un Ballo in Maschera*—the first black singer to be featured in an opera at the Met, when it was down on Forty-Sixth Street and Broadway.

In Harlem, though, there was jazz culture. We lived right down Seventh Avenue from Small's Paradise, which I never went to, because I was a kid, but I knew it was there. Or the Red Rooster. They were places my parents and their friends went. I knew the Lafayette Theatre had once been right across the street from where I lived, but it wasn't now. Orson Welles had directed plays at the old Lafayette. My mother told me how she'd gone there to see the black actor Canada Lee in Welles's all-black production of *Macbeth*, when she was a young woman. Harlemites called it Blackbeth, so that's what I grew up thinking was its actual title, till I saw some posters for it on display at the Museum of the City of New York.

My childhood was massively and miserably contradictory. I'd been singled out as a smart child almost from infancy. Back in 1947, when I was five, I'd spent six weeks with my mother at the Vassar Summer Institute for the Gifted. The institute was very near our Duchess County summer home in Hopewell Junction, New York, and my father would drive out to visit us on the Vassar campus on odd weekends. My mother had a sense that I was a really bright kid, and I thrived on the institute's music, drama, and science programs.

Yet from ages eight to sixteen, I had to go twice a week to special tutors and psychologists who tried to help me with my appalling spelling and often incomprehensible writing. The psychotherapy continued till I was twenty-three. There was this bewildering contradiction between my clear intelligence and my extreme dyslexia. And nobody understood why. The fact that I was a black kid from Harlem in a private school full of white kids added its own tangle to the general confusion. In Jill Lauren's book on dyslexia and learning disabilities, *Succeeding with Learning Disabilities*, I'm used as a case study, along with my daughter, who's inherited it.

Paris Review: You were an adult and a published writer when you first came upon the word dyslexia and realized it described some of the difficulties you experienced with writing. Did having or not having a word for it make a great difference?

Delany: To answer that in any detail, we would have to reanimate the whole discussion over the Sapir-Whorf hypothesis, the notion that the lack of the word in the language means it's all but impossible to entertain the concept, while a detailed vocabulary, such as the Inuits' alleged fifty-plus words for fifty-plus different types of snow—powdered, crusty, hard, soft, blown-into-ridges, et cetera—enables you to perform intellectual feats of winter negotiations unthinkable to temperate-climate folks like you and me.

What's wrong with the Sapir-Whorf hypothesis is that it fails to take into account the whole economy of discourse, which is a linguistic level that accomplishes lots of the soft-edge conceptual contouring around ideas, whether we have available a one- or two-word name for it or only a set of informal many-word descriptions that are not completely fixed. Aphra Behn clearly describes the "numb fish" and its calamitous effects on other fish, animals, and human beings, so that we all recognize it as what we call the "electric eel" today. But she did it in the mid-seventeenth century, well before anyone had thought of electricity or Franklin had sent his kite up into the lightning storm. Thus falls the Sapir-Whorf.

Discourse is a pretty forceful process, perhaps the most forceful of the superstructural processes available. It's what generates the values and suggestions around a concept, even if the concept has no name, or hasn't the name it will eventually have. It determines the way a concept is used and the ways that are considered mistaken. The following may be a bit too glib, but I think it's reasonable to say that if language is what allows us to think things, then discourse is what controls the way we think *about* things. And the second—discourse—has primacy.

Now that's still a difficult notion for many people to wrap their mind around. But there's a lot of evidence for it. It's what allowed Foucault to say that discourse creates objects. Much of that evidence lies in small perceptual mistakes that we make constantly, every day, when from half a second to four or five seconds we misperceive some object for other than it is—the shadow in the corner that momentarily we take for a mouse, the stranger down the street whom we assume is someone we know till they are four feet away, the bunch of keys left on a workbench that at first we see as a tangle of string. But because an older discourse of perception, consciousness, and presence dismisses them as mistakes in the first place, instead of "important evidence that reveals the way the mind/brain functions," many of us never think about what their greater implications are for the mind.

For a couple of years in my early twenties, I was a die-hard believer in the Sapir-Whorf, though I had never encountered the term, or even read a description of it, which begins to hint at what's wrong with it as a theory. I even wrote a novel that hinged on the concept—*Babel-17*.

Perhaps the largest problem the lack of a single term imposes is that it becomes difficult to individuate the idea. Where does it begin and where does it end in terms of what it refers to out in the real world? The more complex verbal support there is for a concept, the easier it is to critique.

If I'd had the term Sapir-Whorf hypothesis, it might have been easier for me to realize that it was just incorrect—in the same way that when, at twenty-one, I first encountered the word dyslexia, I was able to realize I wasn't the only one with these problems, that it was a condition rather than an individual and personal failure on my part, and the stories I'd read about writers such as Yeats, who didn't learn to read until he was sixteen, or Flaubert, who was so backward in his reading and writing that he was known at home as *l'idiot de la famille* (the family idiot), now made much more sense. The realization of the flaws in the Sapir-Whorf, in that they caused me to begin considering the more complex linguistic mechanisms of discourse, you might say gave me my lifetime project.

Paris Review: How did your dyslexia manifest itself?

Delany: I had, and have, no visual ability to remember how words are put together. I can recognize them when I see them. But unless they're in front of me, I can't recall the vowels they contain. I have no command over whether they contain single or double letters. The closest metaphor I can come up with is that it's like being able to recognize hundreds of different faces but being incapable of producing any sort of likeness of any of them with a brush and canvas. I know all the rules—"i before e, except after c, or when sounded as *ay* as in neighbor or weigh"—and still cannot put down the words correctly.

At the same time, I read omnivorously.

When I was thirteen, I read *War and Peace*—the first two hundred pages over two or three days; then I stayed up for thirty-six hours straight to read the rest, with my father coming in every few hours during the night to tell me to put the light out and go to sleep. Interruptions aside, it was a wonderful experience—though I slept all Sunday. That's the point I decided novels were where it was at.

I read whatever books were lying around—*Freddy the Pig* and William Faulkner, *Raintree County* and Mandingo and Frank Yerby and *Studs Lonigan* and *God's Little Acre* and the *Alexandria Quartet*. I tackled Dylan Thomas and "The Waste Land" before I left the eighth grade and probably every popular-science book George Gamow published. My downstairs neighbor, who was a writer of young-adult novels, in a moment of who-knows-what excitement, enthused to me one afternoon about Colette's *Chéri* and *The Last of Chéri* and Chester Himes, whom he had known personally. By then, I had a library card, so I read them.

The novels that made me want to write them were *Huckleberry Finn*—my father read it to me one winter, a couple of chapters a night, after I was in bed, one of few truly pleasant memories I have of the man—and *A High Wind in Jamaica* and *Great Expectations*. And *Pale Fire*, a novel that reinspired me to want to make more such books in the world. *The Song of the Lark*, *My Ántonia*, and *My Mortal Enemy*, along with all of Cather's stories and nonfiction writing. *La Princesse de Clèves*, Madame de La Fayette's wonderful seventeenth-century psychological study on which Radiguet modeled his *Count d'Orgel*, or *Sentimental Education*, or *Lost Illusions*, or *Mrs. Dalloway* or *The Waves* or *The Years*. They are all books that have made me—and, oh, yes, others—want to write still other books.

The dyslexia didn't much hamper my reading. What it affected was my writing. I couldn't spell anything! In an early short story I wrote, a woman who works in a five-and-ten at one point exclaims, "Customers! Customers! Customers!" All three were spelled differently—and all three wrong. I could not spell the word "paper" three times right in a row!

Paris Review: But you were already serious about writing?

Delany: I don't think I was ever any more serious about writing than I was when I was twelve and thirteen. Of course I wanted to do lots of other things besides. I wanted to be a musician—that is, I wanted to be a composer. I played the violin back then. I wrote a violin concerto, from unrequited love for a young violinist, a prodigy my age who was playing solo concerts, named Peter Salaff, who went on to be the first violinist with the Cleveland Quartet, and whom I had met at a kids' party up in Croton-on-Hudson, given by a girl I'd gone to summer camp with, Barbara Finger. (Her younger brother, Greg Finger, eventually ran a summer camp my daughter went to.) I choreographed dances, wrote stories, directed plays. It was all terribly serious. At seventeen, for a winter, I took ballet lessons. But, one after another, probably because I had a sense of the seriousness of each, I realized you can't do it all. Finally, writing more or less drifted to the top.

I had already tried to write a novel, something called *Lost Stars*. It was about a very lonely young man named Erik Torrent who wandered around the city, *looking* at things. I started it when I was fourteen, though it had chapters that I had written the year before at Dalton. The hero was modeled on a boy in my freshman class, named Jimmy Rivers, a boy in my class whom I was infatuated with—and myself. (Torrent . . .? Rivers . . .? Get it? Image of someone nudging you in the side *much* too sharply.) He was the earliest of my nail-biting heroes. It had about everything wrong with it such a narrative could have. People were very nice about not telling me that. I suspect they were just impressed I'd filled out that many pages with words.

My literary model had been *The Notebooks of Malte Laurids Brigge*, which I'd read and thought was . . . strange. But I didn't see why I couldn't do it, too.

I hope you find the idea of a fourteen-year-old—any fourteen-year-old, no matter how bright—trying to rewrite *Malte Laurids Brigge* funny. I do. But much of the early intellectual life of any prodigy is a comedy—and a slapstick comedy, too.

Paris Review: In my opinion, Asimov's *Foundation Trilogy* seems to have had a much wider and more transformative influence than has generally been acknowledged. That's something else you read when you were thirteen. How did it affect you?

Delany: Well, certainly that's an opinion we share. The first volume—with malice aforethought on Ike's part, I'm sure: the SF club he belonged to when he was seventeen, the Futurians, was a hotbed of hyperintelligent teenage Trotskyites—taught me what historical materialism was. By the end of the third volume, I had a pretty dramatic picture of what's wrong with historical determinism, so that when I encountered Popper's *The Poverty of Historicism*, say, I'd seen the whole thing on the big screen, as it were, in full color and with stereophonic sound. Why do you think nobody's ever made a film out of it? It would make Marxists—or, at any rate, small-m marxists—out of every bright thirteen-year-old in the country. Personally, I think that's preferable to the demagoguery of Ayn Rand.

Paris Review: When you write about high school at Bronx Science, it almost comes wrapped in gold. The image you give of Dalton is very different from this cornucopia of creativity in the West Bronx.

Delany: Whatever its problems—and certainly it had them—Dalton was an excellent school, as was the Bronx High School of Science. But Dalton was a relatively small, private institution of no more than three hundred and fifty students, while the other was a sprawling city public school, spread out between two buildings and catering to several thousand. I remember thinking, when I got out: You haven't learned anything at Science that you didn't already learn back at Dalton. Science was an excellent school, but, with few exceptions, what they were doing in effect was going over all the things I'd already been exposed to.

One of those exceptions was music. Science had a wonderful music-appreciation course, in which I learned all about the Second Viennese School. It changed my life. We listened to a part of Berg's first opera *Wozzeck* and, after we listened to Webern's "Passacaglia," heard the story of his death—how Webern had been shot by an American soldier when he went out on his front steps for a cigarette after curfew. Webern and Berg have been among my favorite composers ever since. A lot of the students, when our music teacher played the last three scenes of *Wozzeck*, began to snicker and wanted to know, "What is that? That's just noise! What kind of music is *that*?" But I was knocked out by its expressivity. All I could think was, *Wow!* Our music teacher explained the twelve-tone system to us, and I went home and started composing a twelve-tone piece that afternoon.

Paris Review: Did college not excite you in the same way? Why did you drop out?

Delany: I wasn't smart enough. By that I mean I lacked a particular kind of organizational discipline or intelligence. I had the reading under my belt. I had the analytical chops. I was a magpie for picking up facts and dates. But to do well at college—there's no way around it—you have to be able to organize your time, which I could not do to save myself. I'd get started on one thing, and twenty minutes later I'd be off on another, in the midst of which I'd pick up some book on calculus or archaeology or Galois Theory and read the odd hundred pages about *that*. I was intellectually all over the place. I was writing music, directing plays, acting in them, singing in folk groups, choreographing dances, and if I had a paper due next week, there was at most a one-out-of-five chance I would finish it—some of which, yes, was the bad side of Dalton, because they'd been fairly accepting of that sort of thing and had often been willing to cut me some slack. But I didn't have the discipline. Still, not once did I ever think, Hey, I'm superior to all of this! I never thought, I know more than these people. When I flunked out of my first year of college, I flunked out miserably, spectacularly, and I was mortified. I thought, the truth is out—I'm an idiot! Now everyone knows.

It took me a while to realize that if a teacher had taken me aside and said, "Come on, Chip, sit down, let's talk, this is how you have to do this," probably I would have learned how to negotiate it. But nobody did.

Paris Review: What would they have said?

Delany: Well, when I started as a comparative-literature professor at the University of Massachusetts, I wrote an essay explaining how you do it—"How to Do Well in This Class"[1]—and I still give it out to students who are having problems of that sort. Basically, it's about what's gained by living your life in end-stopped time units, both for work and for play. Some of the students I've given it to have found it helpful. I wish I'd had it when I entered college.

Paris Review: You have suggested that the writers who influence us "are not usually the ones we read thoroughly and confront with our complete attention, but rather the ill-read and partially read writers we start on, often in troubled awe, only to close the book after pages or chapters, when our own imagination works up beyond the point where we can continue to submit our fancies to theirs." What were some of your "ill-read" books?

Delany: Proust—until I finally got around to reading most of it in my mid-twenties. *The Recognitions* for the first thirty-some years of my life—I had my first copy at fifteen—until, in 1975, I got snowed in at a Buffalo motel and, over a couple days, lay on the bed and read the whole thing. Early teen-aged stabs at getting through *Nightwood*—which, though a wonderful poet, Marie Ponsot, had given me a copy when I was sixteen, I didn't manage to get all the way through till I was twenty. (Today, it's the novel probably I've read more times than any other.) *Moby-Dick*, once I realized it was, intentionally on Melville's part, a gay novel and that at the end of Father Mapple's sermon Melville swears to the reader to tell us the absolute truth about the relation between male sailors—and does. *Sons and Lovers*, *The Rainbow*, and *Women in Love*—until I sat down and read them through in preparation for a class I taught on them at the University of Massachusetts—along with Lawrence's great story "Odour of Chrysanthemums."

Any book you have to work yourself up to read. Walter Pater's *Marius the Epicurean: His Sensations and Ideas*, which I've now read four or five times and taught twice, and his *Plato and Platonism*, which I also teach. It took me two years to get into the first. I devoured the second over two evenings. When such books influence you, if that's the proper word for what I'm describing, it's what you imagine they do or that they don't do, that you yourself then try to effect in your own work—that, to me, is what's important. What these books actually accomplish is very important, of course! But the whole set of things they *might* have accomplished expands your own palette of aesthetic possibilities in the ways that, should you undertake them, will be your offering on the altar of originality.

Before I read Robert E. Howard's *Conan the Conqueror* books and stories, I really expected them be the Nevèrÿon tales, or at least something like them. But I discovered that, vivid and colorful as they were, they weren't. So years later I had to write them myself.

Paris Review: You open *Atlantis: Three Tales* with a very rich story about your father as a young man.

Delany: When I was seventeen or eighteen, before I'd gotten married, my dad had told me that the main reason he had come to New York from Raleigh was to see the skyscrapers. He hadn't turned eighteen yet. It was just after Thanksgiving, 1923. His older brother Hubert met him at Grand Central Terminal. They didn't even come out of the station. They went immediately into the subway and got out at 125th and Eighth Avenue. My father looked around, but he saw only two-story buildings. He was very disappointed; he'd expected New York City to be *all* skyscrapers. He said to Uncle Hubert, "Shoot, this ain't no different from Raleigh. And there, at least, we got a building six stories high what got an elevator."

And Uncle Hubert, who was a twenty-three-year-old law student at NYU at the time, turned to him, laughed, and said, "You are a *real* country nigger, ain't you?"

When my father told me this, it was just a funny story. But he was so disappointed at not seeing the skyscrapers right away, I decided, thirty-five years after his death, to include the anecdote in "Atlantis: Model 1924." Family stories provided most of the proairetic material for the tale.

Because Dad wanted to see the skyscrapers, someone told him he should walk across the Brooklyn Bridge. Back then, of course, Brooklyn was nowhere near as built-up as it is today, and as he got to the other side, he saw a big cornfield—where Borough Hall is now—an immense cornfield stretching off into the distance. His first thought was, "They told me Brooklyn was supposed to be part of New York City. But coming off the bridge here is like walking right back into North Carolina!" That's how he told me the story.

In 1993, when Dad was dead and I started to write my story, I realized that was the same time—year and season—that Hart Crane had moved into his new home at 110 Columbia Heights, in Brooklyn. The first thing Crane did was start writing the poem "Atlantis," which would become the final section of his poetic sequence *The Bridge*. There's a reference in it to corn and another to fields. It struck me: That's got to be the same cornfield my dad saw! It's *got* to be—!

When Crane looked from his window, he must have seen the same corn my dad saw when he crossed the bridge. So that's what gave me the idea—and the title. Why, I thought, don't I write a story about the two of them meeting each other on the bridge?

Paris Review: You wrote the novella "Atlantis: Model 1924" and your essay on Hart Crane at the same time?

Delany: I wrote the novella first, then the essay.[2] One led directly into the other. That's because I had all this extra information—specifically textual—that didn't go directly into the story, and I thought, I've got to do something with it, since I read all those books.

Even before the autobiographical impulse, what started "Atlantis" is the idea that the paradigmatic works of our time were *The Waste Land*, *The Cantos*, and *Ulysses*. A vast intellectual armamentarium is presumed to stand behind each one, an armamentarium of cultural references and literary allusions. They're drenched in intertextual references, to the point where you wonder: *Could* a writer do all the things that Joyce and Pound and Eliot are presumed to have done in these works? Is this really possible, or is this all critical hype? So I thought, Well, let me try it on my own.

I went and got as many books on Hart Crane as I could. I invaded the library at UMass Amherst, where I was teaching. I wrote down hundreds of phrases I wanted to work into the story. There are so many references to other texts, I can't remember them all! In my story, Crane cries, "Any dull seamy era can throw up an Atlantis." Well, "any dull seamy era" is an anagram for Samuel Ray Delany—and, yes, the other thing I had in mind was "Vivian Darkbloom," Quilty's biographer in *Lolita* and an anagram for Vladimir Nabokov. Nabat and Kalit and the lines just before them are the code words and phrases the terrorists use to gain admittance in Oscar Wilde's early play *Vera, or the Nihilists*. The tale is filled with references to all sorts of obscurities, most of them things Crane might have known. The subway signs on the subway cars, for Naugahyde and Sloan's Liniment? Well, when Crane worked for Sweet's Catalogue Service, those were among the accounts he had to write. The subway car Sam and

Hubert ride uptown in is, in effect, Crane's own world . . . except for the Coca-Cola sign.

Paris Review: Now, you've said you don't do research—

Delany: "Atlantis: Model 1924" is the exception. There I read the weather reports for every day the story covers and reflected it in the narrative. That year saw a blizzard on my birthday, which is in the story. I got hold of astrological ephemerides for the time and read them. The references in the tale to the transit of Mercury and those other astrological occurrences are accurate. I looked at street maps. I knew the nights when the moon was full and when it was crescent. That tale contains as much research as I could get into it.

Paris Review: Was it fun to write?

Delany: No, not at all. It was a game but it was tiring. And I was aware that it wasn't reaching after any end. But at least now, when somebody asks, "I wonder if Joyce could have done all the things he's supposed to have done in *Ulysses*," I can answer, "Yes, he could have. I know, because I tried it myself. It's possible."

The next question is, of course, *Why* would he have done it? These are very conservative, backward-looking literary experiments, you see. They are experiments that start with a hypothesis, and the text is used as a way of working out a task, to see what the result is. Other than trying to weave the work, in a practically magical way, into the rest of the culture, I don't know why. The only reason I can think of is because he wanted to see if he could.

Paris Review: You describe a moment of transition, around the age of twenty, between conceiving of writing as the transcription of a sort of mental movie to becoming a writer who felt the presence of blocks of language, so that you were no longer just describing images and ideas but creating a string of sentences and paragraphs with verbal particularity and rhythm and so forth. Has that transition continued?

Delany: Arrogant and self-flattering as it is, today I really like Lessing's description of genius from his wonderfully suggestive *Laocoön*—the ability to put all your talent into the service of a single idea. That's usually what I'm *trying* for these days, rather than merely describing a movie in the mind—though I still lean a good deal *on* diegesis, that movie in the mind, as a strategy to focus it.

To assume that "putting all your talent into the service of a single idea" necessarily involves something fundamentally different from concentrating on the precision, energy, and ekphrastic force of the single sentence is to commit one of those logical slips Orwell described so well in his essay "Politics and the English Language," the one he calls "operators" or "verbal false limbs," assuming there are differences and oppositions where there are really developments and continuities. It's just a way of starting to talk about the larger project, the bigger picture—and critics are always slipping into the false notion that there's a conflict between the bigger picture and the details it comprised, when there isn't. That's one of the ways they mystify the artistic process. Sometimes these are honest mistakes. More often, however, they are symptoms of lazy reading and lack of thought about what the writer is actually saying.

Paris Review: You—and, indeed, several other SF writers—have called Bester's novel *Tiger! Tiger!* the greatest science fiction novel from that period. What so excites you about Bester?

Delany: I picked up *Tiger!* first when I was fourteen or fifteen, in its initial 1956 *Galaxy Magazine* serial publication, and thought it was the greatest thing I'd ever read. *Tiger! Tiger!* is an extraordinarily colorful and inventive novel. One whole chapter utilizes bizarre typography that sprawls all over the pages. In the climactic chapter, the hero is in the basement of a burning cathedral—St. Patrick's, in New York City—that's collapsing all around him, and the man experiences this through synesthesia, where he hears smells and sees sounds and tastes what things feel like. It's Bester's version of the end of Gaddis's *Recognitions*. Besides the nods to Gaddis—he was Bester's Greenwich Village neighbor and published *The Recognitions* the year before *Tiger!*—and Joyce, it's also very much an homage to Rimbaud's *"dérèglement de tous les sens."*

Later on, when I was about twenty-four, I read Bester's book again and realized, while it was very good, it wasn't the greatest thing I'd ever read. But because of its overall color and energy, *Tiger! Tiger!* projects a sense that, just over the novel's horizon, someone is thinking seriously about important modernist questions. What is the relation of the ordinary working man to the privileged man at the pinnacle of culture? (Do, finally, they contain each other? Can the rage of one of them at the oppression of the 1% finally release it?) What causes modern warfare today? What is the relationship between economics and war? Bester was very definitely a leftist writer, with a sense that economics was behind all wars. For him, wars were the playing out of economic-cum-industrial conflicts.

Still later I found out that Bester himself had been reading and rereading *Ulysses* for a year and discussing it weekly with two close friends. You could easily say that *Tiger! Tiger!* was his attempt at a book for bright fourteen- to seventeen-year-olds, with some of *Ulysses*'s textual playfulness. I wanted to see whether I could write something that would be as interesting for a twenty-five-year-old as this had been for me at fifteen. I'll never know whether I succeeded.

Paris Review: In *Nova*, your reimagining of *Tiger! Tiger!*, Prince Red and Ruby Red have an almost incestuous relationship.

Delany: Yes, they do. You have to remember the book was written before 1968, the moment when innuendo ceased to be a legally necessary literary technique.

Paris Review: Did you intentionally want to make something the reader could only speculate about, rather than be certain of?

Delany: Certainly as far as the incest goes. Suggestion *is* a literary strategy. But it has played a different role at different historical moments. (There's a brilliant and persuasive little book about how, in Hawthorne's *Scarlet Letter*, "adultery" is a coded way to write about incest in the mid-nineteenth century; I wish I could remember who wrote it . . .) When, by 1968, works like Henry Miller's *Tropic of Cancer* and *Black Spring* and Lawrence's *Lady Chatterley's Lover* were legally publishable in this country, the age of innuendo and the coyly placed line of white space, as the hero envelops the heroine in his arms, ended. Fifteen years later, AIDS rendered them permanently obsolete.

Today, I watch seminar rooms full of graduate students misread both Bester and Conrad, because they no longer have to wonder about the possibility of such illegal elements occurring in the story and the compensating possibility of suggestion as a writerly strategy for specifically representing both sex and violence—strictures that were in place in both the 1950s and sixty years before in the 1890. In *Tiger! Tiger!* the demonic antihero, Gully Foyle, invades Robin's exploded apartment and stalks across her living room to where she cowers away from him on the couch. There is a line of white space . . .
    At fifteen I knew perfectly well Gully went on to rape her. Many of my students, however, miss it. But the rest of the book bears it out. As readers who've learned to read with texts written largely after 1968, my students are unfamiliar with that order of narrative suggestion. Writers aren't constrained by law to use it today and many young readers, under thirty-five, have forgotten how to read it—if they ever knew.
    Like *Tiger! Tiger!*, Conrad's novella *Heart of Darkness* was another magazine serial, first published in the February, March, and April issues of *Blackwood's Magazine* in 1899. My students reach the second of its several climaxes in *Heart of Darkness*, when the pilgrims stand at the steamer's rail, firing their rifles at the natives on the shore, fifteen or twenty feet away, "for some sport." An appalled Marlow begins to blow the boat's horn to frighten the Africans off, back into the woods. Some of the natives throw themselves on the ground, but among them stands Kurtz's black mistress, her arms raised toward the boat that carries Kurtz away. From his bed in the wheelhouse, the sickly Kurtz watches through

the window—which Conrad has made clear has been left open. At the boat rail, the white men go on firing, and, with a line of white space, the scene ends . . .

Year after year, more than half my students fail to realize that the white men have just killed the black woman Kurtz has been sleeping with for several years; or that Kurtz, too weak to move, has had to lie there on the cot in the wheelhouse and watch them do it.

(The current Wiki plot summary is a mess: incidents are out of order and the writer[s] completely miss the murder of Kurtz's mistress. She does *not* "walk back into the bushes"! She's *dead!*)

When you ask, later, the significance of Kurtz's final words, as he looks out through this same window, "The horror! The horror!," it never occurs to them that it might refer to the fact that he has watched his fellow Europeans murder in cold blood the woman he has lived with and slept with (and, yes, had marital squabbles with). Suggestion for them is not an option. Earlier generations of readers, however, did not have these interpretive problems. Conrad could not have spoken about this directly, either. It had to be hidden—absorbed by a line of white space in the text, in the same way as Robin's rape—the rape of a black woman by a white man—sixty years later. Done explicitly, however, both would have made the texts illegal.

"If he raped her, why didn't the writer say so?" "If they shot her, why didn't Conrad show her fall dead?" my graduate students ask. It makes me wonder what other techniques for conveying the unspoken and the unspeakable we have forgotten how to read over four or five thousand years of "literacy."

Another canonical work that lists toward the incomprehensible for the modern reader under the weight of modernist criticism is Kafka's "The Metamorphosis."

Paris Review: How do you mean?

Delany: I've read interpretations that see the tale as Kafka's prediction of World War I or II, and it has to stand up beneath interpretative phrases like "that great portrait of the sickness that was Europe." I've even heard one academic give a rather involuted explanation about how the story depicts the encounter of a family with the inexplicable. Well, that's true, in the sense that a heart attack, a stroke, a crippling accident is, itself, inexplicable. But that sort of occurrence—schizophrenia or some mentally or physically crippling disease—is still the tenor of Kafka's metaphor.

Whatever you say about the story's all but infinite higher meanings, just at the level of plot, "The Metamorphosis" is an allegorical tale about a family, one of whose members, presumably the one who's responsible for bringing in most of the money, is suddenly stricken by a catastrophe, a debilitating disease that—overnight—renders him homebound and largely unrecognizable as the person he once was and tells what the experience might be from the point of view of the person to whom it happens.

This was a fairly common experience for families before World War II, and it still is. Kafka himself was such a person. His tuberculosis rendered him such a person in his own family, and it struck me as a chillingly accurate picture of the whole process of the transformation that occurred when my own mother was felled with a major stroke that, in an instant, rendered her wheelchair-bound, paralyzed on one side, and without language for the last eight years of her life.

The way the remaining family both recognizes and does not recognize the new and wholly dependent creature as the person he or she once was, and the way the invalid has to be treated—physically and emotionally—as a kind of insect . . . well, it's a hugely cruel story, even as it details how love for the person metamorphoses, under pressure of the transformative situation, into annoyance and a feeling of entrapment. The title refers to the family's transformation as much as it does to Gregor's. When the invalid finally dies—as my mother did, almost a decade on—Kafka explains how at last there is a feeling of freedom and even rebirth.

When we were coming back from the cemetery after my mother's funeral, my sister, who truly loved my mother—as, indeed, did I—said to me, "Chip, that is the end of eight awful, *awful* years," and a breeze blew momentarily through the trees. I had to answer, "Yes, it is." And I remembered Gregor's sister, in the last sentences of Kafka's tale. That tale is a portrait of the human processes which constitute that awfulness.

I'd never argue that the historical resonances so many analysts see in the tale are not there, but I point out that what I have described as the events of the story and their general significance is how those historical suggestions manifest themselves. How we treat our invalids—our mad, our physically or mentally compromised family members—does tell you something about who we are politically, historically, culturally. But until we can respond to the story as an allegory on that level, those historical suggestions are just not anchored. The commonplace reading, under the "supernatural" event Kafka has given us, is what keeps the meaning-generating mechanism of the tale functioning.

I can believe that Kafka intended to tell a story that commented on his own situation as an invalid in his own family and the story of other majorly debilitated men in a similar predicament—even perhaps young women. I cannot believe he intended to predict a World War; though it may read that way—and read profitably—with hindsight.

Paris Review: Like *Birth of a Nation*, *Dhalgren* tells the story of a black man who is believed to be a sexual predator and whose act of transgression becomes a fixture in the public conversation. Why were you interested in unpacking that particular story?

Delany: What can I tell you? Many black writers, from Richard Wright in *Native Son*, to Chester Himes in his novella "A Case of Rape," have tried their hand at it. The fact is, it is a many-layered process. I wanted to give the several participants, the white woman and the black man, the opportunity to speak where desire can freely articulate itself, without the judicial pressure of capture or incarceration.

Paris Review: Forty years ago, when you were traveling on the West Coast, you lost a notebook with some forty-two pages of a late draft of *Dhalgren*. What was it like to reconstruct the novel? Did the story change as a result?

Delany: No. I plan things out pretty meticulously. It was simply three weeks of hard, boring work, re-creating the lost pages. If the National eighty-page spiral notebook had ever turned up in the back balcony of the Empire theater on Market Street in San Francisco, where inadvertently I'd left it, many (many; not all, but most) of the paragraphs would be, I suspect, all but word-for-word identical with the reconstructed version now in the book.

Paris Review: What led you to write *Times Square Red, Times Square Blue*?

Delany: I had written an academic essay called "Street Talk/Straight Talk," and an editor at *Out Magazine* happened to see it and asked whether I would like to pursue the topic for general readers. I wrote them a not terribly specific profile piece that described the corner of Eighth Avenue and Forty-Second Street, just before they started tearing things down. But the editor, as I recounted in a preface to the book, said, "You've mentioned the theaters. Let me see what goes on in them." I asked, "Are you sure you want me to do that?" and she answered, "Yes," so I said, "All right." I tried for a representative range because I had thirty years of visits to tap. The second essay, "Times Square Red," is the theoretical underside that supports the general observations in the first half, "Times Square Blue."

Paris Review: In your 2007 novel *Dark Reflections*, the protagonist is haunted by embarrassment over a gay pornographic novel he once wrote.

Delany: Yes. As was common in the 1960s, a friend of the main character, Arnold, gets a contract for a porn novel, which he actually gets Arnold to write for him. During the '60s, pornographic publishers often turned to young poets and writers who were not making any money to speak of and hired them to write sex novels. Some of the results were quite astonishing. David Meltzer, Diane di Prima, Gregory Corso, Michael Perkins, Marco Vassi, and Alexander Trocchi are some of the ones who did. Others, like Arnold's, were done anonymously.

Paris Review: A number of critics have called the work autobiographical.

Delany: Oh, the differences between me and Arnold Hawley could fill a book! In fact, they already have filled a book—*The Mad Man*; and it's a book three times the length of *Dark Reflections*.

Arnold Hawley is married for not quite twenty-four hours before that relationship falls catastrophically to pieces. For the rest of his life, he lives alone. Since I was a teenager I've always been partnered with someone. Maybe four years in my life—from 1975 to '79, when I was taking care of my daughter—I lived as a single man. But Dennis and I have been together for twenty-one, going on twenty-two, years. I've seen him through a serious drinking problem and his recent half-dozen years of sobriety. He's seen me through prostate cancer and a few other medical emergencies. I've always lived in open relationships and generally had lots of sex. I've been quite lucky, with some small public reputation.

Arnold is an adjunct university instructor and a poet. I've been a full professor since I started full-time university teaching in 1988, and I'm a prose writer. Really, my life has been the opposite of Arnold's. Certainly when I conceived Arnold's story, I wanted to write about somebody who was as close to my opposite as possible. The only way I could have made him any more different from me was to make him white—and perhaps a woman. But I really wanted to write about another black gay male writer, a different black gay male writer from myself.

Paris Review: In some of your real autobiographical writings, you've taken care not to name or identify others who appear in the text.

Delany: Back in the mid-1960s, I lived for six months in a Lower East Side commune, called Heavenly Breakfast, named after a rock group I was part of, which lived and rehearsed there. I kept a journal at the time, and a few years later, after he'd accepted a short story of mine, Theodore Solotaroff, the editor of *New American Review*, suggested I next write a nonfiction article for him about commune life. I broke out my old notebooks, and soon I had a ninety-five-page article on life in and around Heavenly Breakfast. It took about a year to assemble, but by the time I'd finished, *New American Review* had gone under. There was no chance of it appearing there. I didn't show it to anyone for a couple of years after that. When I did, I had moved back to New York City. More on a lark than anything else, I showed it to my editor at Bantam Books, at that time a young woman named Karen. I was surprised when she announced that she'd fallen in love with it and wanted to publish it.

Much of *Heavenly Breakfast* deals with the day-to-day minutiae of minor drug sales. As much or more deals with sex—much of which was polymorphous. Since some of our activity was illegal, as a matter of course I changed the names. Besides, as I made clear in the introduction, I had not kept characters strictly apart. There'd been a fair amount of fictive mixing and amalgamating.

I was a little surprised, then, when I ran into a woman who had been a character in the narrative and who, as we stood on the corner of Sixth Street, somewhere in Alphabet City, told me how much she'd enjoyed the book. Then, after a moment's pensive silence, she added, "I wished you'd used my real name. That way I could prove to some of the people I know now that we really did things like that."

Not long after that, I ran into Eeyore, called Grendel in the first edition. He was back selling pot off this bench or that in Tompkins Square Park. "Hey, man—that was a really cool book you wrote."

"You read it?" I asked.

"Yeah, sure. But how come you called me Grendel? Nobody believes it was me." He, too, grew pensive. "You know, I ain't done a lot to be famous for. About the only thing anybody could know about me who ain't one of my customers is being in your book. It would be nice if I could point to that and say, Hey, that's me. People who read it would see my name and know." So in the next, Bamberger Books edition, when I next got the chance to change it, I did.

Paris Review: Do you revise every day?

Delany: Pretty much so, except the days or the hours I devote to writing a first draft. Eighty-five to ninety-five percent of my work is rewriting and revision. Probably that started as a strategy to deal with the wages of dyslexia. Now it's habit, but it was a fortunate habit to acquire.

Paris Review: Is it a difficult regimen?

Delany: Finding time to work is the main problem. That's why I want to retire—so I can really get to work. One of my favorite quotes is from Goethe— "As soon as a man does *something* admirable, the entire universe conspires to see that he never does it again." This is frighteningly true. You write a decent book, and you're hired as a creative-writing teacher. The next thing you know you're director of the program, which basically means you get less time in class and more administration, which nobody likes, so that you can hardly write anything anymore.

Paris Review: Your teaching gets in the way of your writing?

Delany: It doesn't completely halt it, but it slows it *way* down!

Paris Review: Is the teaching worth it?

Delany: No. It's not.

Paris Review: Why not?

Delany: I'm not that good a teacher. I'm decent, maybe even better than average, but I believe I'm an even better writer. The trade-off between doing a job that you only do moderately well for one that you do very well can't be justified simply because the former pays the bills. When I was thirty-five or forty, I envisioned myself doing a kind of ideal version of the teaching that a Lacan or, yes, a Foucault did in their French seminars. That was before I had a steady position as a professor at UMass. I was going from research institute to research institute. Here, I was senior fellow at the Center for 20th Century Studies at the University of Wisconsin, then I was a senior fellow at the Society for the Humanities at Cornell's Andrew Dickson White House, then I was a guest at the Center for Humanities at Wesleyan, next the Institute for the Humanities at the University of Michigan. The pay was usually munificent.

And I'd think, this is going to be it! They'll give me a lecture hall and some graduate students and turn me loose. I'll be able to do some real thinking and some significant teaching for them. Then I'd get there and discover that maybe three people had read any of my scholarly nonfiction, and while they had talked it up a great deal to the others on the faculty, what the school wanted me to do was to take a class of freshmen and sophomores and introduce them to American science fiction—which, of course, was Asimov and Heinlein and Bradbury and maybe Pohl and Kornbluth's *The Space Merchants*. "You're teaching that, aren't you? We had a graduate student here nine years ago who begged us to let him teach a class in science fiction, and when we finally did, that's what he taught. So I guess that's an important book, right?"

They were sure that's what it was all about, because fifteen or twenty years ago perhaps they'd actually read some. Their views of SF basically came from some monumentally uninformed articles on the genre that would appear every ten years in *Harper's* or even, slightly less so, *The New Yorker*.

Or they'd want me to teach a creative writing course for undergraduates.

Most were surprised—and, I could tell, resentful—when I'd explain, "These are all moderately interesting, middlebrow texts. I have nothing against any of them, not to mention Philip Dick, another entirely middlebrow writer. But none is rich enough to support the kind of reading I want to do with my class." A few times I got to sit down and argue my way through to something a little more interesting. Repeatedly I got Sturgeon and Bester, Zelazny, Russ, and Disch on my reading lists—and not just single stories by them, but two and three books by each. Eventually, though, I learned that the kind of teaching I wanted to do just wasn't supported in this country. Even in France, Foucault complained repeatedly that there was never really time for post-lecture discussion.

Once I was invited to give a lecture at MIT. David Halperin invited me, and I warned him it would be a three-hour talk, with only a ten-minute break in the middle. He must have thought I was crazy. Still, he said yes. I delivered it to a jam-packed lecture hall, with students sitting up and down the aisles. It went over very well—I've talked to a few people who still recall it from twenty years ago. From the student response directly afterward, I got a sense that it was what they were hungry for.

But I'm seventy, now, not fifty, and arthritis prevents me from standing for more than twenty minutes at a go. Were I offered that sort of lecture venue today, I'd have to turn it down. Even my public readings at universities these days have to be done seated. But that was back when I was thinking seriously about teaching.

My book *The American Shore*, an analysis of Thomas Disch's brilliant and exemplary short SF story "Angouleme," was an attempt to provide something I felt could stand up to the new approaches to reading that were burgeoning all around me back then. In at least three classes, *Shore* provided me with my own theoretical textbook, before I made the transition, in 1988, to professor of comparative literature at the University of Massachusetts at Amherst. *The American Shore* and *About Writing* are my two stabs at creating textbooks for my own students.

Paris Review: At Temple University, where you currently teach, you place a lot of importance on the individual sentence.

Delany: Yes. It goes back to the notion that what happens in the mind of the reader when the reader moves his or her eye from word to word on the page—*that's* what a story actually *is*. What the language calls up in your mind can make you think in a rich and vivid manner. How it makes you think about what it evokes, including its place in the world—that's particularly important. And how it makes you think about it must be supported by certain discourses. If those discursive models are rich enough, they inculcate the sophisticated idea of discourse itself that I'm striving for. For forty years, that has been and remains my project.

Frequently, those discursive models are in conflict with simpler discourses. When that happens, for some people it will be as interesting and as exciting as a good chess game. Others will not pay that much attention to the discursive clashes. For them it's not so interesting. But, as I did, listening to the students after my MIT lecture and reading what some of them went on to write me about the experience, I have the impression that a certain number were hungry for the kind of experience they had there and took from it something I can recognize as what I'd wanted to give. It's not a message, but an experience of seeing the world and the topics it comprises at a certain level of complexity, of potentiality, of relationship—a complexity and relationship that intricately entails, even as it empowers, the perception of suffering, ignorance, and cruelty and the pursuit of beauty and joy.

—February 16, 2011
New York

NOTES

1. "How to Do Well in This Class" is included in Samuel R. Delany, *Occasional Views,* Volume 1 (Wesleyan University Press, 2021), 320–23.

2. See "Atlantis Rose . . . : Some Notes on Hart Crane," also in Delany, *Occasional Views,* Volume 1 (2021), 122–95.

12

The Mirror and the Maze, I

For some years, "The Mirror and the Maze" has been the title of a week-long writing workshop I teach each summer at Naropa University's Jack Kerouac School of Disembodied Poetics. It comes from my sense of what the walls of the Prison House of Language look like and within which Nietzsche so wryly and accurately noted we dwell. Between those annual four sessions, for over half a dozen years now, the students and I read and reread works by two or three writers from a list including Heraclitus, Friedrich Hölderlin, Georg Christoph Lichtenberg. G. E. Lessing, Novalis, Gérard de Nerval, Sigmund Freud, Willa Cather, Robert Hayden, Robert Duncan, Theodore Sturgeon, Lorine Niedecker, Joanna Russ, John Keene Jr., and Robin Blaser. I mention this because at least three of these names have already surfaced in the papers prior to my comments here.

The attempt to grasp the workings of the physical universe, how the world functions, is, if we follow Baruch Spinoza, an attempt to grasp the God presumed to stand just outside those walls. As Professor Scott writes in his paper, in the poem "Patmos," one that I return to regularly over the summers, Hölderlin notes that it is hard—if not impossible—to do. While none of the readers here have attempted to wrestle directly with the seven-year project that is my most recent novel, *Through the Valley of the Nest of Spiders* (2012), those who have read it will have recognized that my sympathies—as much as those of a committed atheist can (the grandson of a born slave, a slave who had gone on to become one of the first two black suffrage Episcopalian bishops in the United States)– lean in that direction.

I don't remember exactly when I first decided that someday I would use that title for something. But it was before I had any specific idea of what to fix it to—or had any encounter with Nietzsche other than the obligatory seventeen-year-old's tussle with the Apollonian and Dionysian reductions of *The Birth of Tragedy from the Spirit of Music*, and while I was still happy enough to categorize myself to my professional acquaintances as "young."

When Robert Reid-Pharr proposed a selection of academic papers to celebrate my fifty years of published writing, I was minded (as, with his combined accuracy and eccentricity, Dr. Thomas Browne might have written) of an anecdote that, for the first ten years of my career, formed part of my general self-presentation.

My seventh novel, *The Einstein Intersection*, appeared in March of 1967. The biographical squib inside the front cover mentioned I had been born in New York City in 1942. When the novel had been out six weeks, a photographer and self-taught expert at industrial carpeting (and sometimes super at the Met [Ed McCabe]) in his late thirties or early forties visited our fourth-floor East Sixth Street flat and, among a group of friends, picked up the published volume from the wing of the typing table in the kitchen corner and opened it. A moment later, he was frowning. "1942 . . . ," he said, loudly. "1942 . . . ? No one was born in 1942."

In 1967, that was funny. Everyone in the room laughed.

In 1986, when I was a few years older than the photographer had been, as an anecdote, it only evoked a moderate smile from any collection of new or old acquaintances, and I realized that it could not even be trotted out any more as a historical curiosity. Today, it is all but opaque and mysterious when recounted by someone who is clearly the eldest in the gathering. I do much better explaining directly: "For so many years, I was always the youngest writer present—now, on the far side of seventy, often I'm the oldest."

What had once been a mirror of recounting had turned, with time, into a maze that had become too tangled for anecdotal negotiation. A lesson had gone along with this: At the risk, first, of bemusement and, finally, obscurity, age simplifies one's style. This is a good thing.

It also highlights a certain bravery on the part of the writers who, gathered here, have plunged into that amorphous collection of texts which fall under that—at least to the writer—confused rubric, "fifty years of production." The scholar-writers here have risen to the challenge of reading their selected texts through the lens of half a century's cultural and political change. I am grateful to them for taking it on.

Thus, "The Mirror and the Maze" is also the title I have displaced over to the energetic and astute work of this symposium. Now that I am a bit better at figuring out things for it to mean, I hope I get a chance to use it for a handful more. It will only surprise my new readers, but I don't believe we intend meaning "into" our language. Rather, we train ourselves, educate ourselves, to produce language for certain situations, many of which situations are themselves linguistic or even mental/linguistic ("Good morning; how are you?" "Fine, thank you. And you. . . ?" Now, how shall I greet the next person I see this morning?—a model for all talk from phatics to physics lectures), which we listen to, as we produce it, and are either satisfied with the meaning or meanings we find in it, or are dissatisfied—and try the process, in part or in whole, again.

It can take five seconds. It can take fifty years—which is why the very concept of "fifty years of production" is so treacherous; and which is why I am so willing to forgive anyone who looks into those words and for a moment (if only that) sees anything other than what she or he expects to see.

The only proper response any writer can have to such intelligent attention and the effort this symposium represents must begin with thanks. That thanks goes not only to the four contributors but also to Professor Robert Reid-Pharr for putting together the entire project, as well as for his introduction that so clearly illuminates the four subsequent papers relation to each other; it goes as well to Professor Gordon Hutner for overseeing the whole enterprise and providing such a welcoming home for the work.

Professor Keizer gives an account of the application of Freud's therapeutic techniques to what she sees is necessary to move some of my major characters from illness to health: to a "final freedom . . . the liberty to experience desire without the shadow of coercion."

Personally, while I believe that there are sick and healthy bodies, sick and healthy minds, that there are more or less free people, more or less oppressed ones, I do not believe that particular sort of sickness or health, that particular sort of freedom or oppression, exists. That is because bodily health is a bodily freedom, and freedom without power is an illusion—an illusion almost always in the service of oppression. Oppression without power is, sadly, the same illusion.

I saw Gorgik, my political protagonist, as one formed by the social forces around him that rendered him most able to take advantage of the niche in which he found himself, and who would be believably drawn to do what was most efficacious to alleviate the pains abroad in his society. That is to say, I thought, with all his "perversions" (the opposite of "neuroses," as Freud tells us), he was quite healthy enough. I am convinced the only things human men and women can sexualize are Imaginary (in the Lacanian Sense) signs of power differences—because that is what, at the level of the signified, holds the Prison House of Language together. (Anything else is the Real; and that is power not strength run wild without reason.) Another name for it is discourse. Because, at the (Lacanian) Symbolic level, the arrows on those power vectors may run in different directions and at different strengths from those they appear to manifest in the Imaginary (and thus take some careful explorations of both the mirrors and mazes around us to understand their Symbolic workings), our lives are the interesting game of specific aporias and general surprises that they are, which we are always learning and relearning to negotiate—that is, learning how not to be taken in by their seeming familiarities, how to find our way into and out of them. Another way of saying the same thing so that it cleaves more closely to Professor Keizer's text is that because "shadows" are what they are and function as they do, the utopian turn that draws her sentence and the opening movement of her argument to its end—"desire without a shadow of coercion"—I believe is neither possible nor useful, thank the Big Other, *Deus sive Natura*. The shadows of power (and power, unlike strength, is always a shadow) pulse there, vital and vivid, for either and all genders, much of the time without particularly getting in the way. But they don't vanish—they are constitutive.

I enjoyed following her argument, nevertheless. The last lines of her paragraph that ends on page 6 ("First, I want to make it clear that in using terms such as health and recovery I am not evoking a set of traditional norms . . .") may be an attempt to mitigate a feeling of constriction that, for me and possibly for her, now and then arises from her paper. Eventually she may find other paths through Freud more useful for her literary explorations. Thanks to this attempt, she may now be closer to them—and I think that is a good thing. I want to thank her; and I am happy if my humble inventions were its possible occasion.

Professor Scott interrogates the anonomastic resonances that my marginal divinity "of erasure and absence, of silence and forgetting" might set loose among the tales in the series *Return to Nevèrÿon*, or the characters in *Phallos* (2004).

What does it mean when an atheist writes about divinities, anyway? Is it purely the assumption of a mask, a persona, through which to respond to the hunger for God, which I freely admit to having—though my atheism means I do not believe it can ever be satisfied by anything other than humanly engineered social constructions? I don't think it's an accident when the pursuit of origins leads us to the names that have been associated with the earliest thinkers or writers we possess in one genre or the other; that is to say I don't think it is an accident that both Professor Scott and I find those 124-odd fragments attributed to the "obscure philosopher," Heraclitus, so fascinating. Two of those fragments particularly intrigue me; one I have dwelt on for many years. It forms the epistemological focus of my novel *The Mad Man* (1994), which Professor Scott has taught over a number of years and written about with great insight. The fact that it is first quoted for us in Diogenes Laërtius's history of philosophy, one of the least trustworthy sources possible for ancient accuracy (a popular second-century entertainment for gentlemen farmers of the time, which includes dozens of prepostrousnesses—letters, quoted as authentic, back and forth between men living centuries apart; stories of men leaving the house one day, going to sleep in a cave for fifty or more years, to return, having aged not a day—offered with a perfectly straight face) makes its authenticity flicker

and flutter, even as it draws us back again and again with its clarity and simplicity, that clarity itself a mark of the doubtfulness of the text, which is, after all,
supposed to be from the "obscure philosopher [emphasis mine]," though it is
not particularly obscure at all. One word in the Greek is clearly misspelled by a
letter or two (hotei, "by which"?), by which certainly we can suspect a copyist's
slip—likely Laërtius's. But often a writer so ready to include anything for a
good tale (which is certainly Diogenes L.) is correspondingly careless when it
comes to detail accuracy:

> Wisdom is a single thing—the knowledge of the plan which pilots all things
> through all things.

The second fragment is, indeed, quite obscure enough to fit its presumed author, obscure philosopher Heraclitus, and is quoted by Clement of Alexandria,
whose writings are thought to be as accurate as he could make them at the
time. Its opening words are almost identical to the other:

> Wisdom is only a single thing—what is unwilling and willing to be called by the
> name "Zeus."

The question is: What is their relation? Are they the same textual fragment,
misremembered by the men writing them down?

Is one notably more accurate than the other? If so, which?

They are different enough so that they *could* be two entirely separate sentences
from two entirely different parts of Heraclitus's famous single treatise, excised
from separate arguments that have nothing directly to do with each other.

Or—and this is the possibility that interests me the most, though we have
no more evidence for it than we do for any of the others—are they contiguous
moments from a single rhetorical progression, that might have run something
on this order?

Wisdom is one thing . . . the knowledge of [P . . .]

Wisdom is one thing . . . the knowledge of [Q . . .]

Wisdom is one thing . . . the knowledge of [R . . .]

Wisdom is one thing . . . the knowledge of the plan which pilots all things
through all things.

Wisdom is one thing . . . the knowledge of [S . . .]

Wisdom is only one thing . . . it is what we fail to know and what we know,
[which, taken together,] we call by the name "God" [Zeus].

Have Laërtius and Clement both recalled—or, at any rate, both been struck
by—different moments in one progression?

Ex pede Herculem . . . (From the marble foot of Hercules, we reconstruct the
entire statue—the nickname for a beaux-arts eighteenth-century art students'

exercise.) If that is indeed the structure Heraclitus asked his language to con-form to for a page or so of his *Peri Physeos*, it opens us to interesting speculations about the complex subject that so tended.

It also suggests that Heraclitus is, in some ways, congruent with Spinoza—a suggestion, naturally, I like.

Still, of course, all evidence here is even less solid than Wilde's for the iden-tity of Shakespeare's presumably cherished young actor, "Mr. W. H." Yet, if you do read Wilde's astonishing critical divagation carefully, while you may come away with nothing solid about "Mr. Willie Hughes," you will know a great deal more than you did when you began about the text of the Sonnets. That is useful.

Professor Tucker has taken two texts—two different versions, a longer and a shorter version of a tale, separated by more than twenty years—that suggest, in many ways, mirrors, one of the other. Through a careful pursuit of the nomi-nalism that remains as the two are allowed to filter one another out, they reveal a more mazelike relation than we might have suspected upon first entering with him into his researches. If we bracket his unweaving of my nominalism, its purpose would seem to be the delight in description for its own sake, a delight that extends to one of my earliest pieces, first drafted forty-nine years ago, and for which—if only because of that—I am touched.

Professor Nyong'o takes a 1979 essay that I am still very fond of, "Heavenly Breakfast," and explores the largely apophantic topic of the endeavor—music—through his own meditations on musicians like Joni Mitchell and, finally, his own lyric divagations on the material. It's a lovely piece. It recalls the unstated musical context around that essay—Country Joe and the Fish, Cream, Big Brother and the Holding Company's *Cheap Thrills* and the early Bee Gees album *The New York Mining Disaster 1941*, and self-titled albums by Randy Newman and The Band, music we were listening to back then. (Alas, we had little time for Mitchell herself, possibly to our loss.) I and, I hope, my readers are happy for the reminder.

For all five of these interpretive endeavors, I am grateful. I hope too that in all cases they are early steps to propel our five Scholar-Writers on to works that will be more useful to them on all fronts than considerations of my poor fictive inventions. I said we must begin with thanks—and we must end with it as well.

Thanks to you all.

—2012
New York

13

Brudner Prize Lecture, I

A View from the Valley's Edge, Part 1

This is the transcript of a letter written to Professor Steven Schivero that was the basis for the first of two Brudner Prize lectures, which was presented at Yale University on October 17, 2012.

184 West 82nd St.
New York, NY 10024

Dear Steve,

Since my St. Mark's Place reading,[1] I've been rising at four in the morning beside a snoring Dennis. I feel around for my iPhone on top of the pile of books on the glass-topped night table and press the indentation at the screen's bottom. In the dark the rectangular lights tell me that's the time. Leaning away, I kiss his bare shoulder—more frequently, squeeze his hand—push aside the covers, then lurch from the bedroom and down the hall—into the kitchen, where the light is on all night.

When you come in, you see two leaflets for local leather-repair shops taped to the kitchen door, a small yellow one for Aris's Boot, Shoe, and Bag Repair and an eight-and-a-half-by-eleven flyer for Angel's Jackets, Boots, and Bags, which had just moved to Columbus Avenue when I first put up the signs. (Neither has actually been at those locations now for more a dozen years, which tells you how long ago I taped them up.) As I bumble, naked, heavy, barefoot (two hundred eighty-plus pounds: "It's the diabetes," the doctor tells me, "probably it will be hard or impossible for you to lose it") around the kitchen, over a blackened floor closer to what you'd expect in a cellar than in a fifth-story New

York apartment, I get cold water from the Brita pitcher in the refrigerator to fill the "Mr. Coffee" on the book-and-paper-cluttered table, and glance out the uncurtained window, five stories down, to the dark sidewalks and Amsterdam Avenue, shiny with rain I remember whispering on the sill outside the bedroom window—but that stopped an hour back.

The lights change, and reflections along the card shop window, the kids' store, and the Thai restaurant shift colors and shadows. Behind its bank of flowers (mostly white, red, yellow, and peach roses), the corner bodega across from us still has an hour-and-a-half before its 5:30 a.m. opening. Under the string of unfrosted bulbs along the awning edge, one squat Mexican kid who runs the night shift for the 24/7 flower business sits up on the platform near the corner street light, head back against brick, asleep (I can see, even from up here). The other stands, hands in his jumpsuit pockets—the May night is cold—waiting for blue to seep over the buildings above.

I got the cylindrical Maxwell House can from the freezer door (it lay on its side on the shelf) and sat with it at the kitchen table, opened up the plastic cap—I keep both measuring spoons in the can, and have for years—and measured one, two, three coffees into the fluted filter, and slipped the black plastic hopper into the rather grubby white plastic drip-coffeemaker.

When I pressed the button on the base, the green light came on; as I stood up to leave the room, it began to gurgle. Back in the book-lined hall I walked up the row of bathmats we used for hall runners—green, maroon, yellow, orange, and blue, and all rather dusty. (It's a pretty good way to avoid splinters in your bare feet from these ancient wooden floors.) In the bedroom, Dennis was grunting his way through a bad dream—his first in almost a year. I swung in, came through the dark and got one knee up on the bed, found his naked shoulder in the bunched-up quilt, and shook him. "Come on . . ."

"Unnn . . . unng . . . no . . . stop . . . get away . . . oh!" As he came closer to the surface, his words grew clearer. I bent to hug him. Like a hand breaking the waters, his fingers gripped mine and held.

"Wake up. You're okay. Wake up. It's just a dream. You're all right. You're safe."

"Oh . . ." He raised his head sharply, then let it go back down, slowly, onto the pillow. "Yeah . . . I was having a bad dream."

"I know you were." I chuckled. Two years ago, he'd had them regularly—all involving his mother beating him, yelling at him, or leaving him, sometimes all three.

"You're all right now . . . ?"

"Yeah," he mumbled, already half asleep again.

Again, I hugged him.

Two naked old men in the dark, or rather one old man, seventy, and another aging, at fifty-eight.

Standing, I went on into my office, where I called up the first of the post midnight's e-mails on the computer screen—a thank-you note that I had to answer in like form from the "Delany at 70" conference that Christina Hanhardt, V. J. Spanos, and Marilee Lindemann had arranged out at the University of Maryland, a late graduate student evaluation still hanging fire, then three in a row that, not exactly spam, I could still delete. When I finished, I went back in the kitchen, poured myself a mug of coffee, and got some half-and-half from the refrigerator into it. As they swirled into each other, I carried my mug (it says "Dennis") back down the hall beside the dark wall of books—again to the office.

I start with something from the observed world because it's the best way I know to keep this fundamentally abstract meditation from slipping into the tone of one of D. H. Lawrence's rants from his last years; though that may be one danger of the confluence of age and ideas. (Not that Lawrence had the excuse of age—since he died at forty-four in 1930, a rabid fascist, wanting to install a pair of dictators, one man, one woman, for the working class.) Perhaps it's one of the basic beliefs that makes me a novelist, but I've felt for many, many years that information that gets too far from the landscape that produced it loses much of its force.

As I hope is clear from this letter, here on the far side of seventy where, rather surprisingly to me, I have been dwelling for a handful of weeks now, I have been thinking a lot about Writing; though I confess I have not been writing much. There is so much I want to write, which I probably will never get a chance to even begin, much less finish, that I can get quite depressed—since the book came out, I have been prescribed Zoloft; the first time in my life, since I was on Stelazine for a month, when I had a two-week-long breakdown at twenty-two from overwork, I've been on any sort of psychotropic medication.

Civility demands that I thank you for your kind and moving letter about my novel, which I received the night before last. It's thanks easily proffered. You are thoughtful and gracious and it's a pleasure to thank you.

I know you understand that, in what follows, in no way do I mean you personally. But deeply I suspect that heterosexuals—or more accurately, many of the actions that take place unthinkingly (no matter the sexual orientation of who performs them) within the discourse we can call heteronormativity—are going to destroy the planet as a human habitat; and they are going to accomplish that destruction specifically through the privileged relationship so many heterosexuals as a group believe they have with procreation and patriarchy.

If we do not all begin to think deeply and supportively about that "village it takes to raise a child" and the many people and the many kinds of people who inhabit it, and must inhabit it, if it is to be in any way efficient, our "village" does not have much chance of survival, as a civilized space or as any other kind—not as long as people younger than both of us are still following the politico-salvationist dictum, "Go forth and multiply," especially when some of our largest institutions, in the name of religious freedom, follow a tradition of forbidding both abortions and contraceptives. (I am thinking of the Catholic hospital in Buffalo, New York, where, as recently as two years ago, my daughter, now Dr. Iva Hacker-Delany, M.D., worked in the emergency room but was forbidden to mention birth control to any of the women, mostly poor, overwhelmingly black and Latina, who availed themselves of the hospital's services, emergency or otherwise, regardless of their own religion, even when the women inquired about it.) That is the hidden (or not so hidden) agenda that makes wars and supplies our country with most of its voluntary cannon fodder, while at the same time producing on the home front a significant population who is both the relatively unskilled workforce—itself an unsustainable idea in the modern world—as well as much of the criminal class, and at the same time a group which is all but uninterested in analyzing the fragmentary narratives the media regularly presents them with, nor do they have the leisure or lack the distracting anxieties that allow them to reflect efficiently on their own socio-political situation.

I am sure you are aware of one of the most troubling recent statistical social sketches: When the number of abortions goes up, fifteen to twenty years later in the same locality the crime rate plummets—as the number of unwanted children has dropped. The most recent notion that conservatives want to ignore: an inverse Durkheimian relationship obtains directly between early love and later social malfeasance.

When I was an adolescent, I talked with a number of straight working-class young men, who were just starting out on their sexual lives, whose chief desire was to get as many girls pregnant as possible—guys who would carry condoms with holes carefully put in them, so they could fool women into sex that would lead to pregnancy—and who were firmly convinced that they could pursue this life goal obsessively for a decade or more without consequence. (This is the unstated reason that, of course, control of contraception must be in the hands of women.) And every three months, amidst his endless televised paternity tests, Maurey Povich does a morning show in which a dozen twelve and thirteen-year-old girls yell and scream at their mothers for an hour that their single goal is to get pregnant as soon as possible—they do not care who the father is—and have a baby: that is the only way they feel they can achieve a significant sign of adulthood, which will force people to leave them alone and cease telling them what to do or at least pay them the respect due a full human being.

Really, Steve, I feel that is fundamentally a large part of the world we are currently playing the game of social culture in. Its international ramifications are the "population explosion" itself. Currently there is not a small country going, from Romania to Uganda, whose government does not seriously worry when its birth rate goes down—and that is insane.

Somehow the obvious fact that the nation that can dissociate sex from procreation the most efficiently is the one that will most likely endure; it is not evolution that terrifies our spiritual rulers so much as it is the evolutionary rule that nothing evolves to fulfill a single purpose—and that includes sexuality.

Now, to believe that a novel can create a significant intervention in such a system is, of course, equally insane. But I do believe a novel can help stabilize a counter discourse that must eventually be set in place if we are ever to make the infrastructural changes that can bring a sane world into being.

I've used it before—and I've used it again in this book: my most needed SF speculation is a birth control method that is given once to both men and women and is temporarily counteracted by a pill (or a shot) that both must take, together, when they agree to have a child. It changes conception from a "systems on" situation where accident militates for pregnancy to a "systems off" situation where accident militates against pregnancy. That alone is going to bring down the population. If they do not take it at the same time, pregnancy cannot ensue—and I believe major efforts must be directed toward developing it.

It's the center of *Trouble on Triton.*

It's the center of the science fictional extrapolation of *Through the Valley of the Nest of Spiders.*

Through the Valley of the Nest of Spiders is a very different kind of novel from the "causal" novel that even the smartest readers in the Delany Listserve were expecting. It's as different from, say, Lionel Shriver's *So Much for That* (to take a popular American "problem" novel, a respected bestseller dealing with the nightmare of American health care, a finalist for the National Book Award in 2010, and a book that still sells well and boasts fifty-nine "Customer Reviews" at Amazon, all but six of which are three, four, or—the vast majority—five stars) as Sade's *Justine* is different from Richardson's *Pamela*, as *Juliette* is from *Clarissa.* That is to say, *Through the Valley of the Nest of Spiders* is not a "causal" novel. Little the characters do—or, to make a more direct contrast with, say, Shriver—little the characters know or don't know cause to happen the various events that are presented for our consideration. Rather it is an associative or accretive novel—even agglutinative. In your own clear and accurate words, it is a novel "in which nothing happens"—at least on the causal level that the genre-fictive roots that happily I acknowledge as my own would lead many—such as the readers in the Delany listserve—to expect.

Through the Valley is a book about sex—and how we learn to negotiate sex that is always, already, in excess of that which will lead to procreation. In the book, there is not one description of any act that, if transferred between men and women, could effect procreation by itself—even up until the very last encounter directly described between Shit and the young man who has been called in to father Lacy and Orchid's (yes, the name is intentional) child. This is not an accident. The book presumes that sex itself is an interesting topic at the level you characterize as "the motion of light in water" and in the way that it has to be integrated into one's life, not as something abstract but in the here and now of beds and rooms and the sounds of footsteps over boards or carpets and sunlight or rain and weather in general. It does not presume that the only thing interesting about sex is whether or not it turns one or another individual on—which is what controls the heteronormative approach and finally controls the boredom of most of the listserve readers: they can't imagine any other literary use for it save that it turns them or a character on (or off). The idea that by reading about it (in either Delany or Sade) they may be able, later, to save themselves or their friends or their children or the children of their friends considerable confusion or discomfort does not even enter their heads. That is to say, discursively it does not represent a collection of rhetorical figures that can be associated with "the good," however much lip-service we give to the idea that "sex is a good thing." Rather, it is judged through the discursive filter of "too much sexual rhetoric is boring, and boredom in art is an aesthetic failing," even though, as has been repeatedly proven, the average man thinks (with his own personal rhetoric) about sex throughout his daily life starting at the beginning of adolescence once every twelve seconds and, after age sixty, once every thirty-five seconds—and women only seconds less frequently in both cases. But as art is supposed to turn our inner lives into a conversation with the outer world, we are not eager, at this point in history, for it to happen (usually that's what boredom defends against), though I suspect we are going to have to become so if we are to survive. The night before last I wrote you that *Through the Valley of the Nest of Spiders* is a book about "freedoms." It is also a highly ironic novel—and perhaps the most important irony is the point which it makes through moral humility alone: Eric decides that he is not an important person, even though he has enjoyed his life. But in a good society (and you have seen and generously outlined to me in your letter the way that the Society that has produced/created/constituted Eric is a "good society") will have to believe that they are (1) happy and (2) not special, if it is, in actuality, "good."

It is the quality of the lives of its ordinary-to-marginal citizens that finally determines a society's value.

And the fact that the Kyle Foundation is willing to dissolve itself is what, for me, marks it, at least in the situation suggested by the novel as far as I can read it myself, as—at least locally—good.

Looking back over my writing life, I realize I am—or, better, have become—a rather conservative writer. I can recall sitting in various Lower East Side apartments, now on 5th Street, now on 6th, between my first and second, my third and fourth novels, and deciding that certain ideas controlled the novel as a form, or rather, controlled whether a novel registered with readers (at least readers such as myself) as solid and rich or thin, flimsy, and inept. I had just emerged from Leslie Fiedler's *Love and Death in the American Novel*. One of Leslie's sons, Jay Kurt Fiedler, was two years ahead of me at the same high school, and though I didn't know him at the time, that, along with the republication of a chapter on Huckleberry Finn from *Love and Death* in the *New York Times Book Review*, and the release of the whole as a Dell paperback, led me to read his father's entire book.

Up until that time, I had assumed what made a novel great was a matter of its aesthetic form, and that form extended from the texture of the writing to the organization of the book's incidents—an idea I'd picked up from the paperback "Introduction" to Melville's *Moby-Dick*, which I had read in a Signet paperback when I was seventeen. But Fiedler had argued—convincingly, as far as I was concerned—that for the novel to register as a rich readerly experience, the form of the novel had to take in a range of social representations: *Ulysses* was not a great novel only because it portrayed so meticulously and with so much rhetorical innovation eighteen waking hours, but because those eighteen hours encompassed both a funeral and a birth, both eating and defecation, both carnal desire frustrated and carnal desire fulfilled, both labor and recreation, all of which had to be artfully (i.e., aesthetically) placed in relationship to one another—indeed, *Ulysses*, which I'd also just read (along with Stuart Gilbert's study, then one of the first Vintage paperbacks), was my particular (seventeen-year-old) example, not Fiedler's, though the idea was his. It had to be about something of human significance—an idea later confirmed for me by—surprisingly—Flaubert. (He admits it almost shame-facedly to Louise Colet and George Sand in letters.) That range of human social portraiture, balanced within its aesthetic frame, is what gave a novel its sense of human relevance, import, and what I can only call density and weight.

I have always been a writer fueled and excited by criticism—whether Leslie Fiedler's or Northrop Frye's, Erich Auerbach's or Theodore Adorno's, Sontag's or Derrida's, Barzun's or Barthes . . . not to mention yours!

Three ideas that I had already picked up included (1) that the novel will feel the most grounded and generally register of greatest interest—an idea gleaned, probably, from among the meditations of Edmund Wilson, though I can't be sure—if the central conflict can be presented as occurring between characters from different social classes. This is what gave life to Stevenson's *Kidnapped* and Kipling's *Captains Courageous* as well as London's *Martin Eden*, Austen's *Emma*, and Thackeray's *Vanity Fair*. This seemed somehow to be related to what I took to be Fiedler's idea—though now I know it is much older than that—of social richness as an index to the aesthetic greatness of the individual novel. But, kicking and screaming all the way, I had finally accepted (2) that the structural material of the novel was fundamentally social rather than poetic. Indeed, in the novel the "poetic" was like the brightness control on the TV. Yes, the ideal Reader of the Novel was likely to be most engaged when the poetic was turned high—rather than left dim, gray, and unclear. But, by extension, the poetic must never become an overload, an external overlaid complexity. Rather it must be an imminent clarity, arising from simplicity and observation. (Sturgeon's lesson.) By now I was also convinced that (3) character is given its defining or highlighting features by money—or, at any rate, by the necessities money links us to: food, clothing, shelter, and the labor people must expend in order to acquire any and all of these. Thus, to explore character is not fundamentally a psychological enterprise, but rather a matter of exploring a "character's" individual relationship to all of these in some detail. (Plot is basically a structure to move the character from one situation to another in which aspects of various of these ideas must be dramatized.)

The idea that anything of true novelistic interest can be shown without recourse to all of these is simply not to understand the novel as a form—and probably to write it badly.

This is where I was at twenty, when I started to think seriously about how I wanted to write novels. Because I had sold that first one at nineteen and had to sell the next few, I had to think seriously about them, what made them good—that's the thought that went into the science fiction novels that still remain in print.

Today, when I teach Balzac, Flaubert, Cather, Conrad, Woolf, or even Lawrence, this is what I teach. This is what I see all of them knowing deeply in their bones and displaying across their pages and what supports their greatness—all six of them. I suspect it is what makes me a very conservative novelist.

If you want to write, your words must produce an effect. Moreover, among your most intelligent readers, that effect must be strong enough to spill over into articulation. If you can't do that, you might as well pack it up and do something else.

Producing an effect is different from satisfying an appetite. Appetites are created by genres, and there are many, many more genres than most of us can name. Any time we imagine a kind of fiction—a kind that we might like to read—we are locating a genre. And those same intelligent readers, no matter how effected they are by generic appetites, know the difference between appetite and effect.

I still feel that, no matter how experimental a given novel is—and, yes, I think of *Through the Valley of the Nest of Spiders* as an experimental novel (today, any novel in which "nothing happens" is more or less experimental)—that is what holds it to the world that is the case. It explains what I have been doing since I was twenty-one, and what I have been trying to teach—and often failing at miserably, because my students are convinced there is some deep mysterious thing called "psychology" that is the true field of fiction, though no one is ever able to seize it directly without writing about what makes people suffer—food, clothing, commodities of all kinds, and the relationships of men and women to having them or not having them, being able to acquire them easily or only with difficulty; or having to go without them.

I do feel—which is why I always teach him, as I teach Woolf—that Flaubert is important. He is the writer to formalize the hypotactic lessons of the "motion of light in water," as you call it. That, really, the closest we can get to thinking, is the whole point of Woolf's *The Waves*—the closest we can get to actual "psychology." Different characters have different relations to the flickering web of perception—and that is absolutely fair game for the novel as well.

But the fundamentals (and *Through the Valley of the Nest of Spiders* is a book about what I feel is fundamental in life, in art) are imperative, despite how dull people want to declare the source of such happiness to be, in order to excuse never pursuing it.

But now we'll see if anyone feels it's worth learning how to read it. If not, it will dissolve and wash away in the cascade of forgotten language. Projects that have taken far longer than the seven years I put into this book have been even more quickly forgotten then this one may turn out to be, despite your generous observations on it.

Thank you so much for your attention, your intelligence, and for remembering it as you have, Steve.

It's minutes before six in the evening, two days after I started this letter. Outside on Amsterdam Avenue, aluminum poles clink into other aluminum poles, as, downstairs, they start to dismantle the sidewalk booths: a street fair has been going on all day—guys standing on podia, sloshing water around their sneakers as they demonstrate their "Wonder Mops" and middle-aged women in pony tales and T-shirts, leaning over tables piled with cucumbers, celery, and tomatoes, to demonstrate the speed and agility of Ginsu knives, among stands of linens and baskets and underwear and silver rings and Pashmina scarves and wallets and checkbook covers and electronics parts. I haven't had quite what it takes to go down the five flights and walk around on my cane among the people with their plastic cups of beer and the flannel cake venders with tins of powdered sugar, kids selling roasted corn, smaller kernels near the Cobb's point capped with black and the whole shiny with fake butter, the guys at their stands making sausage sandwiches on their grills bronzed by the blue flames below, onions piled at one side, peppers at the other, white jackets pushed up tattooed forearms, the slow movement of people wandering by in Bermudas and tank tops. Dennis went down, however, and has just come back up, to listen to some Patsy Cline in the living room. I've got to start dinner—chicken, which I put out to thaw a couple of hours back, with some zucchini and onions.

In the words of Rachel Pollack,
Love, luxury, justice, and joy—
Chip Delany

—October 2012
New York

NOTE

1. A video of Samuel R. Delany reading from *Through the Valley of the Nest of Spiders* at St. Mark's Bookshop in New York City on April 23, 2012, with an introduction by Brian Evenson, can be viewed at: https://www.youtube.com/watch?v=H3Pdxp7QD78/.

14

Brudner Prize Lecture, II

A View from the Valley's Edge, Part 2

Delivered in New York City on October 18, 2012, at 7:00 p.m., at Club Quarters Midtown, 40 West Forty-Fifth Street, after a 6:00 p.m. reception, and after introductions by Professor George Chauncey and Professor GerShun Avilez, to a gathering largely of gay Yale alumni and friends.

A drizzly September night in Philadelphia, and I have woken up at three. No classes tomorrow. Dennis is up in New York. Out the second floor living room window the leaves under the streetlight glisten and drip. I wander from kitchen to bathroom to bedroom, back to the living room, sit down at the worktable and wonder what I am going to speak about in October. One idea is to start with a list of questions various interviewers have asked me over the last half dozen years. It might be interesting to confront a few of them that don't usually fall together. Some I'm truly eager to engage. They call up memories and associations that still have their own energy and life for me. Moreover, they suggest an intelligence that excites me before the prospect of immersing myself in the questions proper. I want to move right into them.

A few, however, evoke my uneasiness, my discomfort, even my embarrassment. You may be surprised by which these are. They're not questions about sex, or interrelational behavior, or even ones that announce themselves as interrogations of choices in areas usually thought to be personal or private.

Unilaterally the ones that trouble me are questions about art, questions it seems to me the interviewer should be answering rather than asking—questions that should be focused not on my work because I am the subject of the interview, but rather on works of his or her own choosing from that bookshelf of the mind that has inflected the interviewer's own life with meaning.

Questions such as, "What do you think your legacy will be? What do you feel you have accomplished? What place does this or that work have in the greater scheme of things?"

To begin, I am an artist, a fiction writer, not a scientist, not a scholar. This means I have reflected a few elements from my life—reflections always incomplete, always distorted—as well as a few facets—also distorted and incomplete—from the world and lives around me, from which I have tried to construct one intriguing pattern or another.

A question such as "What is your legacy?" asks me to tell you what I have given you. And the fact is, I have no way of knowing. Only someone else can answer that; only someone else *should* answer it. If someone finds a pattern that has something to do—at whatever level of suggestion, of correspondence—with the true and the functional, only that person can say—not me. I can hope that the patterns are useful, as I can hope that they are beautiful. But any pronouncement I make about their value is simply arrogant wish-fulfillment—a distortion and a waste of time.

I can't answer it—nor would I feel comfortable trying to. So that is not the kind of question I am going to take up here.

Across the table from me, an interviewer[1] from 2010 materializes: "Your reaction," he says, "to those sorts of questions is interesting because it brings to the surface some differences, perhaps, between interviewer and interviewee. As I do my own work, sex education, research, writing, community mobilization, organization/institution-building, I often think about my legacy. I'm thinking about what will I contribute to the long history and tradition of liberatory struggle and social justice work and political art. I want to help in moving those traditions forward. I want to add my little brick to the structure. So I could answer the question about my legacy from that perspective—sort of a vision and mission statement for myself.

"But also, in how I am approaching you in these conversations. I see you as a model for my professional life and career, a mentor in the traditions I have embraced. I am asking you to be vulnerable with me and I am committing to being vulnerable with you in this process, this intimacy."

I answer: I suspect you are thinking of the changes you would like to see in the world. I think about them too. But as an artist, I know the best I can do is outline a discourse that might *stabilize* the infrastructural changes necessary to bring about the changes we both desire.

But that is all.

What makes me uncomfortable is not the intimacy or the vulnerability, but the question's assumption that the future is predictable. Surely you've heard the old saw, "Life is what happens when you're making other plans." Well, the future in general is what happens while you're planning out your legacy. Major problems today may be swept away in a moment of historical or technological change. Things that it never occurred to you might be problems very easily could bloom and recomplicate into galaxies of problematics that it never occurred to you could have existed.

Take the great and extraordinary work of Magnus Hirschfeld, educator and sex researcher from the end of the nineteenth century through the Great War. He really believed homosexuals were a third sex, half way between male and female—a totally lunatic and obfuscating idea, we now hold. His idea only stands in the way of the any real understanding or exploration of any of the aspects of human behavior that make it seem that such a notion might somehow be relevant.

Certainly he was a "great spirit," and his heart was in the right place. He also put out tremendous energies assembling a sexual museum, which the Nazis destroyed at the start of World War II. *That* might have been a useful legacy, had it survived.

But it didn't.

I am not a sex educator. I am not a scientist. I am only provisionally an academic. To repeat: I think of myself as a writer—specifically, a fiction writer. That is to say, I am an artist, not a scholar. I could not begin to claim to educate anyone about anything having to do with sex, gay or straight. Quite secondarily, I'm an English teacher. All I can do is describe some of the things I have seen occur in the world around me and talk about some of the things I have done and some of the thoughts that I have had about them. For me, the notion of the sort of legacy you describe is—if I may be blunt—absurd. I have seen enough things change already in seventy years to know that.

Above and beyond phatic civility, I must live my life according to Thomas Mann's insight: About the worth of my own work, I cannot know and you cannot tell me.

That means also: I cannot tell *you*.

A few abstract notions, such as more sophisticated ideas of discourse in general (readings, reactions, understandings, responses . . .), might, if we are lucky, make it easier to negotiate the possibilities and contradictions inherent along the rhizomatic rollercoaster tracks of change. And that, yes, has been the philosophical underpinning of my project for forty years. But a positive legacy?

As an intellectual notion, the truth is, I find that—as asked of the artist—at its best a silly notion and at it worst an evil one.

Possibly what you're talking about is socialization. I'm involved in that when I teach a class in creative writing, as I do twice a year at Temple University, in Philadelphia, and every summer at Naropa, in Boulder, Colorado. I was involved in it while bringing up my wonderful and exciting daughter who graduated from medical school last year and recently got married to a wonderfully warm and loving husband. If you ask me, what I want my students or my child to be, I can say: "I want them to be good people, effective citizens, who are emotionally equipped to strive for their own and others' happiness. I am involved in that, when I teach them how to behave in a workshop. I was involved in this when I dissuaded my three-year-old from running into the kitchen and turning on all the gas jets from curiosity and excitement, then sprinting into another room out of boredom.

There it was a matter of life and death, mine and hers—and we are both still around today and even, from time to time, go to the movies together.

But while both of those might contribute to the content of narrative art, neither, in itself, represents the form of narrative art, which is only restricted to patterns that evoke the aesthetic emotions that fall on the spectrum running from intrigue to beauty.

In the dark Philadelphia living room, in the midst of the city's "gayborhood," I realized now *that* interviewer had been displaced by another:

"Clearly," she begins, "there's a link between your award-winning short story 'Aye, and Gomorrah' and some of the memoir writing you've done about that period of your life in the early 1960s, when you were touring Greece and Turkey. Can you talk about some of the work you've done? Not just because of the locations, but because of the free-flowing sexuality of the time and some of the experiences you had—your story '*Citre et Trans*' is another good example of what I mean."

Well, to reiterate, I'm an artist, not a scientist. That is to say, I deal in suggestions, generalizations about facts. But suggestions are very important if we are to go on to establish facts in the world, though it is equally important not to confuse one for the other, suggestion for proof.

On October 18, 1965, with a straight friend of mine, Ron Helstrom, whom I'd run into the previous spring when we were working on shrimp boats out of Aransas Pass, Texas, down near Corpus Christie and Brownsville, I took off from New York City on an Icelandic Airlines prop-jet to Luxemburg, for a six-month stay in Europe that lasted to mid-April of '66. Ron and I were simply friends, although many gay men that I met on the trip, in Paris, in Venice, and in Athens, and with whom I did have sexual relations, were very generous to us. Ron and Bill Baluziac—another straight young man who joined up with us on the plane over, and traveled with us for a few months—had a much better time than they would have, had the third member of their traveling trio been straight.

On the second day of our two-week stay in Paris, when the three of us were living at the small Hotel St. Louis, on the Ile St. Louis, next to the Hotel Olinda (at the time, its reputation was that of the cheapest hotel in Paris; and the next cheapest, by a few cents a night, was ours, right next door), I went out cruising that evening, leaving my two straight friends back at the hotel. A little after midnight, in the Tuileries Garden—the park grounds just in front of the Louvre—I ran into a very tall, very black, very handsome and full-featured African in a dark suit, white shirt, and tie.

In the shadows, he was sitting on one of the side benches, one leg crossed over the other, masturbating.

I sat down with him, as if I'd met him on Central Park West in the same way, where I had been a few nights before—in the same way and with the same intent. We fooled around with each other. With my very poor French, I discovered he was a medical student, from Senegal, studying in Paris, and whose mother was a tribal queen.

His name was Bernard Lusuna—about twenty-seven years old, that is to say, four years older than I was.

Yes, Bernard was an African prince!

At his suggestion, we walked back to his small, ground-floor Latin Quarter room—where, in other apartments in his building, various other of his gay, African friends also lived. Prince or no, Bernard's room was about eight feet by eight feet, with a table on one wall and a double-decker bunk-bed against another. Bernard slept on the lower level of the bunk and used the upper for storage. In her tribal regalia, a photograph of his impressive mother, the Queen, hung on the wall, as well as others of his family—his father and uncles and multiple mothers and aunts and many half-brothers and -sisters.

Bernard and I spent a pleasant night together. The next morning, one of his friends in the building—a shy, stocky little fellow with bushy, slightly brownish hair, also from Senegal—came by and we all had coffee and pastry at Bernard's. I explained that I was traveling with two other North Americans—and that they were straight. Then Bernard invited us all over that night for dinner. His friend had a working stove in his room, Bernard explained to me, and they often prepared dinners together.

His friend seemed shyly eager and enthusiastic.

Back at our hotel, on the Ile next morning, I conveyed the invitation to Bill and Ron. They were surprised, but accepted. I didn't mention how I'd met Bernard—but only explained that we had started talking, and that I had ended up staying over at his apartment.

We were expected at seven o'clock.

I suggested we bring a couple of bottles of wine—which we did. That's what I would have done in New York and it seemed a reasonable thing to do in Paris. We spent about four dollars each on two bottles of wine—today that would be about the equivalent of forty or so a piece.

I'm very glad we did.

Dinner began with pâté-stuffed mushrooms and olives and went on to a spectacular lamb roast, with lots of wonderful vegetable dishes and a glorious salad. The Africans recognized the wine as extremely good, and we got points for it! We were six for dinner: Bill, Ron, and myself, and Bernard and two of his African friends from the building. (The one I hadn't met yet was tall, soft-spoken, smiling, and—I finally realized—very smart and level-headed . . . enough for me to recall it, forty-five years on.) We all sat in Bernard's room, some on the bed, some in chairs around the wall, balancing a five-foot-by-five-foot square of plywood on our legs, while Bernard flung up a white table cloth that momentarily filled the room, a spotless sail, that billowed down to cover the board so that, laughing, we all pulled and slid and pushed and adjusted it under the edge and over our knees. Bernard went on to lay cloth napkins and gold-edged china on silver chargers (at that time, they were the first chargers any of us North Americans had seen!) and cut crystal glassware for wine and water, and a wicker basket of French baguettes—and a silver ewer of peach and pink roses. Then Bernard and his stocky friend from the morning—I remember he wore a French sailor-style shirt with a traditional boat-neck, three quarter sleeves, only with horizontal olive and mustard stripes (rather than red and white or blue and white)—carried the food in from the apartment next door.

Somehow not a glass of wine was spilled, and when we were in the midst of things, I couldn't help thinking with all that silver and bright china, and flowers on the table, we could have been at the Four Seasons!

It was an extremely fine, classic French meal, ending up with fruit and good cheeses, and I remember thinking—*only* gay men could have brought this off! These men truly enjoyed food and cooking. Today the whole evening stays with me as a prime example of serious international camp—a combination of elegance and student poverty overcome.

As dinner went on, with conversation in three languages (French, Senegalese, and English), Bernard's short friend (all three were gay) became quite taken with Bill—to which Bill was oblivious. Though Canadian, Bill spoke no French, and Ron and I had to translate for him; therefore most of the evening's sexual overtones escaped him. Bernard's friend contrived to sit next to Bill and, with a big smile, kept putting his arm around Bill's shoulder, who would—with a bemused smile back—shrug it off.

When we left and were walking in the street back to the Ile St. Louis and our hotel, the first thing Ron said to me, was: "They were gay, weren't they?"

And I said, "Yes."

Ron said, "Yeah, about halfway through, it dawned on me that something wasn't . . . well, quite what I thought."

And Bill said, "Gay . . .? What do you mean? My God, that was a good dinner. That was so nice of them, too, just having us over like that, and not even knowing us . . . !"

But this was four years before Stonewall . . . and another world.

The next day, I went back and Prince Bernard and I spent another pleasant afternoon in bed. But, though he shows up—by name—as a tertiary character in *Nova* (at the Von Rays' dinner party at Sao Orrini), you'll note none of these are incidents on which, a year later, I chose to model either of my stories about matters gay from those years, "Aye, and Gomorrah" or "Time Considered as a Helix of Semi-Precious Stones," however coded—though I'm sure it would have yielded a more interesting, certainly a more characteristic, and probably a richer story than the more traditional ones (in literary/thematic terms) I actually wrote.

But the fact is, *none* of the writing I published, about that time—or during that time—gives a direct portrait of my sexual life back then. To repeat, this was three, four years before Stonewall. Back then you didn't write about things like that, except in code. You left clues that people could—sometimes—read, between the lines. But it was actually dangerous to write about them. You could get in real trouble. You could get your friends in trouble. So you didn't do it— not in journals, not in letters, not in fiction. A few brave souls, like Ned Rorem or Paul Goodman, were exceptions—and some years later on, I tried to fill in a few incidents myself. But basically, that wasn't me.

I tell you this, because it's important to remember, when considering fiction—like "Aye, and Gomorrah"—just how wide a gap can fall between life and literature—and how social pressures control that gap, so that, in looking at, say, the two award-winning stories of mine that deal with matters gay from the second half of the '60s, you have to realize they are finally fairy tales in the way my anecdote about the African medical student cruising the park and his friends is not—even though the Science Fiction Writers of America, who handed out the awards, doubtless felt that they were congratulating me for bringing a new level of "mature realism" to the genre, simply because I was dealing directly with something they thought of as sordid and probably wouldn't have recognized it at all if I had presented it in any other way.

Now, something like *"Citre et Trans,"* written twenty-four years later and well on the other side of Stonewall, at least tries for a sketch of what was going on during some of my time in 1966 in Athens—perhaps five months after the incident in Paris. But you have to remember as well, even that piece was *written* two dozen years after the fact, in September of 1990, which, as far as gay politics is concerned, was a different era.

Not all of my gay encounters led to dinner parties with Senegalese tribal princes. But many of them—now with a Dutch journalist a couple of days later in Paris, now with a young Greek student who wanted to learn English in Athens, now with a young Oxford student on summer vacation in Greece—led to social interchanges that I profited from or, in some cases, not only helped me out but repeatedly helped out both my North American companions. The vast majority of my sexual encounters—often two or three in a day—were pleasant and friendly; so that, when, eventually, back at that little white stone house above the Plaka in Athens, the two Greek sailors my older British roommate brought home one night raped me (described in *"Citre et Trans"*), all that other was the context which gave that unpleasant incident the meaning for me it had. But the context was not a bland, unmarked progression of heterosexual encounters with their usual betrayals and break-ups and cheatings. It was a context in which the vast majority of the thousands of sexual partners I already had picked for myself had ranged from friendly and helpful to, at least, sexually satisfactory to me—at their worst!

Yes, that unpleasant experience was a warning that I had to be more careful with whom I associated. Ever since, I have been. By the same token, however, the good will and general pleasantness of the many, many others on both sides of it, before and after, are why the scars that remain from it are nowhere near as deep or debilitating as they might have been.

Now we jump to the near side of the start of the AIDS epidemic. Only a few years after that various African leaders were famously declaring homosexuality did not occur in *their* country.

Needless to say, it was impossible for me not think: How odd, then, if there are *no* black African homosexuals, that I ran into a rooming house full of gay African men on my second night in Paris, with some of whom I and my friends had a lovely dinner on my third.

Now running into a rooming house in Paris full of gay Africans does not prove anything.

One person's individual experience cannot prove any generalized experience. This is just one of the things wrong with the whole process that tends to be demonized under the term "prejudice." But it certainly can suggest things that are then accessible to further statistical exploration.

From time to time, for a year or two here or a year or two there, I have found myself somewhat notorious for writing of how my own personal experience suggests various things about behavioral transmission routs of the HIV virus. Again, no one is more aware than I of the fact that such experiences on the part of individuals prove nothing. I have also written, in articles such as "Street Talk/Straight Talk" and "The Gamble," in the same essays in which I have detailed my own experience, about the woeful lack of further reputable scientific exploration. But a "woeful lack" is not the same as none. And when all the reputable scientific exploration supports the suggestions from individual experience; and, at the same time, all the scientific information that contradicts the suggestions (I am referring, of course, to the oral transmission of the AIDS virus) can be shown *not* to be reputable *because it can be shown to incorporate hearsay*, then we have another situation in which the only choices you have are to bet on the science that has been done properly, or you bet against it and try to do the best you can to live something close to an abstinent life (which again and again has been shown for most people to be about as difficult as sticking rigorously to a weight loss diet), and the hidden and acknowledged failures of which only go further to muddy the epistemological waters.

It waits for books such as Marc Epprecht's *Hungochani: The History of Dissident Sexuality in Southern Africa* (2004) or his *Heterosexual Africa? The History of an Idea from the Age of Exploration to the Age of AIDS* (2008), to give statistical confirmation to what we must not be too quick to call common sense—though, in this case, what we know of the Big Other and *Deus sive Natura* could well confirm it by other routes.

From still another interviewer: What do you believe writers contribute to a society like the United States?

Samuel R. Delany: We are its archivists, its analysts, and its speculators.

Interviewer: What do you think your long-term lovers would say about you as a lover?

Delany: Let me quote Dennis from last night (and we have lived together for almost twenty-three years now), when the chicken stew I had started rather late, at around six-thirty, was finally done near ten: "Hey, I like it when the two of us are just living here alone by ourselves."

To which I answered, "Me too. So do I."

Interviewer: What was happening in your life at the time of your writing *The Mad Man*?

Delany: Well, in 1988 I began teaching in the Comparative Literature Department of the University of Massachusetts at Amherst. The steady paycheck—really, the first I'd ever had in my life, in terms of one that I knew I could count on for years—produced a flurry of creative work: the interviews in *Silent Interviews* (1994) and a number of pieces in both *Longer Views* (1996) and *Shorter Views* (2000)—as well as some others I'd still like to see collected. My series of short, analytical fictions, *Return to Nevèrÿon* (1979–87), had drawn to a close. One of the minor projects that makes up *Return to Nevèrÿon* came from my middle 1970s exposure to Derrida's *Of Grammatology* (1965) and to various essays in his *Writing and Difference* (1967): to use conscientiously a metaphoric system in which writing was always given primacy over speech—and I think, from passing comments to the major structures of the stories, I succeeded. As readers of the early Derrida work will know, that contravenes the entire metaphoric history of Western philosophy. I've never seen a reviewer comment on that aspect before, but certainly it's there, if anyone finds it of interest. But once that was out of the way, I was beginning to feel the urge to write more fiction—not fantasy this time, but something more grounded.

While a financially regular life made short pieces easier to conceive, execute, and bring to fruition, also I began to experience how the regularity of teaching responsibilities got in the way of the creation of longer work.

In June of 1993, I read a two-part *New Yorker* article by Harold Brodkey. Brodkey's article became his brief memoir on his losing battle with AIDS, *This Wild Darkness: The Story of My Death* (1996). The first pages of the article and, only slightly less so in the published final book, present a maddingly impossible medical scenario of how he contracted the disease. By this time, I had lost too many dear friends myself from AIDS. (Eddie, Ralph, David, Steve, Michael . . .) In a rage, I flung the magazine across the room (several times as I read it), went to my work room, and that afternoon started *The Mad Man*. The novel begins with a variant of Brodkey's opening sentence. Brodkey's book began: "I have AIDS. I'm surprised that I do . . ." Mine, *The Mad Man*, begins: "I do not have AIDS. I'm surprised that I don't . . ." Fairly soon, I had finished the book's first movement.

An extremely kind woman named Barbara Wise used to invite me regularly during the summers to her Cape Cod home in Wellfleet, where I got a good deal of the opening work done on the book. We were great friends and I will always be grateful to her for her kindness and support. For several years, we traveled around doing readings from *The Tale of Plagues and Carnivals* (1984).

Then I took a year off from teaching—and immediately realized I wouldn't be able to support myself and Dennis, when, like something out of a fairy tale, another very good friend of ours inherited a rather astonishing fortune in the millions.

I had told him our problem, and to my even greater astonishment, he said: "Hey, I'll support you guys for the entire summer. We'll take you up to our country place, turn the cellar over to you and Dennis. At five o'clock, I will bring you a martini, and if you will come up for dinner and socialize with whoever is there for an hour, an hour and a half, that's all I'll ask. Dennis, if he likes, can help my partner who is working on our garden."

And that's exactly what they did. Three days later they came by in their car, picked us up by the scruff of our necks, stuck us in, and drove us up to Canaan, New York. And I wrote for the rest of the summer. *The Mad Man* is dedicated to them. And I learned something dreadfully important. For years, I had been telling myself that my ups and downs in creativity were entirely self-generated.

But now I realized, No. They had to do with how much money I had available. And when I had, as it were, a patron, I had the most creative period of my life.

For those three months I wrote like a crazy man! The only six weeks I've had comparable to it were the weeks, in 1999, when I was fellow at Yaddo. Apparently, I'm an artist who responds remarkably well to patronage.

Barbara was an extremely generous friend, without whom I would never have been able to do a number of the projects I did—though they tended to be more performative than compositional.

Really, I only had what you could call a patron that one time—and it was wonderful, marvelous, magical. Since I started full-time teaching, I've felt more and more that teaching and writing were in a fight to the death!

Interviewer: Who was your mentor when you were growing up?

Delany: Until I was an adolescent, I never knew I had any gay adult friends. When I was seventeen, in 1959, a friend of my soon-to-be-wife Marilyn Hacker, a young painter and sculptor, David Logan, introduced me to a married gay man named Bernard Kay, who lived on West End Avenue. He was multilingual—one of the few people I've known who could speak conversational Latin, French, and Spanish . . .) and in a matter of weeks he was my mentor; soon he was mentor of Marilyn (my teenage confidante and, at nineteen, wife) as well.

Though we only went to bed once (on the eve of my wedding, actually), Bernie and I were very close until his death from lung cancer in 1982, when I was forty. He was widely read—he read science fiction regularly, as well as literature. (He had read Proust in French, and written a novel—unpublished—about ancient Uruk in Sumer.[2]) Though he was white and the son of a New England minister, he was best friends with Harlem Renaissance writer Bruce Nugent; they had become friends at ages nineteen and twenty-three in New York and stayed friends until Bernie's death. Bernie knew many black actors and performers, including the young Gladys Knight, Earl Hyman, and the black actor and composer Lorenzo Fuller. You might meet anyone of these, in his living room and later in his office down on the nineteenth floor of the Candler Building on 42nd Street, when you dropped in; in the early '50s, he had taken over the part of Casio in the famous Paul Robeson production of *Othello* with Jose Ferrer and Uta Hagen that had premièred at the Metropolitan Opera House; and he had directed Marlon Brando in his first Broadway appearance, at age nineteen, in a children's play called *Bobino*. Certainly he was the most important adult male in my life—and Marilyn's—throughout our adolescence and adulthood. Whenever I was in New York, I saw him often several times a week, either at his house or at his office.

Interviewer: Was Bernie the first person to facilitate the process of creativity for you?

Delany: Well, a person who was wonderfully supportive of me before and during my marriage was the poet Marie Ponsot. She lived in Queens with her painter husband Claud and their gaggle of children. She gave me my first copy—hardcover—of Djuna Barnes's *Nightwood*. Today it's the single novel I have read more times than any other in my life—that's at least thirty-five. She managed to get me a scholarship to the Bread Loaf Writers' Conference when I was eighteen, through a friend of hers, Margaret Marshal, who was then an editor at Harcourt Brace, on the strength of one of my early novel attempts. From the first to the third year of my marriage, there were periods where I visited her at her house almost weekly.

Still later, when I got back from my first six-month trip to Europe, and the painter Russell FitzGerald (another friend, and, indeed, mentor of Marilyn's; a married gay man) was more or less a mentor from the time I first met him till he moved to Vancouver with his family in late 1968.

We also had some very important straight friends, such as Dick and Alice Entin.

Among gay male friends, Bernie Kay was the earliest and most important. He was also a child psychologist and a musician. One of his many "adopted" children had grown up to be a Catholic father, director of music in the Catholic church in the northeastern U.S.: Father Fred, as we knew him. Bernie was a committed atheist, but to show his affection for Fred, Bernie composed for him a *Mass in D-Minor*, and for three months I and my friends, Marilyn, who played the piano, and a fine musician and singer named Ana Parez, would arrive at Bernie's house at five in the morning, all of us sitting around the glass dining-room table, copying parts and writing out the score for three hours every morning, before we went off to school, now at the Bronx High School of Science, now at City College. For another overlapping three months, we met in the evening with a small group of singers to learn the choral parts. The *Mass in D-Minor* was eventually performed in a Brooklyn Church, with Lorenzo Fuller conducting and performing the baritone solo—one of the earliest of Bernie's fascinating projects with which I became involved. Bernie and his wife Iva lived at 845 West End Avenue and a 101st Street, Apartment 4-B. When I first met Bernie, he was forty-seven at the time, and had just come back from a vacation in Puerto Rico. An actor as well as a practicing child psychologist, he had run and directed a traveling theater company out of Manchester, New Hampshire, for several years during the 1930s and '40s. He had gathered a group of young men around him, black, white, Latino, a number of whom, many of whom, came from hugely distressed families and, for various lengths of time, officially lived in what had once been the maid's room in his sprawling apartment as part of his family. Indeed, his group included a few young women. Many of the actors who had been in his theater company were still his friends. I must have seen him on an average of once a week from the time I first met him until he died of lung cancer at seventy-six, when I was forty-two. Even though he was married, Bernie was gay, very openly so. For a young gay black man, who had a pretty troubled relation with his own father, it was an incredible relief to have an adult friend—to repeat, Bernie was a practicing psychologist, among other things—with whom I could talk about such topics.

When I first met Bernie, one of his adopted "children" was a neighborhood fellow named Eddie Serano, whose spoken English, at nineteen, was quite serviceable, but who had simply never mastered reading in either English or Spanish. Bernie had arranged to give him three-times-a-week English reading lessons, and these had been going on regularly for several months when I first got to know Bernie.

One day, I came in, and David Logan answered the door. Bernie and Eddie were sitting at the big, glass dining-room table, his papers and books spread around them. "Go on," Bernie was saying. "Now read the whole sentence out loud . . ."

Following his finger along the page, Eddie read out, "For . . . break-fast . . . I . . . had . . . a . . . big bowel . . . no, bowl . . . of . . ." But here he was stymied.

"Come on," Bernie said. "You're doing fine. See if you can sound it out, like we did with some of the other words."

Eddie sat for another five, ten seconds. Then he blurted, "Oh-at-me-al . . ."

And Bernie, David, and I all laughed, and—fortunately—so did Eddie.

The black actor Earl Hyman had also become one of Bernie's protégés during his adolescence. Those of you who never saw Hyman perform live on Broadway or Off-Broadway will likely still remember him as Bill Cosby's father, the elder Dr. Huxtable, on *The Cosby Show*. Though I'd heard him tell this story several times before, often to groups of people at Bernie's apartment, the last time I heard this tale of his meeting with Bernie, back in the '40s, when Bernie and Iva lived in an apartment on Gramercy Park West, was when he was one of the eulogists at Bernie's memorial service and he told this story to those of us who had come to honor Bernie's memory, while I sat next to Bruce Nugent.

At the time of their meeting, Earl was sixteen—a year younger than I was when I first met Bernie. Earl had been in some community center theater project in Brooklyn (it was 1942), where a friend of Bernie's had noticed him and seen that he was particularly smart and talented—and sent young Earl to meet Bernie, much the way, seventeen years later I was sent to meet him in 1959. Earl described himself as a black kid, born in North Carolina, now living in Brooklyn's Bedford Stuyvesant, who had never yet been across the river to Manhattan, and who found himself sitting in the very elegant Gramercy Park living room with crocheted doilies on the mahogany end-tables, the white shades on the brass lamps, under the endless bookshelves, where, at the time, Bernie and Iva were living. To put at his ease young Earl—who was speechless with awe—Bernie said, "Here, let me bring in some in hot chocolate for us. We'll have a cup together, and you can tell me all about yourself." So, Bernie went out into the kitchen and, in a minute, came back from with two cups of cocoa. He handed one cup and saucer to Earl, and went to sit down across from him, with his own cup.

Earl looked down at the cup on his knee, overcome with adolescent embarrassment, and started to pick it up—the handle slipped from his fingers, the cup slid from the saucer and fell to the hard wood floor, spilling cocoa all over!

Mortified, Earl said he wanted to melt into the chair cushion. With his ears burning, he looked up—

But, in his seat, Bernie suddenly overturned his own cup, spilling his own chocolate on the floor and laughed. "Oh, don't worry! That's how we *all* do it, here. Now, sit back and tell me what you're doing out in Brooklyn in the show that I've heard so much about?"

Earl said, that, in spite of himself, he began to laugh. They talked for another three hours—back and forth across puddles of chocolate on the floor. And from that time, he and Bernie became wonderful friends till Bernie's death forty years later.

But that's the sort of man Bernie was. I've said he was a close friend of the Harlem Renaissance writer Bruce Nugent—they'd been best friends since Bernie was nineteen and Bruce was twenty-three. I first met Bruce in Bernie's living room, a few months after I met Bernie himself.

But Bernie is definitely another gay man whom I very much admired and wanted to be like.

All told, Bernie Kay was by far the most important adolescent mentor for both Marilyn and myself. Our daughter is named after Bernie's wife, who had been an actress in Bernie's theater company and who worked for many years in New York as the executive secretary for the Association of the Junior Leagues of America.

In the dark living room, the wind gathers outside, raindrops clatter on the pains, and branches lift and fall before the street light. When I look back across the table, I see another interviewer who has taken the place of the one I was just remembering.

What, he asks, brings you joy in your private life currently?

Delany: Those experiences which, after some thought, alone in a room by myself, I can figure out how to express economically in language. Yes, it's a way of staying out of trouble.

Interviewer: What are you looking forward to accomplishing? In what ways will retirement from teaching be an accomplishment for you?

I think for a moment. Then I dare what is probably the riskiest statement in this talk: I would love to retire from teaching and write another couple of novels.

Thank you very much.

In the words of writer Rachel Pollack:

To you all,

love, luxury, justice, and joy.

—*October 2012*
New York

NOTES

1. Dr. Herukhuti, whom I met through my librarian friend, Steven G. Fullwood, then at the Schomburg Center for Research in Black Culture in New York City.

2. *The Walls of Uruk*, a copy of which should still be in my archive at Yale. A well-known editor, Herbert Weinstock, had asked for revisions—but Bernie had never been able to find the time to make them. This was an historical epic that centered on the story of Gilgamesh and Enkidu. Several times Bernie read sections of it to us out loud.

15

A Note on William Gaddis

For all practical purposes, *The Recognitions* is a novel I grew up with. Published in 1955 by Harcourt Brace when I was thirteen, in an edition littered with typographical errors, it did not receive particularly good—or incisive—press or wide distribution. I read about it because I was an obsessive reader of book reviews back then. But the first time I was really aware of it was three or four years later, when my older cousin, Barbara, who was in medical school, acquired a red-headed boyfriend named Fradley Garner, a young man who lived in a Greenwich Village apartment, at the other end of the hall from . . . a writer. One evening, Barbara, then in her middle twenties, and her rambunctious teenaged cousin, Chip (yes, that was me), dropped in at Fradley's apartment on MacDougal Lane in the West Village, and I noticed on his desk was a thick book. On the back cover was a praiseful endorsement from British poet Robert Graves, some of whose poems I'd read—comparing the book favorably to Eliot's *The Waste Land*.

A month before, I had read an entire book by Graves, *The White Goddess*—a poor man's (or bright adolescent's) *Golden Bough*—in the 1948 edition.[1] The book had made the rounds of some three-quarters of our junior-year high school creative writing class. It makes a good introduction to *The Recognitions*, and is a good way to find out why the hero's name starts off as Wyatt Gwyon, before he vanishes from the text entirely. Fradley said something to the effect that the book had been given him by its author, his down-the-hall neighbor, Bill. "It's all about various religions and how they're all really versions of each other and stuff," Fradley said.

So, I thought, was *The White Goddess*.

Fradley went on, "Bill explained to me how, early in the book, a character at the railing of a boat tears up a letter and tosses the pieces out on the wind, which blows them away, over the water, and Bill describes them like white gulls flying off in the sky. Then, at the end of the novel, on another boat, a bunch of white gulls fly away from the ship over the water, and Bill describes them as looking like pieces of a letter someone has torn up and tossed into the wind."

That struck me as fascinating. "I'd like to read it," I said.

"I'd lend it to you," Fradley said. "I've started it a couple of times and I don't think I'm going finish it any time soon. But Bill signed it to me—so I don't think I better let it out of the house."

"Oh," I said. And sure enough, on the title page, were a scrawled signature personalized to "Fradley." A few years later when the Meridian paperback came out, I bought my first paperback copy of *The Recognitions* from one of my earliest trips to the Strand.

I wish I could say I read it through immediately. But—deeply grateful for the corrected Meridian trade paperback, which, since, has fallen in and out of print—I read the first hundred or hundred-and-fifty pages and recognized it as a retelling of the *Faust* story with art critic Rectal Brown playing the part of Mephistopheles, preceded by his scrappy black dog and accompanied by the smell of smoke. Although eventually I read all the chapters in the book, reading them *in order* defeated me. That had to wait till late winter of 1976 and the mass market Bard Books edition Peter Meyer gambled on at Avon. I was thirty-three and visiting Butler Chair Professor at the University of Buffalo—and snowed in at a Buffalo motel over a three-day blizzard. I started on page one, and three days later I finished it—as Stanley makes his way to the church with the organ he has been in search of (mistaking a men's room momentarily for a sacred chapel, the theme of the mistaken identification ringing out over the novels landscape until the end), and his ignorance of Italian condemning him to death. He plays his composition with its grand bass passage on the foot pedals of the organ—

And the Church of Fenestrula, unable to remain standing around it, collapses—killing the composer and ending the cascade of damp-down Jamesian stylistic data and conceptual music that constitutes his retelling of a modernist *Faust* tale.

I am going to read you here a little of *The Recognitions*, followed by a letter the twenty-six-year-old Gaddis wrote to his Harvard friend Charles Socarides, which first puts forward his vision for the plot and development for the entire book. (Socarides would later become one of the villains of the history of Gay Liberation Movement; a psychoanalyst who maintained through most of his career that homosexuality was an abnormality and a disease that, contradicting Freud himself, could be cured by psychotherapy, though paradoxically he believed that, at first, the patient needed to accept that no moral onus accrued to the condition, presumably because it was an illness like alcoholism or depression, before it could be altered.) The scene I will read has stayed with me from that long-ago defeated first reading, before, a hundred pages later I . . . simply gave up. But it was the first scene where I recognized the novel contained something specifically for me.

"Chapter IV" is one of the shortest in the book—and was the scene in which I realized that the novel did hold some treasures for a youngster already trying to write novels, though I knew—at seventeen—I was going to have to come back and do some serious digging and thinking to grasp it.

After a stint in Greenwich Village, as a young writer who has friended and been befriended by the tortured painter of meticulous forgeries, Wyatt Gwyon and his wife Esther, in an attempt to garner some real experience of the world, the young writer Otto (aka Gordon) goes to central America, to live for a while on a banana plantation and work on his play (to imitate real writers, as it were) and work further on his pastiche of overheard witticisms that have impressed the young fellow in various Greenwich Village parties back in New York, in which a character named Gordon says one crushingly witty thing after another, to the beautiful, sophisticated, and wholly appreciative Priscilla, who, scene after scene, act after act, plays his straight man.

The setting, from the first paragraph of "Chapter IV":

In the dry season haze, the hills were a deep blue and looked further away than the sun itself, for the sun seemed to have entered that haze, to hang between the man and the horizon where, censured and subdued, it suffered the indignity of his stare. The heat of the day was inert as the haze which made it visible, and it only mitigated with the dessolution [sic] of the haze in darkness.[2]

Interrupting Otto's work on his play, an all but illiterate sailor, Jesse Frank, enters, shirtless, barefoot, tattooed, spitting on the floor, looking for some one talk to.

"Read me your play," he tells Otto.

Otto obliges. But Jesse does not think much of the effort.

"You want something to write about?" he demands of Otto, after offering himself as the reasonable subject for a good, exciting tale.

"OK. Take this down. Gordon was the kind of guy that walked into . . . shouldered his way into a bar. He came in and got what he wanted. If anybody wanted to make trouble . . . no. He was a nice guy, but if anybody wanted to make trouble . . . you got that?"

"Yes," Otto said with a pencil.

"If anybody was lookin' for trouble . . . no, that doesn't sound so good. Leave that out." He watched Otto's pencil to be sure it was marking out. "O.K. now start with this. I was around in Chiliano Bay in Columbia with no money of the country, see? I had some money. I had about a hundred dollars, but no money of the country, see? But I have to have a little to get around the country. I was on a boat with a contraband cargo. So I run into a chuleta. You know what a chuleta is?"

"No, I . . ."

"Then you're not so smart, are you. Just because you went to college. It's a money changer, a guy who changes money and takes some out for himself. O.K. So a cayuga come out to the ship, wanting to buy her cargo. But no sell. Worth too much see? You got that?"

"Yes, I . . ."

"O.K. now where was I?"

"A cayuga came out to the ship . . ."

"Yeah. So this guy is only wearing a pair of dungarees, tight-fitting, see? He's well-built, wearing a pair of tight-fitting dungarees. You got that?"

"Yes."

"How do you say it?"

"He was a well-built-fellow wearing tight-fitting dungarees."

"O.K. So he goes into town and finds a girl in a bar. She wants to go to bed with him. But he can't take no chances on account of the cargo. The police, see? The girl visits him at his house, but he can't take no chances. So he tells her, take it easy . . ." Jesse stopped and looked at Otto. "You're goin to get paid for this and I ain't goin to get nothin."

"I never sold anything yet," Otto said.

"Yeah. Well you can sell this, see. This is what people like to read about. Where was I? O.K. So she wants to stay, but he wants everything he has in his mind for shark fishing. Chiliano Bay, that's the place for shark fishing. So he dives for sharks. The white ones and the nigger sharks. Those are the black ones. They don't kill the white ones. But he'll do it, see? He's not scared. He'll dive for any shark. Period."

Otto waited.

"How's that?" asked the author.

"Well, it isn't quite a story yet . . ."

"What do you mean it isn't a story. You think I don't know what a story is? This is what people like to read about, realism, real men doing something, not a lot of crap in fancy trimmings. You get me?"

"Yes, I . . ."

"You're goin to get paid for this and I ain't goin to get nothin." Jesse returned to admiring his chest.

Otto stood and walked over to the bed. He scratched his arm to give his hand something to do.

"Yeah, you're pretty, all right. Where'd you get hands like that. They aren't men's hands."

"They just grew," Otto started to reason. "Like yours did . . ."

"Like mine!" Jesse made a fist as Otto sat down again. "Yeah, you got to wise up to yourself, see?" Jesse approached with the flat bottle in the palm of his hand,

and stopped swaying over him. He made the motion of smashing the bottle in Otto's face, then stood laughing.

"I have to go to bed, Jesse."

"Yeah, you have to go to bed. Look, rabbit, I'm looking for a shack job, see?" Otto sat still.

"Get me?"

"I get you."

Jesse stood swaying for a moment. Then he said, "I gotta go dump my bowels."

"Well, I'm going to bed," said Otto. He stood, stretched as though at ease, yawned a feigned yawn. Jocularly, man-to-man, he said, "Good night, Jesse. I don't want to seem to throw you out but . . ."

"Throw me out! Why rabbit, you couldn't throw me . . . You just try, if you want me to kick you from one end of this room to the other. Throw me out, rabbit, that's a good one . . ." said Jesse, out the door carrying the bottle, leaving the dirty glass.[3]

What struck me, in this scene, was how familiar its content was. Structurally it is a sign for the same order of growth as the scene with the much younger Stephen Dedalus in *Portrait of the Artist as a Young Man*, who, as a little boy going to sleep, sleepily realizes that a rhyming quatrain recited backwards, with the rhyme scheme reversed, is no longer a poem.

I had by now declared myself a writer, and was slowly willing to declare it to others. (Hell, I'd even published some novels.) And already, at least three times now, I had run into one or another Jesse Frank, who'd wanted me to write his story for him, and who had tried to tell me his "story," with no more sense of "what a story was" that Jesse himself. What I'd recognized specifically in Gaddis's glimpse of the underside of this saraband of forgeries and attempts to create meanings that may or may not be there in imitation of a God who may or may not be there Himself, and when clearly Gaddis did not have much faith in any of the formal organizations through which He was supposed to manifest, is that the reason all art *is* a forgery and *must* be borrowed is not because we take the content from others, but rather that, to make it comprehensible at all—to make it a story—we *must* steal the substructure that allows it to signify. This is absolutely and universally inescapable.

Because it had already happened to me—and happened to me repeatedly—I was pretty sure it or something very much like it had happened to Gaddis as well; and this was why I was so interested to read his 1948 letter to Charles Socarides, from the Panama Canal Zone, that gives the wondering twenty-six-year-old writer's first overall view of his theme and the structure of his extraordinary novel to his former Harvard friend, seven years before it was published.[4]

Dear Charles,

First—please don't be alarmed by the weight of a correspondence which I may seem to be thrusting on you. But when you write a letter like this that I have just received, honestly I go quite off my head with excitement. Am fearfully nervous now.

All because I have been away for 3 days, on a neighboring island, working frantically on this novel. Which looks so *bad*. But here: you see, what you say in these letters—most *specifically* this last—upset me because the pictures you draw, the facts you offer, are just as this novel is growing. It is a good novel, terrific, the whole thread of the story, the happenings, the franticness. The man who (metaphorically) sells himself to the devil, the young man hunting so for father figures, chasing the older to his (younger's) death. And the "girl"—who finally completely loses her identity, she who has tried to make an original myth is lost because her last witness (a fellow who takes heroin) is sent to jail—the young man ("hero") the informer. Here's the frantic point: that it all *happened*.

Not really, maybe, but with the facts in my recent life and my running, it *happened*. All the time, every minute the thing grows in me, I "think of" (or remember) new facts of the novel—the Truth About the Past (alternate title). (The title is *Ducdame, called 'some people who were naked.'*) But this growing fiction fits so insanely well with the facts of life that sometimes I cannot stand it, must burst (as I am doing here). And *then* I *ruin* it by *bad writing*. Like trying to be clever—this perhaps because I am afraid to be sincere?

But I watch myself ruin it. And then—because when I was writing in college I went so over board, now it must be reserved, understated, intimated. Or bad bits of writing just run on. Look: "There are few instances when we are not trying to control time; either frantically urging it on, or fearfully watching its winged chariot ragging by, spattering us with the mud that we call memory." Isn't that *awful*.

You see, it just happened, was out of my control until the sentence reached the period. To be facile can kill what *must* be alive.

That is why I hated Wolf [Wolfe]—that he cried out so. Because my point is, no crying out, no pity. We are alone, naked—and nakedness must choose between vulgarity and reason. Every one of us, *responsible*. Still, those lines you quote excite me horribly. Not to have Forster's understatement. No room for Lawrence's lust. Perhaps Flaubert or Gide.

(At the mention of Gide, I inject an auxiliary comment. Even at seventeen, after reading the opening two hundred pages, I was sure Gaddis had wanted to call his great work *The Counterfeiters*, but had declined to because, with *Les Faux-Monnayeurs*, Gide had beat him to it—another volume that, by then, in its early Vintage paperback, had made its way from hand to hand around a third of our Bronx High School of Science creative writing class.)

But I am not good enough as they. It is sickening this killing the best-loved work.

Now I should like to see you, if you could look at this thing, flatly condense (parts of) it—the writing, exposition. God I know all this fear, but have no sympathy with it. Fools. I can not afford to be one.

As though your letter anticipated what I am just putting down as fiction.

(Here I elide a paragraph on the young writer's need for money . . . and the Spanish-speaking girl with the "splendid nose" who has caught his fancy; anyone who reads the letters of any young writer has read about both before, whether Joyce or Lawrence or Mansfield or Pound. It ends, however, with an aphorism worth noting:)

. . . It is hell not to have either the time nor the money to live.

Then there is a man here with a sailboat going to Sweden. And if the novel suddenly looks too *bad* I may go, he needs someone to work, a very small boat, sail boat.

God the running, running. You *understand* it, don't you?

(Another auxiliary: this sense—I think most readers feel it—of running, of pursuit, obtains from beginning to end of the completed *Recognitions*.)

I almost do. But if I can't make a *good* novel then I must keep running until I know all through me—not just as a philosophical fact, as truth which I "believe" and am trying to sell—but can sit down and know without having to try to sell it [writing] to *everybody*.

Thanks. I shall *write* you.

W.

(Socarides was a Harvard friend. This is the earliest letter to explain the essential idea and plot of *The Recognitions*.)

I do not know if Gaddis had yet met his Jesse Frank—or one of his many Jesse Franks—in that landscape that his scene and his letter share; though I suspect it is impossible to be an aspiring writer and not meet at least one such every two or three years, minimum. (Three days ago I ran into one in the line for the bus to Philadelphia where I teach—a very hung-over lawyer, recently disbarred, who, I'm am pretty sure, had not taken his medication for the last few days, and who could tell me things about the housing market in Philadelphia that would make us both a million dollars, if I would only turn them into a book.) But Gaddis wrote the letter from the landscape in which he would stage one such meeting in *The Recognition's* "Chapter IV."

I reiterate: one point so richly and beautifully suggested throughout *The Recognitions* in resonantial relation to many others is that the reason all art—all true art—is forgery is not because the *content* is borrowed or stolen, but because the form that makes the content recognizable as art *must* be taken from other works, whether on purpose or inadvertently. Otherwise, like Jesse's string of pointless incidents, it would simply not be recognizable *as* art.

Jesse's incoherent evening ramblings yield one of the few scenes in the novel that parodies the aesthetic disaster that ensues if, in effect, one *fails* to "plagiarize"—as Otto's vapid "society" drama, there in the Central American jungle, displays what happens when one "plagiarizes," or copies from life, the wrong things; like the most ineffective jar possible placed in Tennessee.

A decade later, an explosion of intertextual studies burgeoned from the general interest in high modernism until it had spread through the hall of the humanities. But this is one of the earliest novels in which we were given to watch a writer wrestle as seriously as possible with the glory and humbling terror of this truth.

—*February 19, 2013*
New York and
Philadelphia

NOTES

1. Robert Graves, *The White Goddess* (Creative Age Press, 1948; amended and enlarged edition: Noonday / Farrar, Straus and Giroux, 1966).

2. William Gaddis, *The Recognitions* (Penguin, 1993), 154.

3. Gaddis, *The Recognitions*, 156–58.

4. William Gaddis to Charles Socarides, Pedro Miguel, Canal Zone, February or March 1948, in *Letters of William Gaddis*, edited by Steven Moore (Dalkey Archive, 2013), 88.

16

Interview with Reed Cooley

Reed Cooley: In the book *Times Square Red, Times Square Blue* you indicate that the porn theaters actively encouraged sex and masturbation in the audience. How so?

Samuel R. Delany: Perhaps it would have been better to say they passively encouraged it. *Most* of the porn theaters, of course, actively discouraged it. That discouragement was usually one or two guys with flashlights, walking up and down the single aisle (rarely did such theaters have more than one) between every five and twenty-five minutes, shining them on this patron or that one. If anyone looked as if he might have been masturbating or about to, the guy would bark, "Hey . . . Cut it out, fella! This ain't that kinda place," or some such.

If the management did NOT do that, soon the theater gained the reputation of a place you could go, sit, watch the movie, and beat off. But for most guys, it didn't take a lot of "public shaming" to make them put their privates back in their pants. If it wasn't discouraged in the same way, guys who liked giving blow jobs could join someone sitting in the audience, bend over, and orally service him. Sometimes you were told to go away, but many times guys let you go ahead or, if you asked, whispered, yes. Thus, if you were an active fellator (and I was), you could have three, ten, fifteen guys in an afternoon or evening. This is simply how the different theaters evolved (with pay-offs to inspectors and/or police to look the other way, arranged by the owners), so that men who didn't like that sort of thing—and most basically didn't care—found another theater, and guys who did like it made a practice of showing up. Often you saw the same people returning again and again. That meant, of course, low-level—and sometime not so low-level—drug dealing often went on in places that were more permissive. Active or passive, guys who wanted to spend an afternoon at such a place often liked to do it with a dime bag of weed. Since the police were always on the lookout for such business, this could create other problems.

When, in the '80s, crack moved into that world, it was a much bigger problem—for a whole number of reasons that would take a book of its own to detail. But some of the theaters became regular crack dens.

Toward the end of the reign of the porn theaters, more than once I would be in a theater that "wasn't that sort of place," and when the man patrolling the aisle would shine his light on a customer, especially if it was big guy, and bark his, "Hey—cut that out!" he would get a surprisingly rough answer back: "What the fuck for? You're showin' them damned movies. What you expect us to do? Get that fuckin' light out of my face, now, or I'll piss in your fuckin' ear! Don't get your undies in a twist just 'cause mine's three times as big as yours. YOU cut it out and lemme pull on my dick!"—or some such. A couple of times, the customer like that got put out. But in a couple of cases, to avoid trouble, the "guards" shook their heads and left him alone. And, having grown comfortable with this sort of public display, more and more men who patronized such places came to regard it as a natural right. It simply followed the path of least resistance before bodily desires—that were, after all, in such venues, harmless.

Cooley: One of your hopes stated in the preface is that new venues and institutions that allow and encourage public sex proliferate. For those who haven't read the book, why would such places be good for a city's social life?

Delany: Well, with now and then an exception, by and large such spaces were pretty friendly. They catered to a range of folks from a wide range of social classes. You could start a quick physical encounter with someone in the theater, and they could turn out to be a doctor or a dentist as easily as a truck driver or a window washer—or, in one case, I recall, an opera singer. Part of the thesis of the book is that interclass contact is particularly good for the quality of life of a city.

Cooley: To your knowledge, have any such institutions emerged in the last fifteen years?

Delany: Manhattan is pretty much devoid of such activity today—at least in any movie theaters that I know of. In Brooklyn and Queens, I've heard several porn theaters have opened up (or converted to porn, e.g., Cinema, 711 King's Highway), where indeed there is some activity. In Philadelphia, in at least two theaters such activity went on when I started teaching there in January 2000. After half a dozen or so years, a remaining one out on Market and Twenty-First closed down (The Forum). But though the other theater—the specifically gay Sansom Street Cinema, on Thirteenth Street just down from Sansom—did a complete physical renovation a couple of years back, it's hard for me to tell how well it's doing. Also, I'm notably older, by more than a decade, from when I wrote *Times Square Red, Times Square Blue* in 1998. For more than two-dozen years now I've had a wonderful partner, as well as a small circle of "fuck buddies" and at this point I'm simply interested in other things.

—February 24, 2013

17

Notes on *Heart of Darkness*

A Facebook and Email Thread

Samuel R. Delany: In order to establish a jumping-off point, let's assume that Conrad's 1899 novella *Heart of Darkness* is precisely the sort of political intervention that some of its detractors, such as Chinua Achebe and others, have taken it to be—that is to say, a political intervention. Achebe and others assume that is what the story is and that, as such, it fails disastrously. But that is to beg the question, which is: What is the logical structure of its intervention?

Conrad had been to the Congo in the 1880s, and seen horrors that might well have been intense enough to make anyone want to do something about it: He's walked beside roadways and trudged by mountains of black, right hands—or, occasionally black heads—as high as a two-story house. So what, a decade later, when he sets a story in this landscape, does he decide to do?

If you pay attention only to the Kurtz story as it unfolds in Africa, once Marlow arrives, you have a mildly anemic adventure in what would seem to take you farther and farther into darkest Africa, where—as Achebe complains—there are simply no African characters to speak of so that it becomes absurd to hold the book or the tale up as an any sort of study of life in Africa at all—and pretty much justifies his complaints.

It also suggests that as much as two thirds of the book would seem to be more or less padding.

I would suggest that precisely that padding is what contains the "heart" of *Heart of Darkness*; and that a careful look at it reveals a story that poses itself against all the easy assumptions that most readers—in spite of the text—tend to make about the story, in expectation of certain sort of "inarguable" generic conventions, starting with the assumption that (1) the "heart of darkness" itself lies, somehow, in Africa and is (2) what the story is trying to plumb, in the middle of the "untamed" African landscape, despite the lack in the text of any black Africans looked at in enough detail to say anything about their character and internal subjectivity or any portrayal of any African culture in enough detail to determine its own central structure or heart to which, somehow, this dark "heart" metaphor may assigned.

As far as racism is concerned, I would hazard that it is the readerly assumption that the heart of the story—of the title—can be found in such an anemic, even nonexistent, presentation of character and culture simply because it's black: that is the only racism that the story inarguably "contains."

And that, I would hazard, is not Conrad's—or his collaborator Ford Madox Ford's.

If we pay attention to the text as written, another story emerges, which, I would argue, is much more coherent—and meaningful—in terms of the interventions that Achebe misses; though it is not the one he's looking for, either.

Mark Fuller Dillon: Vincent Czyz—Yes, I did remove the nuance from your *Heart of Darkness* comment, and I apologize for that. But I have to agree: to call it a travelogue does reduce a complex novella into something less than it is. And to say that it gives "short shrift" to plotting seems equally reductive: the plot is there, and it matters.
Yesterday at 2:37 PM · Like · 1

Vincent Czyz My claim throughout the essay, and even in my last comment, is not that books like *H of D* or *To the Lighthouse* have no plots, but that plot is NOT the hook; plot is the hook in a Dickens or a Jane Austen novel: characters want things and there are obstacles. The characters DO things in those novels and their actions and choices have consequences relating to their goals and to other characters. Marlow doesn't do much. Kurtz does, but it is all off-stage. He's not even a character really. Marlow is mostly a voyeur (hence my travelogue comment). What does he want? What does he do to get it? These things don't drive the action . . . and the action is just a steamboat going upriver. There's much more classic plotting in *Moby-Dick* though one still doesn't generally read *Moby-Dick* to see whether or not Ahab catches up with the whale; it's just not that kind of book. I'm not saying—never did, even in the essay—these books have zero plot (this is almost always how the essay is interpreted) but that plot, as one aspect of the novel, is not the one that stands out in the novels I have found memorable, including *Dhalgren*, perhaps my single favorite.
23 hours ago · Edited · Like · 4

Vicki Silkiss . . . and Chip, your writing—in prose—almost more than any other's—has made me resonate with the precision of phrases, the poetry of paragraphs, the crystallinity of words. Thank you for that.
Yesterday at 6:16 PM · Like

Dodie Bellamy Thanks so much for this.
Yesterday at 6:51 PM · Like · 1

Samuel Delany One of the things that makes *H of D* so difficult for most students to read—and it *is* hard for them: I've taught it numerous times and the number of students who are honestly bewildered by what's going on is often more than fifty percent, even intelligent graduate students—is that they don't notice WHERE the story lies in the novel. It has almost nothing to do with Mr. Kurtz, for example. It takes place almost entirely among a bunch of un-named characters, the various "Pilgrims" and the Manager of the station, the Manager's nephew, the Engineer, etc., and happens during the endless delays when Marlow is trying to fix the boat. In a sentence, the plot is about all the in-efficient, self-aggrandizing, blow-hard lies Marlow MUST tell—which is what the "Pilgrims" do all the time—to get the materials needed to make the boat river-worthy so that he can go on up-stream . . . the lies this man must tell who "hates a lie more than anything." It's about how, in the course of the journey, he is transformed into what he initially despises.

The Kurtz thread through the story is largely symbolic (as Conrad him-self wrote in his journal), and is only a commentary on what the story of the Pilgrims has been about, and the revelation of their essential "hollowness" that has finally "infected" Marlow himself—letting us know that the "Heart of Darkness" is not black but a white emptiness. It is the Pilgrims who are hollow—and finally Marlow himself, which is why he lies to Kurtz's beloved at the end, back in England. (See T. S. Eliot's poetic commentary on the tale, "The Hollow Men.") Basically, ask anyone who's just finished reading the story what color the heart of darkness is and what's within that heart. Unless they can say pretty definitely that its color is white and it's empty, they've missed what little plot the story has, probably because they were paying too much at-tention to the Kurtz current—and thought that the actual story was secondary, so didn't pay attention to it. (And it is by not paying attention to them, when they happen to us, that they have the same effect.) It's not secondary. It really is the fundamental point.
13 hours ago · Edited · Like · 2

Jeff VanderMeer I have discovered that I think about my fiction as being about character and structure, not plot per se. Plot feels to me like a reader's way of looking at story and not, for me at least, a writer's. For me, it's character

doing whatever character does and then whatever structure that's encased in. Progressions and beats are the things inside the structure—the micro structure. Which simulates what might be called "plot" if you've got to call it plot.
23 hours ago · Like

Dave Ryan Going back to *Dhalgren*, I was thrilled when I read it almost forty years ago at how it undermined my stock "reader's expectations" with a more explosive artful effect. The other novel at the same time with similar impact was *The Four-Gated City*, which jettisoned the end of a five-part *roman-à-clef* with historical texts tracing out the post-apocalyptic heroism of characters we'd known in naturalistic guise for thousands of pages. (Both on my to-reread list)
23 hours ago via mobile · Like

Mark Fuller Dillon "One of the things that makes *H of D* so difficult for most students to read. . . is that they just don't notice WHERE the story is in the novel."
And again, this is what fascinates me about an A. E. Coppard story like "Dusky Ruth": the actual story is behind the frontal story, and implied by details presented in that frontal story. If you assume that the protagonist is the character who *perceives* events, then the story seems inconclusive, undramatic. But when you realize that the actual protagonist is Ruth, then the plot begins to make sense and begins to take on emotional weight.
23 hours ago · Like

Vincent Czyz Though I haven't read *H of D* in . . . 27 years, I'm going to go out on a rickety board here and disagree that the darkness is hollow & white. The white-shirt-wearing accountant is hollow, empty—"a *papier-mâché* Mephistopholes" . . . because he is not actively evil, he is passively so. Kurtz fell to committing evil acts, was actively barbaric and therefore I don't think was characterized by mere hollowness. Personally, I don't feel (wrong though I may be) the darkness has a color at all or that it can be clearly pinned down as one thing. it's a multi-entendre . . . it's the darkness of the unknown (for years Africa's nickname was the dark continent, for centuries I suppose), the alien, evil, the unconscious, the instinctual/bestial—it's all of these things and probably more. It's as hard to pin down as the whiteness of Melville's whale. Marlow drops this hint when he famously tells us the meaning is not inside, like a kernel in a nut, but outside, only as a glow brings out a haze, in the likeness of one of these misty halos that sometimes are made visible by moon light . . . or something like that.
23 hours ago · Like · 1

Vincent Czyz I should probably read it again with whiteness in mind.
23 hours ago · Like

Mark Fuller Dillon "Though I haven't read *H of D* in . . . 27 years"—I'd like to suggest that it's not helpful to comment on a story unrevisited in such a long time. Memory can play tricks.
23 hours ago · Like

Craig Brewer A question for the writers: why is it that "plot" so often gets discussed as a secondary, even "low-brow" thing . . . almost as if it's just too "science fiction"-y. And we know how bad that is.

I see the same in academic circles. To elevate a piece of writing, it's often an early move to downplay the "plot" in order to discuss more ethereal things. Or, when it does get discussed, it somehow gets translated into "narrative structure" and "narrative moments" rather than simply story. I just always worry that there's something going on which suggests that the simple readers are supposed to like plot while the subtle and smart readers are supposed to like . . . other things. (Not that I disagree with what Vincent has written—I agree in many, many cases. Nonetheless, this discussion seems to repeat itself quite often.)
20 hours ago · Like

Mark Fuller Dillon I would never consider an interest in plot "low-brow," nor would I dismiss the joy that a well-tuned plot can bring. But I think that for many writers, plot is the least "creative" aspect of the craft. The process of developing a plot is quite different from the process of writing a story; I suspect that it requires different skills and a different mindset. For that reason, it can feel "mechanical," more like developing a logical argument than like typing up a dream that unfolds as you watch. On the other hand, some writers love that process. It all depends on the person.
20 hours ago · Like · 2

Mark Fuller Dillon As for academic circles—I can't comment on these; I was a farmer, not a teacher. But plot is what it is: it's right there, as plain as a snake on cement, for anyone to see, and that makes it a less interesting topic for discussion than other aspects of writing.
20 hours ago · Edited · Like · 1

Craig Brewer Easy to see, hard to make elegant, perhaps even harder to make "poetic." Prose, a way of phrasing a sentence, creating an image, any and all good writers do that. But to turn a plot into a poem while keeping it a plot? That seems like magic to me.
19 hours ago · Like

Mark Fuller Dillon It would be like making a flow-chart poetic.
18 hours ago · Like

Craig Brewer I know some programmers who can do just that. Not every programmer, but the good ones. And there are certainly people who can make a story itself into "art": Dunsany, Wolfe, Budrys, Le Guin, Dick, and so many others. If I'm going to overgeneralize, I'd argue that what makes "genre fiction" worthy of being called literature is its ability to turn story and story-elements into things that last and that are worth returning to, that affect us. Sure, some writers just slowed down a bit and thought about sentences and characterization. But at its heart, I think, is a feeling for story. A dragon or a space ship isn't wondrous by itself; but it's wondrous because of the story it promises and, ultimately, of the one it delivers.

In the end, though, I just hate either/or's. And discussion of the value of plot always seem to want to make us choose.

18 hours ago · Like · 2

Mark Fuller Dillon I agree in principle; all I can add is that sometimes a story is not about what happens, but about something else, something hard to pin down. Not much happens in "The Lady with a Lapdog," and yet, if you look at it from a different angle, the promise of that final paragraph is enough to raise goosebumps.

18 hours ago · Like

Samuel Delany Jeff VanderMeer, I couldn't have said it better—and tried to say it, probably not so well, in *About Writing*. Thanks. (Kurtz's story is entirely subplot, Vince, not plot—and the plot is as carefully structured as *The Good Soldier*'s, the novel by Conrad's collaborator [Ford Madox Ford]—who claimed, by the way, that he was a major factor in *H of D* as well. And I suspect he was. The fact that none of the characters in the plot have names, any more than do the listeners on the deck of the Nellie, completely disorients many, if not most, readers the first time—or even after several times—through the novella.)

12 hours ago · Edited · Like

Vincent Czyz However intricately *H of D* is plotted, I don't think plot is what they are burning in the furnace to get upriver. Just me. Perhaps unhelpfully, I didn't distinguish between plot and subplot in my comments. That said, I can see more Aristotelian plotting—much more—in Kurtz's implied story than in Marlow's explicit & detailed narrative; and I believe that is much of the point . . . NOT to see this through Kurtz's eyes, which would have made this pretty close to Greek tragedy and good but not great. Then again, maybe, as Mark points out, that's the lensing effect of 27 years.

10 hours ago · Edited · Like

Samuel Delany Terms like "plot" and "subplot" are provisional, used to indicate what I'm pointing at—not to name something that can be fixed and bounded. (I'm the guy who doesn't believe "plot" as such even exists.) But sometimes you have to appropriate a less precise vocabulary to make clear to people what's going on. Otherwise you're stuck with the really pernicious notion that any story can mean anything—which, while it is literally "true," doesn't take into account probability, usefulness, and coincidence with the text, which means that some interpretations are more useful and more arguable than others.

10 hours ago · Like

Samuel Delany Try reading it again, Vince, and pay particular attention to what Conrad spends most of his pages writing about, in the course of the "story": what happens when the boat is stalled and needs to be repaired. In short, the point of the novella is not primarily about where he's going and what he does when he gets there but what happens to him and the transformation he undergoes while he's en route.

7 hours ago · Edited · Like · 1

Samuel Delany I think my argument about *H of D* is as strong as your argument about *Moby-Dick* as a retelling of *Paradise Lost*, with Ahab as Satan and the white whale as God's manifestation, the sailors as the rebelling angels, etc.—an interpretation which you have totally convinced me of, by the by.

10 hours ago · Edited · Like · 1

Vincent Czyz I don't think I'm arguing what *H of D* is about . . . I think I'm arguing that I'm willing to read it a 4th time because what actually happens in the narrative, the events, the plot, whatever you call that stuff, isn't the story's strength. I'm going to read it again for the reading experience . . . which for me (3 times so far) has consistently bordered on hallucinatory, dark at that (and absolutely no punning meant there).

9 hours ago · Like

Mark Fuller Dillon Still, I prefer "The Secret Sharer," which, in its quiet way, is even more hallucinatory—and often downright strange.

9 hours ago · Like

Frank Giallombard Don Levy you may like this literary discussion. Nisi Shawl I still think a good plot is important to a work of fiction to keep the readers' attention and to get the editor to publish it. This goes for the literary novel as well as the commercial novel. Plot definitely comes from well-written characters. What does the main character want? How will he/she get it? Will the person get it? Success or failure. My favorite plots came from characters' goals. H. Ellison, Tolkien, Dickens, Rand, London, Shakespeare, B. Traven, etc. I guess my favorite plot in all books is from *The Treasure of Sierra Madre* from Traven's novel. I'll put that book up against any plotless meandering literary yawn.

8 hours ago · Edited · Like

Nisi Shawl Well, we have different tastes, Frank. I suspect yours is more on the main sequence than mine, but I don't find fault with either tendency. To me, plot is *lagniappe*, and it's really not what I care about as a reader. As a writer it is sometimes an afterthought for me, sometimes an element I knowingly steal from someone else. It's never what motivates me to write.

8 hours ago · Like

Nisi Shawl And by-the-by, I read very little so-called literary fiction. Mostly genre, and when I stray from SF/F I read Victorian novels: Dickens, Trollope, Gaskell, etc.

8 hours ago · Like · 2

Frank Giallombard OK, well, I simply want my fiction to "go somewhere." Plot is at least a kind of compass and blueprint.

8 hours ago · Like

Jeffrey Lemkin Great discussion! I'm with Nisi Shawl, who, in an earlier comment, extolled the virtue of character. For me, if I care about the characters—and that's a tricky thing that I'm not sure I'd care to try and define—then I'm going to read, finish and—often—enjoy what I've read. It may even make me think.

If I don't care much about the characters, then I end up having far less interest in the story, however it may be crafted.

So, I might say that to me, story is (largely) character. Or stuff (internal or external) happening to characters that I care about in some way.

Frank Giallombard, I agree—I also want my stories to "go somewhere," but I'm far more interested in where they go when they're populated with characters I connect with in some way.

8 hours ago · Like

Nisi Shawl Nicola Griffith had a bunch of Clarion West students come up with metaphors for their writing processes. I was sitting in on the class and did the exercise also. My metaphor: I'm standing on the edge of a cliff, looking down into a wide river valley I want to cross. I have a compass, a knife, a rope, and a water bottle. I cross the valley. From time to time I climb a tree and take a look around. But I have no map. And to me, plot would more nearly resemble a map in this metaphor than a compass.

7 hours ago · Edited · Like · 2

Nisi Shawl I don't know what the compass is. Desire, perhaps.

8 hours ago · Like

Mark Fuller Dillon Frank Giallombard—I also want fiction to "go somewhere," but there are many ways to do that, some of them surprising. I prefer short stories and novellas to novels, because the need for concision offers a greater variety of techniques for the implication and suggestion of plot, for narrowing the focus to essentials. That range of freedom is great for writers, and for readers too, because it allows them to use their own imaginations, their own experiences, to fill in the gaps.

7 hours ago · Like

Nicola Griffith For me story is the intersection of a person and her world. (World being setting, culture, situation.) You can plan all you like—I'm going to walk in the woods for one hour, say—but unless you ignore everything unexpected around you, you'll be surprised by something. You'll end up (emotionally, intellectually, even physically) in a different place. You will have changed. That, to me, is story.

7 hours ago · Like · 1

Frank Giallombard How sweet. You guys sound like literary fiction textbooks. Now I get why over the last decade, when I go into a book store, there's nothing I am attracted to buying and reading except George R. R. Martin and Bernard Cornwell.

7 hours ago · Edited · Like

Mark Fuller Dillon That's the beauty of used bookstores: you can pick and choose from centuries of work.

6 hours ago · Like

Samuel Delany E. M. Forster on "Story": "The more we look at the story (the story that is a story, mind), the more we disentangle it from the finer growths it supports, the less we shall find to admire . . . *Qua* story, it can only have one merit: that of making the audience want to know what happens next. And conversely, it can only have one fault: that of making the reader not want to know what happens next. These are the only two criticisms that can be made of the story that is a story. It is the lowest and simplest of literary organisms. Yet it is the highest factor common to all the very sophisticated organisms known

as novels . . . The story is primitive. It reaches back to the origins of literature, before reading was discovered, and it appeals to what is primitive in us.
That is why we are so unreasonable over stories we like, and so ready to bully
people who like something else . . . Intolerance is the atmosphere story generates . . . Scheherazade avoided her fate because she knew how to wield the
weapon of suspense—exquisite in her descriptions, tolerant in her judgments,
ingenious in her incidents, advanced in her morality, vivid in her descriptions
of character, expert in her knowledge of three Oriental capitals—it was yet on
none of these that she relied when trying to save her life from her intolerable
husband. They were but incidental. She only survived because she kept the
king wondering what would happen next."
6 hours ago · Like

Frank Giallombard . . . Ray Bradbury places more faith in the subconscious
than in conscious over-planning. Not that he doesn't believe in plot. But for
Bradbury, plot is secondary to, and determined by, character: "Plot is no more
than footprints left in the snow after your characters have run by on their way
to incredible destinations. Plot is observed after the fact, not before" (139). In
short: if you want to surprise your readers, perhaps you should first try to surprise yourself. Just follow the footprints—and see where they lead.
5 hours ago · Like · 1

Nisi Shawl Well Ray said it. What I meant. Thanks.
5 hours ago · Like

Frank Giallombard Here's another direction >>> the story that has a good
plot but a hollow and crummy ending or denouement. I would like Bradbury's
tales up until the ending which then wasn't satisfying enough for me. Writing
a good ending can be tough. There's gotta be some sort of resolution. Maybe
the tale doesn't have to be totally "over." But I don't wanna get to end of a tale
and say, "That's all ???"
4 hours ago · Like

Nisi Shawl People sometimes criticize my stories by saying that they haven't
ended. I think of swinging on a playground—often I want to leave my reader
on the upward swoop, flying free, leaping out at the top of the arc, rather than
dragging my heels in the gravel till things come to a standstill. That's what I like
to read, so that's what I write.
4 hours ago · Like

Nisi Shawl Sometimes I am surprised to find the ending has been written.
4 hours ago · Like

Nisi Shawl My probably unusual take on what stories are and how they work and what parts of them matter is why I sometimes question my abilities as a critic, reviewer, and editor. But I never question my identity as a writer.
<u>4 hours ago</u> · <u>Like</u>

* * *

Tue, Sep 3, 2013 at 1:16 PM
Vincent Czyz
To: Samuel Delany
Subject: Reconciling the views

Well, Chip, I've gone back and looked over my master's essay, which included *H of D*, and found quite a number of interesting things, including this: "Kurtz turned out to be 'hollow at the core' . . . Kurtz is one of those men in whom 'there was something wanting . . . some small matter which, when the pressing need arose, could not be found under his magnificent eloquence.'"

I gather this hollowness, allied with whiteness, is what you take to be the darkness of the novella. Rereading my essay, I took away a different meaning: Had Kurtz not been hollow, he might have successfully faced the darkness, both inner and the outer (which, in Africa, calls irresistibly to the inner—it is the point of setting this story in Africa, I think). Marlow is at pains to show how various things are used to cover up both this hollowness (the starched collars and vast cuffs of the accountant) and a reality or truth that is difficult to face.

Reading my old essay is just a primer; I'll re-read the novella. But I think it's possible to reconcile—to some extent anyway—our divergent readings.

Vince

Tue, Sep 3, 2013 at 2:30 PM
Samuel Delany
To: Vincent Czyz
Subject: What the text says

Actually, I don't think that's what the text says. The text says very clearly that the inefficient white men in the repair station—who run to put out a fire with water in a leaking bucket, then beat a black man for their failure—are the hollow ones. They are the ones who are always boasting about all the powerful people that they know in the capitol, and back in England—and that is the reason you should do what they want.

Marlow finds out that the only way he can get his boat fixed is by threatening to wield the same kind of power, which is a complete fantasy and fabrication. Kurtz is never described as hollow, but the "Pilgrims" are. Kurtz is not described one way or the other.

When Marlow first lies to the Station Manager about whom he knows in England in order to get the grommets for his stalled boat, that is the real climax of the story, when he begins his transformation into a colonial himself.

Kurtz and Marlow are the only two named characters in the story. When Marlow and the Pilgrims get to the head of the river, and reach the "heart of darkness," they are enveloped in a white fog. *That's* the heart of darkness. And that's what the text says. What is terrifying about the heart of darkness is that it is empty. It is not "yellow," as it is on the maps. It is not black, which is what the cliché would lead you to believe. It is a white, uninflected haze. And the only "hearts" that the text presumes to be able to see into are the whites'—whom it finds second-rate, heartless, and hollow.

I'm only going by what's in the text.

Chip

Tue, Sep 3, 2013 at 3:27 PM
Samuel Delany
To: Vincent Czyz
Subject: The argument

The basic argument of *Heart of Darkness*—which really is a scathing indictment of colonialism—is that the reason it is such a spectacular failure (at least morally; when you walked through the streets of Leopoldville in the year Conrad was a steamship captain there, there were mountains of body parts in the streets, rotting, two and three stories high—right hands, mostly, that had been cut off of natives by more war-like natives so they could get bullets in exchange for the bags of hands to keep the regular natives under control.

You could not write about this in fiction that would be published in England or France or Belgium. Conrad records being taken on a trip, carried by native bearers, because he was sick. His white transporters decided that he would likely die, and so left him at the side of the road. A black woman found him and took him into her hut, and nursed him back to health. This was something else that could not be reported in fiction or nonfiction—though he uses a very similar incident in passing, in *H of D*.

The major reason why you should not treat anyone else this way is because it's immoral and inhuman. But if there were any way to make that argument from the situation, which was literally spread about in the streets, it would have already been made.

So what—if you are Joseph Conrad and appalled—do you do?

The only thing I can do (he reasoned) is to write a story that shows—not how we tyrannize the blacks—but how we corrupt our selves, which allow us to go on and act so inhumanly to those we are supposed to be protecting and saving.

And that's what he did.

The argument in the story runs:

First, we tell everybody that we are bringing the best and the brightest over to Africa to bring civilization to a primitive, ignorant people.

But in reality, what we get are the failures of our own civilization, the ones that cannot make it here in Europe, the second rate, the corrupt, the losers from our own culture, who come over to see what they can do in this primitive land. But we mask that by inventing myths about the ones that go off by themselves, that they are really supermen, who are better than all the rest—like Kurtz. We turn them into gods . . . What Conrad shows us is a bunch of second-rate losers who keep telling themselves and each other how great they all are, and how much power they wield because of their European connections, and Kurtz is the most god-like. And the only way to get anything at all done is to start acting the way they do, to get your grommets for the boat, and to get on with your job.

The problem is, if you start acting like that, you become them. And that's what happens to Marlow.

In the end, Marlow has become as much of a liar as any of them. (He could simply have said nothing to Kurtz's Intended, when he gets back to England. But he chooses to lie outright. And all his subsequent research on Kurtz with Kurtz's cousin and Kurtz's friends proves that Kurtz, with a little talent at a dozen things—very much like Frédéric Moreau in *Sentimental Education*, with his novel *Sylvio the Fisherman's Son* and his German waltzes and his landscape paintings—is just another Victorian loser who is without the determination—not to mention the vision—to become a writer or a musician or a painter—and so has gone off to Africa to become an ivory stealer instead, and may have found some happiness with his life lording it over the natives, which the whites felt morally called upon not to let him have, and so dragged him, dying, back, then murdering (for sport) his black mistress (which, while he is sick and dying, he observes through the boat's window: That is the sight he sees on the shore and his final comment on it is "The horror! The horror!").

This was the same basic decision I made, by the by, when I decided to write my own anti-war novel, *The Fall of the Towers*, between 1962 and '64. I didn't have the basic information to write about what the war was doing to Vietnam, so I wrote a novel about what the war was doing to us—the ones who stayed at home. No, it wasn't very good. But it was the best a twenty- to twenty-one-year-old could do at the time. And it's still in print, for better or for worse.

Hugs and stuff—

—Chip

Tue, Sep 3, 2013 at 3:30 PM
Samuel Delany
To: Vincent Czyz
Subject: PS

PS—The white fog at the head of the river, the heart of darkness, IS on the outside, as you pointed out, not inside. That you got right.

& more hugs—

—Chip

Tue, Sep 3, 2013 at 7:04 PM
Vincent Czyz
To: Samuel Delany
Subject: Darkness

Apparently I misquoted!

Now I will have to re-read.

I know about the river mist, but, until I read it again, I'll find it hard to believe the darkness is a reachable place on a map or that it is even a single, pin-down-able thing. If it is, as I've said, it's rather a disappointment. And from what I've read of my master's essay, it doesn't seem it will be that simple. Conrad isn't just concerned with mere hollowness or heartlessness; he could have set his story in many other places for that. He wanted civilization pressed up against primitive societies. He talks about being accustomed to seeing something monstrous shackled, but there (Africa) you could see something monstrous and free. He talks about the gratification of monstrous passions. He talks about confounding the beating of one's heart with the drums in the jungle.

Still, I need to re-read it.

Vince

PS—I am beginning to see the Europeans in the story as representative of appearance—appearance there to hide unpleasant truths. And civilization as a mosaic of appearances—from starched collar's to table manners—there to hide the id's discontents, as it were. The black natives, for the first time, seem to me representative of a truer reality. Indeed, when the civilized man gets too close for too long to deeper realities, what civilization has given him falls away like rags. There are a number of references to nakedness and frankness. Anyhow, this is mostly something new I've come up with . . . could be all bosh.

Tue, Sep 3, 2013 at 7:17 PM
Samuel Delany
To: Vincent Czyz
Subject: Metaphor

No, it isn't a single, reachable place on a map. It's a metaphor.

But the surprise is PART of the metaphor. Everyone is expecting blackness, the night, etc., and they arrive, and find themselves in a white fog where they can make out nothing. So they stop—and they're at their destination.

Come on, Kurtz is the one with the gratified monstrous desires. That's Victorian code for a miscegenational relationship (that's what "going native" means), which is what they must drag him back from and cannot allow him to go on indulging. It's not in the least simple. It's quite complicated enough. But it's comprehensible.

The hollowness is not simple heartlessness. It's lack of character, lack of determination, inability to be consistently human and responsible to those you are supposed superior to. (That's how it would have been interpreted in 1898.)

Read it and see what you think—

—Chip

Tue, Sep 3, 2013 at 7:43 PM
Vincent Czyz
To: Samuel Delany
Subject: The argument

"The basic argument of *Heart of Darkness*—which really is a scathing in-dictment of colonialism—is that the reason it is such a spectacular failure (at least morally; when you walked though the streets of Leopoldville in the year Conrad was a steamship captain there, there were mountains of body parts in the streets, rotting, two and three stories high—right hands, mostly, that had been cut off of natives by more war-like natives so they could get bullets in exchange for the bags of hands to keep the regular natives under control."

You never finished the first fascinating—and repugnant—sentence.

"You could not write about this in fiction that would be published in England or France or Belgium. Conrad records being taken on a trip, carried by native bearers, because he was sick. His white transporters decided that he would likely die, and so left him at the side of the road. A black woman found him and took him into her hut, and nursed him back to health. This was something else that could not be reported in fiction or nonfiction—though he uses a very similar incident in passing, in *H of D*."

Also fascinating.

"The major reason why you should not treat anyone else this way is because it's immoral and inhuman. But if there were anyway to make that argument from the situation, which was literally spread about in the streets, it would have already been made. So what—if you are Joseph Conrad and appalled—do you do? The only thing I can do (he reasoned) is to write a story that shows—not how we tyrannize the blacks—but how we corrupt ourselves, which allow us to go on and act so inhumanly to those we are supposed to be protecting and saving."

So far, we're pretty much on the same page.

"And that's what he did.

"The argument in the story runs:

"First, we tell everybody that we are bringing the best and the brightest over to Africa to bring civilization to a primitive, ignorant people."

Yes, the "White Man's Burden."

"But in reality, what we get are the failures of our own civilization, the ones that cannot make it here in Europe, the second rate, the corrupt, the losers from our own culture, who come over to see what they can do in this primitive land. But we mask that by inventing myths about the ones that go off by themselves, that they are really supermen, who are better than all the rest—like Kurtz. We turn them into gods . . ."

I think we begin to diverge here.

". . . what Conrad shows us is a bunch of second-rate losers who keep telling themselves and each other how great they all are, and how much power they wield because of their European connections, and Kurtz is the most god-like. And the only way to get anything at all done is to start acting the way they do, to get your grommets for the boat, and to get on with your job. The problem is, if you start acting like them, you become them. And that's what happens to Marlow."

"The change occurs inside," I believe he was warned by the company doctor.

"In the end, Marlow has become as much of a liar as any of them. (He could simply have said nothing to Kurtz's Intended, when he gets back to England. But he chooses to lie outright. And all his subsequent research on Kurtz with Kurtz's cousin and Kurtz's friends proves that Kurtz, with a little talent at a dozen things—very much like Frédéric Moreau in *Sentimental Education*, with his never-to-be-completed novel *Sylvio the Fisherman's Son* and his German waltzes and his landscape paintings—is just another Victorian loser who is without the determination—not to mention the vision—to become a writer or a musician or a painter—and so has gone off to Africa to become an ivory stealer instead, and may have found some happiness with his life lording over the natives, which the whites felt morally called upon not to let him have, and so dragged him, dying, back, then murdering [for sport] his woman.)"

No real differences here . . . well, I wouldn't consider them large differences, but you might.

"This was the same basic decision I made, by the by, when I decided to write my own anti-war novel, *The Fall of the Towers*, between 1962 and '64. I didn't have the basic information to write about what the war was doing to Vietnam, so I wrote a novel about what the war was doing to us—the ones who stayed at home. No, it wasn't very good. But it was the best a twenty- to twenty-one-year-old could do at the time. And it's still in print, for better or for worse."

I don't disagree with all that's in there, but I think there's more.

Now SAVE this email so you don't have to explain all this to someone else!!

You spent way too much time on it and me.
Love ya,
Vince

Tue, Sep 3, 2013 at 7:18 PM
Vincent Czyz
To: Samuel Delany
Subject: Darkness

Condescend all you want (I say that with a smirk, not with smoke coming out of my ears), but if you think the darkness is only outside and only the mist at the head of the river, I think you are quantifiably—as in a math equation—wrong. There are scads of evidence that the darkness is also within, including the gorgeous line about confounding one's white heart with the native's drums. There is so much of this evidence, I'm not sure why you've dismissed it. Even the part about the wilderness whispering to Kurtz suggests it (I think).

Anyway, upward and onward.

Vince

Tue, Sep 3, 2013 at 7:30 PM
Samuel Delany
To: Vincent Czyz
Subject: Hollowness

I admit I'm wrong about Kurtz not being described as hollow.

But I think Kurtz's hollowness is like all the white men's hollowness.

Kurtz's hollowness is what allows him to go native and shrug off his commitment to "civilization."

Believe me, I'm not being condescending in any way. I do think I'm right, though. Conrad's story is not essentially about Africa. He was there. He was appalled by what he saw, and he wanted to write about it, but couldn't do it directly—so he did it indirectly. (Achebe is right as far as he goes: it's not a story that gives any sort of portrait of Africa—of life among Africans. It gives a crushing portrait of whites in Africa.) Or that, he didn't see much of Africa, but only other white people—and the atrocities they effected. It could have taken place in any business office in any country of the world. It's about the way inhumanity develops among people with no real hope, who have nothing of their own to live for—and must aggrandize themselves to believe they're human, and pretend that every one around them is sub-human, in this case the black natives that they hunt down, at the end, over the rail of the boat, for sport. I too think it's a great work. But I think it's about a very specific situation—and not a general foray into metaphysics.

Best—

—Chip

Sep 3, 2013, 7:13 PM
Vincent Czyz
To: Samuel Delany
Subject: The quote
  Chip,
  I've gone back and checked the quote. It is as I quoted it. Here's more: "It
[the wilderness, I believe] echoed loudly within him because he was hollow at
the core. . . ." [ellipses are Conrad's.] He also says, "The wilderness had found
him out early . . . [ellipses are mine] I think it had whispered to him things
about himself which he did not know, things of which he had no conception
till he took counsel with this great solitude—and the whisper had proved irresistibly fascinating."
  Vince

Tue, Sep 3, 2013, 10:17 PM
Samuel Delany
To: Vincent Czyz
Subject: A re-capitulation . . .
  What I started to describe in an earlier email and cut myself off (acciden-
tally) was a situation Conrad saw firsthand but could not write about in a piece
destined for English publication:
  There were two tribes in the Congo, a peaceful Bantu-speaking tribe and
a small but far more aggressive and war-like tribe. The Belgians retained the
warlike tribe to make slaves of and control the peaceful tribe. To effect this,
they gave the war-like tribe guns.
  But they didn't give them bullets.
  The war-like tribe had to purchase their bullets from the Belgians. The
fee for bullets was something like three bullets for the amputated right hand
of a male member of the peaceful tribe. The war-like tribe would show up
with sacks of right hands and claim their ammunition—which, soon, they
needed or they would have been killed by the "peaceful" tribe, who developed a raging fear and hate for the war-like tribe. Pretty soon there were
too many hands to bury, and white and blacks both began to make piles of
them at the street corners—two and three stories high, as was reported by
several inspectors; the stench was appalling. It was estimated that more than
a hundred fifty thousand natives were maimed in that way—with machetes
the war-like tribe carried around for the purpose. Once it got started, no
one knew how to stop it, because the war-like tribe feared for their lives and
so did the Belgians. Yes, Conrad knew that this was inhuman and needed
something to intervene.
  Heart of Darkness was the best he could do.
  Nor do I think it's bad, given the Victorian constraints on him.

Now I've finished my "repugnant" sentence.

Best—

—Chip

Tue, Sep 3, 2013, 11:07 PM

Vincent Czyz

To: Samuel Delany

Subject: A re-capitulation .

Yes, I will read *H of D* again with a mind toward hollowness and white-ness . . . and I will try to do it soon. But if it turns out to be that simple (oh, Brussels, that whited sepulcher), I will be thoroughly disappointed. It will make it so much less complex and interesting for me. That said, Kurtz is most cer-tainly a subplot in any sense of the word as Marlow is our boy, but without that subplot, you barely have a good story, let alone a great one. "Exterminate the Brutes" and of course "The horror! The horror!" and Kurtz's fall from a decent man to something bestial give this story so much of its force. I suspect, though I have never argued this, that Conrad wanted to do a Greek tragedy obliquely . . . Kurtz the hero with a tragic flaw, etc. Through Marlow's eyes, this tragedy becomes far more subtle—and modern.

Vince

Wed, Sep 4, 2013, 8:11 AM

Samuel Delany

To: Vincent Czyz

Subject: H of D again . . .

This is where I think you are missing the point, wildly, Vince! Kurtz was NOT a decent man who fell from grace, as it were, into savagery. He was a loser who rose to some sort of happiness in the jungle—it's not our happiness, but it's the happiness of an exploiter, but it is still something that he thinks is worth fighting to maintain. Back at civilization, all the colonials talked about him as if he WERE a great man who had fallen from grace. (Because he's gone native—presumably because he has crossed a sexual boundary line.) So they have to "rescue" him and bring him back. The truth, however, is that he started out no greater than they are now. Their rescue IS "The horror! The horror!" Kurtz WATCHES THE PILGRIMS SHOOT HIS WOMAN through the window of the cabin, where he is too sick to intervene. He hears them call out, "Let's have some sport." You've fallen for all the illusions of colonialism that Conrad has so carefully set up about Kurtz and then goes to such lengths to undermine. Kurtz's essential mediocrity is what Marlow finds out, once he returns to England. That's the fantasy of colonialism that Marlow ends up supporting with his lie to the Intended. Your version is much simpler (and more optimistic) than the very dark reality the text gives us.

Try to imagine someone writing the following about *Huckleberry Finn*:

"*Huckleberry Finn* is a novel set two or three decades before the Civil War in the western United States, in which two young men, roughly the same age, one black, one white, take a boat trip together down the Colorado River. They spend many evenings talking together about their lives and plans. Now and again they get separated, or run into interesting characters along the way. But they always get back together again. The book is filled with beautiful nature writing, and their exposure to the western landscape along the river banks makes them become more and more thoughtful, mature, and helps them both achieve real adulthood. Throughout the book, the young black man, Huck, is eager to return to his aunt, the Widow Douglas, and tell her about all he has learned on the trip. The young white man, Jim, wants to get home to his family, his wife and his children, for the same reasons. This is a great and beautiful American novel about the force of landscape to change people who will spend quiet time and thoughtful time traveling through our land."

How do you start correcting somebody who reads Twain's novel in such a manner? Can you call it a misreading? The last sentence is absolutely one hundred percent true. Here and there, so are fragments of others. But, when the rest is that far off, does it matter? Or, rather, how much does it matter?

I really feel that not just yours but most readings of Conrad's novel today are just as far off—as most readings of *Moby-Dick* today are pretty wildly off. Conrad sets up the myths of colonialism and then goes to great and careful lengths to dismantle them.

PS—Or, more accurately, all through the story Conrad is dismantling them as he puts them together—by showing how they're constructed. He was there for two(?) years. He took a steam boat up the Congo River to Stanleyville. He had to deal with the inefficiency of the colonials along the way—we have photographs of the boat here and there being repaired—and watched it turn into some of the most inhuman behavior this side of the concentration camps fifty years later—or arguably more so, if not in its numbers, in its cruelty, bloodiness, and violence. He left, and was told it couldn't be written about. No one would publish it. He was not interested in writing a Greek tragedy praising a heroic mad-man who was part of a society who killed black folks for sport. He thought that was horrendous. That's why Marlow blows the horn to scare the natives away from the river's edge when the Pilgrims start firing. Anyway. See what your re-reading nets you—

—Chip

PPS—We don't even have the Victorian model of "character" in our critical armamentarium to help us read various nineteenth-century works that were written with the assumption that the concept of good and bad "character" represented a universal truth, which would always be with us.

When I say the "Pilgrims" are depicted in Conrad's novella as "losers," that's what I mean. They have no "character." They are morally lazy. They tell little "harmless" lies to make themselves look better, to make their lives easier. They have no sense that honesty to others and to themselves is extremely important, and to fail to have it is to set in motion all sorts of social evils. It is to be lazy and lack determination—oh, I don't need to do this today. I'll get to it eventually, if I ever do.

This is the prime flaw in the colonials in *Heart of Darkness*. It is a flaw Marlow has flirted with, if it hasn't completely taken him over. Character is knowing that you should be firm but even-handed to all people you deal with, high and low, but . . . well, I got angry and I hit my servant this morning. Oh, it doesn't matter. The notion that it doesn't matter, no matter how you justify it (he was black, he's uneducated, he doesn't really feel it, etc.) eventually leads to the piles of body parts rotting in the street, which, after all, we—the whites—didn't cut off. (Eventually, they ran out of hands in various sections of the country, so began to accept other body parts in exchange for bullets, feet, forearms, calves, etc. It leads to John D. Rockefeller calling out the National Guard to fire on men, women, and children protesters in Colorado at the beginning of the century—and the National Guard obeying.) We just told other blacks they had to do it, and—how can you blame them—they're just doing it to stay alive. Again, Conrad was there, he saw it, he took part in it.

I can remember moments when Iva learned lessons of character. And they shine out among my own memories. We were on Park Avenue, coming from her private school and we had gotten a slice of pizza, perhaps a block a way, and while she had picked it out, she realized it was not what she wanted (she doesn't like cheese) and was carrying on as only an unhappy seven-year-old coming from her Sixty-Eighth Street private school can carry on. Look, I said. If you don't like it, don't eat it. But she continued crying and leveling invectives at the world— Throw it away, and stop yelling, I said. So she did.

Just then, an old homeless woman passed, looked into the trash basket, and removed the slice and began to eat it. There were no more than three seconds between Iva throwing it away and the old woman salvaging it from the garbage. Iva watched, totally astonished. She was quiet for the next block. Then she said, holding my hand tightly: "I was acting very badly, wasn't I?"

"Well . . . yes," I said. "You were acting thoughtlessly."

This thoughtless laziness is the same flaw that Flaubert blames on the "men of his generation" for the failure of the Revolution of 1848. They lived too much in a fantasy world, didn't think about the consequences and promises of the revolution, and thus it failed. But they were young men who lived their lives that way, as Frédéric and Charles, Martinon and Cisy, Hussonet and Pellerin and the others—except the best and the worst, Dussardier and Sénécal—live. And Sénécal murders his one-time friend Dusardier, because they have ended up on opposite political sides.

It's what keeps them from being artists. (Frédéric.)

It's what keeps them from being effective politicians. (Charles.)

Wed, Sep 4, 2013, 2:24 PM
Vincent Czyz
To: Samuel Delany
Subject: Can't escape the Heart of Darkness . . .

Thinking about it, I think once again we may be closer in views than we appear. I'm saying that Kurtz would have put heads on stakes in Brussels—given the opportunity (power) as well as the absence of a police force and the absence of social restraints to prick his conscience (these last being the weakest; dictators flout them regularly if not daily). The only thing that could have prevented it in Africa would have had to have been found within himself—but wasn't. He therefore clearly lacks character and can be called mediocre, with the exception of his oratory skills. Marlow mentions "the gorgeous folds of a noble eloquence," I think is how it runs . . . and I think the implied comparison to clothing (a trapping of civilization which can be removed or stripped away, which is there to hide nakedness, to cover over) is deliberate.

Random thought.

Vince

Wed, Sep 4, 2013, 4:22 PM
Samuel Delany
To: Vincent Czyz
Subject: Inside out

There you go. I'm not surprised we're closer than it might seem.

Conrad starts to turn the whole traditional way of telling this story inside out with the frame: first we're introduced to a number of people who only have titles, the director of companies, the lawyer, etc. Then, when the story starts, and we expect to get full-blown character portraits, we just get more titles, the accountant, the Station Manager, etc. The naming strategy makes them all equal—which is Conrad's way of signaling that the "colonials" are finally us. Basically, the story has only two named characters, Marlow and Kurtz, and as they come closer and closer, we see Marlow turning into (or being revealed as) a Kurtz, until Marlow fights a sick Kurtz in the dark.

Oh, well, and onward . . .

—Chip

Sep 4, 2013, 5:56 PM
Vincent Czyz
To: Samuel Delany
Subject: No higher power

Yes, I think that is a very keen observation—WE are the nameless colonials. The namelessness always irritated me but now I see the point. Fascinating that a story with so much expository writing in it is still so hard to really pin down. I like to think Marlow is better than Kurtz . . . he is the Ancient Mariner in that he tells his moral tale (we can imagine over and over), but he has sentenced himself to it; no higher power coerced him. (I draw this parallel in my master's essay). It's a confession really.

Vince

Sep 5, 2013, 2:17 AM
Samuel Delany
To: Vincent Czyz
Subject: Confession

Yes, it's very much a confession. But it's a very carefully crafted confession (crafted by Conrad), a confession designed to mimic the way a real person would make it, not complete, that still withholds, here and there, and that's still biased in the penitent's favor. He has started out as a man who hates lies; he ends a man who lies easily to protect the Intended from the truth.

—Chip

Thu, Sep 5, 2013, 3:24 AM
Samuel Delany
To: Vincent Czyz
Subject: Ye Olde Dark Heart . . .

Another comment and (I hope) last PS, this one about your comment on Kurtz's rhetorical prowess. First, the mediocre and second-rate often talk a great game. That's the first "trope" that Conrad, I suspect, was trying to utilize. But at one with that is the fact that Marlow himself—who is not a success among his friends; he has no title—like Kurtz, he has merely a name; he's the wanderer, he's the one they support and like and find interesting, but he's not going to make any money nor has he so far—is also a great talker. The others'—the auditors of his tale—friendship for Marlow is a luxury they can afford. But neither fiscally nor socially does it directly improve their lives. The fascinating story of his hunt for Kurtz, which contains his confession of his own "corruption" in Africa, is the evidence . . . for his secondary social importance and of the part he plays in the story—as the tale's other great talker. And its revelation at the point it's positioned in the story develops the theme of Kurtz-appearing-more-and-more-like-Marlow/

Marlow-appearing-more-and-more-like-Kurtz, as they get closer and closer to their wrestling match—which is clearly supposed to recall Jacob wrestling with the Angel for his birthright and name.

—Chip

—September 3–4, 2013

18

Remembering Pete Seeger

(1916–2014)

Briefly our music advisor every summer for five years at Camp Woodland in the early 1950s, Pete Seeger is easily one of the ten people who have had the greatest intellectual effect on my life. He made me love America's folk music and through it the music of the world. His Hootenannies at the old Pythian Theater in Brooklyn were the highlight of my early adolescence. (Once, I got to sit on the stage with him, while he performed, because there were not enough seats in the theater.) Till I was twenty-five, I wasn't sure if I was going to be a folk singer or a writer—mostly because of Pete. He was the first performance artist whom I loved. His influence was so broad that there is no saying good-bye to it. This is not a good-bye, only a late thank-you.

You walked into Pete's presence and sat down, cross-legged on the grass in front of him, and suddenly you were singing songs in Swahili and Hebrew and Spanish and Hindi and from the Appalachians and the alleyways of New York 19 (in the old pre-zipcode system) that kids sang as they played games on the streets or ran in the fields or walked back home through the woods, or their parents or grandparents sang on their stoops, on their porches, and your world got bigger and richer and more beautiful, and to sing those songs meant you shared something with the people who had sung them before. That was what Pete was about. You learned what had made them laugh or grow pensive, or what had made them angry or sarcastic, as Pete told you where he'd learned them and why they'd been put together, and you underwent a musical agape that changed you, changed you forever . . .

Around a big log campfire, edged with rocks, one July or August night, in 1951 or '52, on the side of Mount Wittenberg, Pete taught fifteen or twenty of us kids "We Shall Overcome" and I heard it for the first time—and sang it, there in the dark, among crickets, trees, and stars. It seemed beautiful then, and it seems beautiful with the musicians gathered at the Garden four years ago on Pete's ninetieth birthday, in the mock-up in lights of the Clearwater Boat representing Pete's ecological project for cleaning up the polluted Hudson.

https://www.pbs.org/wnet/gperf/pete-seegers-90th-we-shall-overcome/820/

Since the night I learned it, I've seen people giggle at the song; I've seen people weep with reinvigorated hope when it was sung. I'm glad it's out there and that, among so many Pete brought us, I can still hear it.

As Pete's fellow Weaver, Lee Hays, said in his own thoughts on the history of their group, Pete was a genius. Hays was right—Pete was a unique hands-on genius. He could have been a newspaper man. He could have been a musicologist—as his mother and father were. And he was a charismatic live performer. He may have made what, today, seem to us to be mistakes. Looked at in their historical context, however, they are pretty explainable. He was both forthright and modest, in a way that goes along with his genius. The young American opera composer, Nico Muhly, whose opera *Two Boys* only just debuted at the Metropolitan, about a gay internet romance and its catastrophic end—well, I don't think Muhly's music would sound anything like it does if it had not been for Seeger and the musicians he influenced. Muhly's use of the folk tradition is one of the reasons I like his work so much. But Seeger's influence has been phenomenal, as everyone from Johnny Cash, to Bob Dylan, to Bruce Springsteen has openly celebrated. That's for openers . . .

Pete is still surprising me, even today. Here is a song I'd never heard him do before this morning—probably many of you who know his Clearwater work well—but I offer a link to it. It's his version of the Dylan song "Forever Young." And look at "The Story Behind Forever Young" as well; because the stories behind the songs were so much of what Pete himself was into making known. As a rule, I'm into owning your own age, and celebrating age and maturity as well as youth. But the truth is that all ages are good metaphors for important qualities that need to be supported. And as the song says at the end . . . well, listen.

https://www.youtube.com/watch?v=Ezyd4okJFqo

and the story:

http://www.youtube.com/watch?v=PW4XxXo6AmA

Yes, after Woodland, I attended Camp Rising Sun ("An International Scholarship Camp for Boys," back then), but Camp Woodland, which I went to for five years, was for me far more important and the far richer experience of people, community, music, theater, and culture. And the music was regularly invigorated by Pete's annual summer visit to camp. Rising Sun tried hard—and is still trying, I gather. When I went, however, it was all-boys and rather elitist. They were very smart boys, certainly. That was a plus; but after the richness of Woodland's community program—we worked with the people living in the Catskill hills and woods around the camp, collected their songs and stories, and their culture—Rising Sun and its "Indian" traditions, without a Native American in sight anywhere in the neighborhood, seemed a bit artificial.

The day I arrived at Rising Sun, Pete Seeger—who died last night at age ninety-four—was the first Rising Sun alumnus whose name got mentioned, in passing, probably by our new music counselor, Allan Sklar. I found that exciting and wondered why I hadn't heard it before. I can't—nor would I want to—speak for Rising Sun today. I wish them only the best and applaud what they have done and been doing; the many changes I know have occurred since I was there can only be for the better. At least today they are coed. By the end of that summer, though I'd had an enjoyable time (by no means was it an unpleasant one; once, before Woodland, I'd gone to a summer camp that was a nightmare), still, I'd pretty much figured out why. At Rising Sun, there was a lot of talk about "the philosophy of camp." Once, at Rising Sun, I asked why we didn't have more to do with the people in the area, and was immediately told that "insurance" made that impossible—which was probably true, but which was also a sign to me something was wrong with the social ecology between the camp and community it sat in. At Woodland, because of the ideals of Seeger and many folks who shared them, including the camp owner and his family, we lived a philosophy and thought about it afterward. We helped out farmers on neighboring farms; we patrolled the edge of a forest fire with other local boys and girls, hiking through a charred landscape on which you could see where the flames had stopped as if their limit had been knifed into the earth. Campers and locals carried water canisters strapped to our backs, pumping out silver streams to hose down the ash-covered logs and fallen, leafless branches.

Campers ran a folk museum in the neighborhood, too, that displayed old farm tools, spinning wheels, looms, and butter churns, or sat on porches in front of a bellied-out screen door, while the people we were helping—or who had donated the handmade quilts or tools or old photos of the land we exhibited—told us about their lives and their families' lives and, while our plastic tape reels turned at the doweled legs of their chairs beside their work shoes, sang us their songs. That was an extension of what Pete was about; though I could say as easily Pete was an extension of what the camp, he so generously gave his time to, was equally about.

—January 28, 2014
Chicago

19

A, B, C . . .

Preface and Afterword to *Three Short Novels*

1. Preface

The Jewels of Aptor . . . The Ballad of Beta-2 . . . They Fly at Çiron . . .
Aptor, Beta-2, Çiron . . . A, B, C, and there's my title.

The subtitle tells what follows: *Three Short Novels.*

This book contains my first published novel, a science fantasy, *The Jewels of Aptor,* much as I wrote it in the winter of 1961–62. Officially it was released December 1, 1962. I saw copies late that November.

As I'd conceived and written the book, its audience was my brilliant, talented wife of those years, the poet Marilyn Hacker—nine months younger than I, but always at least a year ahead of me in school. Walking up and over the school roof to get to classes, as all the entering students had been instructed to do, so as not to bother the elementary school students with whom we shared the building, we'd met on our first day of high school. Two years later Marilyn went on to New York University as an early admissions student at fifteen and finished her classes in three years. When we married on August 24, 1961, she was eighteen and I was nineteen.

Those interested in the invaluable part she played in discussing the ideas in *Aptor* and getting it published—she wrote one of the poetic spells in the book—can read about it in my autobiography, *The Motion of Light in Water* (1988; expanded edition 1992). Without her, it wouldn't—it *couldn't*—have happened. After our marriage, Marilyn's second job was with the publisher, Ace Books. She took my manuscript in under a pen name. That's how it was submitted. That's how it was read. That's how it was accepted.

Only when contracts were drawn up, did she admit that the writer was her husband—and the name on the contracts was hastily changed to mine.

Eventually it got a few (generous) reviews; but the thousand-dollar advance I received—$500 on contract signing in April and $500 in December on publication—back then would have covered fifteen months of our $52 a month rent on our second-floor, four-room tenement apartment—rent for more than a year! (Would that it did so today.) And I could think, "Hey, I'm making my living as a writer!"

And I had a publisher. If I handed in anything that more or less met my editor's genre expectations, I assumed, I could sell it.

For my second book (which today is *They Fly at Çiron*), I took two old fantasy stories and quickly wrote three more. Each section had as a protagonist someone who was a minor character in one of the others. One involved only a name change for a character in one of the already completed tales.[1] Nor were the landscapes the tales took place in much related to one another. Rapidly reading over passages, I decided on a few more things that might connect them and wrote out bridges from one to the next. But I put into *Çiron* neither the time nor the intensity of thought and imagination I had put into *Aptor*.

A few weeks after I handed it in to Ace Books, Don Wollheim rejected it.

Today, I feel that rejection was the most important thing that happened to me in my first year of publishing. I'll try to explain how and why it was *so* useful, *so* instructive, *so* important—though I don't know if, finally, it's possible to describe it in a definitive way.

Understand, I'd had novels rejected before. I'd been writing them since I was thirteen, and from seventeen on I had been submitting them to New York publishers—who'd been declining them. But also I'd been getting a fair amount of attention for them. Two years before, Marie Ponsot, a poet who had been very supportive of both Marilyn and me, spoke to her friend Margaret Marshall, an editor at Harcourt Brace. At Marie's request and on the strength of one of those early manuscripts, Marshall had secured me a work-study scholarship for the Bread Loaf Writers' Conference at Middlebury, Vermont. While attending the workshops and lectures on the grassy and sunny Bread Loaf campus, where, even before the inception of the already legendary conference, novelists as varied as Anthony Hope and Willa Cather had written some of their most critically acclaimed pieces, I'd worked those two July weeks as a waiter in a white-painted dining room with square glass panes in the window doors along one wall. I'd attended the lectures, readings, and novel-writing workshops; I'd talked with writers and editors, new and established, and found two or three who were willing to read my work and were even enthusiastic about it. Both before and since Bread Loaf, I'd submitted my novels. They'd been rejected, too. What remains from those rejections, however, are the hours or even days of encouragement preceding them.

Wollheim's rejection, brief and final, I recall with documentary clarity.

Wollheim phoned me at our apartment at 629 East Fifth Street in New York City. The phone sat on an end table, discarded by my mother-in-law in the Bronx, and I sat on the armchair's arm. He said, "Hi, Chip. This is Don—Don Wollheim. I read your second manuscript this weekend." Somewhere in an office on Forty-Eighth Street in Midtown, he paused. "I don't think they quite make a book, Chip. So I'll pass on them. But I'm certainly interested in seeing the next one you do. Okay?"

I said, "Oh . . . *um*, yeah. Okay. Yes, I see! *Um* . . . thanks."

Don said, "You're welcome. So long."

I said, "Good-bye . . . *Um*, Good-bye," and hung up, surprised and disappointed.

I was twenty. It was still painful when I wrote about it in my autobiography twenty-five years later, so I told it there as quickly as I could. Here's a little more of the tale:

I wanted to talk to Marilyn—badly—but she was out looking for work; so after I hung up I went downstairs and outside for a walk, to think over what had happened. It seemed clear, though.

One reason why I felt it so deeply was because with this particular rejection, the rejection of what would become *Çiron*, I had been turned down by an editor (and publisher) who had accepted something already.

Walking through the chill spring slums, I thought about the differences between the kinds of work I'd done for the book that had been accepted (so enthusiastically too), and the kinds for the book that had been turned down (so summarily). With *Aptor*, before each scene, each writing session at the writing table, or with my notebook, crossed-legged on the day bed, I'd worked to picture as many details of that scene and its physicality as I could. Many of those scenes had begun as disturbingly vivid dreams, so that for a number of them—the waterfront, the jungle, the beach, the temple, and the morning light or the evening light that suffused them—already I had complete images in mind, in some cases unsettlingly so.

Others, though, I'd had to visualize from scratch.

Aptor had commanded high imaginative involvement throughout. I had not used all the results or even most of them. But having them when I needed them seemed to loan the work (for me) coherence and authority.

For *Çiron*, however, I'd taken some odd texts, hastily forced them into what I thought might do for a linear narrative, which I'd realized in the hour since the rejection was nowhere near linear enough. I had read over passages quickly and decided what might connect them to the next and wrote it out; but I'd put into it neither the time nor the intensity of thought and imagination I had put into the earlier book.

For a scene here or there I'd done a bit of the mental work. But the things that I'd felt (that I'd hoped. . . .) had made *Aptor* lively, vivid, and given it momentum, were the things I'd failed to do in *Çiron*. Don had read it, felt how thin it was. Now, so did I—and I realized as well what the world's reaction would be, as exemplified by Don and Ace Books.

I'm glad I saw this—with only a sentence from Wollheim to prompt me over the phone, a kindness granted my second book doubtless because he'd published my first; and probably because I *was* twenty. In those days, young writers starting to sell, when and if they found themselves in that position, often didn't understand this:

It didn't need to be another kind of written piece. It needed to be a better quality piece. The book didn't need more sex. It didn't need more violence. It didn't need more action. It needed to be better organized from start to finish. It needed to be more richly imagined, first part to final. That meant I had to do the work, start to finish, I hadn't done. Had I done it, that work would have suggested better organization because I would have seen the material more vividly along with its many incoherent lax spots. The missing or extraneous material would have stood out more clearly and provided me with a clearer view of how to fix it—delete, insert, rewrite, expand, replace, connect to something earlier or further on, several of them or one, the choice hinging on the clarity and intensity of my apprehension of the whole book.

As I'd read and reread *Aptor*, during its composition, that's how the details had come to me: in further specifics of landscape, characterization, psychology, dialogue, and incidents for the story.

This was the work I hadn't done on *Çiron*.

I thought this, however, not because any of it had been mentioned in the workshops at Bread Loaf or in E. M. Forster's *Aspects of the Novel* or in Lajos Egri's *The Art of Dramatic Writing* or in Orwell's essays or even in Gertrude Stein's *Autobiography of Alice B. Toklas* or *Lectures in America*—books I'd read on writing that already had been, up till then, so helpful. Today I suspect five different writers, each going through some version of this, might go through it in five different ways and arrive at five different conclusions, all of which would accomplish much the same. What seemed most important, however, as I walked through the smells and confusion of our crowded neighborhood was: Think about this seriously. Your life hangs on it. (That's another year's rent you don't have, now. . . !) You can't fuck around . . .

It's surprising how far that can take you—about anything.

Returning from my walk, past the East Side tenements, the fish store on Avenue C, turning into the dead-end of East Fifth Street where we lived, walking over the broken pavement before the parking garage's gaping door, by the plate glass window edged in the flaking paint of the bodega next to it, set back, and up three steps, I thought: If I'm a writer and I want my pieces to place, I have to do that work.

This was not a case of writing the kind of pieces that would place. I could decide that pretty easily. I needed to write the *quality* of pieces that would place. It was neither the acceptance nor the rejection that had been so instructive, but the differences between them and what I knew now I might expect from each, and the information about my future in the world those differences comprised.

I knew what the two kinds of work felt like, behind my face, in my belly, along my arms, in my feet against the floor, my hands moving over the typewriter keys or across the notebook pages as I gripped my ballpoint, which now I could associate each with their different results.

If each had a shape, a shape I could grasp at in the world, even if those shapes were not entirely pensive, spatial, mental or muscular, descriptions of their form or the content that could arrive to fill them out would always be incomplete—including this one. But now I had a nonverbal sense of what each was.

When Marilyn came home, we talked about what I might do. In my journal I'd already made notes on possible projects. One was the barest sketch for a trilogy of SF novels that would show what war was like in its effects on the country attacking, as opposed to the country invaded.

After several conversations with Marilyn, a few days later we walked across the Brooklyn Bridge to visit some friends in Brooklyn Heights for brunch. Walking back, we talked about it more. When we got home, I sat down in front of the typewriter, typed out a title page for the entire project, and began the first of the three-volume series I had planned out with her, and began the work I needed to generate the material necessary to construct its first volume, in order to write the best book that, at that very immature age, I could manage.

Basically I'd decided that if I was going to write something of the highest quality I could achieve, it had best be about something I felt was important. And we were a country at war.

It was a *lot* of work—I've written about it several times. The middle volume was more work than I'd ever imagined it might be. Often, I was afraid the work would defeat me. There are places where I believe it did. But I also knew, by now, that if I didn't do it, not only couldn't I sell it, but I couldn't live with myself either. By now I was afraid to avoid the work or to try for short cuts.

The three books of *The Fall of the Tower* are not here. But they are still in print.

It's worth repeating: The rejection of *Çiron* gave me the chance to compare two things I had written, not in terms of the differences between the surfaces of the texts, but rather the differences between the mental work I had done writing the accepted text and the mental work I had shirked writing the rejected one.

The writing of *The Ballad of Beta-2* came along to interrupt the trilogy, during the time I'd thought, for a while, the second volume would stop me. I began it in the middle of that stalled second book. I wanted to write a short novel unconnected to the War of Toromon, so that I could give myself the feeling of starting and completing *something*. Soon I realized I had to stop (or more accurately realized I had already stopped) thinking about selling in order to attain and sustain the level I was reaching for—and always missing and going back in hope of pulling myself closer. Today I suspect even that conflict muddled the causes of the problems I was having.

The Ballad of Beta-2 itself was interrupted when I managed to get back my wind on the trilogy's recalcitrant book two. After the third volume appeared, I finished *Beta-2*. (Yes, I managed to complete the trio; after volume two, work on the third was as surprisingly easy as, for the second book, it had been un-expectedly hard. That meant—to me—it was time to go on to projects which would be harder.) *Beta-2* appeared as the shorter half of another Ace Double at the start of 1965 and then in an Ace volume containing *The Ballad of Beta-2* and another of my short science-fiction novels, *Empire Star*. In 1982 *Beta-2* was again released by Ace, this time in a stand-alone paperback that remained in print till 1987. Altogether the book had a run of twenty-two years in print, as did *The Jewels of Aptor*.

Although *They Fly at Çiron* was, in fact, the third of the three here to be published (which is how it earns its "C"), while I think of it as my second novel, actually it was my nineteenth published. The reason I published it at all is because in 1991, in Amherst, Massachusetts, I took it out and reworked it end to end.

In 1993, *They Fly at Çiron* had two separate hardcover printings, a trade hard-cover and a special edition, both from Ron Drummond's incomparable small press, Incunabula. Two years later, a hardcover and a mass-market paperback followed from Tor Books.

The above is all to say, whether the effort was wasted, invisible, or has some-how left its signs either in pleasing or in awkward ways, by the time these three were actual books, I'd worked on them as hard as I could—as did the publish-ers to see that they were successful in the marketplace—and I hope it says it in a way that conveys three further facts (the second of which I'll return to in my "Afterword"):

First, with each book, moments arrived in the creation process when the text felt as if it required more work than I could possibly do. I gave up. I despaired. Then I came back and tried to do it anyway. In short, it was a process like any other human task. What made it different, however, was that it was primarily internal: the "shape" of its internality made it wholly of itself and only indi-rectly and incompletely communicable in any rigorous way.

Second, over a very, very long time—tens of thousands to multiple millions and even billions of years, rather than over decades or centuries—a congruence arises between creatures and the conditions that are the landscapes in which they and we dwell.[2] Along with that congruence arises the illusion of a guiding intelligence. (There may be a truth behind the illusion. There may not be. But that is metaphysics, however, and not our concern here.) But that illusion is an indirect effect, not a direct cause, for which the extraordinarily protracted duration of the process is the first, but by no means the only, evidence. The similarly structured illusion of direct animal and human communication through the senses, by the same process imposes the effect/illusion of a metaphysics we arrogantly presume must exist behind our necessarily mediated perceptions to form a reality resonant with our aesthetic wonders and distress, our appetitive pleasures and pain, our political urgencies, disasters, and satisfactions, and their largely unseen structuring forces: another illusion, another effect. The same indirect process that feels so direct to us (and probably to all the animals who utilize it) is what allows wolves to bay out to warn their pack of danger or approaching prey—and humans to tell stories, gossip, and write novels, as well as create cultures: The cultures we form are the only realities we have, however, or can have any access to, and our ignorance of which, when we are aware of it, all-too-infrequently we take as a mandate for both honesty and humility (the engine of ethics at its best), even as these realities of which we are a part create the curiosities, the yearnings, the passions to know so often perceived to be that arrogance itself. That these multiple realities are parsimoniously plural, however (without having been directly caused by evolution; only the ability to construct them and respond to them is evolutionary, not what is constructed), is the first, but by no means the strongest, evidence for their complex relations,[3] however functional or problematic their multiplicity.

Third, the work of art—a story we tell or a novel we write—can be and can exhibit a complex organic structure that appears to reflect some of the world (some of one reality or another; or even some of one that does not exist) because it evolves *from* the world; it mimics it in much the way certain insects camouflage themselves as the bark or the leaves of the trees they sometimes rest on, in the same way that intelligence can sometimes mimic something greater than itself, both spatially and temporally, even while simpler in its details and protracted operations; thus we can camouflage what we have to say as a series of happenings from life. And sometimes something that is not mind but that here and there entails one or millions of minds, at different levels and at different tasks—mind that is as likely to be on the way out (like gigantism in dinosaurs) as it is to be developing into something more useful, the results of which we will not live to see because it (they) will not manifest in any way we might notice or even it itself might notice or comprehend—if ever—for another handful of millions of years or more, is only another wrinkle in the bark or the leaf—another fold in the monad, as Leibniz would have it.

The possibility that from time to time such aesthetic work as I have so inadequately described can create anything of interest is another effect: direct causality between work and result is as much an effect here as it is another sort of communication. But because that interest is communicated and therefore indirect, incomplete, constituted of its own inaccuracy and slippage, already there in whatever education from which we can construct our experience of utterances (including what can be spoken about), or of texts (including what can be written about; and they are not necessarily the same). From time to time, locally or briefly, however, something of interest occurs. We suspect it does mostly because, however briefly and locally, we are interested.

—April 17, 2014
Philadelphia

2. An Afterword

Something happens when a writer's readership grows substantially larger than the dozen odd members of a university workshop or even a full auditorium of listeners at a college or a library reading. Approximately every seven or eight years, with each book of fiction and nonfiction I've written (though not every essay collection), I've cycled through the experiences I'm about to discuss.

I will meet a new person, sometimes a young woman who has just published her first book and with whom I'm giving a reading, or an editor who has recently joined a publishing house to whom my own editor is introducing me in an office hallway, or a stranger who has recognized me a moment after I have stepped from the door of Barnes & Noble onto Union Square North. Over fifty years these people have been male, female, black, white, Asian, Native American, Dominican, Inuit, African, southern or northern European, Haitian, Jamaican, Martiniquais, half a dozen sorts of Latino and Latina; they have been gay; they have been straight; they have been transgendered or cis-gendered; they come from New York or San Francisco, Boston or L.A., from Peoria or Salt Lake City, and many places between; they have been Jewish, Baptist, Episcopalian, Catholic, Mormon, Muslim, Buddhist, atheist, disabled or temporarily abled. Sometimes it's a teacher at a university or a high school where I'm giving a talk, sometimes it's a student—though once, as I was walking down Eighty-Second Street, leaning on my cane, a city sanitation worker in a green T-shirt, who, recognizing me from a picture in a recent *Entertainment Weekly* article, leaped from the back of his groaning truck, ran up and gripped my shoulder with an oily glove of orange rubber, to tell me what I will tell in its time, and, three weeks back, when I was returning to New York from a guest professorship at the University of Chicago, it was the uniformed fellow at the curbside baggage stand outside the United Airlines terminal at O'Hare, who, after I'd gone inside to wait for a wheelchair (arthritis makes getting around airports on my own all but impossible these days), ran in after me, stood in front of me, and declared: "Samuel R. Delany . . . ? The writer guy? I'm right, aren't I? Hey, my absolutely *favorite* book of yours is . . ."

That's what so many of them want to tell me.

This one or that one will name *Through the Valley of the Nest of Spiders*, my most recent novel, or my very first, which you have in this book, or my tenth, or my fifth or my fifteenth, or my book of science fiction and fantasy stories, *Aye, and Gomorrah*, or my book of naturalistic novellas, *Atlantis: Three Tales*, or one of my contemporary novels, *Dark Reflections* or *The Mad Man*, or a science fiction novel like *Nova* or *Trouble on Triton*. It can be a nonfiction work. The book named can be an award winner or a one-time bestseller or something published by an independent publisher that not two thousand people can have read. It can be my twentieth, from a press out of Normal, Illinois, and Tallahassee, Florida, specializing in avant-garde fiction. It can be my twelve-hundred-plus-page fantasy series in four volumes, *Return to Nevèrÿon*, or a ninety-page novella once sold as a stand-alone paperback such as *Empire Star*.

And it can be—and has been, repeatedly, over fifty years as well as at least once over the last seven or eight—each of the novels here.

It pleases me to think there might be a connection between that experience and the way I write. Do I know there is? No, I can't know. No writer can. (So we decide—or hope—it's because we're quite smart . . . as we take a wrong turn, lose a laptop, drop and step on our reading glasses, or inadvertently call a business acquaintance the name of someone she or he despises, who, the moment we met, came to mind—or something else stupid.) Because such indications of popularity, however poorly they correlate with quality, hinge on reception rather than creation, they suggest—even if it's never a sure thing—a reason to gamble on reprinting.

The forty-five-odd experiences over the more than fifty years from which I've culled these instances might seem a lot, because I've crammed more than half of them into not a page-and-a-half, with a number doing double, even triple, duty—the woman outside of Barnes & Noble, the most recent one to mention *The Jewels of Aptor*, was a Mormon here in the city with her brother (who'd never heard of me); the last young man who liked *The Ballad of Beta-2* was a student and an African Muslim (in a motorized wheelchair). Sometimes three or four such encounters have happened in a year. Some years have gone by, though, with no such encounters at all. Were you waiting for the next one, you'd be more frustrated than not.

Here's something that better suggests how little public attention that is: Only three times in fifty years have I seen someone reading a book of mine in public. Once, while I was sitting on an IRT subway car in 1964 or '65, I saw woman across from me reading the second volume of my *Fall of the Towers* trilogy. Once, when Marilyn and I were returning from London a week before

Christmas in 1974, coming through Kennedy Airport we saw a book rack full of just-released *Dhalgren* and, minutes later, a sailor in unseasonal whites relaxing at his flight gate reading a copy. (With his knees wide in a tubular chair that they used in airports back then, he must have been flying to somewhere in the Caribbean or Central of South America—as we walked by with our daughter in a stroller.) Finally, on a Philadelphia bus, three years ago, I saw someone, certainly a student at Temple where I teach, reading a trade paperback of *Atlantis: Three Tales*, a week after the publishers had released a new printing.

Three times in fifty years.

It doesn't seem so many now, does it?

*   *   *

Not just *Aptor* and *Beta-2*, but all three here had a run of well over a decade in bookstores—and that was in a book environment where the average life of a new volume on the store shelf was under three weeks. That interests editors and marketing folk, trying to anticipate how this book will do. I'm interested in that peripherally, of course—but not centrally. "No man but a blockhead," said Dr. Samuel Johnson, the poet, scholar, and writer who put together the first comprehensive English language dictionary, "ever wrote, except for money." A surprising number of writers since Dr. Johnson pursued the life of writing, however, have been blockheads—many of them good writers, too. You have to think about too many other things while you're writing that drive such considerations from mind, so that dwelling on money is distracting, intimidating, and generally counterproductive. Also, the number of people who, if they were not calling me, personally, a blockhead for wanting to write at all, thought I was nuts, strange, or patently out of my mind for doing it (and it was never a munificent living) seemed at the time innumerable—starting with my dad. When I won a prize in high school or a scholarship, he was proud. And when his best friend, our downstairs neighbor, who wrote and published children's books for black kids like myself but made his living editing immense economics textbooks he called "doorstoppers," read some of the work I'd written at sixteen or seventeen and told my father I would probably be in print before I was voting age (back when that was twenty-one and the drinking age was eighteen. Since then, they've reversed), Dad even paid the sixty-seven dollars to have my third novel retyped by a professional typist in Queens—the one that got me the Bread Loaf Writers' Conference scholarship I mentioned in my Preface.

It never appeared.

Mom had a more liberal attitude. She wanted me to do whatever would make me happy, and from childhood on she encouraged me in all my enthusiasms. Clearly, though, she shared Dad's misgivings. Except for intermittent relapses—which were most appreciated and probably the only reason Dad and I had any positive relationship at all—generally my father argued and raged about those enthusiasms. My mother mulled over them and looked glum. They had lived through the Great Depression. Like many parents in the 1950s, they were concerned about security and their children's livelihood. They had seen many disasters themselves. We, who were too young to remember those disasters firsthand, however, felt the manifestations of their fears were the harshest parental oppression. I wish I could say eventually I learned they were right, as they kept telling me I would. ("Just wait. You'll see . . .") In truth, however, they weren't. Some things were much worse. Some things were far better. Many were different. The world had changed—including the speed of its changing.

Novel writers, short story writers, science fiction writers, and many writers from the "unmarked" category, which bears the genre mark "literary," have told me they cannot read their past or early work. When they try, many say, they feel something akin to pain.

That's not me, however.

Possibly it has to do with how I write—though I can't be sure.

I'm dyslexic—severely so. Therefore, to put together a manuscript that's readable, much less printable (by my own standards), I must read it and correct it and reread it and correct it again and reread it again; not three or four times, but twenty-five, thirty-five . . . Some sections I must read forty-five times or more. (Now you know one reason so many people—not just my parents but teachers and friends—thought I was nuts for wanting to write at all. Clearly I was so bad at the basics and everyone around me was better.) It's the first five or so readings, however, I find painful. Among them, someone who is not dyslexic has to read it too and mark those places, usually with underlining, where the words are out of order and often incomprehensible or even missing, where I've spelled words so badly you can't tell what they are, or when I've dropped other words and phrases that must be there for the sentences to make sense.

I'm a grammar fanatic. I have been since I was in the sixth grade—probably to compensate for the other things I did and still do so poorly. Mistakes slip through even now; now and again other readers catch them, for which I am always grateful. (You may find some among these pages.) I couldn't—and I still can't—spell some simple words correctly three times in a row. But I was the best in my fifth, sixth, and seventh grade English classes at diagramming sentences on the blackboard (in those days when blackboards were black, not green) or on school tests. ("If you can do that, I don't understand why you can never remember how to spell 'orange.' It doesn't make sense." It didn't make sense to me, either. But my seventh grade English teacher's sincerity, concern, and honesty made me love her at the same time that it made me feel I was profoundly and irrevocably flawed.) Still, it's why, today, I'm comfortable using both formal grammar and informal grammar at all colloquial levels. Point out the errors you find, and I can usually tell you why they're errors and often the formal names these errors have or once had and how to correct or improve them. But these are what my dyslexia initially prevents me from seeing. (Today we know it's neurological. Back then we didn't.) In the course of my rereadings, however, phrases, words, or sections that to me are painful—for stylistic and content reasons that become one as the hand falls from the keyboard, from the page, and the ear and the eye take over to judge or to approve or, more frequently, to find fault with what I've put down—I excise or clarify so that, over time, the manuscript moves closer and closer to something I can enjoy. That's how I wrote my earliest books, the ones here; that's how I write them today. That's how I build a text I'd like to read: by way of retardations, excisions, expansions, compressions, simplifications, and rewordings, along with numberless additions and plain corrections. Each layer is the trace of a different "self" as much mine as the self who tries to impose the effect of a controlled voice by suppressing one or enhancing another—to form a text I hope will fall within sight of my notion of the way a "good writer" writes, even though I am not one "naturally."

The only way I can get a text to feel (to me) that it is one my true thoughts might inhabit is through layers of revision.[4] If I try to express anything directly that I believe deeply and intensely without a fair amount of thought beforehand and during a many-layered process afterward, what comes out is banal, overwrought, and riddled with errors in which clichés and imprecisions mock anything one might call intention.

Another way of saying the same thing is that the unexamined "I" in an unexamined "world" is boring.

I'm much too much like everyone else—because, presumably, the world has made me so: more venal than I would like to appear or admit, shy, deluded by clichés and common-places, eager to be liked, and for accomplishments, intellectual or social, that most of the time I feel I do not possess.

Possibly this is also why, ten or fifteen years after a book of mine has appeared, when I pick it up and again start reading, I find sentences that strike me as pleasant, scenes that seem well-orchestrated, passages that appear to project their ideas with clarity, or an observation on the world that registers as true for its time and that goes some way toward delineating, if not recreating, my feelings, or other passages whose grammar and logic convince me they are the utterances of a single mind rather than the dozen deeply flawed selves I had to be shattered into by the world to live in it, much less to write about it. (Is it the layers of correction or the illusion of unity that does the pleasing? I can hope. But I can never know. They are the same thing seen from different sides: an effect and what creates it.) If they please, they please to the extent I have forgotten how the disjunctive cataclysm that I am wrote them—though also I know that so much rereading can, as easily as it might produce excellence, fix the mistakes in a text in our mind so deeply that, when we come back to it years on, we skim errors in expression and thought without seeing them because unconsciously they are so familiar.

Neither the writer's pleasure *nor* pain justifies returning a work to print, however; nor is either a reason for letting a text languish. (Sometimes a work is about something no longer of current or compelling interest, but that's another tale.) All language is habit, as I remind my writing students regularly, speaking or writing. You learn to write badly, to overwrite, or to write dull, banal stories much the way you learn to write well—well as a given epoch sees it. (Lacking a National Academy of the sort France, Italy, and Spain have had for centuries, America finds the surface criteria changing radically every twenty or thirty years.[5]) I do believe, however, that the amount and quality of mentation that go into the fictions I find interesting are different from the amount and quality that go into the ones I find thin. Only hard-won habits can fix the difference within us—if we're lucky. And no one can be sure it has—ever. As well, I believe the writer must look at the minute places where her or his relationship to the world is different from most, for me personally to find that relationship of interest. (Often I've wished I had broader tastes.) To find what deeply engages us, within a field of our apparent differences we must interrogate our similarities for the sake of potential and possibilities, either good or bad. That can mean, for the same ends, the writer is trying to dramatize a feeling of difference within that field of similarities, so that often the writer has a sense of having undertaken a more difficult analytical dance than anticipated. The writers signals both differences and similarities by additions to the text, by organization of the textual elements, or by absences in the text, vis-à-vis the average productions of that day or era—and, as much as they are frowned on today, by direct statement of emotions, most effective when they are used indirectly. How to distinguish between which texts are better and which texts are worse is, ultimately and finally, anyone's guess, and the shifts in criteria, decade after decade, century after century, even place to place in what we always assume is a more unified culture than it ever is or could possibly be, and the general attitudes toward following the various paths of least resistance that mark out the cliché, the cluttered, or the thin *don't* make it easier. Those shifts in criteria, however, all indicate traces of a struggle with those problems, though not necessarily in a manner that either you or I might feel was successful. That's why it's worth it for both of us to accustom ourselves to the way things were written a generation or two, a century or two, a millennium or two before us, in India or Italy, in China or the Czech Republic, in Timbuktu or Teheran, Portugal or Japan, in Leningrad or Moscow, Brazil, New Orleans, Mexico City, Argentina, or Chicago—which is to say, the ways of reading the texts were written for, at various places at various times—for the pleasure of the game if only because of what, here and there, we can learn about how they made the game pleasurable and use it for our own profit, if it still works today. It's the concert of all these that justify republication, a decision from which, for the reasons outlined here (mostly in dependent qualifying clauses, or even parentheses) the author, if still living, is always excluded. Only someone else who has managed to educate him- or herself to read the texts of the past, even from only forty or fifty years ago, and is sensitive to the problems and concerns of the present, can make the call—and finally for pretty personal reasons—as to whether or not a text merits republishing. We all hope—readers and writers both—we will be lucky enough to have such editors.

*   *   *

When *The Jewels of Aptor* came back from copyediting, Don Wollheim asked me to cut 720 lines—about 10 percent of the book.

Standing at the far side of his desk, I must have looked surprised.

"Huh?" I asked. "Yeah, sure. But why? Was there some particular place you thought it was too . . . loose?"

"Oh, no," Don said. "But it has to fit into a hundred forty-six pages. It casts off at 720 lines too long." He would do it for me, if I wanted—

"Oh, *no!*" I said. "No. . . . That's all right. I'll do it!" I reached across the desk for the manuscript in its red rubber band.

Completed when I was nineteen, contracted for not quite a month after my twentieth birthday (since the copyright laws changed in 1976, the phrase has become "in contract"), and cut down by fifteen pages a few weeks later, the first edition of *The Jewels of Aptor* was published that winter, where I pick up the story:

In 1966, an editor a few years older than I, Terry Carr, joined the staff at Ace Books, the U.S. publisher of all the books I had written up till then except *Nova*. I have written before, as have many before me, that the history of post-World War I science fiction is the history of its editors: Hugo Gernsback, F. Orlin Tremaine, McComas and Boucher, Raymond Palmer, Howard Browne, Ian and Betty Ballantine, John W. Campbell, H. L. Gold, on through Avram Davidson, Cele Goldsmith, Don Wollheim, Harlan Ellison, Frederik Pohl, Damon Knight, Michael Moorcock, Larry Ashmead, David Hartwell, Judy Lynn and Lester Del Rey, Betsy Wollheim, Beth Meacham, Patrick Nielsen Hayden, Betsy Mitchell, L. Timmel Duchamp, Steve Berman, Kelly Link, and Warren Lapine. (In this incomplete list, many were writers as well—Campbell, Davidson, Pohl, Knight, Moorcock, Ellison, Duchamp, and Link are *significant* writers, whose fiction remains influential for any real understanding of our genre's development—though their editorial force and direction is central to their careers.) Carr is among those editors. He edited the first novel of William Gibson, Joanna Russ, and Kim Stanley Robinson, as well as Ursula K. Le Guin's *The Left Hand of Darkness* and a dozen other memorable titles for his Ace Science Fiction Special series.

In 1967, Carr did for me one of the most generous things an editor can do. "Chip, I was just rereading your first novel, *The Jewels of Aptor*. I enjoyed it. Don told me we cut it for length, though. I was thinking of doing a new edition. Do you have an uncut copy? I'd like to take a look."

"Actually," I said, "I do . . ."

In the top drawer of a file cabinet in the kitchen of the fourth-floor apartment where we had lived for a couple of years on Seventh Street, I'd left an uncut carbon copy. The apartment had been more or less inherited by a woman I'd known in Athens during my first, six-month European jaunt. Later I'd brought it up to my mother's Morningside Heights (aka Harlem Heights) apartment, where it stayed in an orange crate full of manuscripts and journals in a back closet—and left all the other papers, manuscripts, contracts, and correspondence in the Seventh Street kitchen filing cabinet.

I came up to get it.

As Mom and I walked down the hall to what had been my bedroom when I'd lived there, and was now my grandmother's room, my mother asked: "When are you going to take the whole thing?" Over the years I'd transferred the most important papers and my growing stack of journal notebooks to my mother's bedroom closet.

"Soon," I told her. "I'll take it soon."

"Well, please do."

And I carried the uncut *Jewels of Aptor* back on the subway down to where I now lived, further along Sixth Street.

At home I read it through: I crossed out the odd word or phrase and moved a few more subjects up against their verbs. My personal sense is that this was no sort of rewrite. There was no revising of incident, characters, setting, or structure. Pages went by without an emendation. I wouldn't call it "editing," so much as "copyediting." As I remember, no more than six pages were corrected so heavily (more than five corrections on a sheet) that I put them through the typewriter once more. (This was before there were copy centers or home computers or word processors; even Xerox machines were rare.) The rest were done by hand on that "onionskin" copy, typed with carbon paper. I finished the final work two days later and took it in to Terry Carr that afternoon.

Some time on, I was able to oblige Mom: a letter came from the curator of Special Collections at Boston University's Mugar Memorial Library, Dr. Howard Gotlieb. He asked if I would let his library house my papers. "Thank you," I told him when I phoned back. "I'd be happy to." Dr. Gotlieb and his staff sent a station wagon from Boston to get them from the places around Harlem and Alphabet City where they'd been stored (such as my mother's bedroom closet).

Mom and I stood back while two graduate students in slacks and sports jackets carried the very full crate—yes, made of wooden slats in which oranges had been shipped from Florida, with a dark blue, white, and orange paper label pasted onto each end—to the apartment door and out into the echoing co-op hallway with its florescent lights, to take it down to the van parked on Amsterdam Avenue.

While getting ready for sending things up to Boston, I'd learned that the conscientious super's wife had had the wooden file cabinet, with its four drawers still stuffed with papers, manuscripts, and letters moved to the building's cellar only days after I'd removed *The Jewels of Aptor* carbon. A few months later, the building had been demolished. Everything in the basement had been buried beneath brick, glass, shattered beams, and plaster, to be steam-shoveled into dumpsters and hauled to a landfill, while a new building went up in its place on the north side of Seventh Street. The paper trail of my life till then—contracts, correspondence, completed manuscripts of both novels and stories, along with countless false starts on countless stories and other projects—today is ripped, scattered, soaked, and soiled beneath the mud of the Jersey Flats.

Certainly, I felt *Aptor* read better with the text intact. But I had been prepared for Terry to say he thought the cut version more commercial and that he'd stick with it. When he called me into the office, and I asked him what his verdict was, however, he told me, "It certainly makes more sense, now. And it doesn't lurch quite the way the cut version did a few times. Yes, we're going to do it."

That is the version Ace republished in 1968, which has generally been in print since. Regardless of what it says on the back of whatever paper or hardcover edition, it has not been "expanded," except to restore the missing pages and paragraphs, nor has it been "completely revised" or "updated," other than to return to the initial version, along with one more read-through to make sure it was as close as I could get it to what I'd first wanted. Those mass-market claims on the paperback are Ace's concession to what, at the time, Wollheim felt fans would like to hear, however misleading. But even the actual changes I inserted are no more than any conscientious copy editor might have suggested, the majority of which—the vast majority—were spelling and typing corrections that had slipped through because of my dyslexia.

It's what appears here.

Over the years, Dr. Gotlieb and I exchanged notes between the Mugar and New York, between the Mugar and San Francisco, between the Mugar and New York again. Regularly Boston University's Special Collections archive sent me birthday cards, Christmas cards, update announcements on its other holdings from other writers—and every year or two I would FedEx cartons of my journals and manuscripts and hand-corrected galleys to Boston. Since Elizabethan days publishers have called these "foul papers" or "foul matter" and were happy to be shut of them. In any publishers' storage spaces it accumulates faster than clothes-hangers breed in clothes closets.

I didn't meet Dr. Gotlieb or see the collection in person, however, until a 1982 visit. Elderly, genial, and eccentric, he was a white-haired library science scholar, at home in his office and among the extraordinary things he had gathered about him over the years for Special Collections (today the Howard Gotlieb Archival Research Center) at Boston University. While I was there, I broke down and asked him why, fourteen years before, he had decided to collect me. He said, "I used to pick your books up from the newsstands, read them, and I liked them. As well, I had this dream of making the collection here a portrait of the twentieth century for future scholars: You were part of the second half of the twentieth century. So why not?" That's how my papers joined the collection that includes the papers of Samuel Beckett, L. Sprague de Camp, Martin Luther King, Jr., Dan Rather, Phillip Roth (Roth's mailbox from one country house or another sat on a side shelf in Dr. Gotlieb's office), Isaac Asimov, and Bette Davis—whom Dr. Gotlieb also liked.

Talk about luck.

* * *

During 1999 and 2000, I taught at the Poetics Program at SUNY Buffalo. Henry Morrison had been my agent since I was twenty-three, and by then was also a film producer. At a New York lunch he told me: "As far as I can see, Chip, this is the worst time to be a writer—a regularly selling writer with a market—in the history of the United States. And I mean back to Charles Brockton Brown. I don't see how you guys do it anymore."

To which the answer is, most of us don't. That's why, today, so many of us teach. I would like to be able to say to the young, "You think you have it rough? Well, when I was your age . . ." But I can't. Today's young folks, especially in the arts, have a much harder time than those of us—who now have some sort of track record and, possibly, tenure—did fifty years ago when we started. I wish it were otherwise. It would be healthier for the entire country.

* * *

From January 1969 through '70 and again in '72 and part of '73, I lived in San Francisco. By late '70 I was staying on Oak Street, in something of a commune. The building was a medium-sized Victorian, painted gray on the outside. To the right of the building was an alley less than three feet wide, halfway down which sat a baby stroller missing a wheel. You had to climb over it or really squeeze by to get to the back. From the broad kitchen windows, out over a green board fence, you could see behind us the yard and rear balconies of the San Francisco Buddhist Center. A counterculture artist who'd owned the place ten years earlier had painted the inside walls and ceilings along the halls and in the major bedrooms with pastoral murals.

But not in mine.

Mine was just over the size of the small downstairs bathroom and at the very front of the house. Probably at one time it had been used for storage or a maid's quarters.

In that year's foggy West Coast winter, the Modern Language Association was holding its sprawling annual academic meeting in the Bay Area. One Professor Thomas Clareson had invited me to address the Continuing Symposium on Science Fiction that year—the second oldest of the two continuing symposia in the organization. (Once I'd asked Professor Clareson what the oldest continuing symposium in the MLA was. He'd said, "Oh, it's something like *Shifts in the Umlaut through Two-Hundred-Fifty Years of Upper High German* . . . or some such." I assumed he was joking.) The night before I had been out drinking with a handful of science fiction scholars, including Clareson, who was to moderate the next day's panel on which I was to give my talk. It was my second MLA appearance in three years, though at the time I was neither a teacher nor a member. (You could do that then, but you haven't been able to for the last decade or so.) Apparently he had been keeping track of what I was drinking—I hadn't—and he had driven me home afterward. He'd figured, correctly, that I might need some . . . support getting to my event by one o'clock the next day.

At ten I had opened an eye, squinted at the sun coming through the curtain, and thought, "Oh, Christ . . . *no*, I'm going to blow this off. Can't do, can't do, can't do . . ." and I'd rolled over and gone back to sleep. Stuck in my notebook, on the desk wedged beside the head of my army-style cot, was the typescript of my talk.[6]

In about an hour, though, the doorbell rasped. Loud knocks, now. The bell rasped again. Someone else in the house answered and, soon, called through my closed door: "Chip! Someone's here to see you . . . !"

I had no idea who it might be. But in that haze where you are too wiped not to respond, I sat up, pulled on some jeans, stepped to my room door and opened it.

Looking fresh in a gray suit, a pale blue tie, and a paler blue shirt, Professor Clareson—far more experienced in such matters than I—said, "Morning, Chip. Into the shower with you. Come on, get your clothes on. We'll pour some coffee into you. You'll feel a *whole* lot better!"

I said, "*Unnnnnn* . . ." and then, "Tom, hey . . . thanks. But I don't think I can do this, today—"

"Yes, you can," he said from behind silver-rimmed granny glasses. "It's eleven. You don't have to talk till one. Hot shower, then cold, then warm again . . ." White hair receded from the front of his skull. (I thought of Death . . .) "Come on," he repeated.

I took a breath, looked around, and grasped a fistful of clothing. Tom walked with me along the hall's gray runner, while on the walls oversized shepherdesses loped among blue and pink sheep and, with halos neon bright around their naked bodies, male angels did not look down at me. Clouds and eagles—and one angel who was also a skeleton, refugee from some *Dia de Los Muertos* celebration—drifted over the ceiling. Tom pulled a wicker-backed chair in front of some large shepherd's knee and settled on it, slowly, glancing down at both sides. I think he was wondering if it would hold. "I'll wait . . ." It did. "If you really feel sick, give a yell. I'll help, if you need me." He smiled up at me. "You'll be okay."

"Okay . . . ?" I repeated, queasy, between questioning, confirmation, and the entire conceptual impossibility. I went inside—white tile to the waist, a few pieces cracked or missing, dark blue walls for the rest—and pulled the door closed. A cat box sat under the sink. Kitty litter scattered the linoleum, and a blue plastic toy lay on the shower's zinc floor.

There five weeks, it belonged to the kid who belonged to the stroller in the alley. But the people whose kid it was weren't there that month.

I dropped my jeans, tried to kick them off—one pants leg wouldn't come away from my foot till I sat on the loose commode ring (it had no cover), leaned forward and pulled my cuff down over my heel. Standing again, I stepped into the stall, moved the plastic curtain forward along its rod (it had torn free from two of the odd-shaped metal wires), and—stepping toward the back—reached forward and turned the knobs that looked more as if they were for two outside garden hoses than for an inside shower stall. Between my forearms, water fell.

When it reached reasonable warmth, I moved forward and, for a minute or so, turned one way and another, under the heated flush. A soap bar lay in a metal dish edged with rust and bolted to the blue. I slid the bar free—soft at one side—and soaped chest, underarms, groin, and butt, while warm water beat away the foam. Then, a knob in each hand, with a quick twist I made the water cold—

"Oh, *Christ* . . . !" shouted a committed atheist. (In foxholes and in cold showers . . .).

Outside, Tom chuckled.

Taking a breath, I held it and made myself stand there for a count of three, four, five—then sharply turned up the hot and turned down the cold. It took three, long seconds for the warm water to creep up the pipe and spew from the showerhead.

Again I began to breathe.

Out in the bathroom once more, I turned for my towel, among four others filling the rack. My glance crossed the mirror, and, remembering I had a beard, I was glad again I didn't have to shave. But I wondered—for the first time in years—if I'd look foolish speaking in public with bushy black whiskers.

When I was again sitting on the commode and my legs were dry, I pulled on my dress slacks. Outside the closed door, Professor Clareson went on, "You know, Chip, I was thinking this morning. My favorite book of yours has always been *The Ballad of Beta-2*. I must have read it four, even five times since it came out—but I keep returning to it. The reason, it occurs to me, is because it's about learning."

Inside, I thought: I *hope* I've learned not to do *this* again . . .

I stood once more, stepped over and got the blue toy from the stall, turned, and put it on the bathroom shelf where I noticed my aerosol deodorant. I'd thought I'd left it in my room and would have to go back for it—

"You've told me about your dyslexia. I wonder if that has anything to do with it. Though there's nothing about that in the book. Still, it's about learning—yes. But I mean a particular *kind* of learning, one I have so much trouble as a teacher getting my students to do: getting them to understand texts that don't make a lot of sense unless they also acquire some historical knowledge that clarifies what was really going on, why it was important, even to the point of what actual phrases mean—in Charles Reade, in Spenser, in Milton and Melville. Your book deals with a problem very close to me. And it deals with it interestingly—at least each time I reread it, I find it so. And each time in a new way."

While I finished drying, I told myself I'd take the toy to the kitchen and put it in the parents' mail cubby next time I went in, then started for the door to get my deodorant from my room—with my hand on the knob, I remembered it was on the shelf, turned back, got it.

And knocked the toy—it was a blue airplane—onto the floor. I sighed, left it, took the aerosol can and sprayed under one arm and the other. (The anti-aerosol campaign to help preserve the ozone layer and retard the Greenhouse Effect was a few years off.) It was cool—cold even, but not as cold as the cold water. I put the deodorant can back on the shelf. At least that stayed there.

After pulling my T-shirt down over my head, I shrugged into the dress shirt I'd carried in, buttoned it—incorrectly, I realized—unbuttoned it, breathed three times, sat again and rebuttoned it. Looking around, I realized I had left my socks in my room.

Standing, opening the door, jeans hanging from one fist, I stepped out barefoot into the hall.

Still in his wicker-back, Tom smiled.

I said, "Well, thank you—for telling me." It was at least three minutes since he had stopped talking, and I felt foolish.

The full version is, *Oh, why thank you so much for taking the time to tell me. That's very nice of you.* Before (and since) I've used it in such situations. That morning, however, I hadn't made it all the way through—and had waited too long—and was wondering if the hungover version had only been confusing. Or if I'd sounded *very* foolish. In that state, though, every other thing you do is infected with foolishness, and you spend a lot of time wondering how and why nothing you say or do feels right.

Feeling foolish, I walked to my room, glancing at smiling Tom—who got up and followed. Inside, putting my jeans over a chair back and sitting on the iron stead's mattress edge, I got my socks, shoes, and sports jacket on, reached over, and picked up my notebook and my talk.

We went out and down the steps to the door. I felt foolish because I went out first, then realized I hadn't let the older Tom step from the house before me. I mistook the car he indicated and felt foolish as I walked on to the one, in a moment, I realized was his. Tom drove us to breakfast, and I sat—foolishly—on the front seat beside him, fixated on the fact that my attempt to thank him for his compliment had been so inept.

I was quiet, but my mind kept running on, obsessively, unstoppably, uncomfortably: nobody had suggested I say it, you understand. Rather, after several encounters with people who had complimented me without warning—with the result that I'd felt awkward and clearly they'd felt awkward too—I'd sat down, a few years back, and decided, since probably I'd be in the situation from time to time, I'd better put together a response that let people know I hadn't been annoyed and that acknowledged their good intentions. "Why, thank you so much for taking the time . . ." is what I'd come up with; if I responded with that, both of us would feel a little better and neither of us would leave the encounter feeling . . . well, like a fool. I sat beside Tom, mumbling it over and over without moving my lips and wondered if I should say it out loud again, properly this time—but I was sure, if I did, it would sound . . . foolish. (The next time it happened, months later, it worked perfectly well.) At that point, however, the most foolish thing since I'd waked seemed Tom's preference for *Beta-2*. (Was I becoming a writer who couldn't bear his previous work . . . ?) I hadn't felt this way yesterday.

Could all this be chemical . . . ?

Then we were walking into a San Francisco breakfast place, with loud construction for the new BART line outside, and aluminum doors and mirrored walls inside, on the way to the MLA convention hotel, to join Tom's wife, Alice. She had dark hair and sat smiling in one of the booths.

I ate some toast and bacon (I wasn't up to eggs) and drank some black coffee—and was surprised I could.

We got to the MLA hotel twenty minutes before my talk.

Among the anecdotes above, whether someone is talking about a book in detail or just running up and saying, "Hey, I really liked . . ." and running off again, I have *not* been recounting all this to talk about either popularity or quality.

Because I'm not talking about popularity, that's why, except in one case—to come—I give only one example per person. (That's also why I'm not giving numbers, of people or of books.) Of course it happens with some books more than with others. Those mentioned more often are ones that have been better advertised—though not always—by whatever method or have been simply more available; and we all know what a meaningless indicator advertising or hearsay is for quality.

Well, then, what *am* I talking about?

A lesson comes with someone running up to you, taking the time and putting out the energy to cross the natural barrier that exists between strangers (and though I'd known Clareson a couple of years, I'd only met him in person four times), telling you she or he liked something you wrote. The lesson is not entirely about politeness—or kindness, either. The lesson occurs, yes, when someone tells you why he or she likes a particular work, and—through the fog of your own current concerns (we always have them even if we're not hungover)—it even makes a kind of sense. It also occurs when you encounter a full-fledged academic paper that seems preternaturally astute (or completely wrongheaded).

It occurred fourteen years later, too, on an afternoon when I was at a theater in New York City for the matinee of a musical. I was stouter. My beard was bushier—and largely gray.

And I had a ten-year-old daughter, whom I'd brought with me. (With a music teacher at Columbia and a Chase bank vice president, I'd helped found a gay father's group, which met monthly and now had more than forty members—though, at this point, it has little to do with the tale, in parentheses it will play its part. Marilyn and I had separated for good nine years before, though we'd arranged for joint custody.) Just that week a well-known rock musician had taken over the lead in the show, and at that matinee the rest of his band had come to sit in the front orchestra seats to see their lead singer's first performance that afternoon. During intermission, a third of the audience had moved to the balcony rail to gaze down at them, and, once we stood up, from our own seats in the balcony's rear, both my daughter and I could see that, downstairs, another third, in the theater's orchestra had moved to the front to crowd around the young men, who were being friendly and behaving as if they were old hands at this; but there was no leaving the theater for them to get a breath of air outside, as my daughter and I were getting ready to do.

My daughter attended a school where, if there were not a lot of celebrities, there were a few celebrities' children. As she looked down, she commented: "They're not even letting them leave. That doesn't seem very nice."

"Probably," I said, "they're tourists, and they haven't seen a lot of famous people before."

My supremely cool New York ten-year-old turned away, and we went to the orange stairway and down to street level, to stretch and get a breath before the bell rang, the lights under the marquee blinked (a custom discontinued in Broadway theaters how many years ago . . . ?), and we could return to our balcony seats for the second act.

Occasionally I've written about how rarely our lives actually conform to the structure of stories that writers have been using for hundreds, if not thousands, of years. But, sometimes, they do. A reason I remember that day is because, through coincidence and propinquity, things approached one.

After the show, while we were standing out on Eighth Avenue at the bus stop, the bus pulled up, the door folded back, and two teenage boys got off as I was getting ready to guide my ten-year-old on, to bring her home. (My sister had given us the tickets; back at the apartment, my partner—and Iva's co-dad since she was three—had said he'd make spaghetti, Iva's favorite, that evening.)

One of the young men frowned at me:

"You're Samuel Delany, aren't you? You wrote that book I really liked. What was it, again . . . ?" The young man's friend had read it too and supplied the title.

"Yes, I am. Why, thank you for taking the time to tell me. That's very nice of you." I smiled.

They smiled—and walked off.

My daughter and I got on. We went to the rear of the bus and sat as it started. Then my daughter pushed her ponytail back from her shoulder. "Dad, are you famous?"

I smiled. "Fortunately, no. The band at the theater today is famous. But things like people recognizing me in the street who've read something of mine only happens once, maybe twice a year—sometimes it'll happen two or three times in a week, the way it did right after I was on the *Charlie Rose Show*, or when that article came out in the *Times*. Now, though, it's right where I can enjoy it. Too much more, however, and it would get *really* annoying."

"Oh," she said.

And that's the single time in my life—and my daughter's—where I was able to make such a point, with comparative examples coming within an hour.

Forty-four years after Tom Clareson helped me through a hangover, and thirty years after I took my daughter to the theater matinee, the point is still true.

The lesson, then, is this: there exists a *possibility* of something happening when someone reads a book that is important enough for the person to respond to the writer who wrote it in that manner. And it doesn't happen because of direct communication from person to person any more than sunrise occurred this morning because the sun lifted itself from behind the horizon into the dawn sky.

A possibility. Not a certainty. (There are too many other reasons for running up to speak when you see someone you recognize in public.) The lesson is about possibility and potentiality, not about a probability for communication to have gotten through. It is no more—but no less—than that.

In no way is it any confirmation about communication, even when in practical terms you'd be willing to bet on it. That's because we know that communication *doesn't* actually "get through," any more than the sun actually "rises" in the morning or the moon actually "sets" in the nighttime (or daytime): that's simply how it feels, not how it works. Sunrise, moon-down, and language-as-direct-communication—*all* are effects of something more complex: a spinning planet among other spinning planets in their elliptical orbits about a stellar bole of violently fusioning hydrogen millions of miles away that is releasing immense energy and light—which is drenched in information about what created it as well as everything it deflects from in passing. That light spews that information through the multiverse at a hundred-and-eighty-six-thousand-two-hundred miles per second to tell of the workings of other planets, other stars and their planets, the workings of other galaxies of stars or the workings of other minds a few years, decades, centuries, a few thousand miles behind the pages of a book, behind a Nook or a Kindle or an iPad screen, till it passes too close to a gravitational force too large for it to escape and falls into it—while its stellar source millions of light years away goes on creating the heavier elements—and singing about it in its light waves. As we career through the great spaces along our own galaxy's swirling edge, our own sun takes its planets and their satellites, its belt of asteroids, its Ort Cloud, and its comets along with it (which is why so much of the turning moves more or less in the same direction), while our galaxy itself moves along the gravitational currents flung out by billions of galaxies in a veritable net throughout the multiverse,[7] much of whose material is dark matter that light (I use the term loosely for all electromagnetic waves) doesn't seem to tell us about directly, but only by its absences.

Then why *don't* meanings move from me to you by means of the words that I say and that you hear—or that you read? Why do I say that's just an effect, too, like the rising and setting of the sun, moon, and stars? They don't, for the same reason we need a lens—the one in your eye, the one in your camera, the water drop on a spider web—to retrieve the information from the light—something to focus the data and repress the noise, which may or may not be another sort of data that to us isn't as useful or—such as heat when it grows too great—is harmful to organic systems that are largely liquid and ultimately destructive to all systems comprised of solids.[8]

Think about the electrical signals in the brain that are your thoughts and the electrical signals that make your tongue move and your larynx stretch or contract to utter sounds when you push air out over them, and the physical vibrations that go through the air and strike your own and others' eardrums and the electrical signals that the minuscule hammer bone attached to the eardrum's back that shakes as the eardrum vibrates, the tiny anvil bone and tiny stirrup bone transferring those shakings that, in turn shake the little hairs within the spiral of the cochlea, which transform those vibrations into the electromagnetic pulses that travel to the brain where other electrical impulses are created as sound (already a vast over-simplification) and are associated with the meanings of words, phrases, and much larger patterns of language *already lodged in the mind/brain* of the hearer, the reader—patterns that must already be there, or else we would say that the hearer does not know the language yet or understand it. (In the late 1920s and early '30s, a Russian psychologist, Lev Vygotsky [1896–1934], observed that children tend to learn first to talk and only then to internalize their own speech as thinking, though it's a continuous developmental process.) And because everyone learns his or her language under different circumstances, those patterns simply *cannot* be identical for any two of us. That they can adjust thoughts as far toward similarity as they do in many different brains is a result of the amazing intricacy of the learning materials and the stabilizing discursive structures that they are capable of forming.

Rarely do we get a new meaning from the rearrangement of old ones, helped on by language and the part of language (the signified) we call experience. Perceived experience is one of three ways we can "experience" linguistic signifieds; another is through memory, imagination—sexual and secular, practical and preposterous—and generally conscious thought; a third is through dreaming. (And all three relate. And all three are different. And none of this should be taken to contravene Derrida's notion that the world is what language cuts it up into.) But the meanings understood by an other are *always* her or his own meanings, learned however she or he learned them, and never the speaker's or the writer's, though the effect is usually that they are the same—because we are mostly unaware of the stabilizing discursive circuits that we know so very little about, though we also learn those and learn them differently in different cultures.[9]

Unconscious thought, Freud was convinced by a lot of research and study, was a mode of thinking we *don't* experience directly as such. I am pretty sure he was right. (Whatever that level of brain activity is, I suspect it controls the discursive levels of language.) But without unconscious thought, we literally would not know what other people were talking about, even though we recognized the words whose meanings we have already internalized.

And, remember, every dolphin and whale and octopus and dog has some version of this problem and neurological solution, every pig, porpoise, penguin, or porcupine; every bird or four-legged animal or six-legged cricket who "receives" communication with its ears or an ear-like structure, or emits communication by rubbing its legs together or whistling songs or clicking or crooning underwater or meowing or purring or barking or growling—that is to say every creature who has to negotiate sexual reproduction and/or attraction; every creature who, at food source or a watering place, needs to communicate "move over" to a fellow with a push or a shove; every pig, porpoise, penguin, or porcupine; every bird or four-legged animal or six-legged cricket who "receives" communication with its ears or an ear-like structure, or emits communication by rubbing its legs together or whistling songs or clicking or crooning underwater or meowing or purring or barking or growling or crowing to its flock at sunrise or howling to its pack beneath the moon, infants or adults laughing or sobbing, the distinctions between them, and what, emotionally or politically, in a given culture, a given family, a given situation, each is likely to mean.[10] Without something akin to discourse, they (and we) wouldn't be able to tell if the other was attacking or wooing or warning, or if they should hold it till the morning walk or until they reach a public john or do it in the litter box, or if they want their offspring to suckle them or their owners to stroke them—whether it's time to play or to eat or they'd better get off the couch. (The great mid-twentieth century actor couple Alfred Lunt and Lynn Fontaine were famous for owning a pair of dogs named "Get-off-the-couch," and "You-too.") In humans, discourse learning and management are probably among the main tasks of the unconscious mind. But that's speculation.

In short, it's not just humans who communicate indirectly. It's all dogs, cats, bats, birds, and buffalos, as well as every creature who makes and hears sounds and sees movements that are meaningful; every creature who feels a touch or a lick or a bite from another.

With the sound-making/sound-gathering system we communicate within our species. With it we communicate between species. With it we "receive communication" from plants—think of all the information different sounds such as wind in the leaves, can bring us under different conditions (i.e., evokes in us)—as well as from the entire inanimate world: falling rocks, breaking waves, thunder and trees cracking and crashing to the forest floor. But in all cases, the meanings of those sounds and their attendant contexts must be built up *in the mind of the hearer* (or wired in by evolution: some of us animals are *wired* to wire ourselves that way upon the encounter with certain "experiences" or "linguistic signifieds," such as learning to walk upright or learning to speak) through experiences for any subsequent interpretation to take place, whether curiosity or fear, recognition, prediction, or negotiation ("I don't want to get wet. Let's go inside. Listen to that . . ." "I *am* listening. Hey, we can make it to Margaret's before it really comes down . . .") is the function. But mammals in general and primates in particular—as well as whales, dolphins, and octopodia—seem to have a knack for learning.[11] Because, until recently, there has been no pressing need to understand the complex mechanics behind some of evolution's effects, that's why many of us don't—though we are capable of learning and, with the help of writing, remembering. There is also an educational, stabilizing superstructure, however, where intervention can reasonably occur, and where it is possible to stabilize necessary discourses with the help of beneficent technologies—if you allow cultures to learn in their own way. But this must be both an active and a passive process. This is not cultural relativism (which always moves toward a passive approach that ignores learning and tends toward a dominant destructive approach to behavior, which it sometimes confused *with* learning), but cultural respect—which acknowledges that learning/teaching is always an intervention in the elements that comprise culture, during which both sides must learn if there is to be beneficent change. There is a difference between dialogue-and-respect and imposition-and-domination. And if many more of us don't start to understand those process-effects and their imperfections as well as their successes, soon, directly or indirectly, we'll kill each other and ourselves off. It's that simple.[12]) The fact that—from mice (who squeak) to mastodons (who trumpeted), bats to beavers, giraffes (who mostly listen but sometimes mew) to gerbils (who chitter), pigeons (who coo) to primates (who grunt, growl, or talk)—so many creatures share an auditory form of data emission and reception (i.e., hearing and making more or less informative noises; though we all do different things with them) attests to its efficacy for multiple tasks at every level of development as well as to our genetic connectedness over the last 250 million years since the early Triassic and before and the incredibly intricate road to language that a purely synchronic linguistics is inadequate to untangle without a great deal more extension into semiotics, animal and human, and their evolutionary history, much of which is lost.

Given we have separate brains, that we can "communicate" as much as we can is quite amazing—but don't let your amazement make you forget that "communicate" begins as a metaphor for an effect (a door that opens directly from one room to another, a hall that leads from one place in a building to another) but is thus neither a complete nor an accurate description of many things that occur with sound-making and sound-gathering. The fact that so many different creatures have eyes, ears, and kinesthetic reception systems speaks of the efficacy of these effects as well as the genetic relationships among us since before they and their precursors—from gills, extraneous jaw bones, and light sensitive spots on algae and the forerunners of nerves themselves—evolved over millions of generations. That is an index of their usefulness in this landscape. Bear that in mind, and you may start to perceive how complex the process is and why language is *only* the effect that something has passed from person to person, creature to creature, from landscape to creature, whether from speech or in writing or by touch or through any sound—or perceptible signs.[13]

It was Ralph Waldo Emerson who said, "We must treat other people as if they exist, because perhaps they do"—though we've gotten a lot more biological and neurological evidence *that* they do.[14] Because of this, the force behind that "perhaps" has strengthened to a strong "probably," though in theory we haven't gotten much further. The similarities and differences from which—neurologically speaking—we learn to interpret the world, unto birth and death, comfort and discomfort, safety and danger, pleasure and pain, and the existence of other people and other creatures and other minds and—whatever ours is—other sexualities and orientations and the worldscapes we share are all still effects, even as they form our only access to the life, the world, the multiverse they create for us. But they would appear to be extremely useful effects for keeping us alive and functioning in our nanosection of a nanosection of that multiverse—that is, if what many of us take to be failures of tolerance among the general deployments and our own employments of these effects of difference don't lead to our destruction.

*   *   *

Now that we've had a romp through space, time, and a general ecological agape, which—since Poe obliged an audience of sixty with a talk taken from his then unpublished *Eureka: A Prose Poem*[15]—we still expect certain sorts of imaginative writers to indulge from time to time, I can tell the following without, I hope, it taking on more critical weight than it can bear: an anecdote that pleases me and makes me smile. For—largely—that's what it is. (The indirect gesturing toward metaphysics is done with for the nonce. And, no, we can't say anything about it directly, which is probably why it takes so long to suggest anything about it at all; and, no, we are still never outside it . . .)

All three books of my *Fall of the Towers* trilogy sold.

Every once in a while, even today, someone writes about them: "Hey, these are interesting—certainly better than I ever thought they would be . . ."

I don't make too much of it.

Still, the trilogy was the favorite of a young man who wrote subtle and involving avant-garde fiction, published by a very respectable press, and also of a sharp young woman who wrote crafted and exciting science fiction—and, in his green T-shirt and his orange rubber glove, my neighborhood New York sanitation worker.

Before he let go of my shoulder, though, he held me long enough to say that *They Fly at Çiron*—which had just come out in paperback—was his *second* favorite work of mine:

A possibility for a similarity, or even for a partial congruence having arisen from his encounter with the text in his mind and from the very different encounter with it in mine, but no certainty, no identity. . . .

I smiled. "Why, thank you for taking the time to tell me—about both. That's very nice of you."

Glancing at the glove, he dropped his hand back to his side. "Oh, sure. Any time, I guess. You're welcome. I'm glad it's OK . . ." He told me about the magazine in which, two weeks before, he'd seen my picture and read its few paragraphs about me. He was a black American man like myself, which meant we'd shared many experiences and much cultural history. He was a black American man like myself, which meant his world and his upbringing were unique, as were mine. (For all our human species' similarities, if we look carefully enough, uniqueness—finger prints, retinal patterns, the synaptic links in our three billion brain cells, genetic variations in both essential and nonessential genetic material which reflect the different specificity each of us inhabits and our ancestors inhabited (i.e., it didn't kill us in that particular landscape before we could pass it on), even if we live in houses next to one another, or in the same house in the same family—is our most widely shared trait.[16] Did that have anything to do with his stopping me? Possibly. In the twenty-five seconds we spoke, the next thing he let me know was how much he liked Octavia Butler's work. "*Kindred* . . . ? Those stories in *Blood Child*?" he asked. "*Patternmaster* . . . ?"

I nodded, smiling.

"Did you ever meet her?"

"She was a student of mine, many years ago," I told him.

"Oh, wow," he declared. "That's amazing! She was?"

"That's right. She was discovered by a white Jewish-born writer, Harlan Ellison, who was running a special program in Los Angeles and encouraged her to come to the place where I and a number of other SF writers were teaching."

"I didn't know that."

"Well—" I laughed—"now you do."

For a moment he frowned. "Hey, I like his work, too." Then frown relaxed into a smile.

"So do I." I didn't mention how many other SF writers I'd taught over the years—or Harlan had, or any of the other writers and editors who had taught at Clarion, including several times Butler herself, at both Clarion East and Clarion West.

The article had mentioned that I was black—and gay. It hadn't mentioned that my wife and I, though divorced, had raised a daughter. (Or that, for several important years, forty other gay men and their children had helped me.) I was wondering if he had a family—when he added, "Great meeting you. Hey, I gotta get back to work."

I called, "Thanks again. So long . . . !" while he loped off past the blue plastic recycling tubs that had already been emptied, to follow the once-white Isuzu refuse collection truck up the street, on which, above and outside the hopper, someone had wired a big, stuffed, grubby bear.

If you enjoyed *Çiron*, too, I am happy. My apologies, if you didn't. But maybe the extension of this anecdote here will suggest a further explanation for the sanitation worker's reaction, not so different from why Professor Clareson enjoyed *Beta-2*.

* * *

Initially, at the conclusion of this afterword, I'd planned to revert to our A, B, Cs, and to discuss how what started, after all, as a random collection of signs for sounds, developed into such a powerful ordering tool, beginning with the fact that, at our opening, we *didn't* alphabetize the titles of the books, but only the first letter of the final proper noun in each.

Older alphabets, such as Hebrew and Greek, begin, in effect, "A, B, G: *aleph, beth, gamil . . . alpha, beta, gamma . . .*": which suggest a great deal about the history of written language, because so many of those alphabets from that relatively small arc of the world share so many sequences with each other, which means contact between the cultures. The Arabic abjad has several orders, two of which begin a, b, d, (*abjad, hawwaz, ḥuṭṭī*) and two of which begin a, b, t. (We would have neither algebra—which is an Arabic word—nor the use of the Hindu zero, nor the names of so many of our stars, without the Arabic language and its cultural flowering through the centuries, in poetry, science, medicine, mathematics, and astronomy.) Other writing systems, which developed in different places—China and India, Korea and Malaysia, Central and South America—are as rich and as creative as any of the "classic six" (up through much of the nineteenth century, these included Latin, Greek, Hebrew, and Arabic, along with Sanskrit and Aramaic), but work differently, sometimes at very fundamental levels. My first idea was to go on with what an alphabetic ordering could accomplish and what it couldn't.[17] As I began drafting it, however, I got caught up in still another meditation on "social" evolution, an idea I distrust as much as I believe in what we call Darwinian evolution, a distrust for which the huge collapse of the timeframe in "social" evolution is only one bit of the evidence against it—that is to say, which reduces it to a misleading and highly abusable metaphor instead of an efficient explanation of another effect, another illusion, which often contravenes what biological evolution itself so overwhelmingly suggests. But that seemed a bit off topic for where I wanted this consideration to go.

I decided, therefore, to go back instead to some advice I'd encountered by the time, in Amherst, I settled down to do the work—the rewriting—on *They Fly at Çiron*. (I'd dedicated *Çiron* to my life-partner Dennis, and, after twenty-five years together, I include him in the dedication to this omnibus as well.) The advice was helpful to me; very helpful. But, like any writerly advice, it didn't *replace* the work. If I'd only applied it to the textural surface rather than to the fundamental narrative logic, it would have resulted in more confusion (and perhaps it did), whether I was writing fiction or nonfiction. It had to be a guide for where—and the way—to do the work, which, throughout, habit demanded I do as non-habitually as I could. It also suggests why, today, this version of *Çiron* is three times as long as the text I salvaged from the old manuscript I'd carried with me from New York to Amherst, and why it has six characters who weren't in the first version at all.

The 1925 Nobel Prize–winning Irish (though he lived much of his life in England) playwright and critic George Bernard Shaw was a great favorite of an astonishing American writer, Joanna Russ, whom I was privileged to have as a friend from the middle 1960s until her death in 2011. (Though we met only six or seven times, our letters back and forth starting in 1967 fill cartons.) She was an enthusiast both of Shaw's plays and of his criticism, musical and dramatic. From adolescence on I'd enjoyed Shaw's theater, but Russ was the first to remind me of his other pieces,[18] some of which I had been lucky enough to have read before on my own, so that I could reread them in the twin illuminations of her knowledge and enthusiasm.

After she started writing, Russ enrolled as a student at the Yale School of Drama. Among the things Shaw had said, years before, in a letter to a younger friend, which Russ once passed on to me: When actors are told they are taking too much time to say their lines and, because the play is too long, told they should speed up or even cut the lines, often the better advice is to slow things down even more. Frequently, what makes parts of it seem muddy, slow, or unnecessary is that the development is too compressed for the audience to follow. Expand it and make the articulations of that development sharper and clearer to the listeners. Then the play will give the effect of running *more* quickly and smoothly and what before were "slow" sections will now no longer drag.

That can apply not only to reading texts but to the texts themselves. (Not to mention prefaces, afterwords, and footnotes.)

In a world where cutting is seen as so much easier and the audience is far too overvalued—and simultaneously underestimated (the audience is, before all else, ourselves)—this is important advice. One of the things that make it important is how rarely you will hear it or anything like it these days—which is why I've ended with it. It's one way—but only one—to guide the work I must always return to.

A good question with which to begin that kind of revision is: If I set aside, at least momentarily, what I hoped I was writing about when I first put all this down, what is this text in front of me actually about that interests *me*? How can I make that clearer, more comprehensible, and more dramatic to myself? Can I dramatize or clarify it without betraying it?

(And suppose I can't . . .?)

In revising even this sketchy guide through what is finally a maze of mirrors, several times that's been my question here.

If, like me, you are someone who reads the preface and afterword before you tackle the texts between—and often I do, then go on to chuckle over how little they relate to what falls before or after, the world, the text—now, however abruptly, I will stop to let you go on to read the text, the world which contains them and which for better or for worse, however briefly, they are a part of. Who knows if there might be or not be something between these covers that, later, you'll want to read again. Again, I cannot know. But I can hope. We can even think about how my or your hope inspires you, if we will also talk about why it guarantees nothing, neither to the young nor to the old. But that's one of the things books are for. That's why they have margins—which, in a sense, is where prefaces and afterwords (and footnotes) are written. And when you encounter the flaws in the texts here (and you will), you can decide whether or not Shaw's advice applies, or if they require more or other—or simply different—work.

—August 21, 2014
New York

NOTES

1. Like thousands on thousands of young writers before and since, I figured the easy way to write a novel was to write a series of interconnected short stories. I'd even thought of it as an experiment—and I still think it could have been an interesting one. But it was an experimental idea that I'd used in place of doing the necessary imaginative work, rather than a formal idea I had brought to life through the work and the thinking that would have opened up and multiplied its resonances and meanings. It was an idea I had thrown away rather than utilized, because I'd hoped it would be interesting in itself, whatever its content. Forty years later I tried it again, with more success—I hope—in a novel called *Dark Reflections*. (It won the Stonewall Book Award in 2008.) But this reflects on something I find myself writing about even today: though the genre can suggest what you might need, it can never do the work for you, whether you are thinking of the text as science fiction, as literary, or as experimental; though, from time to time, all of us (writers and critics both) hope that it will.

2. Sometimes the uses of evolutionary developments seem obvious. Far more often, though, they are invisible and their uses not necessarily comprehended by the creatures—including humans—who possess them. (This is why the notion that sex is only for reproduction is, itself, an anti-evolutionary notion.) What are earlobes for? Well, they are blood collectors that help supply the ear with blood and keep the inner ear warm in very cold weather. That's probably why they developed first in northern climates and why smaller earlobes developed nearer the equator. Well, then why don't all northerners have large earlobes and all equatorial people have small ones? Because, over the last four hundred years, quite enough intermixing has occurred in both the north and south to rearrange the genetic distribution, which rearrangements can be considered a natural response to the interbreeding of peoples and the movement that goes along with it and is also a long-ago established evolutionary advantage of genetic reproduction itself, which allows such rearrangements in diploid genetic species for blending-inheritance aspects. (Haploid species—some stages of amoeba and paramecia—can mix genes through a process called syzygy, but that's much rarer and takes even more time to develop anything evolutionarily, although it does, some. A science fiction writer who was most fascinated by that process—and one of the great short fiction writers of the middle of the twentieth century—is Theodore Sturgeon. Read him. He's wonderful.) Two evolutionary ideas to keep in mind: First, by the time anything develops evolutionarily, it always has many uses; and that includes earlobes, large and small. No matter how scientists talk about them, anyone who

believes that any evolutionary development has only one use basically misunderstands how evolution works; because the development is slow and gradual, at each stage the development must be useful enough to give a large-scale statistical survival advantage to a group. And those uses change as the aspect develops but the older uses they met don't necessarily go away. (Humans' external ears are highly erogenous—whether individuals use that aspect or not.) If it isn't useful at all, it breeds out eventually. Carrying around excess still isn't an advantage—though sometimes it only looks excessive to us. Second, any aspect of us that is widespread and has been around for a long time almost certainly has some functional use(s), even if we have never stopped to consider what it might be. Humans had developed a circulatory system with veins, arteries, valves, and a complex heart multiple millions of years before the Egyptians in the sixteenth century BCE and with contributions by Romans and Arabs over the three thousand years that preceded William Harvey's assembling a viable model of the whole human circulatory system (as well as discussing a few of its uses; but by no means all) in his 1628 publication, *De Motu Cordis*. And we are still discovering aspects of the circulatory system that have been in place since before we branched off the general evolutionary line along with the other great apes, many of which are common to all mammals, birds, amphibians, and fish. In many of their variant forms they do lots of things very well, and a staggering percentage of the greater "us" (almost all of us who aren't plants or worms—and worms are the major planetary population, remember; though we share still other things with *them*, such as muscles and an alimentary canal) utilize them to interact with the cities, the caves, the rural areas in which they live or have lived, the prairies, the grasses and brambles and ferns, the seas, the sea-beds and trenches and shallow reefs, the deserts, the hills, the tundras, the mountains, the jungles and forests.

3. That multiplicity, thanks to evolution, is always both plural and limited (parsimonious). Their pluralities are the political urgencies, disasters, and satisfactions mentioned above, as they are inchoate to the wonders and distresses, the pains and pleasures, and the symbolic forces that exist only through intellect, from the workings of discourse to the square root of minus one, to the existence of stars, quarks, photons, quasars and pulsars, dark matter, dark energy, galaxies, gravity, and the multiverse they constitute.

4. The larger point: I am as much the person who makes the mistake as I am the one who corrects it. I am as much the person who gets to the place in a sentence or a paragraph where I realize I am ignorant of a date or the name of a city where some historical event occurred as I am the person who, twenty minutes later, returns from the encyclopedia on the lower library shelf or turns from the computer screen after a ten-minute Google hunt to fill it in. Writing above a certain level requires, however, that you gain some understanding of both, not only within your "self" but out in the world. Perhaps this is what has given me a career-long fascination with people who cannot speak or write at all, as well as an equal fascination with poets (which etymologically means "makers" and more recently "makers of things from language"), though the "self" I present the world is neither one nor the other, thanks to the Other that is always there in me, the "I" that "I" am always struggling to overcome. This is the only way I can resolve the *aporia* (the contradiction; and *aporia* was Plato's word after all) as to why Plato, who was such a fine writer in the Greek of his time, in his hypothetical and optative society so famously excluded the poets from his Republic. (The *optative* is

a Greek grammatical mood, similar to the subjunctive, from which we get the word "options.") Plato wanted the poets who were there to be better than they were, that is, to choose the option to be more faithful to the idea of truth—which, when talking about an imagined world, is not quite the same as actually banishing them from the actual. I am not suggesting, as some folks have, that Plato wrote science fictions. But *I* do. That helps me read him—as, doubtless, having written one novel himself (*Marius the Epicurean: His Sensations and Ideas* [1885], a favorite of both Virginia Woolf and James Joyce) and started another (*Gaston de la tour*), helped Walter Pater, seven years later, in his wonderful *Plato and Platonism* (1893), have the insights about the philosopher that he did. Far closer to our day than to Plato's, Pater noted that, had he been writing in ours, Plato could have been a great novelist. The ten-volume set of Pater's complete works—which her father had not allowed in their library when he was alive—was among the first books Woolf bought with her inheritance on her father's death. A favorite of the young readers of the Oxford Aesthetic Movement of the 1880s and '90s, and its Edwardean coda (and one of the great forbidden books of its age), *Marius* is among the first books directly alluded to (by Buck Mulligan), on page 8 of the Vintage International edition of *Ulysses*, through its subtitle ("I remember only ideas and sensations"). Usually such allusions are literary love—though they can also, sometimes, be literary hate. The unconscious, Freud suggested, uses no negatives. Strong emotion is strong emotion. To me, however, this one has the feel of a positive enthusiasm.

5. Modernist experimental French writers in the twentieth century, such as Louis-Ferdinand Celine and Jean Genet, largely used the not quite four-thousand word vocabulary—with bits of added slang—that the seventeenth-century writers Jean Racine and Pierre Corneille used, three hundred years before. This is not the case with, say, American modernists such as Hemingway and Faulkner on the one hand and our seventeenth-century English writers John Donne and John Milton on the other. The difference between the two traditions, French and English, is an effect of the French National Academy in the one and the lack of the same in England, America, and Australia.

6. "Critical Methods / Speculative Fiction": initially I had written this in the autumn of 1969 and delivered it to a group of enthusiastic science fiction fans who met in a house in the beautiful Berkeley hills. That meeting was hosted by a member of the family who made Tanqueray Gin—surely a resonance with what I will shortly write. At that year's MLA, I read a version cut by half. The complete text was published in *Quark/1* (Paperback Library, 1970), edited by Marilyn Hacker and myself. Today you can find it in *The Jewel-Hinged Jaw*, a revised edition of which is now available (Wesleyan University Press, 2010). For the record, that 1969 talk is among the last times I used the term "speculative fiction" before returning to the term, adequate for any critical use I have found myself in need of since, "science fiction." As far as I can see, the basic meaning of "speculative fiction" is: "Whatever science fiction I, the speaker, happen to approve of at ten o'clock Wednesday morning or at whatever moment I use the term," which makes it a very slippery shifter and too vague to sustain a useful critical life in any analytical discussion. I have not used it, except more or less ironically, and then rarely, for forty-five years, though even today I run across people claiming it's my "preferred term." It's not.

7. With some eight thousand-plus others, our own turning galaxy arcs toward the Great Attractor in our super-cluster of the galactic net, a cluster containing the Virgo

galaxy-cluster at the end of one peninsula of galaxies off the parent cluster, while ours is at the end of another, next to it. Till recently, we thought we were part of Virgo. But we're not. Both our galaxy—the Milky Way—and the Virgo cluster are on short chains of galaxies that feed into the major super cluster (more like an unraveled ball of strings than a swarm of bees), which is about a hundred times larger than astronomers thought even a few decades ago. Only this year have they started calling that larger structure Laniakea—Hawaiian for "Immeasurable Heaven." Now it's been measured and is currently among the biggest structures the descendants of our million-times great grandmother (or great aunt) "Lucy" and her many-times-grandson (or great nephew), "Red Clay Man" (the meaning of the Hebrew name "Adam," which tells not only what they thought he looked like but what they thought he was made of) have individuated, mapped, and named—though Lucy and Adam both probably saw fragments of it when they looked up at the naked night, as we can today. It's about a hundred-million light years across. But, about that size, many more link to it, to make the gravity-enchained galactic.net. Google *Laniakea* or *Perseus-Pisces* or *the Great Attractor* or *the Shapley Supercluster* or *the Axis of Evil* or *the Bright Spot*—all galaxy-markers in our expanding map of the multiverse. *All* are impressive.

For all it doesn't tell us about dark matter and dark energy, light carries an awesome amount of information throughout the multiverse, whether from the very edges of the visible or from the leaves fallen by my shoe at a puddle's edge, information that links through evolution to why and how so many creatures—including most humans—have eyes.

8. They burn up, melt, or both, and finally, with enough heat, defuse as plasma, so that even their atoms may eventually shatter.

9. Those discursive structures stabilize our metaphysical assumptions that, as Derrida remarked, we are never outside of and are most deeply enmeshed in precisely when we are critiquing someone else's.

There is a story, possibly apocryphal, about the philosopher Ludwig Wittgenstein, who was wandering one day over the lawns of Cambridge and looking at the sky, when one of his students saw him. "Professor Wittgenstein, are you all right? What are you doing . . . ?"

The philosopher looked down and saw the student. (The novelist in me at this point always assumes Wittgenstein blinked.) "I'm trying to understand," said the perplexed philosopher, "why, when the earth is turning and the sun is—relatively—in one place in the sky, it feels and looks as if the earth is still and the sun is moving around it."

"Well . . ." said the student, perplexed now by the philosopher's perplexity, "it's because, I suppose, it just feels and looks that way when the earth is moving and the sun is standing still."

"But if that's the case," replied the philosopher, "what would it look and feel like if the earth were actually still and the sun *was* actually moving." And on that question, Wittgenstein turned, looked up again, and wandered off across the grass, leaving a very perplexed young man, now looking after him, now squinting toward the sun.

Your words and mine evoke—rather than carry—approximate meaning, already there at their destination, meanings that the order of words alone will rearrange and that must be interpreted further by probabilistic approximation to mean anything at all.

It is only the effect that feels as if they carry actual meanings from speaker or writer to hearer or reader. But if that's the case, what *would* be the effect if they felt as if they only evoked meanings already there by probabilistic approximation . . . ?

Life is made up of lots of "experience puns," with an "obvious explanation" and several "not so obvious ones." Enlarging on this property was the basis for much of the work of the surrealist artists, such as Pavel Tchelichew, Max Ernst, and M. C. Escher.

Our metaphysics arises from assuming perceived resonances are causal when we have no evidence for it, but without which we would be left with solipsism—itself a limit-case metaphysical assumption, but an assumption nevertheless. In short, we can either assume that stuff is there—or that it isn't. (Maybe it's something else, energy, idea, or pure God. . . .) We have no logical proof for any of them. What we have is effects that seem to make us comfortable or uncomfortable, but comfort and discomfort, remember, are also effects. (We can work directly with the brain to change them, both temporarily or permanently.) We seem to be most comfortable assuming the very complex world we live in is there, and that all the complex things that have developed in it over the last five billion years to deal with are, in fact, the case—and many of us feel even more comfortable when we can untangle contradictions in what appears obvious by means of other patterns we have been able to see in other places, with the aid of other techniques. (It's called science.) Explore it, play, have fun and try to learn and understand, even adjust—but is it really worth fighting with it to make yourself miserable about the way other folks want to explore, play, and learn? And most of us seem to feel better when we can help people who are suffering—because we all suffer.

10. Because the situations are so different—situations which always entail a worldscape with conditions to it—that individuals, pairs, smaller or larger communities of living creatures, find ourselves moving through or settling down in, it is not particularly efficient to wire in one set of responses to all situations. But it has been efficient since before the advent of language to wire in the ability to learn to adjust to different conditions, however, both by establishing habits and habit-systems and through more thoughtful responses; both always involve actions and inactions. To the extent these are always patterns, they are what language, rhetoric, and discourse cuts the world up into and discourses in particular stabilize, but have had very little to do—at least up until recently (say, since the development of writing)—with our understanding how the "process" works. Today, in the context of our hugely expanded world population, even over the last five hundred years—as more and more the plurality of our cultures become the conditions within which we must negotiate—our survival would appear to hinge more and more on understanding the process. Pollution is rampant. The climate has changed and not for the better. Because, as part of our cultures, we have already made such changes, along with our population expansion, in our so-varied worldscapes—the atmosphere, the ocean, the mined hills and fishable rivers, the arable lands and the slashed-back rain forests—it is imperative we do something about it or as a species we will suffer far worse consequences than we have already started to. Types of bees, certain species of starfish, as well as tigers and wolves—and dozen of fish, birds, and butterflies—have become endangered species over the last three decades. Our own human population numbers are out of hand and the inequities among us controlled

by stupidity or mistaken for reason are only going to do us and the planet in. We need to bring the population down, slowly, over generations, and with consent, though genocides, direct and indirect—both of which seed our own destruction—become more and more prevalent.

11. The evolutionary journey from blindness to the ability to visually recognize individuals and places is as amazing as the journey from deafness and muteness to spoken language, if not more so. (And neither journey has been completed. Consider the importance of the overlap in the past five thousand years.) But it couldn't have happened if we—and I include all of humankind's forerunners—hadn't first developed our ability to recognize groups of us by smell, and all of which is innately entailed in the sexual imagination and—if people will let it be—still is.

12. The indirect nature of communication, which we so easily mistake for direct exchange (because it is all we know), especially at the indistinct and misunderstood level of discourse, is the seat from which cultural misunderstandings rise up to rage and shake our fists against an uncomprehending Other. The understandings required are best gained by exposure and participation in the conditions of life (now covered—though clumsily—by the notion of social construction), rather than through observations and explanations of them. Lacking that, the best textual aid is description of the conditions in the form the anthropologist Clifford Geertz called "thick description," where the scribe endeavors to avoid imposing her or his own notions of what's important and what's not. But even this hurls us into the realm of chance. Experience is still all important. But language must organize experience before experience can reorganize language. If that was not the case, there would be nothing or little to reorganize.

13. Even communication of affection and the acknowledgment of the existence of others through touches and nuzzlings and lickings and caresses work the same way. Smell and taste are only slightly more direct, because they start out by depending on the shape of molecules that actually originate with the other, instead of wave functions that are not as material but more process, such as sound or light. But only slightly more so. And once within the thinking-experiencing-interpreting-feeling part of any creature (the brain), all are wave functions again. Smell is still our most intense memory prod. We fight it more and more; we use it less and less. But before you die, watch it save your—and maybe someone else's—life at least three times, i.e., it gives the group a survival edge, which is only one piece of evidence for its usefulness and efficiency. To have evolved, it has to have others. Brain structures have built up to take care of "meanings" at the level of the word, of the phrase, of the sentence, of the topic, and any kind of physical pressure in general for every other stage of interpretation. Primates—not to mention mammals in toto—learn them mostly by exposure and some evolutionary pre-wiring. But learning must precede the "reception" of communication of what has been learned, and in all individuals the associational patterns that comprise learning occur at slightly different times and at different positions in the world and thus the learning process itself is different for each one of us, particularly today among us humans; which is to say, communication by sound is primarily a vibratory stimulation of something already there, not a material (or ideal) passage of something that is not.

This both *is* and *is why* information cannot pass directly between living creatures of any biological complexity. Information is the indirect evocation/creation of congruence, of pattern.

This is what discourse is and controls.

From one side, language can only be explained communally. From another, it can only be experienced individually. That's because "community" and "individual" are abstractions that have been extremely efficient for negotiating lots of problems since writing came along. (Before that, we have no way to know for sure.) But as our population has grown so much bigger in (arbitrarily) the last two hundred-fifty years, it's begun to look more and more efficient to expand "community" from something tribal to something far more nuanced and ecologically inclusive. Some people see this as a return to tribalism. But it's just as much a turn to science. As for "individual," I can even entertain an argument that holds that "logos/discourse" was initially a metaphor put forward by philosophers such as Heraclitus and the Mesopotamian rabbis (which means "teachers") to help stabilize the notion that language is never "our own," but was always from an other, at a time when there was not the technological or sociological support for a model that was, nevertheless, in its overall form, accessible to anyone who had ever learned to speak a language other than the one she or he grew up with, and/or watched a child learn its "own." Most of a century later, Plato called all this pre-learning "remembrance" and speculated it came through reincarnation. I don't believe that was a step in the right direction, other than to nudge thinkers to pay attention to history. But little or nothing that creatures who have evolved do or think has only one use. That's another thing evolution assures. That's what we mean when we say an adaptation is efficient.

14. The German philosopher Arthur Schopenhauer first made a large portion of the reading public for philosophy aware of the mediated (that is, indirect) structure of sensory perception for humans. But the fact is, this is true for all creatures who have senses as well as for plants that seemed to be slowly developing something akin to them. Remember that the next time you take a walk in the woods. Yes, ninety-five percent of our genes are identical with chimpanzees. But fifty percent of them are identical with oak trees. We share genes with lizards, chickens, pond scum, mushrooms, and spiders, not to mention gnats, lichen, elephants, viruses, bacteria, nematodes, and the rest of life's teeming species. That's why we eat each other in so many directions; and it's why a number of species, such as poisonous snakes and poisonous plants, have developed defenses to keep from being eaten. The fact that we share as many genes with everything that lives is one, but by no means the only, bit of evidence for our direct connections. And that creatures with ears and eyes and tactile feelings look, sound, and move as if they are alive in the world and care about being so—that is, they exist as subjects—is another; but, again, by no means the only or determining one. We live in a world constructed of a vast number of suggestions—and a relatively few explanations (relatively few because we only have the ones, however, we've been able so far to figure out, in which there are bound to be inaccuracies and incompletenesses). Many of the explanations contravene the suggestions. The French psychiatrist Jacques Lacan called these two very human orders the Imaginary and the Symbolic. Different cultures have different Imaginaries and different Symbolics. What science says as a larger philosophy, at least to me, is that this multiplicity is a negotiable condition of the world, accessible

to language and its potential behaviors, not an ontological bedrock of the universe: an effect, an illusion if you like that can be explained. I would only add: However you want to talk about it, it damned well better be. If not, we've had it.

15. At the New York Library Society on February 3, 1848, Poe had hoped for hundreds to support his new magazine, *The Stylus*. It was the same month in the same year in which France would erupt in a revolution that, for a few brief months, would result in universal male suffrage and the hope for even more reforms, and which, in the months following it, America would celebrate that victory almost as joyfully as Paris, with fireworks from Washington, D.C., to Pittsfield, Massachusetts, and where, at his Pittsfield home, The Arrowhead, Melville was rushing through *Mardi* and *Redburn* so he could get started on *Moby-Dick*. Initially he'd planned to have a happy ending, say some critics, but all too shortly, within the year, the advances of the Revolution of 1848 had been rescinded—and *Moby-Dick* (1851) was rewritten with the tragic conclusion we know today, possibly on some level a response to the great historical disappointment, suggests the critic C. L. R. James (in his brilliant reading of that novel in *Mariners, Renegades, and Castaways: Herman Melville and the World We Live In* [1952; reissued 1978, 2001]), written while James himself was "detained"—like Cervantes, like Thomas Paine, like Thoreau, like Gramsci—in James's case on Ellis Island, in the first years of the 1950s.

16. That sharing is one of discourse's functions, though it has not caught up to the expansion of population, cultures, and culture encounters that has so increased in our last few thousand years. The dissemination of the unique—through an incredibly complex set of filters that the illusion of intelligence, not to mention intelligence itself, are what we and the world are—is among evolution's most powerful tools as well as its fuel, as long as those filters can receive and utilize energy.

17. Readers of my *Return to Nevèrÿon* series may recognize this as relating to the "Naming, Listing, and Counting Theory" that occasionally crystallizes in one or another of its appendices.

18. George Bernard Shaw's *The Quintessence of Ibsenism* (1891), *The Perfect Wagnerite* (1898), *The Intelligent Woman's Guide to Socialism and Capitalism* (1927), and *The Black Girl in Search of God* (1932) are all still entertaining as well as informative; as is reading the plays themselves and their extraordinary prefaces.

20

A Note on Melville

Once Christmas day arrives and the Pequod sets sail from Nantucket Harbor (and, with "XXIII, The Lee Shore," "XXIV, The Advocate," and its "XXV, Postscript," Melville brings the first 124-odd pages of the novel and the first act of the nautical tragedy to a close), Melville leaves Ishmael and Queequeg to present two chapters, both called "Knights and Squires" (XXVI and XXVII), in which a lush prose modeled after Sir Thomas Browne's introduces us to the internal character of the ship's First Mate, Starbuck, in the one, and its Second and Third Mates, Stubb and Flask, in the other. Then, in a chapter nearly as lush ("XXVIII, Ahab"), we get a more external picture of the Pequod's captain as he might have appeared to Ishmael or to any of the general crew, with a bit of the captain's own musing.

In the three chapters following these affecting character studies, Melville gives the first incident we see occur on shipboard and a bit of its aftermath. Chapter XXIX involves Second Mate Stubb and Captain Ahab: "Enter Ahab; to Him, Stubb." The title, it should be noted, suggests a stage direction from a nineteenth-century edition of a Shakespearean play. There will be numerous others as the book goes on.

Usually (Melville tells us) Ahab is considerate enough not to thump about on the upper deck with his whale bone leg at night. The sailors sleep underneath, and while they are too tired to wake from such noise, Melville hypothesizes that their dreams might be filled with the sounds of "the crunching teeth of sharks." This night, however, Ahab wants to walk and pace the deck. Coming up from below, Stubb deigns to speak humorously to his captain: he's not suggesting the Captain shouldn't be out walking, but perhaps Ahab might stick some tow (candle wax) into the ivory heel of his leg to muffle the clumps.

Ahab responds with what first would seem equal humor. "Am I a cannon-ball, Stubb," said Ahab, "that thou would wad me that fashion." But as he continues we realize the tone is not playful at all. After telling Stubb to get below and go to sleep in the shrouds (where the commonest sailors might sleep on an uncommonly hot night), Ahab finishes, "Down, dog, and kennel."

Stubb is astonished that Ahab meets his good-humored remonstrance with an out and out insult (however mock-Shakespearean the exchange): "I am not used to be spoken to in that way, Sir. I do less than half like it, Sir."

"Avast [*Get away!*],' Ahab gritted between his set teeth," and he moves off violently, "as if to avoid some passionate temptation"—presumably the temptation to strike the second mate for his presumption.

Since Ahab has retreated, however, Stubb stands his ground. "'No, sir. Not yet,' said Stubb emboldened, 'I will not tamely be called a dog, sir.'"

"Then be called ten times a donkey, and a mule, and an ass, and begone, or I'll clear the world of thee," and Ahab advances on him "with such overbearing terrors in his aspect, that Stubb involuntarily retreated." Had a blow from Ahab been imminent, threatened, feared . . . ?

Muttering to himself, Stubb leaves. What's the matter with him? Why did he accept the insult—he has never let anyone else speak to him like that without returning a blow. Should he go back and hit him—or fall on his knees and pray for him? The old man must be mad. He ponders rumors he's already heard about Ahab's sleeplessness. Finally, he tries to put it out of his mind. ("Think not, is my eleventh commandment; and sleep when you can, is my twelfth.") But he was called a dog—and ten times a donkey . . . and Stubb is off again. Finally the mate decides, he must just go to sleep on it, and see what it looks like "by daylight."

In the next chapter, scarce a full page, "XXX, The Pipe," alone after Stubb's departure, Ahab goes to sit on his whale bone stool, and Melville comments that, there in the darkness, the captain certainly looks like "a Khan of the plank, and king of the sea, and a great lord of Leviathans." Ahab takes out his pipe and starts to smoke, then thinks to himself that smoking is a soothing pleasure for calm and contained people, none of which he sees now as himself. He vows to smoke no more—and, if we have not suspected since his unusual decision to pace through night, we know now something is troubling him. Ahab turns and throws his pipe into the night sea, and the Pequod rushes by its bubbles as it sinks in the dark water.

Not two full sides of a page, the next chapter—"XXXI, Queen Mab"—recounts how, the following morning, Second Mate Stubb tells Third Mate Flask about a dream he's had that night.

Queen Mab—Shakespeare's midwife of the fairies from Mercutio's second-act soliloquy of *The Most Excellent and Lamentable Tragedy of Romeo and Juliet*—is not mentioned by name in the chapter. If we look it up in Shakespeare, however, we find, after an exchange between Mercutio and Romeo in which both say they have dreamed the previous night, Mercutio dreaming that dreamers often lie about them, while Romeo holds that this is most likely to happen when the dream contains a truth (The suggestion is that these are probably sexual dreams about lust that the dreamer must not speak of or at least will probably prevaricate some when recounting them.) Mercutio responds:

> O, then, I see Queen Mab hath been with you.
> She is the fairies' midwife, and she comes
> In shape no bigger than an agate-stone
> On the fore-finger of an alderman,
> Drawn with a team of little atomies
> Athwart men's noses as they lie asleep . . .

The more general point, beyond sexual propriety, is, however, that Mab is the sprite who oversees the arrival of dreams that contain some wisdom about the world, whether or not this wisdom is sexually coded. Both are subtle, but I rely on Melville to have picked both up.

Along with the title of the chapter about Ahab's insult to Stubb and Stubb's offence, this title "Queen Mab," is the second suggestion, after the stage directions that comprise the title of chapter XXIX, that will take readers literate in the tradition of English back to Shakespeare (which begin with the chapter titles, "Knights and Squires"). For re-readers of the novel, all these Shakespearean dramatic suggestions presage the various conversations and soliloquies presented in play form among the crew and officers that will come throughout the book, such as "CVIII, Ahab and the Carpenter" up through Ahab's soliloquies complete with stage directions, such as chapters CXX, CXXI, and CXXI, and "CXXVII, The Deck" and on to Pip in "CXXIX, The Cabin" then on through the three days of the final fatal chase, which—though not in play form—is almost all in dialogue among the men.[1]

During the first whale chase, Stubb will jocularly call the sailors rowing his whaleboat both "boys" and "dogs": "Why don't you break your backbones, my boys? . . . Why don't you snap your oars, you rascals? Bite something, you dogs!" I raise this not to suggest that Stubb wouldn't have called them "dogs" and "boys" before his encounter with Ahab; or that he wouldn't "thump and punch" one or another of them about—as, in the opening chapter, "I, Loomings" Ishmael describes the treatment he expects as a common sailor; or that he would not feel deeply offended if the captain called Stubb himself the same dog or came close to threatening to "thump" him.

Later, quite comfortably and jocularly, Stubb will use the same insults with his men. That he will call his own men "dogs" does not imply that he was not sincerely concerned enough about their rest to remind Ahab, though jocularly, that the man might walk more softly. All of these mean only that the structures of respect on a whale ship and their verbal signs are complex and somewhat mutable; Melville has a grasp of them; and he has chosen to dramatize some of this complexity and mutability in his book. But he also shows that Stubb's own critique stops with the Captain's violation of that structure, and does not venture into the ways he himself conforms to it.

Stubb's dream dramatizes, however, a two-step transformation in the mate's own attitude that must have taken place while he was asleep—a transformation almost magical in its total reversal of what he'd felt right after his encounter with Ahab. The dream begins with the combination of wish fulfillment and guilt we are familiar with from dreams. As he tells Flask, he dreamed that Captain Ahab had kicked him with his ivory leg. (Rather than simply insulting him and menacing him, as Ahab did; in the book's first chapter, Ishmael has told us that common sailors are regularly kicked by their officers to make them work harder or faster, and there's no reason to take it personally. It goes with the job.) Presumably because Stubb is no longer a common sailor but an officer, however, he kicks Ahab in return (as he had wanted to return the insult or hit the captain). But Stubb "kicks [his] own leg . . . right off." In short, the kick is rendered ineffectual; and in effect Stubb is revealed to have castrated himself by his failure to strike out at the Captain. Part of his hesitation was doubtless respect for Ahab—for both his age and for the authority he represented—but part must have also been fear elicited by Ahab's irrational "misunderstanding"/"ignoring" of Stubb's initial gesture as well has the captain's failure to back down when Stubb expressed his offence. Despite the loss of his own leg in the dream, somehow Stubb goes on kicking Ahab, and the Captain changes into a pyramid—which Stubb continues to kick! But soon the kick from Ahab no longer seems such an insult. (Explicate the symbolism of Ahab's transformation: He is revealed to be ancient [if not eternal], historical [if not mystical], and what Stubb is kicking at is something that cannot be bested.) As Stubb kicks on, he ruminates that a blow from a hand would have been more hurtful than a blow from a cane, say, and the ivory leg is only a kind of cane. By the same token, the end of the whalebone leg is much smaller than a full, broad foot. The kick he received now seems, in memory, almost playful. But a strange, old humped-back merman takes Stubb's shoulder and turns him around, to ask Stubb what he's about. At first Stubb is frightened, especially by the merman's face ("What a phiz!" he declares to Flask: *What a physiology the merman had!*) but even as the insult implicit in the kick had faded away, so does Stubb's fear of the merman. Stubb now threatens to kick the merman, since he is no longer afraid. But the merman turns around and pulls up the weeds that are his clothes, and shows his "back"—presumably his backside—which is "stuck full of marlin spikes, with the points out." Presumably this *rectum dentatum* convinces Stubb not to kick him, and the merman begins to mumble,

"Wise Stubb! Wise Stubb!" over and over, with "a sort of eating of his gums like a chimney hag." (The sexual—and specifically homoerotic—implications of this feminization of the old merman at the same time as Melville moves him outside of the sexually possible persons are endless.) Stubb decides to go back to kicking the pyramid. But the merman shouts, "Stop that kicking," and they fall to discussing the nature of the insult again. The final half page of the argument progresses:

The merman maintains that Stubb was kicked "with a right good will," by a "beautiful ivory leg," that, after all, belonged to a great man. The merman considers what has happened to Stubb an honor. He describes the induction ceremony of the English Knights of the Garter (recall the chapter introducing us to Stubb's character type is "XXVII, Knights and Squires"), and recounts a part of the induction ceremony that continued up till 1805, when that knightly order was first suspended. The order's motto is the famous statement *Honi soit qui mal y pense*—Evil to whoever thinks evil is there—which is what King Edward III is supposed to have said at a fourteenth-century ball in Calais when the Countess of Salisbury's garter slipped from her leg, fell to the floor; he sniggered, returned it to her. But it also suggests that the kick is only an insult (an "evil") because Stubb thinks it is. (Stubb, or possibly Melville himself, seems to have believed the induction ceremony once entailed a ritual slap from the Queen, that inductees into the order were to interpret as a high honor (though an hour on Google has turned up no reference to it). But whether Melville/Stubb has it right or not, clearly that is where the argument goes: Stubbs should feel honored to have been kicked by such a great man, and such a small kick at that, and from such a beautifully carved leg.

When Stubb asks Flask what he thinks, Flasks dismisses it as foolish, and Stubb concedes that the best thing he can do is keep out of Ahab's way unless necessary—their conversation is interrupted when Ahab calls out that whales are around and exhorts anyone who sees a white one to "split his lungs" with a shout-out.

Ahab has now designated for us the source of his troubles.

In his highly provocative study of *Moby-Dick* entitled *Mariners, Renegades, Castaways: Herman Melville and the World We Live In* (1952), C. L. R. James argues—and argues persuasively to my mind—that Ahab is a dramatic presentation of a dictatorial personality. He is obsessed with his own goals, and more and more ignores the goals that have been set out by the Pequod's owners, Peleg and Bildad (and presumably the investors in the voyage as well, such as Aunt Charity) or simply those in place through the convention of the venture capitalist system. James claims that it is the same personality type as Hitler or Stalin—and what's more, because it was done before either had manifested historically, it is a full and even sympathetic portrait of such a type, though he claims as well that Melville, while he finds the type fascinating and well worth analyzing, has no illusions that Ahab is a good man. (He may once have been a good man but that is the story of another transition which is only hinted at in parabolic moments.)

If he is a tragic hero, he is still a demagogue—self involved, oblivious to the needs, rights, and even lives of the people around him as long as they follow him. How can he take the whole shipload of hardworking sailors along with him to their grave in the pursuit of a self-destructive and finally impossible task?

Though James does not mention it, the first incident and the psychological transformation it shows Stubb undergo is precisely how that will be accomplished with the entire crew. It entails an absolute authority in a situation where, by convention, no escape is possible nor is there any possibility within the law—indeed, without either changing the law or an uprising.

Many critics suspect that, in an early draft, whether he wrote pretty much to the end of it or only plotted it out initially, at one time Melville intended to have the crew stage a more or less successful mutiny that would, like the one Melville himself had engaged in—not on his first whaling voyage on the *Acushnet*, but in his next ship he sailed on—that, after the uprising, deposited him in Tahiti. In preparation for writing *Moby-Dick*, he read about a number of mutinies in several of his source books. Likely Bulkington, the sailor who appears first at the Spouters Inn, was to be the renegade figure around whom the eventual mutiny against Ahab would cohere. ("He stood full six feet in height, with noble shoulders, and a chest like a coffer-dam. I have seldom seen such brawn in a man. His face was deeply brown and burnt, making his white teeth dazzling by contrast; while in the deep shadows of his eyes floated some reminiscence that did not seem to give him much joy. His voice at once announced that he was a southerner, and from his fine stature, I thought that he must be one of those tall mountaineers from the Alleganian Ridge in Virginia.") This stock hero, with his brooding eyes—surely some lost love lies in his past, and which is a stock fictive sign for past sexual misconduct, however minor or serious—is the first physically described sailor to enter the Inn besides Ishmael. The only other thing we learn of him, by a passing comment at the description's end—"I saw not more of him till he became my comrade on the sea"—is that he will be Ishmael's fellow sailor on the Pequod. Certainly it was to have been Bulkington who would save the sailors from Ahab's self-destructive mania and land them in Tahiti (or somewhere like it).

In one respect, that story would have been a more autobiographically accurate account of Melville's own adventures eight years before than the one he eventually published later that year; as well, it would have brought the book closer to *Typee*, *Omoo*, and *White-Jacket*, the three works on which Melville's earlier and considerable popularity had rested. But without further textual evidence, all of this is only speculation.

After a complete draft, or close to one, Melville changed his mind and decided a tragic end would make better art, more interesting psychology, as well as a more important statement about the world—precisely along the lines that James in his study spells out.

This is more speculation of course, though there is circumstantial evidence for it, even if there is no manuscript evidence or direct descriptions of the differences between the older version and the final one in Melville's surviving letters. (Many, many of them were burnt by his family, in several rounds of conflagration, whenever another trove would turn up, over the years after Melville's death.) But I am not the only person to think, from the letters that do remain, and, indeed, from the novel itself, that, as James in his 1952 study and Olson in his 1947 *Call Me Ishmael* both felt, it sounds probable.

How much rewriting Melville did (if he did any), we cannot be sure. Perhaps Stubb's "Queen Mab" dream and the incident of Ahab's insult to Stubb that provokes it was already there. Perhaps it was added once Melville decided on the new direction the book was to take. Unless manuscript evidence turns up, however, we my never know for certain.

In "The Lee Shore" (and "The Postscript" after it) that concludes the novel's opening Act, now Melville decides to drop Bulkington—which certainly feels like a piece of rewriting to me, and at the very least a change of writerly direction. Melville could have gone back and taken him out completely since he only appears in person now in one brief scene. Had Bulkington been omitted wholly, the text would have closed over him more seamlessly than the sea closes over Ahab's tossed-away pipe—but for whatever reason he decided to leave him in—which could have been for any reason from a rush to finish to thematic considerations, in order to announce that, whatever we might have expected, the incipient hero, Bulkington, would no longer figure in the tale; and, indeed, the tale was not going to be the sort that the rhetoric of Bulkington's description makes readers expect even today.

He is never mentioned again.

But if the crew—or at least a part of their numbers—is not to raise a rebellion against Ahab around Bulkington in order to save their own lives, all the men must "half castrate" themselves in the same manner as Stubb does to make their compliance to the fate Ahab commands of them believable.

C. L. R. James claims that such a psychological transformation is undergone in the course of the novel by the whole thirty-man ensemble, including Ishmael and Queequeg. Workers, when they are working and can believe that the authority structure (which includes the society that invests this or that leader with his power) appreciate their work, will change the dangerous conditions and hardships that they triumph over and even the criticisms and insults they receive from the authority into emblems of honor and affirmations of their own strengths and bravery. This is a good deal of what masculinity is about: the heroic. Throughout history, this process will regularly go on to death itself, for a few or for many. (What else is war if not this process in the military precisely?) The problem is: What happens when the authority is psychotic, manipulative, or just lying—or simply fixated on a selfish and egomaniacal goal? One of the things that people are beginning to understand is that in war, there can be no other kind of authority—for precisely the reasons that inspired James to trace out Melville's understanding of these processes and in a non-military setting. Indeed, it is what gives the books—both Melville's and James's—their modern political resonances. For just that reason, it strikes me as somewhat odd, then, that nowhere in his study does James mention this first account of it, presented in miniature but in so straightforward a major key. James does not seem to hold a traditional mid-century distrust of psychoanalysis (so common in that day on the Left). After his extended reading of *Moby-Dick*, he gives his detailed, if briefer, psychoanalytic take on *Pierre* as a kind of necessary supplement to the better-known book. If one wanted to psychoanalyze James's study (rather than what James considers Melville's two great novels), however, one might wonder if James wasn't repressing this extraordinary piece of evidence from the earlier of them that bolsters his own argument.

Pierre had been published in the summer of 1852. In November 1853, the same month that the second and final installment of Melville's tale "Bartleby the Scrivener: A Story of Wall Street" appeared in *Putnam's Monthly Magazine*, another Melville tale, "Cock-A-Doodle Doo! Or, The Crowing of the Noble Cock Beneventano," appeared in *Harper's*. The first paragraph refers to the five years of European political unrest—France's 1848 uprising, then the disastrous reactionary coup of 1851 while Germany underwent its equally glorious, then equally distressing backslide of 1851 in Munich—that were so forward in the minds of concerned folks all over the world, though without giving their names:

> In all parts of the world many high-spirited revolts from rascally despotisms had of late been knocked on the head; many dreadful casualties, by locomotive and steamer, had likewise knocked hundreds of high-spirited travelers on the head (I lost a dear friend in one of them); my own private affairs were also full of despotisms, casualties, and knockings on the head when one morning being too full of hypos to sleep I sallied out to walk my hillside pasture.

Melville is using this paragraph to map out for the reader the same levels—political, technological, and personal—on which he wants the following incident in his tale to signify: the invigorating, life-carrying crow of a "Shanghai bantam," on the farm of a moribund immigrant family.

If we trust C. L. R. James's reading of *Moby-Dick*, these levels are not very different from the ones Melville wanted us to take as the significant allegorical stages for his retelling of *Paradise Lost* in his great 1851 novel *The Whale*, which had gone all but without public notice thanks to the popularity of that far more direct work of novelistic representation, Harriett Beacher Stowe's *Uncle Tom's Cabin*, which had appeared the same year and commandeered pretty much all the nation's literary attention.

In no way can such a passage resolve the questions (1) whether the rewriting of *Moby-Dick* did or did not entail a change in the outcome of the entire story and the bringing it closer to a single literary model or (2) whether at one point Melville decided to salvage that discarded happy ending or even create a novel that was modeled on the sequel to his model, *Paradise Regained*, in the eventually destroyed *The Isle of the Cross*, which indeed precisely a consideration of those "knocks on the head," not only personal but political, being what had decided him in both cases. (Perhaps he'd decided that *Typee* was already his "Isle of the Cross," or that he dare not go into the homoerotic material that he had certainly and clearly broached in the opening act of *Moby-Dick*.) But it does make clear that he was still concerned about them as signifying fields even after he had made up his mind about the work already done.

Written after the final version of *Moby-Dick* but before *Pierre*, it's certainly reasonable to assume that *The Isle of the Cross*, the title of the manuscript he consigned to his fireplace, might have been an attempt to salvage the earlier version with its "happy ending" or "happy continuation" to *Moby-Dick*: the *Paradise Regained* to *Moby-Dick*'s *Paradise Lost*. Beginning with a successful mutiny against a tyrannical Captain and the escaped crew's successful landing on a Tahiti-like island—a situation drawn from his actual life but still not directly made the center of a work of fiction, perhaps it went on to recount how they found happiness—where, indeed, the male/male relation between Queequeg and Ishmael might have continued, as there are hints it did all through Melville's own island adventures? Was it finally too much, however, even for Melville, especially if—for all his willingness to "appal"—his "fear of criticism" triumphed . . . ?

Back when all this research was first being done and exciting writers, scholars, and critics throughout the intellectual community, Malcolm Cowley wrote a letter to Hemingway explaining that Melville's daughter had hated her father and felt he was a crazy old man for whom she had neither love, sympathy, or respect, who had driven one of her brothers to suicide and the other away to a life where his death—from tuberculosis en route to San Francisco—was all too predictable. No one had paid any attention to her father's works at all over the thirty-five years since he died. That a few scholars were now knocking on her own daughter's door was a reason to burn more trunks full of material that had somehow managed to slip through, lest they contain more embarrassments as certainly had the last round consigned to the flames had—and which, today, we can never know about.

In the face of authoritarian dictators, people are often persuaded to start by considering the evils inflicted on them as necessary evils and finally as honors that actually elevate them—until it is too late and the whole nation is toppled.

But to read current biographical work on Melville—Jay Leyda or Newton Arvin—is to learn that huge amounts of Melville's papers were destroyed by his family—trunks full! And not once, but again and again. Some of the destruction was even by Melville himself.

It's arguable that James's method does not admit of such fine-grained or deep-enough readings to include such an argument. In general, while he will introduce history, he avoids explicating allusions.

Though working with what is clearly implied from the text, reinterpreted in terms of actual history, James provides us with a relatively normalized back story for Ahab: he is born:

> about 1790 in New England. He therefore grew up in the period of expanding freedom after the War of Independence. America was the freest country in the world and above all in freedom of opportunity. When still a boy, Ahab chose whaling as his profession and at eighteen struck his first whale. Nantucket, his birthplace, was one of the great whaling centers of the day, in that whaling was on the way to become one of the greatest industries in the United States. Ahab was part of this striking growth of material progress, of trade, and of money.[2]

While the above is all quite reasonable, one notes that James's study is not the book to go to for the biblical tale of King Ahab, his Queen Jezebel, and the Prophet Elijah, whom they tried to murder with all the other prophets of Israel, and whom, according to the *Book of Kings*, after a great banquet to lull them into complacency, Ahab and Jezebel succeeded in dispatching, while Elijah himself escaped to preach against them—or for the King and Queen's own fates. In her finery Jezebel was thrown from the window by her soldiers and both of their bodies, hers and her king's, were licked and mauled by dogs in the street. Melville readers are biblically literate. He could assume his readers would recall this, if not when Ahab's name is first mentioned, then certainly when, at the end of the waterfront vagabond's tale once he's accosted Ishmael and Queequeg on the winter streets of New Bedford, at the end of his interpolated tale, Elijah reveals his own name (in a chapter, number IXX, named "The Prophet," to presage the revelation of *which* Prophet it is: the one who preached against Ahab, and Jezebel, who functions in the allusion as a symbol for unstated sexuality, normal or perverse).

While James eventually mentions the back story that Melville's Elijah tells—of Ahab spitting into the Spanish silver calabash (presumably of Catholic holy water, establishing him as a freethinker)—allowing us to read that story as an originary sacrilege that is already proving the prophecy made by the Gay Head Indian spirit woman Tastig that Ahab, like his biblical avatar, will come to no good end, and appears already to be playing itself out when Melville's story starts. As soon as we reach the streets of New Bedford, by and large James brackets all the Gothic affect Melville gives us with our arrival at the Massachusetts port, so that the first we hear of Ahab comes from the presumably mad survivor of one of Ahab's former trips and the namesake of the Biblical Ahab's antagonist.

What James does impressively throughout his own book—which starts far later in the tale than we have (i.e., when Ahab calls the sailors on deck and promises a gold doubloon, which he nails to the mast, to the first man who spots the white whale)—is to tell a much-abbreviated version of Melville's story, with material taken straight from the text to highlight and even present his own argument using Melville's actual words, but leaving out much of the atmospherics and the rest.

James says Melville "flirts" with homosexuality—which, in the opening movement is pretty much what he does. In *White-Jacket*, James adds, Melville mentions homosexuality directly, if only to decry it. But another point James makes is that, all through his writing career, Melville wanted to avoid public criticism. In *Moby-Dick* Melville goes to the other extreme and romanticizes it to the point where several generations of readers have wondered if that, indeed, was what he was writing about at all. I believe he was, and was doing it conscientiously as a moral choice. (In the last section of Father Maple's sermon, which seems to be addressed specifically to artists, the good Protestant father declares, "Woe to him who would appease rather than appall!" This may be Melville's message to himself, as well as to artists in general, which relates not only to homosexuality but to his new decision about the ending. Because of where it is placed, however, it is almost impossible not to read it as referring to his own decision to write about the narrator's life-bonding with the older Queequeg—about which Melville tells as much or more of its sexual side as any writer could have at the time about any heterosexual pairing—since such sexual parings were common among sailors, especially outside the constraints of the military, and if Melville had been involved in some such, or even seen one (or more) such, either on one of the ships he sailed on or in Tahiti afterwards, and decided to use it as a fictive model or fictive material—even if the one he chose was not so gloriously permanent or economically egalitarian—certainly I wouldn't be surprised. Probably they were all around him, whether or not, however long or briefly, he was part of one himself.

Since we are talking about the subject, however, it is worth remembering that Queequeg drowns in the end—so the relation cannot endure beyond the catastrophic end of the Pequod's voyage. If we want to get further back and

look at the famous (infamous?) "whole picture," (even without in anyway contravening James's own interpretation) the entire novel becomes a machine set
in motion to kill off the narrator's non-Caucasian lover (who already believes
that "fate" has it in for him and that he cannot escape; rather prescient, I'd
say)—in the manner of any of twenty-five if not fifty gay novels written over
the next 125 years. Moreover, Queequeg's self-sacrifice—allowing himself to
die as the single person who might tell more about Ishmael to the world than
Ishmael might be comfortable with—is what saves Ishmael's very life. (The
coffin is not used for Queequeg, but bobs up and becomes Ishmael's means
of survival.) Was this perhaps more than an unhappy political allegory? More
accurately, it seems a truth-drenched political allegory for its times and ours.
Only Queegueg's death allowed the book its modicum of readership and attention—possibly publication itself—if not its eventual ascendancy in the English
language pantheon of great novels.

Moby-Dick was written and published five years before Freud's birth in 1856
and forty-nine years before the publication of his monumental *The Interpretation
of Dreams* (1900), well before even Freud's early work of the 1880s on hysteria.
But Freud's often reprinted contention—that where he had gone with clinical
observations, artists and writers had regularly preceded him in their fiction and
poetry—could easily have included Melville, at least in terms of homosocial
male psychology. (In that sense it also might be Ishmael's "perversion" that sets
Ishmael aside enough from the hetero-normative male mainstream that allows
him the critical distance to write the novel whose critique of the workings of the
world James celebrates throughout his study. He seems to be able to reconstruct
that critique, rather then be swept down into it, even if to do so takes the death
of his partner—economic (recall their pledge of a fifty-fifty split in Queequeg's
much greater "90th lay" than Ishmael's "300th lay," which possibly cements as
well their physical relationship: not exactly hustling, any more than marriage
is sexual prostitution, but close enough, in both cases, to have raised many
eyebrows throughout history), probably physical, and certainly emotional. In
that light the lack of success of *Moby-Dick*, whose cause is regularly assumed
to be the runaway popularity of Stowe's *Uncle Tom's Cabin*, published in the
same year (1851), as well as a public that was made uncomfortable precisely
by any direct view of homoeroticism, and the way Stowe's success in bringing
the negative sides of racism to the country's attention masks the positive view
of potential racial equality and even the superiority of the non-Caucasian
sailors—specifically Queequeg, Tashtego, and Daggoo—in the labor structure
on the ship and, and if only through somewhat Adlerian glasses, its possible
inclusion of homosexuality, both of which turned readers away, vis-à-vis Stowe,
becomes far more readable.

Despite his own psychological acumen, Melville does not have access to
Freud's use of *Nachträglichkeit*—which Freud introduced in 1895 in the earliest

paper in *Studies on Hysteria* and returns to use again in his case history of *The Wolf Man* (1918)—to explain as Freud does, when all is said and done, the formal way the specific mechanics of peer and social pressures work on people over time, causing them to reinterpret past events (especially sexual ones) in a light they did not necessarily have when the event initially occurred. Nor does Melville have access to Freud's much more important theory (IMHO) of the way transference situations of power work, where the young can either internalize as character neuroses or sexualize as perversion (though rarely both). Freud came to feel that, in most cases, perversions were a healthier and less troubling occurrence for the individual than a character neurosis. The drawback for perversions was that you only had to deal with the social stigma and peer pressure of the perversion, and the sexual interest, if it wasn't completely mangled by the power structure around you, could give you the drive to deal with it. It put the problem at a distance so that it was not an ego-structure problem per se. Thus, under the proper circumstances, it could be easier to negotiate, especially with communal support. The other Freudian theory that Melville is historically cut off from is Freud's conviction that "abnormal" sexuality develops by the same fundamental process that "normal" sexuality does, only in a different social power-structure matrix, in which the varying situation of the subject is an inescapable factor, as is the world around her or him. But like evolution itself, much of this was generally accessible to a combination of observation and introspection—and, if I may say so, of precisely the sort that novelists and fiction writers often indulge in.

The decision to follow a tragic structure rather than a comic one (in the classical sense) is the main tether holding the story even closer to the tale of the fall of Satan and his attendant angels in Milton's *Paradise Lost* than Melville began with. As sympathetic as Ahab (and Satan, so famously) is, Melville knows in the final measure, like Satan himself rebelling against God, Ahab is on an immoral, selfish, egomaniacal quest that destroys himself and all around him. That is why, once the book was done, Melville could say, "I have written a wicked book." And it is what justifies C. L. R. James's comparisons between Ahab and a range of modern, ego-maniacal, nation-destroying politicians. Like so much neurosis, it is not the fundamental structure of the logic it followed but the inappropriate intensity with which that logic is followed, is imposed on others, is at the center of a demand to ignore all other things in life, unto compassion, kindness, comfort, and safety, that produces the harm and suffering to both the self and to others. Though they may start with the best of intentions, the position of power in which they find themselves corrupts them into a too-small vision in which their own gain is more important than the gain of the nation and, if not initially, eventually they choose their own desires over the good of the society—and society, the Ship of State, founders if not sinks.

Melville had written such a book. It is a tragedy. But, as James makes clear, it is a very modern one.

* * *

Melville Chronology

August 1, 1819: Melville Born

Herman Melville is born to Allan and Maria Gansevoort Melvill (his mother adds the "e" to their name after his father's death) in New York City. They live first on a house on Pearl Street. (Near Pearl Slip; the street no longer exists.) He is the third of the couple's eight children. His sister Helen is the oldest. Then comes Gansevoort.

1830: Father Goes Bankrupt

Allan Melvill's import business goes bankrupt. The family is forced to leave New York City and move to Albany in order to escape his many creditors.

1832: Father Dies

Shortly after an Atlantic crossing, Allan Melvill dies at home in Albany (where his wife's parents live), leaving his wife alone with eight children. Herman and his older brother Gansevoort must drop out of the Albany Boy's Academy and take a series of odd jobs in order to support their family. Herman's include that of a young bank clerk (at thirteen); over the next few years, he holds a clerk's job in a store that sells fur jackets and caps. At seventeen, he also begins to publish newspaper articles.

1839: Merchant Marines

Melville decides to go to sea. He makes his first sea voyage with the merchant marine ship, the *St. Lawrence*.

1840: Travels West

Melville travels with his friend Eli Fly—a brother of a friend of his sister's, and another aspiring newspaper man—along the Mississippi River to Illinois, where his uncle has settled. When they discover that there are no jobs for them in Illinois, the young men return to New York City.

January 3, 1841: Life at Sea

Melville signs up for the whaling ship *Acushnet*, which sets sail from Fairhaven, Massachusetts. Melville signs on for what is supposed to be a three-year journey.

July 1842: Life in Polynesia

Melville abandons the *Acushnet* and spends three weeks living among the Typee natives of the Marquesas Islands. He leaves the island on another ship bound for Hawaii, and spends most of the next two years at sea.

October 3, 1844: Back on Land

Melville returns to New York after his final sea voyage on the frigate *United States*. He begins writing a series of semi-autobiographical novels about his time at sea.

1846: First Novel

Melville's first novel, *Typee: A Peep at Polynesian Life*, is published. It is an account of his time among the Typee natives of the Marquesas. Readers love it.

His older brother Gansevoort dies the same year.

May 1, 1847: Second Novel

Melville's second novel, *Omoo*, is published. It is also about life in Polynesia. In it, Melville criticizes the proselytizing actions of white missionaries. This book is also a success.

August 4, 1847: Marriage

Melville marries Elizabeth Shaw, the daughter of Massachusetts Supreme Court Chief Justice Lemuel Shaw.

1849: One Year, Two Novels, One Child

Melville publishes two novels this year, *Mardi* and *Redburn*. The Melvilles' first child, son Malcolm, is born.

1850: White-Jacket

Melville's novel *White-Jacket* is published. He is struggling with the draft of a new novel about a doomed whaling voyage. On a summer trip to the Berkshire mountains, he meets writer Nathaniel Hawthorne, who becomes a friend and inspiration. Melville purchases a home named Arrowhead in the Berkshires and moves his family there.

1851: The Great White Whale

Melville's masterpiece is published. Though the story of Captain Ahab is eventually considered an American classic, sales at the time are disappointing. The Melvilles' second son, Stanwix, is born. Melville names him for his grandfather, Peter Gansevoort, who was known as the "Hero of Fort Stanwix" for his efforts in the Revolutionary War.

August 6, 1852: Another Critical Flop

Melville follows with the novel *Pierre*.[3] The public reaction to the book is summarized by a critic who calls it "utterly unworthy of Mr. Melville's genius."

1853: Short Story Attempts

The Melvilles' daughter Elizabeth is born. Disheartened by his reviews as a novelist, Melville tries his hand at short stories. His first piece, "Bartleby, The Scrivener: A Story of Wall Street," appears in *Putnam's Monthly Magazine*. Melville publishes fifteen short pieces in popular magazines over the next three years. Readers are confused by the stories, which are often experimental and metaphysical.

1855: Final Child

The Melvilles' fourth and final child, daughter Frances, is born.

April 1, 1857: The Confidence Man, *Losing Confidence*

Melville publishes a novel entitled *The Confidence Man*. When it fails to garner attention from critics and readers, Melville quits writing as a profession. He takes to the lecture circuit and spends three years giving talks at lyceums.

May 1860: Sets Sail Again

Melville agrees to sail around the Cape Horn with his brother Thomas, the captain of a clipper ship. He makes it to San Francisco before changing his mind about the voyage and returning home in November.

1863: Sells Home

Deeply in debt and behind on his mortgage payments, Melville is forced to sell Arrowhead to his brother Allan. He moves with his family back to New York, the city of his birth.

1864: Visits the Front

Melville visits the front lines of the Civil War, an experience that leaves a deep impression him.

1866: Customs House

Melville takes a job at the New York Customs House, where he works for the next twenty years. The job pays $4 a day. He publishes a collection of Civil War poetry entitled *Battle-Pieces and Aspects of the War*.

1867: Son Dies

Melville's oldest son Malcolm shoots himself. It is unclear whether the fatal shooting was intentional or accidental.

1876: Clarel

Melville's uncle funds the publication of this 16,000-line epic poem. Critics bash it and readers ignore it, and publishers are forced to burn the many unsold copies.

February 23, 1886: Second Son Dies, Retirement

Melville's son Stanwix dies of tuberculosis in San Francisco. Melville retires from the Customs House after twenty years of employment.

1891: Death

On May 5, in New York, Andrew Carnegie's new concert hall on Fifty-Seventh Street opens with a five-day festival. Pyotr Ilyich Tchaikovsky conducts his "Marche solonelle" on opening night, and a few days later his Piano Concerto Number 1 in B-flat.

On September 28, Herman Melville dies at his home in New York City. He is buried in Woodlawn Cemetery in the Bronx.

1924: Billy Budd

Melville's final novel, *Billy Budd, Sailor,* is published, helping to rehabilitate Melville's legacy as a great writer. The finished but unpublished manuscript was found in Melville's desk after his death.

Resume: Melville's Work Experience

Bank clerk (c. 1832)
Clerk, fur and cap store (c. 1832–1839)

Farm hand (c. 1832–1839)
Teacher (c. 1832–1839)
Sailor, Merchant Marines (1839)
Sailor, the whaler *Acushnet* (1841–1842)
Sailor, various ships (1842 –1844)
Writer (1845–1876)
Customs inspector (1866–1886)

—July 21, 2014
New York

NOTES

1. I suspect these mini-dramas that occur throughout *Moby-Dick* are what gave twenty-five-year-old Norman Mailer permission to use such playlets in his debut military novel, *The Naked and the Dead* (1948); and when, at seventeen, I read *Moby-Dick*, certainly they are what, for better or for worse, prompted me four years later to include the playlets I used in the second volume of *The Fall of the Towers*—not to mention including a scene in the first volume inspired by a family trip (again, when I was seventeen) to Gay Head, in the black section of Oakbluffs, during a Martha's Vineyard vacation.

2. C. L. R. James, *Mariners, Renegades, and Castaways: Herman Melville and the World We Live In* (Allison & Busby, 1953, reprint 1985), 6.

3. As published, *Pierre* consists of two versions, one inserted into the middle of the other, which tends to destroy all sense of continuity in either form of the novel, which has been seen by some as Melville's attempt to sabotage the readability of his own book. At least one edition has been published without the insert. (I have not done more than skim either version.)

21

Absence and Fiction

More Recent Thoughts on *The American Shore*

A Facebook post with responses, occasioned by the reissue of my book *The American Shore: Meditations on a Tale of Science Fiction by Thomas M. Disch—"Angouleme"* (Dragon Press, 1978; Wesleyan University Press, 2014). Disch's novella was originally published as a section of the novel *334* (MacGibbon & Kee, 1972).

Fiction can do two things extremely well that, indeed, experience can also do: It can dramatize how incidents, occurrences, and aspects are related. Also, it can dramatize how incidents, occurrences, and aspects are not related, especially when people expect them to be. To do either, however, it must bring the incidents, occurrences, and aspects that relate or do not relate into the same attention field. This is how a discourse is established. This is how a discourse creates a discursive object. After we encounter a few examples of those incidents brought together, and see how they associate or disassociate, then, when we encounter either set of incidents, occurrences, and aspects we tend to recall the other set—because that's what discourses tend to make us do. (A "discourse" is an attention field and the things that fill it and how they relate—or don't relate. Other things outside the attention field we say are outside the discourse. This way a discourse establishes two levels of absences: absences which are within the discourse and absences that are not within the discourse.) If we remember the experiences or the fictions in which this occurred, often we remember that these things are related in the particular way the fiction of the experience describes, or we remember that these things are not related in another way because this is what rhetoric, of which discourses are constituted, can also do.

I will say here that I distrust writers who use their own work as examples for anything. You should, too. For me that distrust means I listen to such examples with a highly critical ear—not that they are necessarily wrong. But I am still on the alert. So be highly critical of what I am going to say: As many as a quarter of the reviewers who reviewed my last novel, *Through the Valley of the Nest of Spiders*, especially among those who liked it, when they described the incidents of the novel's first thirteen pages recounting the morning of the day Eric's stepfather drives him from Atlanta to stay with his mother in Diamond Harbor, wrote that Eric goes out and has sex with a number of homeless men under the highway before returning to talk with his friend Bill, then to have breakfast and help pack the car before taking off on the drive with his stepfather to the coast.

Though I am only one reader of the book (who happens, very arbitrarily, to have written it), I suggest that they are incorrect—all of them—in their account of what happens in those pages.

On page thirteen, which describes the end of Eric's time under the highway, the text says, "He walked around another five minutes, but as happened once or twice a week, that morning *no* one was out" (emphasis in original). In short, while over the previous pages Eric has remembered various sexual encounters under the highway in the summer weeks so far, that morning he returns home unsatisfied. He has had no sex at all. To me, this seems important for what happens in the book over its first eighty-nine pages, devoted to the account of that day—the most pages devoted to such a short time span in the book (i.e., slightly more than ten percent of the novel). Most people when they go out looking for sexual relief and don't find any are even more (I believe the word is) horny than when they started—especially the young. What happens—or rather does not happen—in that morning search for sex explains why, six or so hours later, when Eric and his stepfather reach Turpens Truck Stop just outside Diamond Harbor, why Eric is as . . . well, as receptive as he is, when he goes with Jay into the truck stop's active men's room.

What happens to him in the men's room when he is in that state changes the rest of Eric's life and initiates the motivating forces that impel the novel's remainder. But I wonder what it means that so many readers, even sympathetic ones, cannot apprehend even this much of the plot development.

In the late 1980s and through the '90s, when I was teaching literary theory in the University of Massachusetts's Comparative Literature department, one of the largest difficulties I had while teaching graduate students the early books of Michel Foucault—*The History of Madness* (aka *Madness and Civilization*), *The Birth of the Clinic*, and *The Order of Things*—was that a repeated rhetorical structure Foucault employs is as follow: Here (he will write, either directly or in effect) is the most coherent form I can give of the argument counter to my own. Then, for half a page, three pages, or in at least one case almost sixteen pages, he will produce an all-but-airtight argument—before he takes on the job of dismantling it. Regularly, I alerted my students that this was Foucault's method; nevertheless, students would still come away from the text convinced that Foucault was saying the opposite of what he was actually arguing for, not even because they agreed with the counter-argument or because he had won them over by the force and clarity with which he'd framed the opposing side's position, but because it was so hard for them to conceive of a larger argument that respected the counter-argument enough to present it at all, much less present it so well. In short, they couldn't understand why they were reading it if it was wrong; or why he was trying so hard to make it sound right.

They could not understand or even read these gestures of respect for his intellectual opponents.

They could not understand or even read the importance he was rhetorically trying to impart to his own rebuttal by taking his opponents so seriously.

They could not understand or even read the seriousness he was trying to convey for the entire argument by such respect and importance.

I can only suggest that they were more comfortable (i.e., familiar) with a discourse in which one laughed and made fun of one's intellectual opponent or tried to show him or her up as so self-evidently wrong as to be ridiculous. While in no way am I suggesting that my fiction is as rich or as skillfully presented as Foucault's nonfiction, nevertheless I sense some relation—that is perhaps too easy to call a failure of reading—between my graduate students and the reviewers who are so eager to say things happened in the foreground of a novel that were only thought about or remembered. Eventually many of the students "got it." But it took far more of my skill at close reading with them than I had initially imagined it would. The only general point I can make, however, is to quote a line by Roland Barthes that I first used as an epigraph for the last chapter of my 1983 novel *Neveryóna*: "Those who fail to reread are obliged to read the same story everywhere" (*S/Z*, 16) That is another effect of discourse when we lose track of its rhetorical particulars. As well, it retards discourses from changing in necessary ways. Sometimes this retardation is useful. Sometimes, however, it is lethal.

—July 24, 2014
New York

*   *   *

Chris Watts: Though I don't teach graduate students, my eighth graders all but refuse to consider defining other arguments when building their own. It appears this refusal to see or consider goes beyond the erosive properties of immersion in the larger culture (age, or time spent). Maybe peer expectation?

Or are we training minds for something other than perception? I'm glad to see it's not just me, but saddened as well.

Josh Lukin: But . . . but . . . that Eric has no sex that morning is the *point*! How can people miss that? Well, I *do* have a friend who read the initial pages of *Sexuality* v. 1 and thought Foucault was endorsing the Marxist view he describes . . . and of course, I know you could offer a dozen more examples of misreadings of your own books alone. Readers do seem to develop a strong emotional investment in certain kinds of rehearsed responses.

Alfred Corn: Authors can be very cogent critics of their own work. I always listen to what they say about it. But their views can't be airtight summaries of what the work actually does.

Samuel Delany: Do you want me to quote three reviews . . . ? I only hesitate because they're all highly favorable reviews at that, and the idea isn't to shame people who want to be, as it were, my allies. (With all due respect, I don't think reviews are that important in the greater scheme of things—unless they are very careful pieces of writing. The care with which they are done and thought out ends up creating their importance and literary strength—at least I'd like to believe so.)

Josh Lukin: Me? I take your word: just going Eek.

Samuel Delany: Absolutely, Alfred—that's why I say in the center of the piece I distrust writers using their own work as an example and invite the reader to distrust me, since I'm about to do just that. Maybe I'm an incompetent writer and just miffed it. Josh says he got it, but I also know—because I've discussed many books with Josh over the years—he's an extraordinarily fine reader, and not only because Josh reads me correctly. But such knowledge can only bring a heightening of probability to what I "know" about my own book, never a certainty . . .

Dan'l Danehy-Oakes: I don't want you to quote reviews; I take you at your word. But it is astonishing to me that anyone could think that Eric has sex in that scene; do reviewers not read carefully . . . ? I must suppose not: when one has a deadline (especially when one has a deadline and a very long book to read), skimming becomes the order of the day. Which is not good news for those who consume reviews . . .

Samuel Delany: My suspicion is that they're skimming even more than you think and just quoting each other, because the other has said something specific about the book—that's the unkindest reading I could give of it, but it's also the one that to me seems most probable. I'd love to be proved wrong. When you DO pay careful attention to the rhetoric of anything (like the rhetoric of book reviews that repeat each other), often it tells strange tales, or at any rate makes some strange suggestions.

David Gerrold: I sympathize. I wrote a book once—which I will not identify here—which was intended to satirize a form. Most readers took it straight, which was fine, the one or two reviewers who recognized the form thought it was imitation, not meta-. O well. Lesson learned. Next challenge—learning how to be subtle, but not so subtle it's missed.

Michael Swanwick: I have great respect for reviewers who take their work seriously, given how little money and respect they receive. One such reviewer told me that some of his fellows laughed at him for actually bothering to read the books for so little payment.

Greg Burton: Most books don't require close reading. Most readers don't understand close reading, and even fewer have learned to play on the apparatus. That's the way it is, and that's ok. Not everyone is a mental gymnast. A forgivable miss—more so than, say, missing the medical terms "heterotopia" and "syrinx" when they show up in blinking letters on the pages. And the pages are clearly labeled "playing with the limits of technical language ambiguity (that's a multiparse phrase) in and within the conventions of genre fiction." (I use the term "multiparse" to refer to elements where the ambiguity resolves to "yes, and" instead of "or") . . .

On a related topic—has any critic discussed how optical chain is the result of playing a glass bead game?

Gregory Feeley: Perhaps "most books don't require close reading," but you can't tell for any given book until you have read it closely.

Samuel Delany Josh Lukin, the quick answer to your question is that there is a discourse of pornography, and in that discourse sex happens. It isn't remembered, thought about, or considered. And my book is often read through that attention field (or within that discourse, to use different words), even by sympathetic critics.

Samuel Delany: <u>Greg Burton</u>, no, no critic has, as far as I know. Full disclosure, that's one I wasn't aware of myself till today—though I'd read Hesse's novel. (Heard of it before I wrote *Dhalgren* and read it a few years after—though I had read *Siddhartha* before.) But that's why it's good that we all have personal quirks in our discursive structures. Point them out—the textual objects that share some attention field of our own—and they become shared structures, at least for a while. Finally, of course, their endurance will depend on how useful they are and what one does with such rhetorical overlaps, often in another piece of writing of one's own.

Chris Watt: I think your eighth-grade problem is similar to one I remember reading about (in an article about Foucault, during the same period) on high school pedagogy. That is to say, it was noted (and I've seen it noted since) that high school students of the time, if asked to read several articles on some controversial topic, when asked to summarize someone else's papers or articles they were using for research, they tended to suppress all sense of conflict in their accounts. Their papers would come out with the argument all for one side, or all for the other.

I suspect, pedagogically, what you're seeing is an early form of what led to that a year or three later.

Bill Wood: Perhaps if you could convince the students to believe that their parents wrote the essays, then they would have an easier time disagreeing with them.

22

The Mirror and the Maze, II

I.

I am the first African American science fiction writer to come up through the commercial genre that coalesced around the pulp home of science fiction before and after the term "science fiction" began to appear more and more frequently in Hugo Gernsback's magazine *Amazing Stories* between 1929 and 1932.

Octavia E. Butler was the second. She was briefly my student in the summer of 1970 and my friend until her death in Seattle in 2006. We read together at the Schomburg Library in New York City; shared panels at the Franklin Institute in Philadelphia (where I also interviewed her at Temple University before a large and enthusiastic student and faculty audience), at a book fair in Florida, and twice in Atlanta; and once we presented together for the Smithsonian on a rainy D.C. night.

But we need some ghosts for our own discussion to make sense—ghosts who come from the (I use the word advisedly) genre we call "the literary," itself a genre collection (a collection of usually recognizable practices of writing that include poetry, drama, the short story, and the novel, and others, as they are thought of by most "literate" readers). For an idea of how much literature has changed in the U.S. since I began to publish science fiction in 1962, or perhaps since 1966 when I attended my first science fiction convention, the Tricon in Cleveland, consider first what the academy—which gives us our sense of what literature is—teaches today, and then consider how that differs from what it taught in 1966. In that year, there were no black studies classes (much less programs or departments); there were no film classes, no women's studies classes or programs, and no gay studies or queer studies courses or programs.

That year, less than two dozen university science fiction classes were actually taught throughout the country. (Today there are many hundreds.) The *New York Times* copyeditor would have changed the sentence two before this to "That year, fewer than two dozen" and emended this one to read "*The New York Times'* copy editor." "Negro" was the only proper word, noun or adjective, for a black man or woman, in speech or in print. Neither "African American." Though "colored people" existed, "people of color" did not. Black was considered insulting and colored only slightly less so, except among some older black intellectuals who had campaigned *against* (not for) Dr. Du Bois, who had wanted "black" as the word—without a capital "b"—because it was equally provisional and as inaccurate as white. On the edge of the downtown drug culture, in New York and San Francisco, both black and white men and women had started referring to black folk as spades—and no one took any offense at it. Whites and black used it equally and it felt very convenient. I used it in my home neighborhood in New York City with black folk as they did with me, as well as with whites, who also used it easily with both races, but I also knew that, above Twenty-Third Street, it was probably best to leave that one downtown. And I certainly wasn't taking it with me to a new city such as Cleveland. As a coastal urban solution to the designation problem, "spade" would persist among blacks and whites for the next two years, until in 1968, it was replaced by "black" in one three-month period, pretty much as I described it my novel, *Dark Reflections* (2007). By 1807, when Hegel published his *Phänomenologie des Geistes*, someone purporting to have read him might have said: "All these minute changes amount to no more than a hill of beans." By 1969, when Foucault published "*L'Archeologie du savoir*," someone purporting to have read him (which in 1976 I did) might have said: "The sum of all such changes—unto the metaphor of the bean hills by which you designate them—are one with the culture, the times, and, in their larger units, form the apparatuses of history." Backward- and forward-looking ghosts, from another genre . . .

But it was 1966, three years before Stonewall.

I was twenty-four.

I was on my way to my first World Science Fiction Convention, the Tricon.

Over the previous six years I had sold and published seven science fiction novels.

The evening before, on the overnight Greyhound bringing us into Cleveland, I'd had sex with a sailor about my age whom I'd started talking with in our seats toward the back. In his whites, with cap folded and stuck in his back pocket, he was coming up from Key West for a spell with his family, and had spent most of the previous week "with some guy who writes plays, Tennessee something . . . ? I never heard of him. Everyone around him seemed to think he was a big deal, though." (I have no memory which of us, at that point, moved across the aisle to sit with the other. I think it was him, though.)

I told him he was right: Tennessee Williams *was* a big deal. The guy was surprised *I'd* heard of him.

Later, in the unlit bus, as violet rouged away the dark along the bottom of the window above the seat across from us, he tugged his whites back up under his butt. (We were both commando, as they'd say today, and last night both of us had grinned at each other with the discovery.) He buttoned the two sides of his belly flap with sun-browned hands roughened by paint scraping and disinfectants from deck scrubbing. The uniforms were originally intended to be worn without underwear, he'd explained to me—but now most of the other guys did anyway, unless they were after quick sex, a blow job, a butt fuck, a jerk in the john, and, during our two-and-a-half sessions between midnight and four-fifty a.m., both of us had pretty much covered them all. He slid his feet in their white socks into his black shoes. I buttoned my shirt as telephone pylons swept by outside. A dozen empty seats in front a woman got herself together, stood up, and guided her four-year-old along the dark aisle toward the bus restroom behind us. By the time they came out, he'd gone to sleep, head on my shoulder, and soon I was out myself, both of us hoping to catch a few hours between dawn and our scheduled ten-forty arrival.

An affectionate white guy, he'd been a fun encounter, though the sex had taken place in rigid silence, because of the fifteen- or twenty-odd passengers toward the front. I'd told him neither that I was a published writer nor why I was going to Cleveland—not because science fiction was a devalued genre but because I'd learned, over the last six years, that for anyone under thirty in this country—and I'd spent six months abroad, where it was somewhat different—to tell pretty much anyone else that he (or, I'm sure, she) was a published novelist was to bring all social communication to an embarrassed halt. They thought you were lying or, if you weren't, you must be too weird to be trusted in ordinary society.

And later, at the convention, I did not meet a single person with whom I was even momentarily inclined to share the incident. If something happened along that line today, probably this would not be the case.

An incident that I lifted from my life as a black child, and used as the basis for a scene in the (non-SF) novel *Dark Reflections* (2007), will characterize those times: When I was ten or eleven, I'd spent a night in the hospital for observation. While I was there, I'd asked a young white doctor, probably an intern or resident, how many homosexuals there were in the population. (I'd figured out I was homosexual; I wanted to know. It was a question I was afraid to ask. Maybe he'd suspect my motivation. But curiosity won out.) He laughed and told me it was an extremely rare disease—no more than one out of five-thousand men carried it, and in case I was worried about myself, there were no medical records of any black males so afflicted.

Because I was black, I didn't need to worry!

But while, even then, I spent a lot of time jotting down (gay) sexual fantasies in my journals, despite what a few folks had all but whispered to me about the Kinsey report on male sexual behavior (I didn't know yet there was a companion volume on women), it never occurred to me that I could or should enlighten anyone at the Cleveland Science Fiction Convention about what I'd learned from observation—even in the name of science.

In 1966, however, though from time to time I'd fantasized a happier world that was almost entirely reactionary against the one that existed (and thus not esthetically very interesting but only sexually so to me), I still assumed such widespread ignorance protected me—since there were no protective laws, and same-sex activity was officially both an incurable (and according to some, fatal) disease and a crime for which I could be arrested.

II.

In 1966 *Dune*—a novel consisting of *two* three-part serials, *Dune World* and *The Prophet of Dune*—had started to become available to the science fiction community of readers in 1963 and continued through 1965, available in the largest-selling science magazine of the time, *Analog*. In 1965, *Dune* had appeared in a large, one-volume hardcover edition from Chilton Books.

Since the 1960 change in the title from *Astounding* to *Analog*, it was supposed to be self-evident, at least to the science fiction community, that future-based stories were analogues of (that is, analogous to) what was going on in the present. (Had *Analog* been a literary magazine, it might have been called *Allegory*.) That year, *Dune* tied for the Hugo Award for best SF novel with Zelazny's *And Call Me Conrad* (aka *This Immortal*); but within the part of the community at the convention, *Dune* was a fairly tired old warhorse that had been around forever—and its radical ecological message was wrapped in enough conservative monarchistic trapping, and if not racism then something awfully close to it, and homophobia, not to mention awful prose, that I could never get too excited over its sexist and political back slidings and obfuscations. For me *Conrad* was the far more exciting book—and over that 1966 weekend it was clearly far more exciting for most of the people who attended the convention. That's why—at that convention—it tied with *Dune* for the Hugo. (That's one reason, in 2016, it will be included in a pair of Library of America volumes devoted to important SF novels of the 1960s.)

Over the next few years, the world outside the science fiction community, of course, would react very differently to *Dune*. Me, I still find the book, along with much of Philip K. Dick's science fiction, badly written, about not very interesting societies. The ghosts above—all literary ghosts—have more or less alerted

their readers to the fundamental harms caused by poverty, social and imaginative blindness (innate or imposed), physical punishment, and the hypocrisy of
others, as well as to how small-town propriety chastens and destroys, and how
big-city impersonality isolates and alienates. To undertake the specificities of
black marginalization—that social construction, with all its material and historical underpinning we think of as blackness—yes, the writer, black or white,
may have to invent a few new ones. And certainly we writers better keep our
eyes and ears open: Look at the laws. Look at the land. Look at the men and
women living on and with both, as they resisted and as they adjusted. What was
there to hinder them? What was there to help them? And, however unsettling
it still is, how, sometimes, is it the same as ours? One listens—and listens hard
and carefully, to tales from one's parents, one's grandparents, strangers on a
bus. One can even be outraged at the inadequacy of a metaphor vis-à-vis the
historical research. But, yes, while you have to create and, even more, observe,
sometimes you have to reinvent the whole writerly machine to show what you
know; paradoxically, if you try too hard, likely you'll fall all over your own feet
as not—again, black, white, or any other Other.

But do not let that stop you—the energy of the effort can often count for
much.

Because you have, among all your other tools, the sentence, the syllogism (or
inference, articulated or suggested), chronological order, and narrative progression, both to use and to violate (both a tool of the master and an apparatus of
the subaltern, with thanks to Audre Lorde and to Gayatri Chakravorty Spivak
both, for their clearly contrasting warnings), you arrive with tools that have all
been used before to portray joy or injustice, or the daily island life, as Gertrude
Stein called a third of English literature, to explain how any of the three constitutes a general or a specific situation, and what in any of the situations is
in excess of the others. (Two thirds, I always read her as suggesting, is always
unknown until someone does it.)

III.

The first white U.S. writer who wrote a black character I personally found
believable—and I read lots and lots, both inside and outside science fiction—
was Thomas M. Disch, in his 1966 new-wave novel *Camp Concentration*, seri-
alized in the British science fiction magazine *New Worlds*, recently subsidized
by the London Arts Council. The first of its two installments appeared in the
magazine's initial *New Yorker*–sized issue. The force and power of Disch's black
prisoner Mordecai—only a step away from the situation of the government's
Tuskegee experiments on black sharecroppers from the 1930s to the '70s in

Macon County, Alabama—is one reason I think it's such an important book in science fiction's history. At that first Convention I went to, it was months away from being published; Disch was in London. But five months later, that book passed my own Turing test, the test of a gay black kid who'd grown up in Harlem till age nineteen and who'd then moved for half a dozen years (with six months out in Europe) to the East Village; it passed it in a way that, for me, Faulkner's black characters did not—as, indeed, many of his white characters failed to, as well, though I'd always found his language exciting and exacting, even when it was also exhausting. Neither did those in Burroughs's Tarzan stories. (I'd already noticed that Henry James hadn't even tried, though Gertrude Stein of all people had given it a shot.)

Disch told me later that he'd modeled Mordecai on a black classmate of his in the Midwest, but—boy!—did I recognize Mordecai from my memories of myself and my black friends on the Harlem streets around me.

Till that point *all* of the white attempts to do this, in my experience, *had* failed. But James Baldwin's hadn't. My Bread Loaf acquaintance John Williams hadn't, in *The Man Who Cried I Am*. Neither had Ishmael Reed in *The Freelance Pallbearers* (and back then there was a lot of talk about where Reed's novel should be classed: *Was* it, somehow, science fiction . . . ?) or Amiri Baraka in *Tales* or in *The System of Dante's Hell*—such black-authored works seemed to be coming out all around me. (Nor did Baraka fail in one of his finest and more recent poems, "Patmos" aka "The Patmos Poem" aka "Fashion This from the Irony of the World" [the poem's opening line]—the poem exists under all three titles and when I first heard him read it at Naropa in summer 2013, he announced it as "Patmos.") I believed the black characters in John O. Killens's *Youngblood*, largely because they wanted what I did. More ghosts. More discourse. But, yes, the experience seemed to me quite important enough to interrupt this disquisition. But both literature and science fiction have regularly produced such experiences of that sort, in my life. More discourse. Yes, they were black writers. But somehow, in 1966, this incredibly smart, white, white, *white* writer—I loved Tom, but Tom was *so* white; as well he had all the sex appeal of a boiled potato—Disch hadn't failed either. I find interesting that the ones who succeeded, including Disch, did it in such different ways—to me that's more interesting than their shared narrative success (which is only to put them into category, to give them an identity, as problematic as that of any race).

But that's narration. That's science fiction. That's literature—or perhaps that's a place where, sometimes, instead of trying to strangle one another, the three become, however briefly, congruent.

It also suggests that the way to succeed is a matter of a writer's observation, intelligence, and creativity working within an awareness that the more clichéd the character is, the more likely (though without any certainty of it) they are to

be unbelievable, while at the same time they can't be so idiosyncratic as to be irrelevant (equally uncertain), and that is finally what's more important than the
race of the writer. And it was interesting too to learn in my forties that, along
with his program to bring sweetness and light to the masses (like a Wagner *avant
le lettre*), Matthew Arnold had said the same things when he was considering the
novel back in *Culture and Anarchy* (1869). But by and large, writers do not learn
these things from criticism. The positive effect of criticism, more often, is to
confirm what the writer has already figured out—from reading other writers
who'd figured it out even earlier . . .

Go figure.

Camp Concentration was written for what was then Berkeley Books and was
submitted as the fulfillment of the second part of a three-book contract. The
publisher (also, then, its editor-in-chief) rejected it. Disch was actually proud,
and several times I heard him tell the story of how, when he came to pick up
the manuscript, the man did not simply hand it to him but threw it at him
over the desk, so that he had to gather it from the floor where it had scattered
and put it back together before he carried it from the office. Tom took this as
incontrovertible proof he'd done something right.

Only recently, I learned it was rejected by the Library of America board for
the upcoming collection of novels that the editor had selected as important SF
works of the 1960s.

And again Disch's ghost (Disch killed himself in 2010) bends to gather the
pages of his novel from the office carpet . . .

And again I agree with him about the correctness of his reasoning back at
its 1966 rejection from Berkeley Books; because that is the person I was and
that is the person I still am.

Camp Concentration takes place only an indeterminate ten or fifteen years after
it was written—in short, it has already undergone the transition all science
fiction is doomed to, from historical speculation to historical fantasy. Disch
makes no attempt to extrapolate even fifty years into the future, much less a
hundred. The U.S. is fighting a war—which may be an extension of the war in
Vietnam, or another in Malaysia; it's deliberately unclear. Our protagonist is a
conscientious objector and a poet. The book is his journal, kept at the request
of his jailors. It opens with a riff about Mormons and not a very pleasant one.
His guard is a Mormon, whom he has nicknamed for his own purposes "young
R.M." (Rigor Mortis, for his unshakable smile).

Only a few days ago I re-read part one of *Camp Concentration*. In 1966, after
it had failed to find a U.S. publisher, I first read it in its *New Worlds'* two-part
serialization—again, I was in London. I can locate two things that were then
unthinkable. The first was that, fifty years later, we would have a black president. By 2005, however, that was very thinkable. By Obama's election in 2008,
Morgan Freeman had played the current president of the U.S. in a series of

successful films, more than any other American actor in the previous thirty years, with at least two other black actors representing the POTUS on various TV series. If you consider the way popular culture works as an image stabilizer for the nation, hindsight makes Obama's presidency seem more inevitable than a surprise.

Regardless of his social origins, the novel's narrator, Louis Sacchetti, conscientious objector, is a pretty splenetic fellow. In 1966 such spleen had its humor and thus its charm. (In the age of Facebook, remember that Disch is also the SF writer who writes about the social takeover of "The New Sentimentality" as a national aesthetic in his *334* novella series, the same series in which in 1972 he predicted gay marriage; think about that the next time you move to press "like" under a six-second cute puppy video.) In 1966, the general population did not see those ideas as inchoate to the voting middle class, and we have less patience if we perceive them as coming from someone out of the 1%, angling for the most powerful position in the country.

But that spleen was also Disch's.

Disch characterizes R.M.: "for all his orthodoxies, [he is] serious minded, a man of good will [but] . . . it is R.M. and his like who perpetuate this incredible war, who believe, with a sincerity I cannot call into doubt, that in doing so they perform a moral action" (17). But whether it's about Mormons or anyone else, isn't that the crux of the problem? Finally, Disch suggests that R.M.'s problem may just be stupidity. Today, I believe we'd be more inclined to rack it up to a lifetime's misinformation. And tomorrow (also growing out of the computerized information tsunami and individual exhaustion that Disch has not yet seen) the question will be, "Is that misinformation theirs or ours?" But the question has always been there. The computer landscape of the twenty-first century renders it a much, much bigger question, for many complicated reasons, for many, many more people.

In *Angouleme* (1972), Disch was the first and only science fiction writer to conceive of gay marriage as lying in a foreseeable future. I'd suggested it slantwise in a couple of my own science fiction narratives, but personally I'd already worked through my interest in marrying and was pretty sure—at least in its traditional form—it was not an institution for me.

These ghosts, today, hover around my first science fiction convention in Cleveland, the Tricon in 1966, not especially causal ghosts (some of them arose after it and only help, today, to explain it), but let me describe another book because it *had* already been so important to me before I arrived at the convention. No, this author was not at the convention, though I met him at another in New York City a few years later.

I'd been very taken with Theodore Sturgeon's *More Than Human*—an SF novel I'd first read in the 1950s, before I'd ever thought about writing in the field. More accurately, it made me wish I could write something, anything, as vivid and of the same consuming import as Sturgeon's had been for me. The vivid particulars of its portrait of the socially marginalized, homeless, and mentally delayed Lone dominate the book's first third. Almost mute and without any human socialization until, as an adult, he meets the Prod family, Lone is a white kid brutalized by both nature and the world. My white friend Robert had said it was the most important book he'd ever read; and pretty soon I was sure he was right. (On our first day at school, back in the five-year-olds, I'd seen Robert brutalized almost as horribly as Lone by the other children, simply because he had a slight motor impairment, till a teacher ran in and stopped us. Yelling and jeering at him, we'd been trying to hound him out a fifth-story window.) I read the book's first eighty pages half-way up a movable wooden ladder on a track along the wall of books in our tiny middle school library—not even the big one down on the third floor, where you could sit and read math books—while the middle school librarian, Mrs. Fisher, did *not* tell me to get down or to stop or to go away, but worked at her desk while I hung across from and above her, paperback opened on the wooden wrung at eye-level, reading through two class periods. The book's force—at least with me—was because more and more people, black *and* white (I'm sorry always to be stressing this; but that's because I don't believe the differences can make sense until you have a field of similarities that contain them) were always telling me, as I grew up, Lone was precisely who I wasn't; but because everything Sturgeon mentioned about him or around him or noticed him going through, I recognized—recognized so clearly—it only made me surer and surer that, somehow, I was him.

More Than Human gives an equally intense portrait of Janie, an unwanted eight-year-old white girl during World War II. In the first part, when Janie befriends the black twins Beanie and Bonnie, who live with their grand-father in the basement, Janie's mother comes in from work one day. "Oh Jesus be to God," she exclaims, "she's got the place filled with niggers." As I stood on the ladder, I knew exactly what it meant and felt no discomfort with it at all—thanks to Mark Twain and my father and Tarzan and the Harlem streets.

When the kids sit down together in the old house, they find a locked library, and read some of the books to each other. One they read from is Leopold von Sacher-Masoch's *Venus in Furs*. At ten or eleven I didn't recognize it. But at fourteen when I reread *More Than Human*, I knew what Sturgeon alluded to—and why. Nor did it bother me anymore than it bothered Janie and her juvenile reading group. As well, in the book there's Gerry, an outright orphan who doesn't know *who* his parents are ("I ate from the plate of the state and I hate"), any more than Lone did. In the second part, once Lone is dead, Gerry and Janie must kill the group's new white protectress, Miss Kew, because she wants, first, to separate them from the black twins who are part of their "gestalt" and, second, to send the seemingly mentally delayed Down syndrome "Baby," the core of their group, to an institution. The last two incidents the group manages to undo. But the lack of challenge that Miss Kew eventually surrounds them with, Gerry can only deal with this through an ultimate violence, from both fear and love. (For one moment as Alicia Kew left her childhood, she was Lone's lover but, because of it, she'd been traumatized by her father out of all future sex but not out of love.) I identified with Gerry because he was in therapy and because in Lone, Gerry actually had a better psychotherapist than he did in Stern—who, I recognized, was too much like my own four therapists (five if you count one woman diagnostician)—as well as like my own father.

True, the black girls Bonnie and Beenie, in Sturgeon's triptych of novelettes, don't have much weight as characters—they are problematic from the time Janie sees them out the window to when she assumes they are as unwanted as she is, and basically kidnaps them, to take them with her into the forest. (Well, she is only eight.) Certainly, they are not put together as thoughtfully as any of the men or Baby or Janie herself. But they figured in a general fictive field where, at the time, almost no black characters were visible at all.

However, the micro portrait of Miss Kew's black maid Miriam, who changes her attitude to the children once she sees the white ones fight to preserve their bond with the black ones, is a surprisingly stereoptical moment in the book, for all its summary distance.

Sturgeon's portrait of Miriam's change of attitude is the *most* distanced of portraits, something that Gerry himself takes "years" to understand, but it's highlighted by an immediacy which the reader, black certainly and white probably, will likely "get." (One only wonders why it took Gerry so long. But that was the 1950s.) Miriam is the character who remained with me from the book's first reading.

All the experiences that were used in my own stories and books were black experiences—why? Because they were mine. That includes my readings of white authors' books. In my own books, sometimes the central characters were white—as in *Trouble on Triton*. Sometimes, as in *The Fall of the Towers*, *Babel-17* (where the main character is Asian), *The Einstein Intersection*, *Dhalgren* (where the main character has a white father and a Native American mother), or the *Return to Nevèrÿon* series, many or all were non-Caucasian. But I believe Sturgeon's personal experiences of marginalization and blackness are as validly reflected in his books as mine are in mine. Sturgeon's position and mine really were at that time *two* positions on the cultural map. And I see people who should know better misreading mine all the time today. Those positions still are, too. But both have shifted. They are different from what they were, yes, *because* Sturgeon was white and I was black. But I still could recognize his. And more than once in his lifetime he claimed he could recognize mine.

IV.

The first person to call me a nigger was not a white man or woman. (Though before I went to my first science fiction convention, some had. We'll get to the first of those, too.) In my case, like that of many, many, many blacks all throughout this country of my age, the first person to call me a nigger—whenever he got frustrated with me—was my dad.

Today I'd want to emend that sentence: "He was a black man—and a black man from North Carolina, born before World War I." We were not poor. But we were nobody's rich, either. And when my dad got really riled, I became a "stubborn thick-headed nigger." It was the same phrase the white villains used with the African natives when they thought the Africans were resisting them. My dad used it when he thought I was resisting *him*. But other than that, I didn't think too much of it. It was one of the most common words on the street on which I lived and played, where clearly it had many more meanings than that: those were the ones I was interested in learning, though I knew I wasn't supposed to say it—at all. No, we were not poor, but we certainly were not wealthy. Other students in my largely white private school were. In that school my sister and I were both scholarship students and could not have afforded to attend had we not been. And I was certainly not supposed to say it at my school, which was just off Park Avenue at Eighty-Ninth Street. (And if I said it at my fairly integrated leftist summer camp, probably I would have been sent home—and I would have expected anyone who said it there to suffer the same.)

So I didn't.

But it prepared me for the first time a white person did—which we'll get to.

Both my parents were proud of their black heritage—and both had made me feel that they had reason to be. But I didn't feel any greater contradiction between Dad's saying it and my not being allowed to say it than I did between his occasional "damn" or "shit" that also occasionally slipped past his own proscription on cursing. I thought it was hypocritical that I wasn't allowed to say any of those words in his presence—but I never thought the word was evil, any more than when it emerged in *Huckleberry Finn*, which Dad read me chapter by chapter over a six- or seven-month period, often breaking out in laughter at the jokes, whether made by Huck, Jim, or anyone else. Nor would he have thought of bowdlerizing it for our bedtime readings. He knew Twain's book was on his side. Though, when we got to the end, he pointed out how some of Tom Sawyer's notions about what to do with Jim didn't make a lot of sense. But with the help of Mark Twain and the Harlem streets, my father taught me that words take their meanings from context—which was probably why I found it so easy to see Cratylism as an error in thinking, when we moved into the age of theory.

Here is something that I think of as an almost purely black experience (the fact that racial experiences are never truly pure restricts "purity" to a metaphor at best and keeps it a distant and distorting approximation at worst), one that I've told many of my black friends, fewer of my white friends, and written about fairly indirectly in my *Return to Nevèrÿon* fantasy sequence and directly in the opening novella in *Atlantis: Three Tales*, transferred to a character based on my father. Given what he looked like, I can't believe it didn't happen to him too.

In late September or the first days of Indian summer (I was still in elementary school, so I was probably ten or eleven), I was sitting on a Central Park bench, school notebook open over my knees, doing math homework, when an unkempt blond with sharp blue eyes, a guy maybe twice my age—today, from his jeans and sneakers and T-shirt you'd know immediately he was homeless, although "homeless" was not then part of our vocabulary—walked up in front of me, and smiled over not very good teeth. "Hey," he said with the thickest southern accent I'd heard in a while (like any other twenty-year-old talking to a ten-year-old), "you a nigga, ain' ya there—huh?"

I blinked, surprised.

"Yeah, you a nigga. I can tell. Tha's cause I come up from Alabama. Hitchhikin'. See I always tell. You ain' gonna get nothin' by me. I can see it, right in yo' face there. The mouth, the nose. All that—naw, I can see it. You ain't gonna fool somebody like me, get away with nothin'." Then, chuckling, still grinning, he turned and walked off, through the sunny park.

And that was the first time a white guy called me a nigger—though I think any number of people would accept that he hadn't "called" me anything; he'd only used the word—a southern drifter (maybe or maybe not out of his teens) coming up to an urban black kid sitting on a park bench doing homework.

But it taught me something. First of all, he was right. If anything, getting recognized as black was something of a relief, especially with so many white people around me who often volunteered equally out of the blue that they couldn't tell and, I assume, most of whom at that time felt they were telling me something that for some reason I'd be pleased to hear.

Pretty much between once every year and once every two or three, when I was sitting somewhere in public, minding my business, some strange white person would come up to me and explain—with or without saying nigger—that they recognized I was black. Sometimes they sounded local. Often they had regional accents. They could be of any class, actually. But it was regular factor of my life as a black kid in New York, probably *because* our city had so many visitors on all levels from so many places. By the third or fourth time, however, I would say "Yes. That's right. I am," just to end the conversation. (About a third of the time, they didn't want it to end. But that's a whole set of other stories.)

And sometimes it happened with black folk . . . yet more stories. What are you going to do in a situation like that? Declare (to both father and stranger), "I am not, because *you* used a bad word!" Maybe there are white kids who would do that today. Maybe even some black kids would. But that's not the way language works—and certainly not the way it worked for black ten-year-olds between 1951 and '52.

You either have to understand the point I'm making, or you have to take it on faith. In both cases I experienced the word as falling on the far side of propriety. But in the first case it had been spoken by the authority figure in my life—who, after all, relatives around us regularly claimed loved me, even if more times than not I doubted it. I knew as well, even at ten, he would be the first one to tell me, "Don't let any white man call you a nigger!" But I wasn't about to stop this white kid, both because he projected no harm or hostility by his comment, and because he gave every indication of speaking a truth that I very much wanted to hear, bad word or no—a truth that today has been a useful one, and one which, if I hadn't gone on to hear it again regularly, would have left me far more neurotic about how I appeared to others.

At this point, I don't remember whether it was the fifth or sixth time, but after one of the men or women left, frowning after them *I* said to myself (and I've said it more than once): You thick-headed nigger, you *better* stop believing all those white assholes who keep telling you how white you are, because obviously there are a whole lot of white people in this city—and in the country (for it had happened a couple of times outside New York by then)—who have nothing else to do but go around on the lookout for any black person they think might be racially passing, and remind them that they can't.

More recently—for the last decade or so—I've wondered if the white obsession with reinforcing the demonization of the "nigger" isn't finally a tool to drive a wedge further between the white classes, to separate the ignorant from the educated, the poor from the rich. A couple of years ago, an extremely smart, sensitive, and sympathetic white reviewer[1] pointed out she felt uncomfortable reading my latest novel *Through the Valley of the Nest of Spiders* (2012) on the bus, in case the black woman beside her should look over her shoulder and decide she was reading racist porn. Need I point out that this, historically, is precisely what being black can feel like—the anxiety that, on the bus, other people will assume you are less than what you are because of your race, whether it is a matter of dark skin and black features, or because of features that are no more distinctive, certainly, than those that allow you to notice someone is Irish, Asian, Italian, Native American, Scandinavian, Boriqueño, Mexican, Polish . . . Indeed, that order of cultural appropriation is one with white privilege and becomes an exploitation of blacks for the benefit of the most insecure strata of the white middle classes. (Certainly that's how the word has worked largely until now. Using the word in that way is *also* white privilege.) The only group that regularly rebels against this is the black hip-hop movement in some of its social behavior.

I stress the above not as a call to action: the argument here simply does not contain the information necessary to decide such courses, all of which hinge on needs and materials. In this context it is rather a delineation of a small but important way two races, white and black, constitute and perpetuate each other.

Now easily I could hear my critic saying, "Chip, there's no winning with you, is there . . . ?"

To which my response would be, "It's not a matter of winning with me or with anyone else. It's a system of which we are both parts. Like a text, it *has* no outside. But it changes its shape internally. That is the condition we are condemned to work with and within. We can make local improvements. We can initiate major catastrophes. We can hope that the local improvements hook up to form more stable ones—and some of them will."

Sitting in a park, when someone comes up to tell you they've noticed you are black (not all that unlike sitting on a bus, reading, anxious that someone might think you are someone you're not), these are life experiences—which I've rarely seen written about. At least by anyone other than myself—and my critic. And I suspect that my critic writing about hers is fundamentally a good thing. But that is because mine can't be unique to me.

At least once in a work of fiction I assumed that something like that had happened to my dad. It's hard to believe, given what he looked like, it hadn't. I have no idea where the kid from Alabama came in on the intelligence scale—rather higher, I suspect, than some would have put him; and he *was* observant, though he'd been socialized to use it in a manner very different from mine.

Over the years that order of experience has been gradually replaced by another. Today I'm seventy-three, and the last time *this* happened was about five months back, when I was coming down on the train from Dover Plains to New York after a weekend's visit to a fuck buddy I have known even longer than I have my life-partner of the last twenty-six years, Dennis Rickett; my fuck buddy is himself married—and has been for five or six years now—to a man from the Dover area. They live in local trailer park. They seem to be at least as happy with one another as, unmarried, Dennis and I are.

On the train home a woman beside me started up a conversation. (I was reading a book, but as she seemed eager to talk, I listened.) She was a retired, white psychiatrist—yes, she'd begun as a medical doctor—and a year younger or older than I was—at this point I don't recall. Eventually, as do many people who just start talking to me, she asked my ethnicity. I told her I was African American.

Why do you say that? she wanted to know.

Well, both my parents were black. I grew up in Harlem, in New York. I always assumed I was. Why in the world shouldn't I?

Because, she explained, you can't be. (She wore a textured cloth coat—"a good cloth coat" my mother would have called it.) I look at you and *I* don't see you as black . . . The stress was not so much insistent as interrogative, confirmed by the lift at her sentence-end, as though she was wondering why I wouldn't accept that her perception explained the whole thing.

As politely as I could, I suggested she consider rethinking. We talked about the one-drop rule. She said that was silly.

I said, "It is. But I didn't make it up or set it into law. It's controlled most of my life since well before I was born. It's the life I've had."

She, of course, was quite willing to throw the law along with three hundred years of American history out the speeding train's firmly sealed window and couldn't understand why I wasn't ready to do the same.

But for the next twenty minutes, as we rumbled toward Grand Central Station, she explained why I couldn't be black.

I'd read books that she'd read. (We'd talked about two.) I didn't have a black attitude. (Probably I should drop the "a.") She knew that because she'd had both friends and clients (she explained to me) who were black. (Some of her best friends . . . ?) I suppose I could have cut it off—I don't feel any compulsion to educate people who are either rude, ignorant, or simply disagree with me, but I was curious where this would go. We only had twenty more minutes into the station. Nor did I feel offended: my own self-respect is too well anchored to come loose before the confusions of a somewhat isolated retired psychiatrist (and her sense of personal isolation was something I was beginning to intuit) any more than it was likely to come loose before a nineteen-year-old white kid in an airport with a pouch full of pocket *New Testaments* to hand out, explaining to me that surely it was self-evident that God was responsible for all the different species of animal, and equally so that I could never be happy or good if I didn't come to Jesus.

Since the summer of that Alabama kid, I've talked to white and black folk from the North and from the South whose every tenth word was nigger and whose every third word was fuck, shit, or worse. Some of the men I've even gone to bed with—a few of them more than once. No, they were never people I wanted to live with. Nor did they want to live with me. And you know what? All of them were interesting. But if my self-respect was not going to be wounded by that, certainly it wasn't going to be wounded by forty minutes of conversation with this woman.

What I found—and it was interesting enough to think about writing a story around it—was a bisexual older woman who'd recently wanted to experiment sexually with an older woman friend of hers but had never been able to bring herself to do it or even admit it to her friend—yes, this is the second decade of the twenty-first century, weeks away from the legalization of same-sex marriage—and (but you know this) I also found racism.

I have compassion for the woman. I have compassion for the racist—and the racism of the woman on the Metro North train in 2015 felt to me the same as the kid's in 1951, hitching up from Alabama, when I was ten. Both seemed basically nice people as far as I could tell on first meeting. But both exhibit the same *systemic* form of racism.

Its name is "white privilege."

Have I written about it before? Read "The Game of Time and Pain" in my *Return to Nevèrÿon* series. That's only the first in a list.

It manifests as the conviction that, as a white person, male or female, they have the right to tell anyone else not only that he or she *is* black, but that he or she *cannot* be black. (I've known both to be directed at the same person—sometimes only hours apart.) One is simply the underside of the other: both of them together ground that privilege and the actions and the behaviors and the lack of thought that grow out of it.

I would say, today, the experience of white privilege is a form of experience mostly black folks tend to have—and that people who are however provisionally a part of the "unmarked" hegemony are not likely to. (I'm glad you brought the term in, though we're beginning to realize that very few people can live there all the time, and are likely to experience some of their lives as outside it.)

How did it come about historically? Read Du Bois or Gilroy—or, if you want it neat and straight from a white, Knoxville-born poet who went to explore it back in Alabama in the mid-1930s, where that long-gone drifter on the loose in Central Park claimed to hail from (before he hailed me, "You a nigga, ain't you . . ."), read the appendices "On Negroes" and "Landowners" in James Agee's *Cotton Tenants: Three Families*—an ur-version of his later and denser *Let Us Now Praise Famous Men*. Hell, read the whole book. It's not that long—and it's brilliant because the material that inspires it has been observed and analyzed so accurately. Or if you want the same analysis expanded to hundreds of pages and historified from the Civil War on, read Du Bois's *Black Reconstruction in America, 1860–1880*, and consider the details of all the things that had to be destroyed to bring into being the situation Agee writes about a mere fifty years later.

But these are all only more reasons why I feel racism is a system—and an overwhelmingly destructive situation. And while points of both discursive intervention and (sadly fewer) points of infrastructural intervention can be found, blame (and the discursive habits in which blame lives and thrives) belongs to the problem, not the solution.

Simply as philosophical psychologists, Christ and Buddha both had that one figured out—and don't omit Muhammad. It's the core of all of the Abrahamic religions, but others have arrived at the same insight. And others have not.

Capitalism is fueled by all seven of the deadly sins, and supported by greater and greater alienation (the material and cultural distance between rich and poor), and it does nothing to keep them in check, especially among the rich during hard times for the poor.

But the fact that there were attempts to deal with all of these—racism, sexism, even homophobia—are the things that drew me to science fiction before I started writing it; and they are what kept me there after I'd joined that community as a writer—as only the gay atheist grandson of a slave-born Episcopalian bishop in this country can be kept. But very few of the thoughts here are ones that others have not had already or will have again, in time, about a similar situation, however the context varies. Thus, to talk about any part of this community as a void which I entered alone and worked in by myself is, at its best, the most provisional critical strategy to talk about an aspect so evanescent it could not exist and, at its worst, is naïve, uninformed, and dishonest. Science fiction has always been cited for being ahead of the pack—not only in technological speculation—but in sociological willingness to look beyond. Often it does not remain there long. But its small, self-critical structure promotes that in a way that the sprawling, looser field of the literary does not or, when from time to time it does, it cannot support and reinforce in the same way—sad puppies notwithstanding.

And as usual, by latching on to the failures in that system because they are the ones it recognizes most quickly and easily, the media makes them appear more like the larger structure that has isolated them and ghettoized them. This is the same process that you have seen in the criticism from black groups. "If we have a peaceful protest, you ignore us. (And ignore how unfairly our peaceful protests are so often handled.) Only when we become violent is any attention paid at all—which is used to justify resisting the peaceful resistance." The systemic point of course is that resistance is resistance and the hegemony doesn't like it; and will always settle on the most effective method available of discrediting. Usually this has nothing to do with what an individual wants. As I have written before and—probably—will write again: There are no racist, sexist, homophobic decisions to be made. The system makes those decisions for us. There are only anti-racist, anti-sexist, anti-homophobic decisions to be made. And at the decisive level, they can only stabilize what the infrastructure supports—otherwise they are without power because no strength underlies them.

V.

Only four or five years ago, when a white heterosexual couple, in their twenties I assumed, decided to have sex in the back seat on an 11 a.m. Tuesday bus I was taking to Philadelphia—like the one to Cleveland, it was not that crowded—within ten minutes, through a general whisper net, every male on the bus, of at least four ethnic types, as well as one stolid young black woman, knew it was happening and were making regular trips to the back—many to the john—to stop off and watch for ten, fifteen, thirty-five seconds: the woman looking at them was quiet, but when she returned to her seat and some friends, she seemed to be thinking it was appallingly funny. Her laughter filled the bus—and the couple themselves were not particularly quiet.

On my own trip back, I saw that the woman in the pair was on the bottom, face up, eyes closed (no make-up), hair a kind of strawberry blonde confusion. Her skin was not the best. Backpacks were wedged down on the floor between their seat and the back of the empty seat in front of them. Her knee was up against their own seat back beside and above his hunching butt. (His skin wasn't that great either, at least on his pimpled and brown-furred buttocks.) His feet—in socks, of course—were up on the window, heel in, knuckles to the glass. She still wore her bra—at least I think she did. She had remnants of blue polish both on fingernails and toenails—one foot down on wrinkled red canvas. As I went into the back john myself, I thought: Wouldn't that have been easier, female superior? After I finished urinating, I zipped up and returned to my seat without really looking again.

A few days later, I saw the same young man—that's Philadelphia—after brunch (I assumed, from the plates on the round, aluminum-topped table), outside a restaurant on Locust Street off Twelfth. He was with some older male friends.

The woman was not there.

It started me thinking: over the five or six odd times in my life I've tripped over displays of public heterosexual sex (two black couples, three white ones, and only one interracial—and that not really public because it was at a party and involved five people, three black men and one white woman and one white man, and no violence I could see), the men except in that one interracial case seemed so much more grounded than the women. The woman was a friend of mine and I consider her still so today. The men remained: the women left or vanished.

The gay man in me is relatively happy with the memories of the men. The writer in me really misses the woman in the bus couple, though—and in a way that leaves me uncomfortable.

I want to talk to her. I want to ask relatively simple questions. Did you enjoy that? Did you not enjoy? What was fun? What was not? This is because, as a writer, I have asked similar questions of men and women for years. And I have often gotten surprising answers. Things you would think no one liked at all were sources of hope, pleasure, and relief. Things that one found in what looked like ideal spots of bourgeois satisfaction left the women and men there in suicidal misery.

I want the answers to these questions, however, so that I can make comparisons—my encounter with the sailor against the experience of the couple on the bus. But is the similarity entirely illusory? Forty-five years has passed between them. Manners, mores, the whole array of social information has changed. Other discourses would seem to have remained rather frighteningly in place. (Organizing my library for an upcoming move, three days ago I found a book called *The Republican War Against Women*, dating not from the last election but from the last century—in the 1990s!) Is this simply a comparison between apples and pears? Can any comments be made about the pleasures of fruits in general? Or does context sever them?

Somewhere I remember a phrase from Foucault, "The tyranny of the singular . . . ," and I am sure such tyranny must hinge on the notion of identity. The point, of course, is that retiring the concept doesn't retire the problem. At best it's a way of reminding us that thinking about things in such terms (there is a category, "sex on the bus," that can tell us some likely things about what's going on with the subjects involved if only in terms of probabilities . . . ?) will possibly trip us up.

The point is these are the kinds of things nature and culture both—and all the ghosts that comprise them—are always giving us to compare, are always asking us to reduce to information, until we decide the problem is with the system that identifies either.

Can it be at least a beginning, however?

Can it be the beginning of a discourse?

Can it be the beginning of a map of cultural similarities and cultural variations in which further investigation yields intervention points, not simply for forbidding it but for improving it for everyone—not simply valorizing it. (For men, usually, by taking pleasure and power away from women.) This is the sense in which there is nothing outside the text, nothing outside the event . . .

Is there any way they can't begin one?

And this is what I like to think I have always been interested in using science fiction for, more or less articulately. Because it is what I have always seen others—more or less successfully—do in the genre.

VI.

I'm less interested in how X wields power against Y than I am in the power dynamic that holds X and Y together; how it creates both subjects and objects. To assume that it is ever wielded unidirectionally, without the mediation that either multiplies its effects or mitigates them, is usually another mistake, and often a tragic one. Even a dead body has its weight that resists movement, produces decay products, has its smell, its consequences. For it to work in any mode other than catastrophic, usually power must be a local and humble act—and even then, often it misfires. Mostly it's flailing in the dark and usually creates pain, death, and agony—for several groups or species. That was what Lord Acton was about when he made his famous statement on the tendency for power to corrupt—which I quoted in my first, nineteen-year-old's novel. Despite the generic power boundaries that have traditionally both ghettoized and protected science fiction (and, even more accurately, have not so much prevented ideas and texts from moving back and forth but rather retarded the passage of certain ideas, forms, and images in both directions.

The marginal and unwanted children in Theodore Sturgeon's *More Than Human*, Janie and Gerry, are as shunned as any orphan in an eighteenth-century or Victorian novel. So is the main character, Horton Bluett, in Sturgeon's first novel, *The Dreaming Jewels*. That one utilizes Sturgeon's own experience as both a guitarist and someone on the edge of the circus world, as well as the experiences of a very unhappy kid with his stepfather. It's a tale which strikes up many, many resonances with what, today, we would call transgenderism. *The Dreaming Jewels* (aka *The Synthetic Man*) is one of the earliest commercial science fiction novels to do this—as Robert Heinlein would try his hand at doing in another, years later, and less successfully. As well, in the very first pages we learn that Horty has "a disgusting habit," that, even when I read it at fourteen, I was pretty sure was a stand-in for something some of my friends in school occasionally could be caught doing—and which, in my thirties, I was surprised to learn, when I was cruising in a movie theater in the Village, the now torn-down Roxy, I happened to see someone sitting a few rows down from me and to the left doing. I was surprised to realize it gave me an erection—and only a little later suddenly had the return of a memory of when, in my kid-hood at summer camp, I had had the same response when I'd seen another camper doing the same thing in the ring of campers around the flagpole at the morning pledge of allegiance. Some of my readers will realize this is the same "disgusting habit" that binds my characters Eric and Morgan in my most recently published science fiction novel, *Through the Valley of the Nest of Spiders*. This was a response I realized I *could* have—not that I had it all day every day. But with the discovery, I realized other people could probably have it much more or much less than I did, the way my own sexual obsession—men who bite their nails (even though I don't)—is practically as strong today as it was when I was eight, nine, ten, or eleven. This is simply how (some) fiction works, even as it escapes autobiography.

In the eighteenth century, G. E. Lessing wrote that suggestion was far stronger as an esthetic strategy than is direct statement. The first time I ever heard of Lessing was in the opening pages of Eddison's fantasy classic *The Worm Ouroboros*—and how had I come to be reading *The Worm Ouroboros*? In an occasional essay Sturgeon had recommended it. So I'd gone hunting it up. And where did I first find the Lessing? On a bookshelf outside the door of my second-floor bedroom-workroom in the Trask Mansion at Yaddo, in the summer of 2000, before I left to take up a professorship I'd been invited to fulfill at Temple University.

Yaddo is of course the traditional bastion of literary and artistic endeavor in this country. (It was a wonderful experience, and I learned as much as I ever have about art in a comparable period. For the Lessing alone it would have been worth it.) But what was I doing there? Earlier that year, out of the blue, I'd received an invitation to attend. The fact is, I have never been brave enough to crash any literary gates without an invitation—I've never even filled out and sent in an application. More accurately, any time I have, I've been rejected. So I don't. I tell myself I'm too busy writing, too busy reading, too busy examining the world. (Which has until recently included getting laid—and still does, when I can get to it.) Probably it's a reason I'm a science fiction writer.

The changes in the world which I sketched so quickly in my responses to your first question—changes in literature, in science fiction—are indices of a reorganized world that has shifted greatly. Even though they've never completely blocked the passage of those ghosts from either side to the other in any absolute way (the ghosts themselves change, personally, culturally, with each new reading); nevertheless they retard the passages of those ghosts in different ways and at different speeds at different periods in different directions, and by a process quite as complex as discourse itself because it constitutes discourse itself, another name for which is "understanding," as in a response to the world, or simply to thought.

In pre-platonic Ionia, Heraclitus—as did the teachers (another name for rabbis) of Mesopotamia—called it, in the same three-hundred-year envelope, "logos" to stress its inextricable relationship to language.

(And, contemporary with Plato, Diogenes of Sinope masturbated publicly in the slaves' and workers' market of Athens, and gained reputation for it along with his philosophy that lasts until this day . . .).

In those works, its strength lies not in how it reflects answers but in how it suggests, as Sturgeon said, "the next question," not in the romantic mode of "seeking" but in the far more risky mode of "finding"—no matter the orientation of those who ask it, male, female, gay, straight, Asian, Latino, white, black, Muslim, Jew, or Christian, or even the dreaded atheists such as Butler and myself (another category, another inadequate identity), even if it has, however locally, the *be-spiritedness* to make art of the process, in whatever genre.

Let's go back to that Sturgeonesque vividness and immediacy. By 1962, when I published my first SF novel, I thought I knew—not how to do it, but—how to move my writing toward it. That same year, weeks apart, I'd had it confirmed for me—twice—once in an essay by Chekhov and once in a letter by Sturgeon himself to Judith Merril that she quoted in an article she wrote on Sturgeon for the special *F&SF* issue devoted to Sturgeon that appeared that year. (Often afterward, when I began to teach, I've cited them together to my students, both for creative writing as well as in science fiction and literature classes.) But almost at the same moment, as if revealed by the idea as method, the problems of sentimentality and maturity were there to undercut it, and at the level of popular kitsch, we began to worm our way toward the age of the "inner child" which seemed the natural follow up on essentially the insight that "the personal was the political," even as it tended to repress all considerations of destructive, even fatal, ideologically supported childishness. And here of course is where you begin to experience, from the inside, in that shifting historical system, the dialectical forces that again and again we see change rabble-rousing radicals over the years into die-hard conservatives. They are as convinced as it is possible to be that they haven't moved, or haven't moved very much. What has changed is the system around them, they are sure or they hope; and their "new conservatism" is simply a reasonable response to that. What from the outside looks like reactionary change, from the inside to them looks like consistency and integrity (as well as adjustment to the new realities)—but the point is everything has been in motion, and not always clearly in terms of its trajectory and size and even density and permeability to everything else.

I suspect this is why Robert Heinlein and George Schuyler (a white and a black science fiction writer, one on the West Coast, one on the East, one a part of the community that I was able to enter and work in, and one, unlike me, who remained completely outside it) both started out as far left radicals—and both ended up contributing to the John Birch Society. It is only the similarity that allows you to go on, with real research, to descry out the meaningful differences. (And, no, that's Gayatri Chakravorty Spivak's idea, not mine: mine is only a suggestion of what one might apply it to.)

VII.

I've already cited writers like Sturgeon and Disch. To them I could add Heinlein (his juvenile *The Star Beast* had a tall, lanky black African heroine, who reminded me more of my cousin Nan Murrell, then at the Bronx High School of Science, than anyone in traditional American literature ever had; and I've written several times about the liberating effect Heinlein's make-up wearing Filipino narrator-protagonist in *Starship Troopers* had on me as a kid reading it in Harlem in the '50s—all things that were radically hacked out of the movie, and replaced with the clichéd blond blue-eyed hyper-masculine military hero.[2] But this is how the non-SF community traditionally handles the most radical and subversive elements in science fiction—the "escapist elements" that encourage the reader to bracket this society and try on, if only for moments here and there, a better organized one. Other places I could cite both Alfred Bester and Alexei Panshin. But "Us-and-Them fiction" of any sort has never particularly interested me. That's the subtheme of both *The Jewels of Aptor*, my first novel, and my subsequent trilogy *The Fall of the Towers*, though without much of a sophisticated rhetorical vocabulary to perform them—that is, without a set of writerly tools anywhere as near sophisticated as I needed for the job. (Not to mention my four-volume fantasy series of 1979 to 1987, *Return to Nevèrÿon*.) But I'm more interested in the systems that create the distinctions.

As I wrote sixteen years ago, whether the combat is gentle or forceful, when that combat expands the minority presence notably beyond tokenism, that's when hegemonic folks often get upset. That's not prediction. It's the way the system functions.

Identity is basically a synonym for category, and while categories make language possible, they make problems in life—especially when you try to assign subjects to them. People almost never fit the category you want them in, or never fit it for long.

Black science fiction writer Nora Jemisin talks on a video squib devoted to Octavia E. Butler about going to an SF convention sometime in the last years and finding some thirty-odd black writers there. Easily that could be the convention—Readercon 26—I came back from only a few weeks ago, held in Burlington, Massachusetts. I found it a wonderful and provocative time—as I also found my first, in 1966.

But Jemisin's account is not an account of the first science fiction convention *I* attended back then. There, yes, I *was* the only black SF writer. (In Los Angeles, Butler was not yet twenty.) And what I found were two—count them—*two* black science fiction fans, among thousand of white kids: Elliot Shorter was a big bear of a black guy whom I'd known from New York during my term and a half at City College (though I hadn't known he was into science fiction; people didn't spread that around so easily then); Dee Potter was a tall, dark-skinned, impressive woman who, as did Shorter, appeared to be very comfortable in that world. They were the pleasant surprise, not the white kids. I became friends with both and remained so in the halls of hotels and room-parties of various science fiction conventions for years.

Some context: I had published seven science fiction novels in the years before I walked into the Cleveland hotel. I had written three or four short stories, science fiction or fantasy, but had not yet published any.

I could describe half a dozen events from that Cleveland weekend, from an impassioned request by Harlan Ellison for a story for his *Dangerous Visions* anthology to a dinner with my SF-writing hero Roger Zelazny and his then-wife

Judith; from a young teenage fan, Jerry Kaufman, who volunteered to show me around the convention because I'd never been to one before, then twenty-three years later, as the head of small publishing house, published a book of mine, *The Straits of Messina* (1989), to my learning, from the tumult of applause when Zelazny's name was announced during the welcoming ceremony (louder than for Asimov [whose *I Robot* stories were clearly analogues for the American racial situation, which I've assumed was why Will Smith was so eager to make the film and, as well, starting with the producers, why it was done so ineptly, with all racial analogues buried or removed, and thus why the incoherent mess remaining tanked so abysmally] or John W. Campbell or any other writer, and the only standing ovation of the weekend), that many there also considered Zelazny a hero of language (another pleasant surprise because I also knew back then practically nobody who knew of his work outside the field) or that while I was sitting there, I looked at the name badge of the man sitting next to me and saw it *was* Alexei Panshin, co-author with Joe Hensley of a story I had been impressed with a few years before in the *Magazine of Fantasy and Science Fiction*, "Dark Conception," on the clash between black and white spirituality, and which, when I got up enough nerve to introduce myself and tell him how much I'd liked his tale (atheist as I was), started a friendship that endures today. These were events and people I encountered who changed something about my life and my understanding of it and how it had worked and would continue working.

The way you cross boundaries—especially discursive boundaries—is to cross them. You use what you learned before you crossed them and you try to retain a good sense of why you wanted to cross them. To effect that crossing you use what is there on the other side as well as what you brought with you from the side you left. You do your analysis of how the boundary can be dismantled only after you've dismantled it for yourself as much as you can.

I'd been crossing such boundaries all my life. I'd been a kid from a black working-class neighborhood in a largely white private school—which meant that particular boundary didn't scare me. The main way those boundaries are enforced is through habit and fear—and the fear always begins with the discomfort that comes from habit violated. The rhetoric associated with the discourse will always be used to explain to you that you are right to be afraid and that unspeakable terrors might wait on the other side should you try.

The first time, at twenty-three (only two years before that convention), was when I'd been hitchhiking through the south, in Texas. I walked up to a once white-painted Tex-Mex diner to buy some food and for the first time in my life saw a sign marked COLORED ENTRANCE with a finger pointing off to the side. Yes, I was scared to go in the white entrance: only three or four rides ago some white driver had told me in the car I could have had some black in me. I said, yes, I was Negro. But by then I had learned other things too. White people telling me they had recognized me as black was not an everyday occurrence. As I said, it happened only two to three times each year or two. The fact that it had happened so recently probably meant it was not going to happen again for a while. Also, there were all the white people who now and again said to me, "When I first saw you, I had no idea you were black." By now I knew they were not the same people who came up to me out of the blue to tell me they had known. Though they could be just as racist, they weren't being any less honest than the Alabama kid or the guy in the car who volunteered it on their own. But some people really don't recognize anything more than red hair and freckles as Irish or a hooked nose and shiny black hair as Italian, or a South Philly accent today or a North Philly accent from a family who lived in Fishtown forty years ago. And because I wasn't up to being a whole civil rights protest on my own that afternoon (though I thought about it and weighed the chances I'd be called on it; no matter which door I entered), I carried my guitar in the front (yes, the white) entrance, knowing that both my fear and my attempt to overcome it were what made me black, as for the first and the last time in my life I decided to pass. At the counter I sat down. The waitress, clearly part Mexican, took my order, as I realized there was no marked-off colored section *inside* the place. Maybe it was an old sign, lingering from years in the past . . . ? Besides, I realized, as my heart quieted, if someone did recognize me as black, probably it would look as if I were—perhaps—protesting, since that's kind of what I'd done . . . If anyone called me on that, maybe that's how I should play it out. Since I was scared shitless anyway, in either case and for doing the same thing, I might as well be scared for a good purpose rather than a bad one. (Or should I just apologize and say I'd made a mistake . . . ?) Then the waitress brought me my tacos and refried beans, gave me a big smile—and nobody else said anything—and, when I was leaving, said, "You come back now, you hear." Boundaries have to be learned.

Because boundaries are marked with different rhetorical signs that relate to the discourse—and the law—in different ways, you need a good sense of the difference between power and strength. That comes with familiarity of the particular locality you're in. Strength is guns and fists. Basically power is a language effect. But it can often summon up guns and fists. And you have to learn when and where it will, when it will use them, and when it will only threaten. The other thing that you must not forget is that strength is there to reinforce power, not the other way around—though that can be a very menacing minefield of mirrors to have to get through. You have to remember the differences you've already learned about local rural societies and about more rigid—or differently rigid—urban environments.

I'll end with an incident from that first science fiction convention, two years and a European trip after my hitchhiking jaunt, whichI've often told over fifty-plus years. I recount it here once more, however, because . . . well, because it happened.

(Does this question linger for some of you? Did the sailor on the bus know I was black? [Don't forget him; I haven't.] Answer: I have no idea. He hadn't asked. It never occurred to me to volunteer the information. That too was the times, just as was my deciding to go into the white entrance in Texas.)

In the convention hotel, while I was lingering by a gold-draped wall in the main ballroom, a young man—certainly no older than fifteen, though possibly as young as thirteen—came up, looked at my name badge, then glanced about nervously, and asked: "Um, excuse me—are you the guy who wrote . . . um, that book . . . about . . . you know, the three people . . . doing it, all—together? . . . the woman and the . . . two guys, at once . . . ?"

I realized he meant my then-recent novel *Babel-17*, though I'd never heard anybody—editor, agent, or reviewer—characterize the book that way before. So I said, "Yes, I am," and smiled.

Glancing right, then left, he leaned slightly forward and lowered his voice: "Is that . . . *possible?*"

Now since some of what was behind my account of the three-way sexual relations among the navigators in the book had been based on my most personal of experiences from the past few years, I told him: "Yes. It is."

He pulled in a large breath, let it out with a relief palpable enough for me to feel in my stomach, in the way the back of my throat relaxed. His shoulders went down a little. His mouth closed. (I don't think he smiled.) He stood up fully—he was a head shorter than I was—turned . . . and walked away.

Notebook under my arm, I watched him move off among the youngsters and adults meandering through the hotel lobby, thinking over what had just happened: The boy had done something, I realized, brave. I had tried to be honest. And it's the incident from the weekend that changed me the most.

—*August 19, 2015*
New York

NOTES

1. Jo Walton, on Tor.com.

2. Recently it's made it into print that Heinlein used the rampantly bisexual writer Theodore Sturgeon (1916–1987) as his model for "Mike" (aka Michael Valentine Smith), the hero of *Stranger in a Stranger Land* (1961), in what was certainly the most popular SF novel of the both the 1960s and probably the '70s; that is to say, Sturgeon with all the gay side of his sexuality omitted, just so it wouldn't bother anyone or get in the way . . .

To rethink the book with this reinserted certainly makes it make more sense.

23

Ikky, Kong, Frédéric, Kurtz

Afterthoughts on a lecture on "French-style" narrative structure delivered to Josh Lukin's Temple University class on Monday, October 26, 2015. Ford Madox Ford's novel *The Good Soldier* (1915) appears on several lists of the greatest novels in the English language, but as at least one critic has noted, it is the greatest *French* novel written yet in English. This essay began as a PS to a personal letter to Professor Lukin.

PS: My sense, Josh, was that I didn't get around to talking about the greater political importance of the "French-style" novel over the adventure-style novel, an importance that Roger Zelazny's "The Doors of His Face, the Lamps of His Mouth," our text for the class, exemplifies at the novelette length (and which it mentions by metonymy in both its first and its last paragraph).[1]

So this PS to the lecture represents my more articulate second thoughts on the talk I was hoping to give. The nature of the larger point I was planning to make is that the French story model is more realistic than the adventure model. That's because in life you tend to learn about most things a little at a time, rather than all at once. As well, before you have learned the most important things about one topic, you have already started learning about something else that is going to be important to you concerning the first topic—and so on. That's the structure of "French-style" stories.

Often they require more attention paid to the past than to what's happening in the present. (This is why, as I did get to say, the "French-style" narrative often concentrates just as much on the backstory as it does on the foreground action; and the climaxes of the novel are as likely to be sudden realizations about what something in the past really meant as they are about something that just happened to you which prompted that realization. (That point, I believe, I managed to get over—though, when you're writing (or writing about) the "French-style" novel, often it's good to say it several times and in several ways.

Contrastingly, adventures are based on those very rare situations where you have a problem, and the things you must do to solve it are a matter of having trained well enough at the gym and having had the bad guys incontrovertibly pointed out to you so that by the time you need to beat them up and/or arrest them, you have no problem knowing who they are or that they deserve whatever you have to deal out to them. When it leads to everyone except the villains living happily ever after, with no collateral damage, this does not happen that often, if ever.

I don't remember whether I said this to you or to Ann—or to Beth Mannion when I had dinner with her after the class and was telling her all about it (though I'm still sure I didn't get to say it to your students): The "adventure" is written for an ideal first reading. The "French" narrative (which isn't really French at all) is written for an ideal first reading and an ideal second re-reading. What I would have liked to do is to have pointed out ten places in Zelazny's "The Doors of His Face, the Lamps of His Mouth" (starting with the title and its biblical resonance with the book of Job, 41:14–19: "Who can open the doors of his face? his teeth *are* terrible round about. // *His* scales *are his* pride, shut together *as with* a close seal. . . . Out of his mouth go burning lamps, *and* sparks of fire leap out.") where it was clear something was put in for the second reading, as well as the first: these were some of the underlinings I couldn't find when I was flipping through the text. (And I was all prepared to discuss how the last paragraph, along with the entire experience of having read the tale, changed our reading of the first paragraph on the second time through. But we ran out of time!)

We came close to doing that with our discussion of the first paragraph itself; though I could have been clearer and more succinct.

Most of the time if you handle real-life situations as though they are actually adventures to be gotten through and go looking for something that will serve as a denouement and a resolution that will allow you to get the whole thing, wrap up the problem and forget it, you find that you haven't even begun to set anything right and have just pissed off a lot of people who, often, you really care about, because you didn't take the time really to understand their side or give them some real insight in understanding yours, etc., etc., etc., instead of creating a dialogue and working together (which is what Jean and Carl literally do at the end of "Doors / Lamps"—and why it's so moving) . . . But to the extent you are "a thinking person," you are left with things you keep returning to, keep thinking about.

One giveaway that Zelazny's tale is not an adventure so much as a "French-style" narrative is that the climactic scene is not really the climax at all. Rather the scene where Carl goes under the water and the great beast is nowhere about, but he relives his terrors of the last time he fought the creature, which allows him to realize why his ex-wife must be allowed to have the same chance he did, even if, in a much more skeletal scene, he must offer himself as the beast she must overcome by pushing the button. The climax is simply the symbolic completion of the story, rather than the resolution of the story itself. We will see the same pattern in the other "French-style" narratives we shall go on to look at, Joseph Conrad's *Heart of Darkness* (1899) as well as Gustave Flaubert's *Sentimental Education* (1869) and Peter Jackson's film of *King Kong* (2005).

The passage from Job on Leviathan lends as many resonances to the film(s) of *King Kong* as it does to the text of "Doors / Lamps."

Conrad's *Heart of Darkness* is a prime example of a "French-style" novel written in an English style. (It's no accident that Conrad's unacknowledged collaborator on the story was Ford Madox Ford—of *The Good Soldier*—who guided Conrad (if they did not guide each other) through the French complexities of Conrad's own story of Belgians and Englishmen in the Congo, eighteen years before.) The tale starts out doing everything it can to lead you to expect an adventure, from the title to the apparent content: a man gives a night-long account of his preparations to leave England and travel to France, in order to continue on to Africa, where he proceeds to captain a boat upriver to rescue another white man who has vanished among the natives. But from the very beginning, the book leaves numerous clues that this is NOT what the narrative is actually doing. At first it appears that it's doing the traditional setup of providing a frame story, the way traditional genre fictions so often do (James's ghost tale *The Turn of the Screw*; or Wells's "proto-SF novella" *The Time Machine*)—only something goes majorly off before the frame is completed. Or more accurately, the frame itself is never completed. The characters in the frame are not given names, but only exist as types, even the narrator. A great deal of time is spent describing the civilized world he is leaving. Once he reaches the Congo, more time is spent on the delays and retardations of the trip than on the trip itself. There is anticipation, but it is an adventure without velocity. The encounter itself, in the white fog at the head of the river, then the night on shore, and the retreat with the moribund Kurtz and the vicious slaughter of the blacks by the Pilgrims in the (white) smoke as they stand on the bank, seems confused and confusing.

Only Marlow and Kurtz have names in the story, but by a third of the way through, you should have picked up that Kurtz, at any rate, is simply not the most important character in the tale. Until we learn much more about him, he is a kind of literary MacGuffin. Every new character—secondary or tertiary—is introduced as a type, as a profession, rather than as a named individual like Charlie Marlow, whether the Accountant in Leopoldville or the "Old knitter of black wool" back in England, or even the "old fool" who wants

Charlie to take the measurements of every white man's head whom he will meet there (and who explains, when Charlie asks him why, that he never sees them again, so that it doesn't appear to be important, as far as he says; but why *would* someone, in the 1870s or the '80s want the measurements of all the white people's heads leaving for Africa and then, on top of it, be so lax and inefficient about procuring them . . . unless the inefficiency was the point . . . ? Is it supposed to suggest that he is a primitive anthropologist of the white race, rather than the black, and that maybe these anthropological methods themselves are inefficient, as well as the people employing them? And that anthropology itself grows out of some old, outdated notions of craniology itself, an interesting enterprise fifty years before in the days when Charlotte Brontë was writing, but not with any life still left in them; Conrad was as much aware of the "primitive" white ideas of craniology at the end of the nineteenth century as he was aware of the staggering inefficiency of the colonial program itself, by the time he got back from his months in the Congo. The Station Master, the Station Master's nephew, the Engineer—these are as much frame characters as the ones sitting around listening to Marlow on deck. The story is about the effect of the frame characters on Marlow—how he has to change in order to live with them. Could that indeed be the major point, if not the theme, of the novella? Once I read and *reread* the novella, I found it impossible to answer that question anyway other than "Yes.") And anthropology itself, in later years, was criticized as the study at Oxford and Cambridge you took in place of history, and that was really entirely about how to understand a "primitive" culture just enough to exploit and dominate it, having nothing to do with respecting it. Indeed, only history could lead to real respect. Anthropology was the study of "primitive" cultures that were assumed *to have no history*, but only a primitive endurance without response to the events that happened to them in actuality, especially the treatment by their exploiters and oppressors. What Conrad is trying from the beginning to pin down is where these notions at work in Africa come from in white culture and how they propagated through it—into the primitive ones. As Chinua Achebe said, with both hostility and bewilderment, why are Americans and even the English today teaching this short novel as if it were about Africa? There are no blacks to speak of in it. Neither their culture nor any individual from them is presented in anything like a full portrait. At the best, even they are just types, and unlike the whites, the few who pass by comprise very limited clichés (an African Queen, a couple of servants), types much more limited than the whites.

We're a third of the way through the book and we haven't left the frame tale yet—it's as if the entire book *is* the frame, where the "real" story (certainly in terms of how many pages we spend on it) is taking place. Marlow's pursuit of Kurtz more and more seems a hollow pretense that only organizes dozens of other incidents.

We learn a great deal about Kurtz in the story—and as the story continues on, past his death and through Charlie's return to England, we continue to learn about him; and we learn that much of what we'd learned in Africa about him was wildly exaggerated and, if anything, the opposite of what people thought of him in the civilized world. Only his Intended cherished the illusion of his faithfulness to her (he was not in the least faithful) or his goodness or his genius. For everyone else in England, he was a second-rate ne'er-do-well who could not make it in the civilized land; who fled to Africa because it seemed easier to do something interesting and important there—and what he had done there possibly encompassed the most atrocious of horrors, whether or not he found any redemption in his life among the blacks.

If only from the number of pages that are actually devoted to Marlow and Kurtz, they cannot be very important types. But the point Conrad does go on to make is that, for him, there are only European types. And the question he asks is: Are there any truths to be learned from the careful observations of types? And the answer he begins with is: Yes, but only by the careful observation of types you already know and know well. And for Charlie Marlow, that is the second-rate, self-deluded, and self-deluding English types that he'd already learned about back in England. These are the white men (the Pilgrims) who inhabit the novel: the Station Master, the Station Master's son, the Station Master's uncle, the Engineer (good-hearted though he is), the Man in Charge of Putting Out the Fire, the Russian, or Kurtz's black mistress (the African Queen), and Kurtz's Intended—and both before and after his meeting with her, as he pursues what information he can still collect about Kurtz, Marlow realizes that the man, Kurtz, who was first described to Marlow in Africa as a genius with great talent and accomplishment in so many fields—painting, music, writing—was actually considered in England, which he fled to go to Africa, to be a second-rate dabbler in all those fields, with talent, perhaps, but neither genius nor will enough to accomplish anything, as were so many if not all the types who were most tempted to leave England and take a chance in the colonies, even as they and the English kept patting themselves on the back and telling each other that these second-rate self-aggrandizing fellows were the best and the brightest. It was the best and the brightest that Charlie Marlow had gone to find, that he'd hope Kurtz would be. It was the second-rate and inefficient that he saw, again and again, and that Kurtz himself turned out to be, and—most tragic—Marlow's time in the colonies had only exacerbated Marlow's own tendencies in that direction.

Who is Kurtz? He is Flaubert's Frédéric Moreau, if France had been a committedly imperialist country in the decade just before the Revolution of 1848. Compare Frédéric's half-baked talents (the novel *Silvio the Fisherman* he starts but never finishes; the German waltzes he writes as preparation for some nebulously envisioned great music that he never gets around to going any further with; or the painting lessons he takes from Pellerin in order to be a great artist, but never gets around to painting anything). In two different novels from two different nations: Frédéric with his fantasies of the Far East that he never fulfills, and Mr. Kurtz with his fantasies of becoming a big ivory hunter in Africa, which he fulfills but at what cost we are never really sure, though the novel hints that everyone suspects they are unthinkable, the sign for which is that he has even taken up with a native woman, an act so unthinkable Marlow cannot express it in London. Frédéric has the same order of half-hearted sympathy for the revolution as Marlow has toward the blacks he sees brutalized. In both cases, what characterizes each is that positive feeling is inefficient. Marlow cannot stop the Pilgrims' "heartless" murder of the natives, as the Pilgrims run to the side of the boat and shoot the blacks on the shore for sport. Far more literally than we might have expected. They aren't cruel. They have no hearts *left*. And if Marlow stays, neither will he.

And in *Sentimental Education*, Frédéric's enthusiasm for the revolution is not enough to prevent the murder of Dussardier; he is probably unaware of how, by telling Madame Dambreuse of a nonexistent theft the young worker committed, Frédéric himself is very possibly to blame for her telling this to Sénécal (who is working for her at the time), possibly adding the straw that breaks the camel's back so that, in the police demonstration, Sénécal runs his sword through the one person who cared about his welfare when Sénécal himself was in jail, and who impoverished himself to buy some decent beer for the coldhearted young man and have all of Sénécal's "friends" over to make sure they were there to support the character most distasteful to the rest of the bourgeois crew of the revolutionaries. To Sénécal, thanks to Frédéric's offhand lie about Dussardier, Dussardier himself, despite all his goodness, is only another working-class thief who should be put down.

Only their nations—Frédéric's and Kurtz's—and their national histories are different. But then, isn't that everything? Or is it nothing . . . ?

(The second reading I write of here is, of course, just as idealized as the first. It makes the text *more* satisfactory than the first reading. But ideally we are *never* finished reading such a text. Each time we come back to it, we are more satisfied than we were the first time, but in different ways, ways that might even be accidental or even gifts of the language as well as carefully planned out—of which the writer was possibly aware, or just happy accidents of the language. This is how some of the notes included at the end of Zelazny's tale today strike me on my fifth, six, or seventh reading of the story. Does perhaps the title—and did Zelazny perhaps think it momentarily himself, or even dwell on it, with its doors and lamps—refer not to Ikky but to Ten Square, with its lights and underwater entrances . . . ? So we read again to see if it make sense and is useful to think that, or if things in the text itself contravene it. Aren't many of the unpleasant things that happen to and around Frédéric in some of the climactic scenes in *Sentimental Education*—at the Madame Arnoux's name day party, or even Dussardier's death—actually Frédéric's fault because of his lack of thought, which the multiple-time reader so inclined has time to put together. Some of them jump out the first time through: "You're not very bright," M. Arnoux whispers once to his young protégé who has made a clearly wrong choice in terms of a present to bring, which reveals his infidelity to his wife. Others are more subtle: Sénécal is working for Madame Dambreuse when Frédéric tells her the lie that Dambreuse has stolen the money that Frédéric is borrowing from her to replace. Did she pass this information on to Sénécal, who believed it as well, so that when working for the national guard he was tipped over the edge to commit what is clearly intended to be the most tragic accident for the reader, even if Frédéric himself has no sense of the extent of his possible involvement in the atrocity clearly placed at the climax of the narrative? And this obliviousness to his own guilt is the context against which the terminal discussion of Frédéric's and his old friend Charles's happiest moment at the end of the physical text resonates.)

At the beginning of his "adventure," Charlie Marlow tells us: "The one thing I hate more than anything else is a liar." At the end, we see—we are not told, rather we are shown it—Charlie has become a liar. For the second-time reader, what the story details is not a so much a jungle adventure but how Marlow is taught how to delay and lie, and what you have to do to get anything done among the Hollow Men—the heartless Pilgrims (white people) who have come to the Congo and who have stalled at various places along the river. He has been almost unnoticeably transformed into what he hates most. What must control our second reading, then, is noticing all these encounters with all these nameless second-rate men over the months in the Congo, as Marlow and the river boat he captains (a ruined, leaky, second- or even third-rate boat that is one of the first things turning a possibly decent sailor into a second-rate colonial) move from delay to delay in accomplishing a task that he should have completed in a few months. They sap his patience and prevent him from practicing what he is skilled for, what instead should be—and would be back in England—someone else's job: a good man like the engineer, who rarely gets to practice what he knows; those delays and the men he is repeatedly forced to deal with have turned him exactly into what he hates—and hates "more than anything else."

At the start of our second reading, however, the one thing we should unequivocally know is that it is not the Africans who accomplish this transformation in Marlow. In this, I am completely with Achebe: it is not about Africa. At the end of the African section of the "adventure," its resolution resolves nothing. We think it is a real fight while it happens, but the next day, with sun-up, we learn the real reason Marlow won is because Kurtz was simply too sick—that is to say the wrestling match with Kurtz at night functions like the part of the backstory brought forward in the "French"-style novel. (When they reach the head of the Congo River, the great fog that engulfs them, the heart of darkness itself, is—one wants to say, *of course*—white, not black. And it is hollow like the hearts of the white men on the boat. The thing that makes it a horror story is that their hearts—as they rush to have some "sport" and shoot down the natives from the boat, only fifteen feet away on the shore, and murder both them and Kurtz's mistress—is that their hearts are not filled and replete with some tangible evil: they are empty . . . hollow. How did that happen? How is that emptiness, moreover, so contagious, so that all you have to do is work with it, decide that they have to be put up with, acknowledge for a moment that they're not so bad, that just for a single time [or two, or three] you could use their own techniques against them in order just to get your own job done so you can get out there, that really they are just something to be put up with, a neces- sary evil—and you have already started your transformation.) It is not even the African landscape that causes you to change—or rather it is only a landscape against which we can project our own ahistorical delusions about it, our own historical misreadings, from the fact not that we know nothing of their history, but that we have been taught by our own intellectual tradition (anthropology) that they have none, however seductive those "primitive" misreadings are.

It is possibly the same relation to landscape that, while it briefly excites Frédéric to write a single essay in support of the revolution, it does not excite him enough to commit himself to it the way Dussardier was committed to it, or the way Sénécal (Frédéric's bad conscience) was committed to destroying it. By the same token, it not only makes Frédéric lose the woman he loves, but— through his obtuseness—may even allow him to take part in the destruction of her life, or, indeed, to be a causal factor in the death of the only naively good and positive character in the tale: the single person who appreciates Sénécal more than any other—who arranges a party for him on his release from jail and who bullies the friends into paying attention to the incredibly misanthropic young man.

Why are these tales so powerful?

Because they dramatize the social forces—and the relationship between individual and society—that have constructed so much of our own civilization already.

That is the level on which they are more realistic than the adventure they wave in front of our faces, seducing us into reading and then, by the end, revealing to us what we have been looking at all along.

In Peter Jackson's remake of *King Kong*, Cabin Boy Billy, who is reading *Heart of Darkness* on the boat, holds the novel up to the ship's black first mate, who is Billy's ersatz adopted father, and says, at one foggy moment on deck: "This isn't really an adventure novel, is it, Mr. Hayes?" And handsome Evan Parke, who plays Hayes, the most admirable man in the crew, notably more than the somewhat sleazy German Captain, and whom the boy idolizes, tells him: "No, Billy—it's not."

In that sense, the original 1933 *King Kong* is about Africa and how the forces brought back from there will wreak havoc on civilization. At least it says so. The 2005 remake by Jackson is not about Africa. (Movies, because they are popular culture, have to be more literal.) And it says so. In the full scene just before his death, Mr Hayes/Evan Parke tells the hero, played by Adrien Brody, that he was given a medal of honor by France during the Great War, but was denied any recognition by his own country, the U.S.A. As well, the film was released in 2005, so there is simply no way that a film about the capture of the Empire State Building by a great, black giant won't be read, at least by some, as resonating with 9/11, four years before—even if the building is already in the hands of the enemy and, because film worked differently back then, *doesn't* explode in the third act.

Like Zelazny's "The Doors of His Face, the Lamps of His Mouth," the main character of Jackson's *King Kong* is also named Carl, though that, we will start out by thinking, is pure accident.

One of the reasons I have always thought Jackson's *King Kong* is a great film is that, especially if you look at the full version, with the deleted scenes in place, it's clear, even from the cut version, that the film started out to be an incredibly ambitious portrayal of the Great Depression of the 1930s, when the original film was made, and that, as the characters get closer and closer to Kong and their own version of *Heart of Darkness*, and proceed to return him to the heart of civilization (Broadway!), it is a film about the way the commercial forces of entertainment, as you get closer and closer to that heart, consume and swallow up all attempt at social relevance. And while there is no way you can swallow that the Biggest Blackest Male imaginable has not ravished but seduced the little blonde white woman (in this version, quite a gutsy comedienne in reality, but one who only *plays* for the camera silent, sad figures against the sunset), and what's more the real Black Hero has accomplished that seduction not by waving around the biggest black cock in the Western world at the time but rather by the directors having him climb and appropriate for himself the biggest white one—and he has been successful, so that he has already mastered it. Kong has climbed to the top and carried Ann there with his own Big Black Hands. The script explains that, in *this* version of the movie (Jackson's), Faye Wray was too busy to work with such bozos and simply won't do it. ("She's busy working on a picture over at RKO," i.e., the original production under the "uncredited director" Merian C. Cooper, which will make her famous and lift the film industry out of the Depression doldrums that it slid into largely through doing Welles's *Citizen Cane* and going on to all but bankrupt themselves doing his next film, *The Magnificent Ambersons*—among the first films put together with this level of thought.[2])

In Jackson's film, Ann gets the role because not only is she a good film actress, but more important she is, coincidentally, the same size as "Maureen" (the actress who was going to play the part because Wray was busy making a film over at RKO: presumably the original *King Kong*, or the film that, in this alternate history universe, they are making instead, while we get the real skinny on Carl Denham and the incredibly under-equipped and underfunded film that Jackson replaces it with—and she can fit into Maureen's dresses that have already been purchased, before the intended star pulled out).

If you want to take the appropriation allegory just a little further, by climbing the huge white dick, Kong has, in effect, given it a hand job. While it may not be as observant a film *as Apocalypse Now*, Jackson's *King Kong* is a much smarter film, and along with its self-reflexive running commentary, it's quite observant enough. It starts out practically as a documentary on the times, focusing more and more on the theatrical, and only by breaking through the lowest level—vaudeville—does the film fill up the screen on the lowest level—and in a madcap screwball version—that could conceivably have made *King Kong*, even in the face of all the industries' excesses then and now that it critiques and parodies. If we run over the crew of the Venture (the animal-capturing boat turned film ship, somewhere between an "Adventure" and a commercial proposition, as in "Venture Capitalism," wink, wink, nudge, nudge), it's redeemed by the fact that probably most people don't think that while they are watching, anymore than they think it's supposed to be a serious parody of a commercial film trying to be a serious one (which finally works *because* it is technically spectacular), let's just linger a moment on the crew as significant minor characters in good French-novel style.

Andy Serkis, who plays Kong, also plays a cook on the boat. Equally he is "ass-hole buddies," however far it goes, with the little Asian sailor he is clearly so close to on shipboard. They die literally in one another's arms in the film's restored scene, recreated by Jackson for his remake and also in the 1930s style so that it might be seamlessly re-edited into the 1933 version, along the gorge in the *Valley of the Nest of Spiders*. (Do I know what I'm saying, writing this? You can assume that I do.) This is also Jackson's way of telling us that it won't hurt to look at what survives of the deleted scenes in his version as well. The little white guys in their plane are mad as hell and they want it—that is, "their" big white cock and, incidentally, Ann Darrow—back.

At the end of Jackson's film there is a strange bit of hugger-mugger that cries out for interpretation. It is something I have never seen anyone mention. At the end of Jackson's *King Kong*, the show that Denham is putting on in the theater is running smoothly (in the pantomime on stage, the actors playing natives are wearing the native costumes from the original film, which the original actors used in what was supposed to be the original African scene); Denham is supposed to be reproducing what happened in Africa on the stage for his New

York audience. Jack Driscoll is looking for Ann and comes to the theater. Carl introduces the show, with the actor as the hero, and clearly Ann Darrow will be playing her part as the victim of Kong. (In the back of the theater Driscoll makes a comment to Carl's assistant, bearing a real scar from the African fray across his cheek, that Carl unfailingly destroys everything he loves.)

We see the charade of Kong and the natives played out on the stage. The skirts of the black dancers are identical to the ones the actors wore in the original movie scenes, which were supposed to be real. And a woman in a white dress is chained between pillars, visible only from the back, with her head down. She raises it. And screams, the way Denham had instructed Ann to do on the ship. But it is an actress in a blonde wig—playing Ann—who screams. In the back of the theater, Driscoll recognizes the imposture. What happened to Ann? Driscoll wants to know. He has come for her, of course. The assistant says, "I don't know. Carl offered her all sorts of money [to impersonate herself] but she refused."

Now we cut to the real Ann, dancing in a chorus line, and stepping out of it, as if in a dream. (In the full version we will see her next at a play that is clearly the comedy that Driscoll claimed to be writing for her on the ship—where some of the female parts are taken by female impersonators. Ann is dissatisfied and leaves. She wants to find her true love . . .).

Deprived of the real Ann, Kong revives to full fury, breaks his chains, drives everyone from the theater, leaps into the balcony where he sees Driscoll, and decides that, once again, Driscoll is keeping him from his love. Breaking through the front of the theater, and raging through Times Square, he goes looking for every blonde he sees: could it be Ann? The military is called out.

Ann comes out of the DeLuxe Theater. (I would have to go looking for details again, to find if the DeLuxe is either the theater where she was working in the prologue, before she encountered Denham, with her older friend Manny, or where she went to get a burlesque job which she decides she has not fallen to, yet . . . Neither one would surprise me. But these are the kind of detailed critical questions the "French" form raises endlessly . . . however they are answered.)

Driscoll goes after Kong, whom he presumably realizes is looking for Ann, too. He must save her once more.

Kong and Ann encounter in the street. But now the military is called out en masse.

Briefly Kong and Ann escape from the center of specular capitalism, Times Square and Forty-Second Street, and take refuge in Central Park, where, ideally happy among the trees and Christmas lights, Kong slips and slides with her around the ice. She and Kong can both ignore the cold and simply satisfy each other by gazing at one another.

Only then does a military shell shatter the ice behind him, and Kong, with the blonde white woman still in his grip, swings over the roofs of New York back to the spectacular center of midtown New York, to climb above it all, by means of the white phallus at its center, the Empire State Building.

(It is no accident that, in the 1976 remake, the World Trade Center replaced the Empire State Building, when Kong climbed to the top with Jessica Lange— the same building that was attacked by terrorists and brought down in 2001 and then, rather idiotically, was rebuilt recently as a single tower once more, in order to facilitate the whole drama playing out again . . . , whether in art or in life?)

In Lacanian terms, both Ann and the Empire State Building are the two faces of the phallus, which Kong will be destroyed for having mastered.

The one character on the Venture who does not follow the allegory that the script itself sets out in terms of the classic "French-style" structure is Billy. Billy's backstory is this: he was found in a boat that had come from some place where some terrible thing has happened to the boy, when he was eight or nine. He has never been able to talk about it. At this point, Hayes and the other sailors don't even question it. They assume he doesn't really remember. But because of a few broken bones the boy had, Hayes at the very least assumes it must have been awful, if only because the boy won't talk about it. Anyone who has ever read an adventure story before knows that the boy must have come from Skull Island, and what's more, he is hiding something that will later be a key to their success once they get there, when he is jarred into articulation by whatever event, building, or happening. So we sit back waiting for it, as-suming it will be provided with more or less elegant cleverness. But we want the world to be coherent. In adventures, the world is. Otherwise there's no narrative reason for having the backstory in the first place. Adventures don't have red herrings put there by chance. They have them put there by design from the baddies, whoever they turn out to be. Even if the baddy is entirely a natural force, there have to be humans entailed with it somehow, as there are—the natives that steal Ann from the boat. Ah, so they were the people who brutalized the young Billy. And that's why, when the ship goes to rescue Ann, he is so determined to get back at the natives who once were so awful to him, and from whom he just escaped with his life. (Even adventures tend toward the form of "French"-style narrative.) What will finally make it work, or not, is how elegant or witty or moving the three scenes, one on the boat, and two on the island, each with its quarter-page of dialogue and camera-emphasized visuals to support it, are all presented on screen. It's called a subplot. And you have to resolve it for the same reason you set it up. But if you suddenly decide—at the production meeting—you don't want to resolve it because it takes too much time or distracts away from the main story, then you cut it out along with all its setup, and make the character simply a more or less engaging walk-on, with nothing particular about his position as Cabin Boy. Other cabin boys have been characters in adventures without having been beat up and brutalized as children on offstage mysterious islands.

But Jackson's *King Kong* does *exactly* the wrong thing!

Minutes after we get the story of Billy's childhood mystery, in another scene we hear another story that happened years ago. We've already been thinking about Skull Island because the form demands we do. This story, however, is directly about Skull Island. Another boat was encountered with a dying adult sailor in it. He definitely was from Skull Island. He too was the victim of something awful. He too was not talking about it—oh, that just means I was right about Billy, the audience thinks (and I certainly did so, not only the first time I saw it, but the second and third time as well), so that the eventual lack of resolution to Billy's character arc only becomes more and more striking with each viewing.

I say this is exactly the wrong thing to do—doubling the introductory scene—because it also makes some of the more sophisticated viewers think: Oh, maybe this isn't an adventure after all? (Billy himself will say that, holding up his '20s library edition of *Heart of Darkness*; it's one of the first ones I ever saw in a library in the '50s.) Could this be a slightly clumsy setup for a "French"-style narrative: It only looks like a coincidence? As things go on, and we get to Skull Island, instead of just the return of the vicious natives as a prompt to Billy's revenge both for what they did to him when he was young and what they are currently doing to Ann—which I can see being more than a little racist, and which is the kind of thing that Jackson himself might not like to get entailed in—could it be a setup for an explanation with some psychological nuance?

Coincidences in life happen all the time. There *are* no coincidences in fiction.

In life, coincidences are the sign of nature sometimes indulging in meaningless repetitions. In fiction, adventure or "French," repetitions are the source of all meanings. Repetitions mean that humans have been there and left their signs.

In *King Kong* we are given two similar occurrences: a few years or months apart, in the same part of the ocean, they might well be random events—probably, in life, that's what they would be. In a story, we want them to be a story; a good story. That is why we assume the writer chose to tell it, to recount it as if it was real, or devote energy and time to making it up if it was imaginary. Now an audience, especially a popular mass audience, will go to such a work unraveling from it not the significance it has, but rather the significance they hope it has—and they have been led by the best works of the genre to hope such hopes. That is part of the reception-structure of popular genres. And I even think it's a better structure than encouraging a mass audience, through incompetence or overcomplexity, to take from it anything they want. (Though

I know I am one step away from sounding like a condescending fascist.) I really believe the purpose of art—all art, whether popular or the most sophisticated and refined—is the use of skill, sensitivity, creativity, and observation of the world that (we currently assume) is the case to create an object that allows an audience to critique its own hopes and fear. In popular art, this is always mediated (and the particular version of this mediation we call subversion) by what is most efficiently commercial. In all academic art, these goals are constantly mediated/subverted by what is most easily teachable.

A few years ago, coming out of *Spider-Man 4*, I asked a sixteen- or seventeen-year-old New York Latino, also coming into the lobby, "What did you think of the movie?"

"Aw, man," he answered, with a dismissive grin, "it was terrible! I mean, what kind of hero is that? All he does is cry from one end of the film to another—and he hardly hits anybody!"

I was a little surprised, but not much. I'd actually enjoyed it, though not enough (as they say) to write home about it. But the moment I got his critique I realized that *Spider-Man 4* had been an incompetent portrayal of a religious hero. That's what I'd enjoyed—been able to enjoy, because of what I had brought to the movie, which I'm pretty sure, from his critique, was not what he'd brought to it that early summer Friday morning. But just before I left, I asked him, because it just popped up in my head: "Hey, did you ever see the Peter Jackson *King Kong* that came out—oh, seven or eight years ago now?"

"Yeah, I saw that one. I thought that was pretty good." And we reached the head of the escalator to go down to street level. I got on, and he dashed down the steps beside and ahead of me.

Now as you know, I happen to think *King Kong* is a great film. But to explain why, I have to note something about that young man's critique, there in the movie lobby, of both of them. Before he disappears forever from this piece, take stock of what he did not say. He did not say of either the one he had just seen or the one he had seen an indeterminate number of years before, when it came out and he was eight, or sometime since on a DVD, Netflix, or TV: He did not say, of either, "What I really missed was a young Latino male who was put in the film so that I could have someone to identify with." One could have easily thought that his enjoyment of one and his disapproval of the other—as likewise for the bearded black gay professor, who walked with a cane and was certainly too infirm even to walk down the steps much less run down them the way he did (and who also hadn't missed a black gay hero in either one)—both came from his understanding of the genres, just the way mine had.

Nor am I interested in taking away his disapproval or his pleasure in either.

Now I do think Jackson's film is one of the great popular culture achievements of the first decade and a half, so far, of the century. I can reel off a general list of reasons—especially vis-à-vis *Spiderman*—without trying.

King Kong is a film which is predicated on the situation that everyone in the movie, from the hero and heroine, Adrien Brody (Jack Driscoll) and Naomi Watts (Ann Darrow), down to the most tertiary *en passant* characters running around screaming and trying to get away from Kong on Broadway, are all pushed out of their comfort zones by a greater power than expected from the chained Kong himself. That's lifted straight from Cooper's version, of course.

But what does Jackson add to the film? Both the sexist clichés about women and the racist costumes and visions of native dancing that were part of the original in 1933 are presented in the 2005 version as clichés meant to hide the reality of 1930s Depression life from the people.

As well, from the top to the bottom of the hierarchy of characters on the Venture, from the film people down through the crew, examples are chosen and given more or less rich story arcs that are pretty carefully sketched.

And there *is* a black character on the crew—first mate Hayes, ersatz father of orphaned cabin boy Billy. And I appreciate that he was also a soldier who had been badly treated at the end of World War I. One presumes it had caused him to take up his roving life and single parenthood on the sea, instead of opting for a family and middle-class comfort on land.

Well, one of the reasons I appreciated that character is because I had one of those in my father's family—my father's brother, two up, my Uncle Manross. The family story was that Manross too had been treated very badly by the U.S. Army on his release from the Great War. This was assumed to account for the fact that, in a family of black achievers (every one, including my dad with no college degree, managed to attain moderate middle-class success in his own business) Uncle Manross, the ex-military man, was a drunk, had never been able to keep a job, and more and more rarely tried since leaving the army, which my highly educated black family concurred had not supported him in any way, and certainly not supported him in the way it regularly supported its white veterans after the war. What happened to Uncle Manross was common-place among black veterans before the Second World War, which had been so traumatic it even changed the name of the Great War to the First World War, or World War I. But by the time the Second World War was running down, and had already occasioned the rewriting of history, my mother really disliked Manross, when he would drop by to see my father, inebriated and wanting to get a "small loan" from his younger brother, who, because that was the Delany way with family, never begrudged, at least not to Manross himself. And my mother would complain bitterly to her sisters (these were the overheard conversations, in Brooklyn and New Jersey, in which to me she sounded most recognizably like a black woman): "I despise that man. It's not that he's a drunk, or can't keep a job. No black person in the world hasn't known people like that, all their lives. I have. You have. But it's just that he's such a conceited drunk. He comes staggering up the steps and before he gets to top, he's shouting out,

'Hey, Margaret. How's that boy of yours? How's that boy? I hope you're tellin' him he's a Delany! You got to let that boy know he's a Delany,' and then he's grabbing hold of the bannister so he doesn't fall, and reaching down scratching Butch's stomach"—Butch was my (or the family's, I suppose) dog—"and I'm thinking, though I don't say, but it does rile me: well he's also a Boyd. And so am I. That family is a wonderful family, in some ways, but they're crazy. The way those kids were beaten. And they sit around taking about it together, as if it were the most wonderful thing in the world. We were hardly beaten at all. I wouldn't be surprised if the beatings were most of what Manross's problem was. I'm sure it's part of what Big Sam's"—that's what my father's name had changed to pretty soon after I'd begun to walk, and had become "Little Sam"—"are about."

Uncle Manross was the first Delany, of either sex, to die. It was from cirrhosis or other liver complaints. Compared to Mr. Hayes in *King Kong*, my family's interpretation of Uncle Manross, with the moments of observation that, at this distance, I can recall, are 180 degrees at odds. Nevertheless: both were psychologically wounded in World War I. That wound is a total determinant of what later happens in their lives. Both die, and die early—my Uncle Manross, early in his life, and Mr. Hayes early in the film. But this is the point that everything reverses: It is hard for anyone in my family, whether it was my mother or my father's remaining sisters and brother, to speak of Uncle Manross as anything other than a victim of the state. For my mother, he was an unpleasant one. For my father and his family, Manross was a deeply sympathetic one. Unlike Mr. Hayes, Manross did marry—shortly after the war—to a brilliant woman, my aunt Mary, and remained with her up through his death in the 1950s. Her own death occurred in the early 1990s. She taught at my grandfather's university, and the general sense is that Manross's problem unfairly held her back, possibly even tragically. At least they had never had children. (That "at least" presents as my own reduction of my family's judgment on the relationship of Manross and Mary.) Though once he died, Aunt Mary went on to become friends with various writers and artists, including James Baldwin, and was instrumental with him in founding the Harlem Writers Guild, which she went on supporting after Baldwin's own growing fame in the 1960s and '70s took him away from it, though their friendship endured.

Once Manross had died, my mother's relation with Aunt Mary was of the warmest, until—in 1987—my mother suffered a major stroke which left her confined to a home without speech or understanding or control of her bodily functions for the eight years prior to her death. At my mother's funeral, at age eighty-one, in 1995, Aunt Mary came with the help of my sister and me, and a city-run service for transporting the aged; she was determined to attend, though by now she was a ninety-year-old hoarder on the border of dementia, occasionally found wandering disoriented over the co-op grounds (she had lived, since a decade after her husband's death in a top-floor apartment across a stone courtyard from my mother, at 70 La Salle Street). My own father had passed away in the autumn of 1960, ten years after his older brother, the second Delany of that generation to die.

What other differences do we note about Hayes and Uncle Manross?

If Manross was a victim, Hayes is—at least at a glance that only takes in the surface—a hero, and a tragic one.

If there is a woman's life connected to his, lingering somewhere in the off-screen backstory—the life of a woman either tragic or triumphant—it is not referred to in the script, and certainly we don't see her at any time on screen. This is something I tried to lift structurally from Jackson, as I lifted the title of *Through the Valley of the Nest of Spiders* from his filmic text—it was precisely something that was not in the "original" *King Kong*, that had been left on the cutting-room floor and only retrieved by Jackson, and retrieved in two versions in two bursts, as it were, of concerted *Begeisterung*—while I had tried to urge each of its borrowed elements (black father, white orphan son) closer to an observed reality from my own life, a reality that inflects or in fact actually creates their meaning in my text: that makes a meaning specifically different from Jackson's.

And what about Billy himself? Certainly he is the character that Jackson gives to the young Latino I exchanged my few critical questions with in the lobby after *Spider-Man*, and indeed to me (and anyone else who understands the genre) to identify with, at least once we have enjoyed the efforts of Adrien Brody to play a writer who, moved out of his comfort zone by a fluke of nature, has to play a largely physical hero nowhere near as interesting at the one he would like to write about, if he were left to his own devices, and we enjoy Naomi Watts having to clown and do back flips and pratfalls and otherwise play Stepin Fetchit for the enjoyment of a Big Black (Ahem . . .) gorilla who has kidnapped her, pretty much the same way she had to play the sexist roles for Jack Black/Carl Denham, who pretty much kidnapped her from Western Civilization as we know it, right at the beginning. The first one Watts wants to do, and wants to do badly. And with help of borrowed clothes and a CGI sunset, she does it—and pretty well, we all are supposed to agree. And I did. The second one, with Kong, she *knows* how to do. According to the script, she does it well. It's what she's been doing to survive. Now it's what she has to do in Darkest Africa—to survive. The major difference between the two is that this pantomime is exhausting, both for her and for Kong. At the end, she tells the Big Ape, "Okay. That's it. I can't do any more. That's all there is." He gently knocks her down, as if to tell her, "No, that's what you say. You can do some more. I said so, in my own inarguable way." Cut. On the other side we find both Watts and Kong asleep, Watts curled up in Kong's hand, Kong snoring like a quiet locomotive—as Adrien (The Writer . . . turned Hero) sneaks up on them, observing them through the leaves, wondering how to effect a reasonable (believable?) rescue. As is the entire film, it's pretty choice irony.

The setups are so rich with resonances, it almost doesn't matter how they resolve. Like Hitchcock before him, Jackson realizes his major aesthetic job in terms of the genre is to make each interim resolution spectacular and surprising, so that even if you have the general progression of plot from your memory of the Cooper version, the sheer visual intensity and technological virtuosity of the image construction of the resolution sequence, whatever it is, will . . . surprise you but keep you intellectually satisfied?

Not in the least.

It will start you laughing again. What you are laughing over is the tension between the fact that it is so unbelievable but yet it is done so well!

A later battle between three dinosaurs and Watts, all of whom are falling down a cliff, but are getting snarled in one set of swinging vines after another so that they don't reach the bottom for five minutes, so that the competition between the dinosaurs for Watts's juicy little body is the only thing keeping the struggling—but *still* gutsy—Watts alive—well, if it were filmed live instead of with CGI, the dinosaurs themselves or the actors playing them would have to be as skilled as the Flying Wallendas, or probably better than any Cirque de Soleil routine. The genius that we appreciate is not in any meaning generated by the sequence itself, but simply in who or how anyone, even Peter Jackson, could have thought up and organized such a collection of individual actions, shots, grabs with jaws that miss, swipes with claws that now connect and now don't with vines that hold for one, two, three swipes, then break with the fourth, so a dinosaur, or Watts, drops down, only to be caught again, either on a dinosaur arm or in a net of hanging vines, which a moment later are swinging because another of the dinosaurs has reached out, almost caught it, but it has slipped free of its talons. Then the actions between two other dinosaurs drives them out of our mind and sight for five, seven, nine seconds. Now back to the third dinosaur clawing at the web. Vines break, and Watts plummets down to . . . just another vine layer, and another of the dinosaur's vines snaps and it dives after her—and almost gets her, but . . .

The point is in any sort of synopsis: "For five whole minutes, Ann and three dinosaurs plummet through a net of snapping vines as they fall off a cliff but which delay them till they the last vine snaps and Ann falls on her back on the soft ground, the last five feet, the wind knocked out of her." Perhaps the very last line is: "Through the whole sequence, Ann has managed to keep it more or less together. But now she sits up and . . ." Well, what is that suppose to mean in terms of a series of shots of a swinging actress moving by the several shots of bodies, claws, and teeth of three trapped dinosaurs, who have to be kept recognizable and identifiable if the sequence is to work. Or perhaps that line is: "Through the whole sequence, Ann has been getting more and more terrified, and now, as she tries to get her breath back, coughing and choking, she looks around her, even more terrified . . ." Each of these would probably make major changes in the sequence and content of the hundred and fifty, two hundred and fifty different shots the sequence comprises. And neither gives you any real information of what you will see on the screen. The only thing that will do that is your former experience at one time or another of a similar such sequence in another such film—*Noises Off*, say, *What's Up Doc?* or *What's New Pussycat?*—that's another such sequence, with entirely different content, in some other filmic genre.

The point is, any time a sequence such as this gets done, there is a hostile producer with which the director must already have won an argument: "Look, it's going to go on for five whole minutes. The film is going to be over three hours long, as is. The audience is going to laugh, yawn, and get up and leave the theater . . ."

To which the director's answer must be a form of: "Of course they're going to laugh. I'm going to keep them in their seats with laughter that is getting prompted at an almost unbearably exciting pace and rhythm!"

No matter what you do, in something like this at this point in history, such a sequence *will* register with most viewers as comic—because of its length, because of its sequence of over-the-top choices, because of its ability to keep surprising you with one absurdity after another, and because it clearly takes so much work and thought to bring off. That is to say, it will be comic *rather* than exciting. The only real criticism is: "Why are you bothering to put in so much time and thought in such a sequence?"

And the only answer is: "I'm not going to let them have time to think that. The new viewers will be dazzled because they've never seen it before, and the sophisticated viewers will be dazzled because they have—but they've never seen it done this well.

"Of course the idea of a woman falling off a two-hundred-foot cliff and living, much less falling alongside three dinosaurs who die (or for that matter, get up and walk away) is absurd." A further truth is that, at this distance, though I've watched the whole film five times through and screened parts more than a dozen, at this this distance I *don't* remember the dinosaurs' fate, and would need to watch the end of the sequence once more, to find out. That's because it wasn't a part of the meaning I was allowing myself to construct and revel in.

And—once more—who is Billy? He is the foster son of a black father. He dances his ass off in an Irish jig on deck with Ann and the other sailors, visually reinforcing his friendship with her so that it's believable when he wants to go along with the adult sailors when they take off with their guns to find her—the White Goddess the natives have absconded with. Fascist or not, Billy's filmic context, the whole of his situational surround, means his joining the guys with the guns is not just a fuck-you to the natives we'll eventually see acted out. (In fact, we don't.) His father, his dancing, his reading of Conrad, mean that he is not just one of the Hollow Men firing at the primitives on shore. He loves her—as does Kong himself.

He is also, remember, the one who tells the audience this is a serious film, for all its yuks. (At the same time, he also tells that literary revelation to his black father, who confirms its truth for both Billy and the audience.)

He is the one who mourns his dead black father on the floor of the Valley of the Nest of Spiders—and whose mourning joins that of Andy Serkis for his dead Chinese lover along with the grief any of the audience might bring to the film for any of its thousands of extinguished species that have been obliterated in this continuing greatest extinction of species since the Permian-Triassic. The echoes of all such grief—whether it's for the dozen other sailors who have fallen in (and into) the Valley or the never wholly silenced echoes of that mourning that gathers into the rage of Kong himself, freed by his own strength from the captivity of civilization—carry Watts and Serkis-as-Kong through a moving dance on the ice in Central Park and then up the Empire State Building itself, where he is menaced by the military and the constabulary combined who would rescind his chance to love Ann Darrow, with a rage still supported by grief for the wrongly fallen military or the deluded police on the streets of the city or in the skies above it, for the victims of poverty and starvation or the animals whose antics in the zoo are supposed to entertain us and which we saw in the film's first *faux*-documentary seconds and which we are to recall each time we see the unfettered Kong, who is being hunted and destroyed because his pursuers can't distinguish the difference between loving and wanting to love and the satisfaction both provide in the presence of the person or object loved.

I forgot one last thing about Billy. His origins are a mystery. And that mystery is announced and preserved by a formal mistake in the filmic structure. How neat is that? He could be Kong's brother just as easily as he could throw a gas bomb to help with Kong's capture, which includes original props from the 1933 version that Jackson had collected over the years and kept on set for his own version.

But the damage—the subversion—has already been done. And if some of it isn't as effective as it might have been, it doesn't matter, really: not as long as someone can do another rewrite, another remake. Still, all I can say is that Jackson's is pretty damned good.

All Best—

—Chip

—November 5, 2016
Philadelphia

NOTES

1. "We Are All Bait" refers to a 1952 French film, *Nous sommes touts des assassins*, in which several condemned men in jail are taken away, one by one, to be executed. In *The Collected Stories of Roger Zelazny, Volume 1: Threshold* (NESFA Press, 2009) there are quotes from Zelazny as well as a number of further notes that some, I'm sure, will find of use in reading or rereading, thinking or rethinking the tale.

2. One thinks of Erich Von Stroheim's *Greed* (1924) and even Renoir's *La règle du jeu* (1939), which suffered fates similar to that of Welles's *Ambersons* (though, at least in Renoir's case, not as extreme); or amazingly fortunate wide-screen experiments such as Abel Gance's *Napoleon* (1927), which escaped that fate.

24

Notes on *The City of Green Fire*

I.

Mia Wolff painted her oil-on-linen triptych *The City of Green Fire* between 1997 and 1998 at her studio in New Paltz, New York, where I first saw the paintings in late spring or summer shortly after their completion.[1] It is probably when I saw them again on Church Street in New York City that I first wanted to write about them. (Comic artist Eddie Campbell was also struck enough with them to quote them in *The Birth Caul* that he drew for Alan Moore.) And when she asked me to comment about her paintings in the documentary *Wolffland* (directed by Laura Checkoway, 2016), the triptych always impelled my words, even when I was talking about other Wolff works.

The City of Green Fire is not a Comedy, divine and Dantesque, or human with some Balzacian bevy of social types.

It may be religious, however: the figure off-center in the middle panel is part animal and part human. The fish and flowers that populate the whole of it do not hit me as Christian.

The city itself seems both older and newer than any real ones—that aspect suggests something comic (with a small c), and reminds me more than anything else of Rem Koolhaas's vision of Coney Island in his architectural meditation *Delirious New York* (1978), the experimental try-out area for the shapes then to be exported to Manhattan to create the actual city on its historical base, sometime later.

The artist writes that it came to her in a dream in which she was barefoot, coupled with some photographic sources of the old castle of Prague and a woman—the Patron Saint of Roses—changing roses into fish; the chandelier hung in her New Paltz studio at the time she painted it.

Lights are reflected on its windows. Signs are legible on its walls (but not in English). It's a city of silhouettes, cut out and made visible by light behind them, here and there thrown into relief with decorations and gleams from a more complex palette in its flooded street.

Serious question: Does the liquid over in the city extinguish the fire—or fuel it?

The panel on the left (*The Sea Horse*) appears to be an interior, almost black. Through a window, two portals left and right, and what appears to be a doorway at the end of a cobblestone hallway, a green fire burns.

The middle panel (*The Sphinx*) shows the outside of the city, the sky above it filled with the same yellow-green. The viewer looks down an alley by a sphinx to the left, spurting liquid from her breasts, to spill over a fountain's edge onto the street. Even so, the liquid seems to flow along the ground from the first painting around and into the second.

The third panel (*The Patron Saint of Roses*) shows the city roofs. Then, through a brick arch we see roses, green water, and a female nude (a self-portrait of the artist at the time of the painting); green light still fills the painting's background, but the roses, the fish, the figures here are illuminated by a far more varied and—dare I say—realistic palette than the rest of the work (that is, panels one and two), which of course draws the eye across all three.

II.

In the first of the three paintings, in the foreground we can make out a seahorse—a creature part of the architecture. At the doorway in the back, a wraithlike shadow stands, with fronds and tendrils. Possibly it's a female figure entering the scene. As easily, though, it could be leaving. The figure could be a tree; it could be a silhouetted break between the flames burning at either edge of the door.

III.

In fact, the material actuality of the female figure in *The Patron Saint of Roses* highlights a set of questions and judgments about the figures in *The Sea Horse*.

Is the figure at the hallway's end a positive or a negative space? (No question of that sort needs be asked about the nude with her raised hands.) Is it male or female? If it *is* a positive figure in silhouette, is it entering or leaving?

The larger and closer images of seahorses and fish are specifically architectural; they are images of things painted or carved on the walls as opposed to the realer and realer creatures we see as we move through the three paintings: the more and more unquestionably living creatures are convincingly pictured as we move from the left.

IV.

"The reproach of escapism is seldom aimed at a painter; we do not hold it against Cezanne that he was living hidden away at Estaque during the war of 1870. And we recall with respect his "*C'est effrayant, la vie,*" (*It's astonishing, life*) even when the lowliest student, ever since Nietzsche, would reject philosophy if it did not teach him how to live fully (*à etre de grand vivants*), as Guy Davenport translated.[2]

"It's as if in the painter's calling there were some urgency above all other claims on him. Strong or frail in life, he is incontestably sovereign in his own rumination of the world."

V.

Balthus's *Passage du Commerce Saint-Andre* (1952–54) sets up a distinct dialogue with the middle panel of *The City of Green Fire*. The alley we look down in both paintings is rich with the theme of their artists, Balthus (1908–2001) and Wolff. If Balthus's theme is "the care a culture has for its young" (Davenport, 50)— that is, how the society treats its children, specifically its adolescent girls, with an attention that lapses over into the pornographic, even—Wolff's concern, in a city that recalls Balthus to me, is conveyed in the concluding panel: how its women treat its fish; or, if I can make such a leap, its ecology.

For both painters, in both paintings, these themes are suggested as more or less troubling resonances with sexuality, decentered as much as stated.

VI.

In classical paintings the streets are often the setting for comedy. This is what gives meaning to the fact that in *The City of Green Fire* the paintings are relatively free of direct social life. In *The Sea Horse*, we can't tell if the figure is a single person in front of the flames or a break in the flames themselves. In *The Patron*

Saint, it's a nude woman. Both flank an absence—an empty street, with only a statue spurting liquid (water? . . . milk? . . . oil?) from its breasts—as if to emphasize the lack of living figures.

VII.

The "lost paradise" (of innocence . . . ? of license . . . ?) that Camus wrote about in Balthus may explain Wolff's unpopulated streets in this major work.

VIII.

Writing in 1980 in an introduction to the republication of her earliest story "Acrobats in a Park" (written in or about 1935), Eudora Welty wrote that walls were like families. ("In performance, their act had been the feat of erecting a structure of their bodies that held together like a wall. . . . From points of view within and without, I've been writing about this Wall ever since and what happens to it . . .")[3]

When you look at the brick and stone and dead black walls of all three panels in *The City of Green Fire*, it's interesting to remember that Mia Wolff, after starting as a visual artist, became an acrobat and a catcher in a trapeze act—with a partner. She has described the relationship to me as one as close as a family, and that ceased after an accident when her partner fell because of a piece of faulty equipment, after which she was not comfortable going up to perform with anyone else. Footage of her remains from these days, in the *Wolffland* documentary, though she has taught trapeze work, even as she has become a more and more extraordinary painter. (See her own illustrated children's book, *Catcher*.[4])

IX.

Contemporary art criticism is a criticism of photographs and art books. Even if we spend time with the actual painting in the museum, or on the studio wall, photographic prints or reproductions are likely to play their parts. In my case that's a CD reproducing all three paintings separately, with another of them side by side, which I can put on a computer to review what I have seen so frequently before.

I look at an image presumably shared by the artist who wanted to communicate it. At the same time, though, I am interacting with an image that came
into being though the interaction of what was in the artist's mind with its own
realization on the canvas, an image that grew in a certain way and submitted
itself to certain criteria or just changed so that with her brush and pigments
the artist both made it, then made it look better: painting (the action) and
the painting (the final image the action creates) of necessity have a self-critical
relation with each other and the initial conception in the artist's mind, if the
final look is to be read as encompassing any complexity.

Some of that as a beholder, once the painting is through, I have some access
to, perhaps in the brush work, in a comment the artist might have made to
me, some of which stays and most of which goes ("I wanted to make this seem
darker, and so I . . . ; the correction of an imbalance that did not even exist
before the painting reached a certain stage"), and none of it is present in the
static image of the "completed," which joins the painting even as it creates
itself. ("*The Patron Saint* started as a self-portrait, but eventually I. . . .")

X.

On her liquid-filled pedestal running with water or milk, the winged sphinx
rearing to the left of the central panel spurts multiple sprays from her breasts
in my memory (and in the tiny photograph on the CD case), and appears to be
blind. I see her as a classical cherub, an angel whose ancient form was a centaur
with a lion's body and the torso of a human, another image of the artist herself,
the guardian of the work as well as the city, and at the same time the rector of
all the chaos that the darkness of the painting wrestles with.

The reflections of the city here and there in the water at various distances
comprise the streets from the interplay of dark and light, of colors and cutout
figures, which is what painting is.

In the same panel, a stack of Chinese characters beside another, clearly
not Chinese at all, suggests a private language for which the artist may or may
not have a meaning in mind; in any case they are essentially the same color
as the relatively "realistic" fish swimming through the air and observing or
even reading them, though each rests in different colored hazes of incident and
reflected light.

One fish (in *The Sphinx*) even moves above its own shadow, which gives an
authority to the space between shadow and object. The highlights on the roof
ornaments of the city are another way for the artist to speak directly to us of
space, of illumination, of mind itself.

Can we ask what layer of the painting we are looking at?

When we choose to look at any few inches of the surface, are we looking at an early painted layer or a last? Did it contribute to the organization of the rest of the painting (act) / painting (image) or did the rest of the painting/painting eventually produce it at its climax?

Is it an impetus for the work, or a final layer that reveals a meaning not there at the start?

And can it matter to the viewer that it may be the opposite of the artist's process of creating the image in pigment laid on a ground we do not even see?

The illusion is that we are observing a static picture, but of course we are not. We are looking at an image put together over time—weeks, even months, years if we include the life and education preceding it.

Which again bring us back to the fact that there are three paintings, which we look at all at once—and which were done presumably one after another . . . ? To what extent were they separate?

Did the artist move back and forth between them?

(She tells me she did.)

XII.

The title of the whole work suggests a creative/destructive eruption that must consume and support the artist through the transition of the work's conception to its completion.

Green fire . . .

A city of it. Is the city only named by it? Is it created from it? Is the fire destroying it?

As I write, I can remember two years of my life given over to a trilogy of novels, the difficulties of completing the second book of which simply scared me off conceiving of any work in that form again—even as the toboggan of pleasure that was the writing of the third and final book almost (but never wholly) made up for it.

For better or worse, the memory of my own mental movement over those two years becomes a part of my experience looking at these three Wolff paintings together.

Part of me wants to know if I can find any answers to the lingering despair that was my own experience of the second panel of my own three-volume work in the second painting of Wolff's.

(A circularity is suggested in the third panel: We are looking through one brick arch at still another—a door filled with the eponymous "green fire." Is this, perhaps, the outside view of the door at the end of the corridor in panel one . . . ?)

Imagination being what it is, I would have no problem with Wolff's three paintings, with their questions and visual resolutions as images, on the covers of my own volumes from twenty or thirty years before Wolff's were painted. As easily I could see her response as one of horror at the thought, as though green fire at its most destructive—in the eyes and life of the viewer—was consuming the meaning of her canvasses.

XIII.

The image of the woman making a fish from a rose as it is read to sit at the end of Wolff's narrative arrives with an immense sense of narrative relief.

If we decide to read the work right to left, so that she is placed at the point of origin, it is equally satisfactory. The way she stands out from the background, the way the fire in this panel seems to be closer to resolution or taming, is simply reassuring to anyone who experiences the disruption of the green illumination perfusing the work.

Read in the traditional direction, the three paintings foreground "shadow," "myth," and "body" respectively.

Body is also in the first, though it's entailed in the non-human bodies in the represented architecture.

Shadow is there in the third, in the backgrounds, enfolded in the petals of the roses, wedged in the grout between the bricks.

XIV.

In the first painting, as I return to it on my computer screen, I am reminded (or am I seeing it consciously for the first time?) that there is a great deal of blue in the walls of the building I assume we are within. The liquid running in over the cobbles is as likely to be tar or crude oil as water. (That, I know I have noticed before.) And the decorative fish swimming down the wall on the upper right gives a sense as "realistic" as any of the goldfish (carp perhaps . . . ?) swimming through the air in the other paintings.

XV.

Looking again at the middle picture, the very act of writing about it makes it seem much lighter and livelier than my own meditation transformed it into: the city itself is an intricate city, a city in silhouette, not a heavy city at all, which is how my own ruminations on it pushed it in my imagination.

Looking at it again I feel both disoriented and relieved to have it back.

The particular myth of the sphinx as Mesopotamian angel/monster is, at least in my recent meditations on it, a highly creative image, and one that comes with renewal and—in Wolff's central panel—is painted with it.

XVI.

In the third picture, the chandelier, the bridge shape across the top, the red roof—all these are details that vanished during my reading in note III. The rose in the woman's hands is being transformed into a fish, from the tail forward. The expression on her face as she performs this change in midair is . . . in a word, priceless.

As familiar as I am with these pictures, writing as I look at one of them changes it even now so that every new look is a healing of the violence of interpretation.

XVII.

It is—I almost want to say, "of course"—precisely when I free myself of my own story of the artist's painting these pictures that they speak most directly to my own needs as an eye in time. For whatever reasons and by whatever process, it is an image created. If I lose the why and how (in which only my own uncertainties of the moment can be reflected) and try to fix on the what, the picture is (or the pictures are) more numinous, richer, and more a set of paintings in which I can grapple with what kept drawing me to them in the first place.

XVIII.

. . . what kept drawing me to them in the first place:

The green fire is bright. All the figures walk on the surface of the liquid that grounds them. The sphinx in the central panel has no hands, but paws. The liquid arching and falling from her breasts foams and bubbles in the fountain's pool before her hind claws. She is green, but parts of her body—her own claws,

Mia Wolff, *The City of Green Fire* (1998), oil on linen, 60 x 90 inches.

The City of Green Fire (detail): "The Sea Horse."

The City of Green Fire (detail): "The Sphinx."

The City of Green Fire (detail): "The Patron Saint of Roses."

the edges of her wings—catch all sorts of other colored light from the painting, holding it together . . .

The intelligence and energy in the paintings' details are what, at this viewing, I am responding to the most. And the light.

XIX.

Historically, art seems to move from picturing what we know is there (what we think of as primitive art) and moving on to what it looks like. And somewhere painters such as Wolff come in to paint what is not there and what it might look like anyway. The result is cities or landscapes recognizable as such, but impossible to locate in the world.

This is certainly *The City of Green Fire*, as it is in her most recent series of landscapes.

Under such a regime the works become combinatory, immediately seeming to be in the midst of conversations with other works as soon as you blink at them, infinitely legible.

Thus the way morning or evening comes through my windows in the apartment in Philadelphia where I currently live is the way the light of the Green Fire comes through the windows of the city that bears its name. It's an interesting experience how, over the years that it has been talking to me, I have become so at home in it.

XX.

Clearly physical and conceptual space fall between each of the paintings. Even as there is clear passage between *The Sea Horse* and *The Sphinx*, *The Sphinx* and *The Patron Saint*, there is resistance as well.

It is what gives the city its sense of size.

The interior molding does not get from *The Sea Horse* to *The Sphinx*. The wings of the sphinx do not make it from *The Sphinx* to *The Sea Horse*.

The red illumination in the brick archway of painting two is not continued in the brick arch of painting three. Neither is the sidewalk.

And of course, the massive symmetry of *The Patron Saint* is not continued in *The Sphinx*.

XXI.

Buildings in the city suggest apartments and restaurants, and even possibly places of entertainment, but not libraries or places of business per se.

Clearly, however, there are catacombs, which at least in the neighborhood we are in have access to the surface.

And at least one thing the Green Fire has displaced is weather itself.

The antennae pretty clearly suggest broadcasting. But I doubt the city is as massively online as we are in the present, since—after all—it is a work of the last decade of the twentieth century, not the twenty-first.

XXII.

The tiles and cobbles of the first painting suggest to me sunset, locality, edifices that are utilized largely by the public. Others have recently passed by. Others will soon arrive.

XXIII.

In *The Sphinx* there are two lighted doorways open and exiting onto the street. And there is a larger one that visually balances the sphinx on the other side of the walkway. Out of its half-visible arch, one of the fish in the series swims— not in the water, but through the air.

I find this very hopeful.

In fact, I find this the most optimistic node in the sequence.

XXIV.

In *The Patron Saint of Roses*, a curtain of green fire hangs across one of the doorways, reflected on the water. I am intrigued by the little blue window in the city's upper cupola.

In this panel there are suggestions both of excess and resolution.

XXV.

Guy Davenport translated the Italian version of an ancient Egyptian maxim ("Il paradiso per un uomo e la sua buona natura"): "A man's paradise is his good nature."

Remember that, because often neither men nor women have any other.

Be kind—to people and animals and strangers—because that is how bits of paradise can be spread. Even when you live with someone else who is uncomfortable with all three.

The burning city makes room for such insights, too.

—December 27, 2016
Philadelphia

NOTES

1. Mia Wolff's triptych *The City of Green Fire* (oil on linen, 90 × 60 inches) is composed of *The Sea Horse* (oil on linen, 30 × 60 inches), *The Sphinx* (oil on linen, 30 × 60 inches), and *The Patron Saint of Roses* (oil on linen, 30 × 60 inches).

2. Maurice Merleau-Ponty, translated by Guy Davenport and quoted in Davenport's *The Balthus Notebook* (Ecco Press, 1989), 5.

3. Eudora Welty, quoted by Davenport in *The Balthus Notebook*, 47.

4. Mia Wolff, *Catcher* (Farrar, Straus and Giroux, 1994).

25

Sympathy and Power

A Facebook Post

In his "A Forty-Year-Old Con-Virgin Goes to WisCon" . . . Stephen Gold notes that "Chip Delany . . . was the one who, at the Fundamentals of Feminism panel, finally gave me the straight dope: men can't be feminists. I guess I'll have to settle for being a sympathizer." I can think of more than a score of men who attend WisCon every year without fail; there's no question in my mind that they feel comfortable hanging out in a specifically feminist venue. I haven't asked any of them whether they would characterize themselves as "feminist sympathizers," but I suspect that in 2007 there may well be a valid distinction to be drawn between being comfortable in the company of feminists and being a sympathizer that could not have been drawn back in, say, the 1970s or even in the early '80s. Do you think such a distinction can be drawn, and if so, what does that signify to you?

L. Timmel Duchamp

A sexually active gay man of nineteen, in August, 1961, I married an eighteen-year-old-woman, who had been my best friend since soon after we'd met in the Bronx High School of Science in 1956. Eight months younger than I, she was a year ahead of me in school and went to college at NYU as an early admission student of fifteen. Within a year of that marriage, largely under her tutelage and after many hours of discussion with her and her women friends, I decided that the reapportionment of power between the sexes—women and men—was the most politically important job of all the possible liberatory projects one might take up. The unfair and widely abused power discrepancies between all groups—nonwhites and whites, homosexuals and straight people, children and adults—were all based on the first; and they were fully understandable in its terms and only in its terms.

I believe that today, still—though most of my personal energies now go into addressing the power imbalances between gay men and straight society: living and working in the social niches that I do, those are the conflicts I have the most day-to-day experience with. Those are the ones where I feel I can do the most local good. But I try to keep all my efforts to that end in line with what I still see as the greater political imbalance.

Power imbalances are contingent social constructions. They can be changed; they do change: each handful of years reveals more and more changes in them all. Not everyone is happy with these changes. Nor do many people who are basically pleased by them necessarily understand them.

One of the most confusing aspects of all socially constructed power differentials is power itself—what is it and how does it work? Provisionally the best way to begin understanding power is to realize that, practically speaking, power is different from strength. There are two general approaches to power—or better, axioms about power—one of which is fairly easy for most people to grasp. The problem with it *as* an axiom is that it isn't particularly useful in changing power structures. It might be expressed:

"Power is the social generalization of strength."

Certainly it has its truth. Because some men are stronger than some women, we generally go through our lives, men and women, assuming most men are stronger than most women. And I have seen that argument generalized to a simple statement that men are stronger than women—and, on occasions, have even heard some men generalize it to "all men are stronger than all women." Whether these generalizations are true or not, most of us can understand how these generalizations work or come about.

I had a friend once—Sunny—a fat, extremely strong, brutal, and violent (but also charming) man. Regularly he got into fights—some of which, when he reached his thirties, he was hired to get into by criminals, who paid for his services. He almost always won. He had spent several years in jail. He was over 250 pounds. By his own admission he had killed at least five people, two accidentally, one for personal revenge. The others were "work." He had been caught for none of them.

The generalization of power can actually undo the extant power structure: "I don't get in fights with women no more—never. Strongest person I ever fought with was a woman. I was at the movie theater, the old Academy of Music up on Fourteenth Street," Sunny once told me. "With some of my friends—we was just sittin' there, watchin' the film, and there was this couple in the row ahead of us. So we decided to fuck with 'em. I began makin' these comments about his woman, and suddenly the guy stands up, angry, and turns around. And I see it's not a guy at all—it's another woman, only she's got short hair like a man. And she's dressed like a guy. She ain't even that big, either—not like me. Or one of my sisters." (Sunny was the only boy and youngest child in a family of twelve siblings. His father, physically even bigger than he was, had spent twelve years in a Canadian jail.) "So I figure, it's just some scrawny dyke. I stand up—and this woman hauls back and socks me in the jaw. I went out, like *that*! I didn't come to for ten, fifteen minutes. I lost two teeth—man, that's the hardest I was ever hit in my life! And I been a hit a lotta times by a lotta guys, who were fuckin' serious about it, too! Don't tell me a woman can't hit as hard as men. The hardest I ever got hit, that was a woman. So I don't fuck with *none* of 'em, no more. You do that, and you gonna get your head handed to you. I mean it, 'cause it happened to *me*."

For Sunny, from a single experience that ran counter to the general wisdom, he had generalized this to the assigning of greater physical power to women. Quite possibly some earlier experiences with his older sisters (several of whom had also spent years in jail) when he was a child may have contributed to it.

But the problem with the concept of power as the generalization of strength is that—in general—it doesn't locate the most useful socially effective intervention points.

The other approach-cum-axiom about power does: "Power (unlike strength) is *always* assigned by an Other."

Sunny himself is the Other who, from the point of generalization, reassigned power to women so that he "no longer fucks with 'em." Is that enough to change the balance of power? There was a period, certainly, starting in the middle '60s, when physically competent women actually became a staple of adventure movies, comics, TV, and science fiction, and physical training for women grew much more widespread, which began only shortly after Sunny had his movie theater encounter; incidents of this sort certainly couldn't have *hurt* the reassignment of physical power to women. But it seems to me, today, reflected in films like *Million Dollar Mermaid* (1952) and *Bridge to Terabithia* (2007)— where the strong or competent female is killed off by the film's end—that this period is fast petering out.

Holding on to where the other makes his or her move in the assignment process is still very necessary. In the early 1990s, I was invited to spend a term as Cole Honors Professor at the Honors College of the State University of Michigan at East Lansing. I and my life-partner Dennis went out and, while I taught for a term at the university, we lived together on campus.

For a number of reasons, Dennis and I were housed in a faculty apartment on the ground floor of Yakely Hall, a large building, basically a women's dorm, which faced out on the university's main thoroughfare. To its back was a forested area through which a number of shortcuts ran to other classroom buildings.

I am a short (five-eight), pudgy adult, with a beard. I was in my early fifties and just beginning to walk with a cane. I have—and had at the time—many visual cues about me of an "older man." Dennis, my life-partner of three or four years at the time, was (and is) a slim, tall (six-one) man, who had been homeless and lived on the street for six years before we met, and he had an animal vitality and a body that was all muscle. Twelve years younger than I, Dennis was then thirty-nine or forty, but he carried himself like someone as much as ten years younger.

On several occasions, either when collecting our mail with the young women who shared our building, or going to chamber music concerts or political debates that were sometimes held in the lounge, we found ourselves walking through the dorm halls—which were lined with blackboards. Their repeated messages and warnings had an overriding theme:

"Every six minutes, somewhere a woman is raped!"

"Keep yourself safe. Travel with a friend or friends after dark!"

"The best weapon again rape? Use your head!"

Across all of these hung hand-printed flyers about individual cases of sexual molestation on various parts of the campus. (Once I looked carefully at a couple of them to discover they were dated three and four years ago, and had not yet been taken down!) The blackboards were covered with the addresses and phone numbers of rape counseling centers and rape crisis centers. There were emergency phone numbers for battered women's shelters and numbers to volunteer for work with displaced and homeless women who had been abused by husbands or boyfriends.

As we were walking, looking at all this, Dennis voiced what I was feeling myself: "That's gotta be kinda weird—living someplace where you're threatened with rape every time you step out of your room."

"It probably is," I said. "But then, it's also probably necessary. You remember, the school paper had an article about a rape on campus just two weeks ago . . ."

"Oh, yeah. That's right."

A few evenings later, Dennis went out to see some friends, and I went to a program about gay studies. I got home early and retired to bed. A bit after eleven, Dennis came in.

He was visibly upset—so I got up and asked him what was the matter.

A light snow had stopped earlier in the evening. Dennis had been walking home through the back wooded section, when he'd seen a pair of young black women, some ways away, but both clearly—as was he—headed toward

Yakeley. He wasn't really thinking about them, but he noticed that, now and then, they stopped and looked at him. Then they would whisper together, and hurry on—sometimes moving toward the hall, sometimes away. In fact, he was fairly sure he recognized one of the women as someone he'd seen around the dorm before—and now also realized they were nervous.

The back entrance to the hall was only thirty or thirty-five feet away. Dennis decided to wave and maybe call out something friendly, but the moment he did, he said—he also took a step forward. Perhaps that was interpreted as his starting to run. The two women took off, pell-mell, toward the door. Dennis thought he was involved in some sort of joke, and took a couple of quicker steps after them, to get into the light, and even called, "Hey—it's all right . . ."

At that point, the women reached the door, which had a light above it. One—after yanking open the door—turned to pull her friend inside . . . and Dennis saw that the look on her face was, as he said, one of *absolute* terror!

He stopped dead.

The door slammed behind the two. They were gone inside. Dennis realized that they had thought he was pursuing them. He was very upset. He wanted to go looking for them and explain that he was just coming back to his room, as were they. He alternated between being deeply distressed—and very angry. He was not exactly sure whom he was angry at—sometimes it was at whoever had put up all the frightening blackboard notices. Sometimes it was at the women for being "stupid" and thinking an ordinary gay man was a potential rapist. Sometimes it was at himself, for not making clearer that he was harmless before they'd started to run, or for being so silly as to think that they were taking it all as a joke in the first place—or, indeed, that *he* had been stupid enough to take it that way.

The point here is simply that, because "power is always assigned by an Other," *you*—if you are male—can't get rid of it just by "being a nice guy" or being personally "harmless" as you walk around in the world.

I (and Dennis; and every other male in this society) exercise my male power and prerogatives (which includes the power of a rapist over his victim) just by walking around in the street. The fact that I—personally—believe the reapportionment of power between the sexes (notice I do not use the word gender) is so overwhelmingly important has nothing to do with the power that is assigned me by every male and female who happens to register my presence as I move through this society. This is why changing the power structure is so difficult. The power *never* starts with the one who has it. It is assigned by an Other; and effective change is always a matter of changing the assigner, not the assignee.

(In my ideal world, there is one gender with infinite variations; not two with the variations limited to what lies between them. If there *are* two, they will be assigned unequal power, because—sad as the news may be—unequal power differentials are the only socially meaningful differences that exist. That is, therefore, what *two* genders means. If they weren't of unequal power, they wouldn't *be* two.)

This brings us to your question about being a male "feminist" or a feminist sympathizer at WisCon.

But there's a limit case to all this that I wish I could simply skip over—and I would, had I not had to deal with it directly in the first few years that I was teaching at the University of Massachusetts at Amherst. In my third year, 1990, I drew up a course description of a continuing graduate seminar in the history of the novel called "Male Sexuality and the Modern Novel," which, that term, included works such as Joyce's *Portrait of the Artist as a Young Man*, D. H. Lawrence's *Sons and Lovers*, *The Rainbow*, and *Women in Love*, Musil's *Young Törless*, and Gide's *The Immoralist* and *Strait Is the Gate*. The course description mentioned that we would be looking at some of these texts from a position "sympathetic to feminism." But the secretary who typed up the description for the course catalogue made a mistake and accidentally the course appeared as "Sexuality and the Modern Novel." The result was that a number of young women applied to take the course, thinking it was a course *in* feminism per se. Among the men who registered, one was an auditor, of twenty-three, named Bill, whom I had already met in town, where he worked in Amherst's local comic book store.

Bill was a blond, strapping young man who lifted weights. He was notably better looking than average, and knew it. He was quite intelligent, and during the first class session, when I was telling my dozen students about the focus of the course—and the titling error—as I often do in such classes I asked the students to say a few words about why they had taken the course and what they hoped to get out of it, and Bill was the only one who said he had read several of my books already and was therefore interested to hear what I had to say on the topic. He confessed that he too had made the expected mistake, however, and had registered to take the course because he felt "the position of women in the society" was an interesting question.

When the first meeting was over and we had adjourned, however, Bill attached himself to me for the bus ride back into Amherst and, in the course of our chat, said, "You know, I'm not *really* into all this feminist stuff. But I figured it would be a good way to meet chicks. And even with the mistake corrected, there're still a couple of cute ones in your class. But I guess you have to talk the talk in order to get anywhere with chicks like these."

Needless to say, I was not very happy with this as his opening move—though I chuckled and said, "Who knows. You may even have to learn to walk the walk."

His response: "I don't think there's much chance of that. Believe me—I already know how to handle chicks."

And, indeed, though Bill was often deferential, as our class discussions progressed, it became clear that he had neither any understanding of—nor sympathy with—feminism, and that he thought all of us in the class were basically out of our minds. He made two or three efforts to date some of the women students, then, at the two-thirds point—which he could do because he was auditing—dropped out.

It's always been my practice to teach anyone who will show up. But since Bill could be obtuse and even, sometimes, disruptive, I don't think anyone missed him. In the class meeting before he left, however, one of the women who had long ago lost patience with Bill challenged him: "You're in this class. Do you think of yourself as a feminist?"

Bill had answered, "Sure, I do. I'm a feminist. I like women. I like spending time with them, talking to them. They make me feel good. I just don't think they're generally as smart as men, that's all. And I don't particularly even want them to be—doesn't that mean I'm for women, as they are and as they should be?"

This was, of course, fifteen years ago. But here we are at the inescapable brink of "male feminists" and the power deployment between the sexes.

I don't think we have to spend time discussing whether those men (and women: often the women self-identify as "post-feminist") who believe that the status quo is fine as it is, and that a power reapportionment is neither desirable nor necessary, should call themselves feminists. The point is that some, like Bill, if not many, do.

Please forgive all this contextual elaboration before I turn to your question directly, which is about comfort vs. discomfort, feminists vs. sympathizers, and the change in the relationship between the early 1970s, early '80s, and now, in a venue such as WisCon.

Let me start by saying that when power *is* reassigned, *nobody* is comfortable with it, at least at the beginning, neither men nor women. Some folks—men and women—who have taken part in a careful intellectual analysis of the situation are possibly more likely to put up with that discomfort in the name of something like "tough love." But while there are certainly joys to be experienced from the reassignment of power, they are interlarded with new rights and new responsibilities that are simply difficult to negotiate.

Also, when power is reassigned to one person, that means it is taken away from someone else—and that is always going to be men. Invariably that is experienced as the taking away of former privileges. Nobody likes or enjoys that. And if they say they do, they're lying. But it's still amazing what you can acclimate to. Nevertheless, the comfort of men that you talk about at WisCon is, I'm afraid, basically an index that, while WisCon well may be a gathering of women and men who are highly aware that reassignment is necessary, the comfort most feel there—again, men and women—is because that reassignment has not yet taken place.

When now and again in the 1970s I would encounter social experiments where precisely such reassignments *were* taking place, I remember how *uncomfortable* I felt with them. Once I visited an Oregon commune where the back wall carried a large banner, MOTHER IS A JOB. A condition of my entering and visiting for three days, eating there, and sleeping, was that I had to agree to do a certain amount of child care. And when I said, kind of lightly, "Well, all right. I'll try. But I don't know how good I am at this," the young man who was showing me around didn't return a supportive smile, and say, "Oh, you'll get used to it. And we'll try to make it easy on you and show you what to do." Rather, the look he gave me said: "What's the matter with you? Are you nuts?"

That's the effect of the reassignment of power. And it *isn't* comfortable. For what it's worth, they did help me. I learned a number of techniques that I used with my own daughter (and that led, I'm sure, directly to the wonderfully warm relationship I have with her today, thirty years later, now that she's an adult in medical school). After three days I was a better parent because of the time I'd spent there.

Then there was Grey Rabbit (1971–1983), a collective that ran a bus back and forth from New York to San Francisco. The bus was restroom-equipped, but among the freewheeling young people, especially the young men, on a shaky vehicle with dubious springs, the restroom quickly became un-usably foul, to the distress of the women passengers. The driver happened to be a woman, however, and she was also handy as a carpenter. After the next run, she sawed off a couple of lengths of two-by-four and positioned them across the john space, one just inside the door, one further in, so that it was impossible to approach the commode standing. You had to back in and sit.

She accompanied it with a sign:

> You don't sit,
> You don't piss!

That's the reassignment of power—and most of the guys on the bus were pretty uncomfortable on the first day of the three-day run. At the end, however, even they appreciated the *much* cleaner space. And the rear third of the bus no longer smelled like a stopped-up urinal.

The benefits of reassignment, even in so small a taste as I got at the Oregon commune, were huge. I only wish I (and Pat Muir) had been there longer.

But no one should approach them looking for comfort. It isn't there. Indeed, the sign that they have taken place is initial *discomfort*.

As far as the changes over time from the '70s through the '80s, it's always difficult for me to distinguish the changes that age itself brings—the kinds of experiences that age precludes me from (or, suddenly, includes me in)—and the changes that are transculturally there.

At dinner only last week, a young gay studies professor told me, "Oh, today *all* the queers are the straight kids. The gay kids don't want anything to do with 'queer' any more. It's been completely co-opted." And indeed, I'd noticed only last term when I taught a class in gay studies here at Temple, all the men who registered for the class were straight—and the one who most vociferously self-identified as "queer" also most vociferously self-identified as "heterosexual."

I also noticed something else, though. The class was half men and half women, but the women dominated the discussion. They were extremely comfortable with our progression from *Kinsey* and Kenneth (*Scorpio Rising*) Anger to the Derek (*Sebastiane, Edward II*) Jarman films we screened and our readings of everything from Foucault and Freud and Henry (*Deep Gossip*) Abelove on homosexuality to "Chapter V" of Philip Aries's *Centuries of Childhood* (in today's atmosphere of hysteria over child abuse and childhood sexuality certainly one of the most "shocking" pieces of scholarship, in its findings, that I know of) to my own *Times Square Red, Times Square Blue*. To support one abstract point or another they offered anecdotes about their own bodies freely and intelligently, in a way that, twenty years ago, I'd only found among older gay men and women, while the men in the class . . . what can I say, still sounded like boys—and not what I, at least, think of as adults. (Many of them reminded me simply of quieter and less hide-bound Bills.) Some reassignment of discursive power, at least, had clearly taken place, though whether it was permanent or larger than the accidental fall of the class roster, I have no way to know. Nevertheless, the constantly reiterated message from the young men in the class was, "I never even knew people did things like that—ever. Wow . . . that's just so weird" (sometimes said to me in class, sometimes said wonderingly outside in the halls), while the women seemed to find it wholly nonthreatening and interesting for the ways it suggested the world might one day be rearranged. This seems to represent a change that is palpable over the last seven years since I first came to Temple.

Do any of these attitudes, to the extent they are indexes of comfort or discomfort before the social reassignment of power, mirror anything that you have seen at recent WisCons? And that question, really, is about as far as I can go.

I feel as though I have not answered you with any sort of directness. But perhaps I have given someone younger than I (and someone who has been to WisCon more than twice in twenty years—my own situation) a tool or two that might be useful in working toward an answer. Or, perhaps, I have only displayed some tools, the value of whose inspection is precisely that they have no particular relevance or use to the question. But all intellectual work is a gamble.

I wish you the best of things and the best of words and thoughts to stabilize their best order for you—

—Chip Delany

—*December 22, 2016*
Philadelphia

26

Ash Wednesday

I.

I'm worried about my trip up to New York to attend a sex party.

I worry that I am not traveling with my twenty-seven-year-old assistant who is far more skillful at pushing the buttons on my iPhone (or laptop, if I hadn't drowned the keyboard in coffee and destroyed the damned thing even before I became that comfortable using it) than I am, so that I'm stuck writing my notes with a ballpoint in a small spiral notebook. I worry about the latest Theory of Everything (this decade it's Attention Deficit Disorder) which does such a good job of holding people in their various social tracks, so that someone who is dyslexic (such as I am) is also framed as "having a form of ADD." A third the people at the party, Bob tells me, will have it. Our mutual friend Eric—who is eighty-five and whom we've both been to bed with, separately and in a three-some—says Bob is practically a hoarder, which makes it likely he has a touch of it too. But despite that, I'm on the Peter Pan bus and heading north.

Bob Woof[1] has invited me to one of his Prime Timers' parties on Sunday evening, March 5, 2017; on the phone he's been talking to me about coming to these monthly gatherings for more than a year, but this time I've decided to accept and attend, as well as write a few notes about it.[2] (Manually, in a notebook. I can't handle them any other way on, say, an iPhone.) The hotel is near Forty-Seventh Street; the party is in room 3905 (two rooms and a bath, actually), given over to sex from five-thirty pretty much till midnight.

I'm combining the trip with another visit I've been wanting to make for several years, to see my old fuck buddy Maison Bailey and his husband, Fred

Rinaldi, who live in High Meadow Trailer Park further upstate in Dover Plains. I have been invited for two days: after the Prime Timers party, I'll continue by the Metro North train and stay with Fred and Maison on Monday night, March 6, and Tuesday night, March 7, then return by train to New York City. After a trek across town from Grand Central Station to Port Authority with my gray plastic rollaway and my grubby white Zabar's bag, I'll return to Philadelphia on the morning of Wednesday, March 8, on a Peter Pan bus. Fred has been diagnosed with ADD and is on medication for it. He's told me about a book he's got, which, last night, I ordered online. (*Healing ADD*, by Dr. Daniel Amen.) Fred has also said he has Hepatitis D, which could be a third thing to worry about . . .

They have an open relationship. I've been to bed with both of them on other visits and also with just Maison. On a previous visit, Fred slept in the soft, saggy living room chair so that Maison and I could have the bed for sex. I've been to bed with Fred a couple of times, but both understand I'm more interested in Maison sexually than Fred—an interest that precedes Fred by many years. I enjoy both for conversation—and Fred has a wider range of conversational interests than Maison. Often when I've visited before I've taken them both out to dinner.

But that's getting ahead of things.

The Prime Timers are a group of older New York City–based gay men, who have a sex party every month. Unless you count some of the adventures I had when I first met Maison, back in 1983, when I was forty-one and he was twenty-seven, this will be my first. In short, some of the earliest parts of my relationship with Maison are what has most prepared me for the sex party.

Maison and I met in NYC in the balcony of the now-demolished Variety Photoplays Theater on Third Avenue just below Fourteenth Street. He had come there with his "uncle," Johnny Cadore, his father's best friend since the two had been boys together; Johnny was gay and took it upon himself to bring Maison down to New York to sample the city's gay movie cruising—and generally expose him to the aspect of working-class gay culture that movie house cruising afforded.

When we met, Maison also had an older lover, named Eddie Redick, a black man like myself, only in his middle sixties. They'd been together a few years. On a couple of occasions, Maison took me to see Eddie, who worked as a church organist and lived in upper Manhattan. At least twice, I was invited to Eddie's apartment along with Maison, and the three of us ended up in bed together. It was always fun. And a couple of times Eddie took us to a small gathering of three white friends his age or older. Clearly Maison and I were both supposed to have sex with them—so we did. (I was good at doing what I thought was socially expected of me, and I hope I still am.) I also remember thinking that it was an interesting sexual network, though I had no sense of it at the time as a permanent or stable social structure of which I was a part and which I would be repeating this far along in my life.

Three years later, Eddie died. A veteran, he was buried in the sprawling Veterans' Cemetery. I have failed to mention two things about Maison: he could not read or write at all. As well, he had been born with a decided harelip that went all the way through his nose, and because he had an extreme speech defect, he had compensated with what he described as a pronounced "country" accent.

Once Maison asked me to visit the cemetery with him where Eddie was buried, and to run interference for him and help with the names that had to be looked up and the work that had to be done to find the actual grave. We found it. And as we were standing there, Maison began to cry softly. Eddie had been very generous both to Maison and to Maison's family. (He'd brought Maison's mother a television I remember, which lived in Maison's parents' trailer-park home, now that they no longer lived in their family house in Brewster.) As we stood in the vast cemetery, and I held weeping Maison, fourteen years my junior, I realized I had a much closer friend than I'd thought—and over the years, though both of us went on to partner with other people, we still saw each other (almost always at Maison's prompting) for sex at least once or twice a year, and this extraordinarily loyal friend regularly phoned me every few weeks and continues to do so today.

About a year ago, Bob Woof brought a car full of guys to stop and have lunch with me out in Wynnewood Mall, in a restaurant called Sabrina's. I'd been calling him from the house in Keithwood Road, where Dennis and I had been invited to live. The guys Bob brought were civilized, seemed well off, and friendly. One big fellow in jeans and a jean jacket drove for the group. They were coming back from somewhere to New York City.

One man named John in a navy pea jacket remarked on what a nice guy I was. Bob sucked my fingertip at the restaurant table. Nobody else in the restaurant seemed particularly interested in us. Probably we were recognized as a gay men's group but it didn't seem to bother anyone. Dennis didn't come that day, I remember, for whatever reason.

I'd met Bob at an academic convention on gay comic art, in the downstairs concourse of the CUNY Graduate Center, where he'd walked up to me, put his arms around me, and began to kiss me. He was fifty-five, and I was seventy-two. He told me that he was really mad over "silver daddy bears," and I had long white beard and was clearly a "daddy." With glasses and a short white beard, he traveled in jeans and plaid shirts, as I did. My beard was notably longer, though.

Through the rest of the program, he hung out with me—even though I had come with three younger friends (Mia Wolff, Ann Matsuuchi, and Alex

Lozupone: it was the day I met Alison Bechdel, and we mentioned my part in the formation of "The Bechdel Rule," and met a number of other folks)—and while Bob verged on the annoying, his brazenly direct sexual come-on was intriguing.

What has always interested me about gay male society is the way it seems to operate differently from what one might call normative heterosexual society.

Woof ran a group for men such as myself—the Prime Timers: older gay men. What this had to do with gay comic books, I never really understood; but, well, there was some connection . . . For better or worse, however, Woof seemed to be as interested in teaching me about some of those differences as I was to learn them—and he also seemed well positioned to do it. He seemed naturally kind, concerned, and caring.

In the subsequent year of suburban isolation (a born New Yorker, I'd never learned to drive), I found myself repeatedly phoning Bob for help and knowledge of a different way of living than the one I and my lover of twenty-seven years had fallen into with my daughter and son-in-law. What had been intended as a permanent move from New York City to Pennsylvania turned into a disaster, till after ten months, first me, then Dennis and me, were asked to leave . . . And Dennis and I were back in my old Philly two-room pied-à-terre that my son-in-law had generously renovated for me a few years before. Did Bob think I was out of my mind? "No, it sounded more like what you need," Dennis said when he joined me. "Check it out, if you want." And so through a number of repeated phone calls, and then with a setup with a friend of Bob's when I went out on a trip to do a reading and lecture in Santa Cruz (during which Maison phoned me the same afternoon, while I was in California, waiting for my assistant Beth to come out of a coffee shop with a latte), I spent the night with Bob's eighty-five-year-old friend, and, to my surprise, had the best sex I'd had in more than a decade. Eric also calls up, now and again, with some sort of internal clock not that different from Maison's, at least it feels that way!

There was still a world of experience that, for all my interest, had been slipping by and that I wanted at least to know something about it.

Party manners, Bob has explained, are that when the dozen-plus guests (from age forty-five to age eighty) arrive at the hotel, every one strips off his clothes and has sex with each other. Between seven-thirty and eight-thirty, there'd be a dinner break: pizza plus whatever Bob's co-host, Chuck, could put together. While I was not particularly nervous sexually about what would happen, there was my worsening ADD: the shattering of my self-confidence last year had left me with exactly the kind of uncertainties that Bob prided himself on being able to take care of in the elderly who came to his parties. Would I arrive with phone and luggage intact? Would I be able to negotiate my medications, food? Sleep?

ADD is not forgetting so much as being pathologically absentminded. And it gets worse with age. At one point, I'd had my memory tested. It was "normal," but I have some "cognitive failings." That's my ADD.

Bob Woof turns fifty-eight on March 29, and is six years younger than Dennis, my partner of twenty-seven years. Bob would stay over at the hotel, and has invited me to help him set up for the party and, afterwards, to stay there for the rest of the night once the others have gone home.

(Did I mention I turn seventy-five three days after Bob's birthday?)

The people who attend, save for Bob and Chuck, pay thirty dollars apiece. That includes me. After the night at Bob's, I am planning to continue up to my friends Maison and Fred's mobile home in High Meadow Trailer Park.

(Maison still cannot read or write. I have known him seven years longer than I have known Dennis. I will spend two days and come back to Philadelphia, while I am no longer being looked after by Dennis or Bob.)

(Thoughts on technology: I am bringing an iPhone and a charger with me. Bob Woof brought an ordinary cell phone and laptop with him, that he didn't set up. He brings it because the party hotel has Wi-Fi and if he doesn't have someone staying over, he can get some work done.)

(At home, Dennis has two laptops, one of which he takes with him to the Green Street Café every day, with his iPhone and his Bluetooth device [which, till recently I had forgotten needed a separate charging.])

Worries about getting to the party include:

Will I be able to get back with everything I started out with? (Note to myself: read some of Fred's book on ADD when you get up to Dover Plains. It's interesting that so many people have it, all over the place. Including me and my daughter.)

(The bus has skipped Mount Laurel and is going express to New York City.)

(As a younger man I had a pretty extensive sex life. As a writer, I'm known as a "sex radical, Afro-futurist, and grand master of science fiction," but I am nowhere near as sexually radical as many, and while I have been busy taking care of life on this or that front, lots of things have slipped by on others. Which, put simply, is one reason—ADD or not—I am doing this.)

I haven't yet announced on Facebook that I am going to a sex party of older gay men and after that going further upstate to see my only real remaining fuck buddy. (*Am* I going to announce it in so many words . . . ?) Am I taking this trip for sex, for friendship, or just to be able to spread information to people who need it or might benefit? Or all three?

Some of them all, I suspect.

I'm certainly going to write about it.

I met Maison in 1983.

(Dennis and I met in 1989. Dennis has never met Bob, though when he was most recently in Philadelphia [last autumn], Bob invited us both to come to dinner with him and his older friend, Eric. "You, go," Dennis said. "I'll stay here . . .")

Probably at this moment, I should take my luggage down from the bus rack overhead—maybe after a trip to the john. Or even before . . .

The trees on the far and near sides of the fields beside the roads are all bare, and remind me of underwater sponges. Despite the bursts of warm weather, there is just old grass—some dull green—amidst browns and tans.

A serious historical question underlies this project.

How did I get from a more or less monogamous heterosexuality in my childhood, which I thought all people lived in, to an open marriage with a woman at nineteen for thirteen years, to age seventy-four, with, in the U.S.A., same sex marriages and open relationships, such as Maison's and Fred's, mine and Dennis's, with the death penalty repealed and reinstated, no ERA yet passed, but Roe v. Wade as law on the books, by which abortions are tentatively protected but not by much, and the trammels of ADD wreaking havoc with logic and focus throughout them all.

The woman in the seat ahead on the bus to New York is reading an article in a magazine, "Science and Technology," which shows the familiar spiral of chromosomes. (Is this going to be a journal entry, a Facebook post, or what?) She just turned the page . . .

My old friend Abe, when we were young, would complain I wrote using too many colors. He was a friend in high school and still a friend on Facebook. And yet, back then, the colors were what I loved. Now, true, they don't seem as interesting as they might, if only because this is no longer an intensely colored land.

Everything out the window, from ranks of boxcars to flat concrete buildings, is muted with winter colors. There are no clouds, which to me suggests it's *cold* outside the bus.

All the cars speeding in the opposite lane are gray, black, or white, with a few eccentric reds or blues. This is not an externally colorful era.

Partitioned stone walls keep people from crossing the highway or drivers from being distracted by the landscape. We passed a billboard on the other side of the road for Hooters: a chesty young white woman in a summer halter standing at the side of the yellow sign. We're an hour and four minutes through the presumably two-hour Sunday afternoon trip. It's 12:04 p.m.

Ah, another yellow billboard across the way . . .

Anyway, I'm not worried about AIDS. I *am* worried about Hepatitis D, which Fred freely admits to. That's the first thing I have to ask Doctor Fellow about when and if I get home on Wednesday. Boxcars are stacked to the right of the bus. Newark Airport spreads to the left. Briefly I can see the Manhattan skyline with the single tower that has finally replaced the great tuning fork in the sky—my personal nickname for the twin towers in the years before they came down in opening two hours of a week of smoking ruins. Really, the tower there now is dull, unimaginative glass, and ridiculously phallic—even more than the World Trade Center, because now we should know better. We are getting closer to the tunnel from which Bob Woof said I ought to call him. Okay, I'm ready.

(Phoned Bob in New York. Phoned Dennis in Philly. Everything is on track.)

As we come out of the Holland Tunnel, the driver announces that, at the end of May, Peter Pan and Greyhound busses will no longer honor each other's tickets. That's going to make things inconvenient after all these years.

Ash Wednesday was the first of March. In the Gayborhood streets of Philadelphia, I saw only two people with the cross of ash smudged on their foreheads that day, far fewer than in former years. Are sexual activities (the topic of this meditation), replacing religion, or is there any connection at all?

"Teach us to sit still," Eliot writes in the *Four Quartets*, paraphrasing Pascal. And in the hundreds of hours I have spent on busses and trains and even planes going up and down from Boston to New York, Springfield to New York, Amherst to New York, I have sat still while I was transported along the bland highways and over the landscapes that comprise the northeast parenthesis to the nation. But the ADD pacer back and forth—me—has a far harder time with that than most, unless he or she is actively working on the solution of a problem.

II.

Well, my trip to New York and the Prime Timers' sex party that Bob Woof ran at a midtown hotel near Forty-Seventh Street (two rooms and a bathroom) is finished with. We *were* in room 3509.

Woof and I went up to a pizza place about five blocks to the north and carried back four boxed pizzas to the hotel. (Three in a duffel bag; I carried the one that wouldn't fit.) Before anyone else arrived, Bob and I decorated: I put large sheets of red tissue over two of the lamps, set out dishes of cookies, peanuts, potato chips, popcorn, candy, and soft drinks for the taking, even before Chuck came with the bowls of food, which, during the dinner break, had to be microwaved. Bob said there were thirteen or fourteen guys there. I didn't count them. They were pleasant and all trying to have fun: Paul, Joe, Rich, Chuck (co-host of the party with Bob), Larry, and George are some of the names that stick, but there were more than twice that many. All of us, with the exception of Chuck and Bob, for the first half of the four- to five-hour party were naked and barefoot. My shoes were in the corner. Eventually Bob's clothes came off as well. Because I was there as his friend, I got my own drawer.

There to help Bob out with the logistics of food and cleaning up, Chuck (easily fifty or fifty-five) was the only person who stayed in his jeans, studded belt, and tank top from beginning to end, though he was free with his hands with everybody else and very good natured about people touching him. That night he brought some tasty black-eyed peas and a green curry of Brussel sprouts and rice, both of which were pretty good. He and Bob also put out a dish of almost tasteless fettuccini with a green sauce that was not a success, but edible. Still naked, we ate on paper plates and stood around or sat on the edge of the opened-out couch, talking about . . . well, to be honest, I don't remember. Some of it was about a lecture series one of them was putting together. And there was a general agreement that had been reached to the effect that we would just not talk about Donald Trump, president for three very uneasy months. People stuck to it.

I got the impression nobody knew or cared who I was, possibly because they were not expecting a writer here and possibly because Bob hadn't told them. (Bob told me that two-and-a-half months before, a filmmaker named Charles Lum had filmed a documentary on the group which was to appear in a short fifteen-minute version (*Secret Santa Sex Party*) and a full-length seventy-minute version (*Sex and the Silver Gays*). Although I used my real nickname Chip, and I think at least once said Chip Delany, and though I mentioned I was going to write a brief article on the goings on, since I was taking part and the group was seasoned by the attentions of a filmmaker (many of them had been interviewed for the film) they were not particularly concerned with the prospect.

George and one other guy were uncut. (George was the only person there who was probably older than I was.) It was hard to tell, but the youngest and, by my lights, best-looking character was an extremely fat young man of perhaps forty, who was very active but seemed slightly slow. He was certainly over three hundred pounds and with a working-class face and beard and one of the several people who, at least to me, seemed unremittingly masculine. From time to time, I managed to get a few stories. For a while I sat with Paul, ignoring his claw-like big toenail while he jerked off beside me and gave me a fifteen-minute monologue of petty crimes that, according to him, continue to this day, the telling of which apparently kept him very excited. My part was to listen, seem interested, maintain physical contact, and not leave. I'm not sure whether it was true or whether it was just a sexual fantasy. He was lean, swarthy, with glasses, and said he was in his sixties.

There was a good deal of sucking. (I did my share.) Mark, who was fifty-four, again traditionally masculine and very good-looking, had recently lost a lover in his nineties some months before, and apparently had severe ADD, according to Bob. He was very forward sexually with me and with everybody else in the group. Again, another good-looking man, and I really enjoyed being there and having sex with him and several others at the same time. He did, however, hang around the longest, and next to very heavy Joe was the last to leave and I think put Bob out just a bit by not taking the hint that the party was over.

I spent some time with Larry, who misplaced *his* shoes at one point. Then we spent some time on the bed together while he talked about some more lectures he was planning to give in a couple weeks, again with sexual play all through. I wondered if I was going to have a similar shoe problem, but I found them pretty easily in the confusion of clothes in the corner. Besides me, there was one other tall obviously black guy, not by my lights particularly good-looking, but he was, rather like the cliché, the tallest and best hung in the group. At one point I was talking to him while he was being serviced by someone else. His name was Philip and he explained that he had started coming to these parties when he was thirty-five, and he was now forty-three. Clearly he was having fun and lots of guys wanted to play with him. Among other things, he was shaped rather like a bowling pin and had a deep, irregular, fourteen-inch-plus scar up his belly. He wore large, black-rimmed glasses, and whenever he looked at me, he seemed dazzled. I don't think it was drugs. In fact, I suspect that other than Viagra, no drugs were entailed. (But I'm sure I wasn't the only one there who'd had cataract operations.)

The very last person to leave was Joe, who had gone to sleep on the folded-out couch, all three hundred and fifty pounds of him. Earlier, in the midst of some of his play with someone else, I don't know who, there had been a couple fingers full of scat, and I had brought him a wet towel just to wipe himself off.

Now, as one after the other got dressed and said goodbye to Bob and Chuck, Joe seemed to be passed out and having some trouble breathing. In the other room, Bob mentioned that Joe probably needed a CPAP machine. (Actually, I'd brought my own in my rollaway, though I'd decided not to use it, but Joe's weight seemed to militate for it as something necessary. Finally, we got him up and more or less into some clothes. In the other room, Bob mentioned Joe's obvious breathing problems. I went back in to hug him goodbye, which he returned very good-heartedly. "You know," I said, "you could probably use a CPAP machine."

Still in the hug, he said, "I have one, but the mask is so uncomfortable, I never use it." Moments later, he pulled a wheelchair from behind the door and got into it. (I hadn't realized he had been using one when he came.) He let himself out to roll away down the hall.

At least two people had made it known that they had come twice. While I had fun and generally enjoyed the sucking and affection and some of the stories even more, I had not had an orgasm at all nor was I particularly looking for one. Nor had anyone had one with me. Although I can't be sure, in terms of ejaculations, I suspect it was about half-and-half.

My general take on the group? They seemed like nice guys trying to have fun. I have no idea whether I will seek out this kind of entertainment again or not. Probably I would if it were in my own city—even better in my own neighborhood. This is not a need to experiment. Rather, it's an opportunity to do what I have done before, to find out if it's satisfying and learn what I can. Though I was impressed with the energy that Mark put out—not to mention Joe—by my twenties I had learned in the truck along the docks, movies and in grope rooms at the backs of bars or in bathhouses that orgies while they can become energetic, are simply not wildly Dionysiac behavior, but are some of the most socially constrained and inflected behavior there is. They entail too many people relating at once.

I hadn't taken any Facebook pictures of people, but I'd taken a few of the rooms themselves, the bathroom, the abandoned bedroom after the fact around three fifty-five in the morning. Now I'm going to bed again and will try to stay there. Red lights blink on the hotel's CO_2 detector. I am using both the urinal I brought with me and the actual john, and I have my phone plugged in. By now it's just after four. This time when I went into the john, I noticed there were drops of blood all over the floor in front of the towel that was wrinkled there serving as a bathmat. Bob is now asleep in the other room. I use the toilet to leave a late-night crap and wonder if I should flush or leave it in, so that if he wakes up later, he will know that I've seen the blood. Later on I asked him, "What's your own feeling about leaving shit in the toilet?" As we were getting clothes next morning, he grinned and said, "If it's yellow, let it mellow. If it's brown, flush it down."

"Fine," I said. "I'll try to remember that."

The explanation for the blood drops is a diabetic condition that Bob has that began to bleed earlier when he got up to use the john.

At breakfast in the hotel—Bob had a coupon that allowed us both to get the hotel buffet—Bob explained over his omelet and my oatmeal: "My first private party?" Bob hadn't started "to play" till he was thirty-five. He'd run into an older gay guy who'd taken him to Houston, which was when he'd started this kind of thing ten years ago. Events like Charon Rising and the Celebration of Friends, which are well-known annual sex parties in the history of gay male entertainments, had been where his early interests had lain, but because he had always liked older men (Bob himself is now sixty-two) this was what he enjoyed doing.

Friendship, affection, sex, physicality . . .

Bob wants to care for the old people he finds sexually attractive in order to allow them to enjoy sex with younger men, such as himself, as well as with each other.

Possibly because I know the same group has been the topic of a seventy-minute film with several fairly extensive interviews, I am not too inclined to say more about the individuals than I already have. I'm certainly glad I did. I would call it an interesting evening. But I'm more interested in how it relates to other aspects of my life.

III.

Well, my trip to New York and the sex party at Bob Woof's are done. I've managed to get up to Maison's and Fred's mobile home at High Meadow Trailer Park in Dover Plains.

Did I mention it was fairly cold out?

Maison was waiting at the familiar Dover Plains station, down from the platform, in the station wagon. Once we got to High Meadow, came in, and said hello, I asked Fred about the Hep. Apparently I'd misheard him a couple of times on various iPhone calls. He has Hep C, not Hep D.

That's a relief, though it cost him a bit to get rid of it.

Maison is heavier by maybe twenty pounds—and I have lost more than eighty, without particularly trying. But both seemed warmly happy to see me, and neither Maison's nor my sexual interests seem to have flagged. Maison's car is a brown mustard, probably called gold, four-door jeep hatchback with green and white Vermont plates: GME 819. In his yard, there is a six-door Chevrolet 3500 with orange and black New York plates (GPA 6244), and two other utility trailers with blue and white Connecticut plates, one chained to the trunk of a tree in the yard. Before everybody else was up, I had to go out in the cool damp yard this morning four different times just to copy down the license plate number and make sure it was correct. That's my ADD.

Maison's is the only mobile home I've ever been a guest in—I can't even give you how many times. When we first began to see each other, we spent afternoons in Johnny Cadorre's house—then overnights at motels that catered to truckers. Both UMass, where I taught for eleven years and for one term lived in the hotel above the student union, and my friend Barbara Wise's summer home at Truro were designed by the same architect, Joseph Breuer. When you start to think about the houses you've stayed in and lived in (or the hotels, for that matter), it makes an interesting contrast.

I have no idea how to describe the trailers outside in the yard themselves or the junk each one is holding with any economy. That's because in terms of cars in general and working-class types of tractors, I am effectively illiterate. Back inside, it is almost seven-thirty. In the two days I have been here, I have already gotten one friendly load of Maison's semen and I am quite happy with it. Also, I've received a fair amount of hugs and dispensed both to Fred and Maison. (For comparison's sake, this is the only direct orgasm I've been involved in since I've left home, though I sucked on half-a-dozen cocks at the party. Certainly, it seems the most satisfying.) He's taken to smoking electronic cigarettes, which means his mouth no longer tastes like an ashtray. Fred smells strange enough to put me off doing more than hugging him; he is basically the same age as Dennis. I'm sitting in their living room, Maison gets up in gray undershirt and blue underpants and lumbers in. Fred comes in, rubs my head and I nuzzle his belly. He tells me to call them when I get home.

(Technology: Maison has an old-fashioned cell phone, and he and Fred have a laptop that sits on the back of the couch, which Maison can use, and their friend Doug [with whom Maison also has an affectionate sexual bond, which allows him to have his insurance, and look at my Facebook posts] uses from time to time, at their behest, and with which Fred and Maison sometimes look at my Facebook posts. There's a regular electrical jack hanging from the computer wires, and that's where I've been charging my iPhone.)

Last night, I had been describing Dennis's fears that the moment something happens to me, he will be homeless again. This morning, Maison and Fred volunteer that if anything should indeed happen, they would take Dennis in. To me this is a surprise, and I send it in a text message to Dennis, who messages back for me to thank them. Maison and I are now sitting on the couch. Fred has returned back to their bedroom. Maison asks me to tell him again when the train leaves: 10:56 a.m.

Maison brings me a cup of coffee. We sit on the couch. No one has yet put on the TV in Fred and Maison's bedroom or in the living room, but the four-screen security cameras have already been turned on just below the high-definition TV screen.

Maison has told me about his own family stealing money from him, which is one of the things that, after Maison's mother's death, broke his family apart. Maison thinks that his twenty-seven-year-old cousin Lige (Elijah) was murdered by his own wife. Maison's husband Fred thinks that Lige actually committed suicide by letting his wife poison him with his heart medicine—an overdose of Plavix—which she was responsible for giving him.

Or someone in that case was not so much forgetful as pathologically absent-minded—the classic description of ADD.

I met Lige when he was five years old at a backyard-barbecue Memorial Day celebration back when the whole family lived a few miles south, in Brewster. My next strongest memory of Lige was when he was sixteen, and I had come up to see Maison. Lige and Maison, at the time, shared a room in Maison's mother's mobile home, also in High Meadows. Lige's cat was very sick, and while Maison and I were out doing errands, the cat died. Maison and I found out when we got home. I remember urging Lige to come out with us to have pizza to get his mind off his dead pet, but he was too depressed to do so, so Maison and I went out by ourselves.

I remember Lige wheedling money out of his grandmother, while she sat at the kitchen table over her coffee, and while Maison and I watched: he claimed how he would succeed and she was saying he wouldn't, and then she'd give in, as though it were a game between them.

I remember meeting his little, rather dumpy twenty-one-year-old wife-to-be in jeans and a polo shirt who already had two children by a previous marriage. She struck me as nice enough, and had probably had a rough time, though the moment they left, the rest of the family had nothing good to say about her, from the beginning.

I remember Lige as a bright and lively five-year-old. By sixteen, he was depressive and into drugs. By nineteen, he was married with one child before marriage and a wife with two children of her own.

At twenty-seven, from an incompetently managed heart condition, he was dead. Now he was a memory five years in the past—though we still talk about him.

In the living room, Maison explained: Oil has gone up from 87 cents per gallon on the first of the year to $2.10 in the subsequent months. Gas has gone down, but Maison uses a woodstove now to heat the house. Every spring, he explains, he burns a cleaning log, which keeps the creosote down. I'm dozing on the couch on and off on a lazy Wednesday (March 8, 2017). We leave at twenty after ten, which will put me at the station at ten-thirty. I recognize the smell of woodstoves from my other old friends Leonard's and Sam's place in Canaan in the middle 1980s. Sam was also a sex buddy, and he died of asthma some years ago. And Leonard, who was diabetic and by that time in a home, we've lost track of, though we've tried to locate him. Dennis and I visited them frequently in the '80s. (At one point Leonard inherited five million dollars, and supported Dennis and me for an entire summer.) The smell is also something I associate with my family's four-room summerhouse with an unfinished basement and attic in Hopewell Junction back in the 1940s and '50s.

I go to take my post-breakfast dump in the trailer's rear bathroom. While I'm sitting there a bulb goes on. Is it a timer or loose connection? Should I ask? Dennis has an upper plate, but his lower teeth are mostly his. Maison's teeth are all gone. I really enjoy kissing him, especially now that he's gone to a vapor cigarette. In practical terms, it's like a constant unflavored mouth rinse.

Maison says, "There's no middle class, only rich and poor." I don't think that puts me in rich, but I am in a lot better shape than Maison is. (He also says the bulb was a loose connection. There are timers, but that's not one of them.) Maison gets $18,000 per year for his disability. Now he turns on the oversized high-def screen. And we are watching a Pixar cartoon short that was expanded into a feature: "Nine" (2009), about funny one-eyed creatures who run around in space suits that look as if they are made out of burlap. These kinds of creations are too hard for me to think about, in terms of how they were planned out and put together. I like old-fashioned special effects far more. The sound is broken on the high-def TV. There's no way to turn it up past a whisper. It would cost more to fix it than to buy a new TV. I recognize the "writing" in the cartoon that the characters are doing as the forerunner of the writing in *Arrival*, based on Ted Chiang's *Story of Your Life*. My sciatica has begun to kick in. I am trying to keep my naproxen (Aleve) down to two per day (440 mgs).

I have been sleeping in the back room, which is a total chaos of clean laundry but in piles along three walls and almost to the ceiling. It seems to be all the clean laundry—if not all the clothing—in the house. On the one hand it's not unfamiliar: much of Dennis's and my clean laundry is in piles on top of our bureau rather than inside it, but at Maison's and Fred's, in the back room, this has gotten to *hoarder* proportions! On the bed is not really a sheet but a mattress cover that is presumably clean but so ragged one hesitates to lean on it for fear it'll come to pieces. At home, Dennis and I for many years have slept on towels. I dug out a towel from the piles around the bed and spread it over the ragged mattress cover so that at least I was on a surface that felt familiar. And there were a couple of pillows and something like a very thin duvet as a cover that I pulled over me in familiar patterns to block out the light directly from the bulb shining in my eye from outside the open door.

Then I called Dennis on FaceTime and got him and talked to him about the strange place, on the verge of a hoarder's construct, that I was sleeping in and living in. Afterward I felt better and got to sleep, but was up before either Fred or Maison.

The second night was somewhat easier than the first, and I only made one call home. There was a lot of talk about ADD and the book Fred had recommended to me that I'd already gotten from Amazon. I'll be talking more about it to my own doctor when I get home. Last night, Maison had made dinner: a big pan of sausage and peppers and tomato sauce. Some of it was still out and had been sitting in the skillet overnight. I put some on a slice of bread and found a peach, which I wrapped up in a plastic bag to take home with me for my lunch on the train. More hugging, affection, a bit of sexual play, and finally it was time to leave. I had taken a few shots of the mobile home from the outside and posted them on Facebook.

Hovels & Barracks:

A home is someplace you can leave and come back to when you want. I can more or less do that here at High Meadow Trailer Park. I can more or less do it at Spruce Street where I now live in Philadelphia. I couldn't do it in the last place I lived in, and I'm not sure I'll be able to do it in the next one.

This became the caption of my Facebook post. I don't remember where I came across the distinction between hovels and barracks, but for years I've thought it was a good one. A barrack has one or more single rooms for single functions. A hovel *is* a single room, with living functions carried on in the center and more marginal things consigned to the walls. We live in combinations of the two, but you can still see the principle at work. In Maison's house, the back room, which is the clean laundry room and the guest room both, is also quite marginal to the rest of the house. The living room and the kitchen are basically one, which happens more and more these days in all but mansions. Some areas, especially in Maison's and Fred's, are clean. Others are unbelievable filthy, and still others, it's hard to tell which is which.

In former years before his marriage, when Maison was still living with his family, and I would visit, sometimes he would introduce me to other men—usually older—that he was having sexual relations with. None of these introductions ever resulted in group sex with me. I always wondered why it didn't, or whether I should have been more forward. But that was more than twenty years ago now.

One exception to this pattern was a man about Maison's own age, a workman with the nickname Spanky, whom Maison said was available, and that they had an *en-passant* sexual relationship. Though he was on the heavy side, Spanky was short, stocky, and fulfilled half a dozen of my personal fetishes so that, when I asked Maison if he thought I had a chance with him, he laughed and said, go ahead, ask him: "Sure, ask him the next time you come." Of course I was inquiring on my return trip home. Three weeks later, I learned—over the phone—that Spanky and Maison had some major falling out, having nothing to do with sex, and then—less than a month later, Spanky moved out of the trailer park and nobody knew where he'd gone.

Then, in New York, I met Dennis, and while Maison and I certainly didn't drift apart, our friendship moved to a new phase.

It is very easy to divide the world into binary groups, and then a supplementary group is postulated as a mediator: friendship, affection, sex, celibacy. Raw, cooked, boiled, burnt . . . Hell, purgatory, paradise, nirvana. Conscious, unconscious, dreaming . . .

Maison drove me back to the train station, but the train coming back from Southeast (the northernmost station) was an hour late (a car ran along the tracks and stopped on a side track, within sight, which didn't seem a good sign at all), so I called him again, and he returned and took me all the way down to Brewster. (This, I believe, has happened before.) Brewster for Maison was his hometown. He remembers when everything in the city was different. He remembers different physical structures that are no longer there, restaurants that are gone. Because of my ADD, Fred had told Maison to make sure that he saw me onto the train, and he did, after parking his brown-gold hatchback on the other side of the tracks.

When I walked across from Grand Central to Port Authority, I missed the bus I had booked online, so I had to pay another $20 to get on a local bus home (gate seventy-three, rather than the usual gate sixty-six), and which took three hours instead of two. Had to show my passport, in order to do it. (That was something that Dennis would not have been able to do online at all.) On the bus, across and one seat ahead of me, was a kid (somewhere between twenty and thirty) leaning forward on his knee jutting into the aisle, playing Facebook voraciously. He was far more adept at thumb typing (and everything else!) than I was. In the bathroom at the Filbert Street bus station, we kind of bumped into each other again, and I said something about his enjoying his Facebook, and he looked up and nodded. Then I came out and snapped a picture of Dennis, who immediately began to grump at me for taking pictures of *everything*, and we walked home while I dragged my rollaway, and my white tote bag, through a pleasant Philly night, where Dennis had sandwiches and ice cream waiting for us both at home.

The clean, clear ending that society keeps looking for is impossible to find because of all the various modes of memory: writing, and other forms of supplementation. New kinds of social formations are always growing up, even within the most rigid that already seem to contain us. I do not know whether I am ever going to see Maison or Fred again. I hope I do. What use will I make of what I have learned from Bob and his older gay male circuit party that I attended? Sex-radical, Afro-futurist, and grandmaster of science fiction that people are happy thinking of me as being cannot preclude the fact that there are people more radical than I am, more alert to what is going on in the social interstices between cultures already or in seemingly marginal communities, such as science fiction, which are changing day-to-day, or just those who know what buttons to push.

I didn't start availing myself of public sex until I was eighteen—though I went out looking for it and almost found it in Herbert's Museum on Forty-Second Street when I was fourteen or fifteen.

Both Bob Woof and Eric Carruthers say they were in their thirties. (And it suddenly hits me as unusual that I never elicited a detailed sexual history from either Dennis or Maison. Dennis has already surprised me at least once in the past year. I didn't know I was the first man he'd been to bed with, and I wonder what Maison's story is. I've never asked him either. [I just phoned him while I stood outside the Green Street Café and asked when he'd first started having sex with men. He laughed and, over the cell phone, told me, "Eight." That was a surprise. I would have guessed ten, twelve, or fourteen. He didn't try women till much later, but [he explained] they always stole money from him, so he dropped them. That was interesting and I stored it away.]) Still later, I would ask Maison if he minded so many specifics such as his license plate number and his address. He said it didn't bother him, and Fred added, when, outside in the street, I asked him on my cell phone, "If we were ballsy enough to go down and get our marriage license at the Dover county courthouse, why should something like that worry us?"

I think of myself as somebody who is interested in the differences, the differences between straight society and gay, the differences between male and female, but all of those presuppose a set of similarities on which those differences have to be marked out. Beginnings and endings are the hardest part for thinkers who utilize such structures. Perhaps that means the best way to end this essay is to say, as of yet, it is not finished.

—March 1–March 12, 2017
Philadelphia
New York
Dover Plains

NOTES

1. Also known as Bob Torres.
2. Pictures also originally accompanied this essay. They can be found at https://www.samueldelany.com/ash-wednesday/.

Acknowledgments

With thanks to my assistant William Wood, without whom the two volumes of *Occasional Views* would never have been completed or appeared in this form.

Many of the essays in this collection were previously published, sometimes in earlier versions.

"The Gamble" was previously published in *Corpus* 3, no. 1, edited by Robert
   F. Reid-Pharr (The Institute for Gay Men's Health, 2005).
"A Note on John Ashbery" was previously published in *Annals of Scholarship* 15,
   nos. 1–2 (1989). The poem "Parergon" is from John Ashbery, *The Double Dream
   of Spring* (Ecco Press, 1976).
"Samuel R. Delany, by K. Leslie Steiner" was previously published on the
   pseudopodium website (www.pseudopodium.org/repress/KLeslieSteiner-
   SamuelRDelany.html), © 2005 Samuel R. Delany.
"More and Less Than Human" has not been previously published.
"Acceptance Speech at Temple University" was delivered on the afternoon
   of April 20, 2008, at Mitten Hall in Philadelphia upon receipt of Temple
   University's Faculty Award for Research and Creative Achievement,
   presented for *Dark Reflections*.
"Fiction's Present: A Brief Note" was previously published in *symplokē* 12,
   nos. 1–2 (2004).
"Two Introductions to Junot Díaz": The first of these was read at the Lannan
   Foundation in Santa Fe, New Mexico, on Wednesday evening, January 21,
   2009. The second was read at the presentation of the Norman Mailer
   Distinguished Writing Prize at the Norman Mailer Gala, held at the Central
   Branch of the New York Public Library on October 17, 2013.
"A Lost Lady and Modernism: A Novelist's Overview" was previously published
   in *Critical Inquiry* 41, no. 3 (Spring 2015), 573–95.
"Interview with Matthew Cheney" was previously published as "The
   Jewel-Hinged Jaw: Matthew Cheney Interviews Samuel R. Delany"

on Amazon.com's book review blog *Omnivoracious*, posted on August 24, 2009.

"Three Novels: *Great House, So Much for That*, and *Parrot and Olivier in America*": These commentaries have not been published previously.

"*The Paris Review* Interview by Rachel Kaadzi Ghansah" was previously published as "The Art of Fiction, Number 210" in *The Paris Review* (Issue 197, Summer 2011).

"The Mirror and the Maze, I" was published in *American Literary History* 24, no. 4, edited by Gordon Hutner (Oxford University Press, 2012).

"Brudner Prize Lecture, I: A View from the Valley's Edge, Part 1" was presented at Yale University on October 17th, 2012.

"Brudner Prize Lecture, II: A View from the Valley's Edge, Part 2" was delivered on October 18th , 2012, at 7:00 p.m. at Club Quarters Midtown, 40 West 45th Street in New York City, after a 6:00 p.m. reception and after introductions by Professor George Chauncey and Professor GerShun Alvilez, to a gathering largely of gay Yale alumni and friends. This piece was also posted on Facebook on October 20, 2012, at 9:03 a.m.

"A Note on William Gaddis" was presented on the evening of February 20, 2013, at The New School for Social Research in New York City on the occasion of the publication of *The Letters of William Gaddis* (Dalkey Archive Press, 2013).

"Interview with Reed Cooley" has not been previously published.

"Note on *Heart of Darkness*" is a collation-facsimile of a Facebook discussion and a subsequent email exchange from September 2, 2013 (see www.facebook.com/samuel.delany/posts/10201995273471227).

"Remembering Pete Seeger" was posted on Facebook on January 30, 2014, at 10:52 a.m.

"A, B, C . . . Preface and Afterword to Three Short Novels": These essays were published previously in Samuel R. Delany, *A, B, C: Three Short Novels* (Vintage, 2015).

"A Note on Melville" has not been published previously.

Absence and Fiction: More Recent Thoughts on *The American Shore*" was posted on Facebook on July 24, 2014, at 4:13 p.m.

"The Mirror and the Maze, II," not published previously, is from a continuing seminar (informally called "The Mirror and the Maze") that Delany gave over several summers at Naropa University.

"Ikky, Kong, Frédéric, Kurtz" has not been published previously.

"Notes on *The City of Green Fire*" was previously published as a January 11, 2017 post on https://wolffbrain.blogspot.com/.

"Sympathy and Power" was published previously in *The WisCon Chronicles, Volume 1* (Aqueduct Press, 2007).

"Ash Wednesday": A different version of this essay was published previously in *Boston Review* (May 9, 2017).

Index

ABOUT THE AUTHOR

Samuel R. Delany is the author of innovative fiction, essays, and memoir, including more than twenty-five novels. He has received four Nebula Awards from the Science Fiction Writers of America, for *Babel-17*, *The Einstein Intersection*, and two of his short stories. He received Hugo Awards for the novella "Time Considered as a Helix of Semi-Precious Stones" and his autobiography *The Motion of Light in Water*. His most recent SF novel is *Through the Valley of the Nest of Spiders*. In 1985 he received the Pilgrim Award for Lifetime Achievement in SF Scholarship. Along with fellowships at numerous institutions, he has taught at the University of Massachusetts–Amherst, SUNY–Buffalo, and Temple University. His honors include the 1997 Kessler Award for LGBTQ Studies, the 2007 Stonewall Book Award for his novel *Dark Reflections*, and the 2015 Nicolas Guillén Award for Philosophical Literature, and he is the subject of a 2007 documentary film by Fred Barney Taylor, *The Polymath*. In 2002, he was inducted into the Science Fiction Hall of Fame, and in 2016 was inducted into the New York State Writers Hall of Fame. In 2013, the Science Fiction Writers of America named Delany a Grand Master of Science Fiction.